The Allure of Immortality

UNIVERSITY PRESS OF FLORIDA

Florida A&M University, Tallahassee
Florida Atlantic University, Boca Raton
Florida Gulf Coast University, Ft. Myers
Florida International University, Miami
Florida State University, Tallahassee
New College of Florida, Sarasota
University of Central Florida, Orlando
University of Florida, Gainesville
University of North Florida, Jacksonville
University of South Florida, Tampa
University of West Florida, Pensacola

LYN MILLNER

THE ALLURE OF IMMORTALITY

An American Cult, a Florida Swamp, and a Renegade Prophet

UNIVERSITY PRESS OF FLORIDA

Gainesville · Tallahassee · Tampa · Boca Raton · Pensacola
Orlando · Miami · Jacksonville · Ft. Myers · Sarasota

First cloth printing, 2015
First paperback printing, 2019

24 23 22 21 20 19   6 5 4 3 2 1

Library of Congress Control Number: 2015938069
ISBN 978-0-8130-6123-8 (cloth)
ISBN 978-0-8130-6440-6 (pbk.)

The University Press of Florida is the scholarly publishing agency
for the State University System of Florida, comprising Florida
A&M University, Florida Atlantic University, Florida Gulf Coast
University, Florida International University, Florida State University,
New College of Florida, University of Central Florida, University of
Florida, University of North Florida, University of South Florida, and
University of West Florida.

University Press of Florida
2046 NE Waldo Road
Suite 2100
Gainesville, FL 32609
http://upress.ufl.edu

publication with a grant from
Figure Foundation

a necessary verb curve dawn

For Jesse

Idealism . . . led them up strange backwaters and provided them with fantastic hallucinations. . . . It is better,
perhaps, to be slightly mad with a sound heart, than to
be sane without one.

Mark Holloway, *Heavens on Earth:*
Utopian Communities in America, 1680–1880

Contents

Preface

In New York State in 1869 lived a charismatic man named Cyrus Teed, who believed he was a prophet. He was thirty when an angel came to him in a vision and told him he was chosen to redeem humanity. Teed was distantly related to Joseph Smith, the founder of the Mormon Church, and no doubt influenced by his cousin's success. He had hazel eyes, a bushy beard, and a determination to find followers, which he did, though much more slowly than he would have liked. Through a series of events and against great odds, his people, the Koreshans, came to southwest Florida to build a socialist, religious utopia. At its height, in 1903, the community numbered two hundred people. The last believer died in 1974.

The Koreshans quit their comfortable lives to follow a man to a hot, humid wilderness where they battled mosquitoes, snakes, alligators, wild hogs, freezes, fires, hurricanes, and illness to build a city. They left jobs, sold businesses, surrendered their possessions to the group, and, in many cases, deserted their families. Most of the followers were women, several of whom left their husbands.

They were not rough pioneer types. Their photos attest to that. They read Greek and formed an orchestra and took voice lessons and painted. They were educated, cultured, well-off, and yet their view of the world seems outlandish.

For one, they believed we live inside a hollow earth. "We Live Inside" was a slogan they printed on lecture announcements, lapel pins, and on the sign in front of their settlement in Florida. This motto was accompanied by an illustration of the earth, hinged open to reveal the continents and cosmos inside. Sometimes the Koreshans added a touch of humor to We Live Inside: "Drop In and See Us."

The Koreshans were celibate, and the men and women lived apart. Today people point to this as proof that they were not forward-thinking. How did they expect the community to survive, people ask, if they didn't have children? The answer is this: the Koreshans believed that by conserving and redirecting their sexual potency, they would transform themselves into immortal beings. Having sex, by contrast, would ensure their mortality.

Inevitably, there *were* some children, and today there are living descendants who recall that their grandparents and great-grandparents were quiet on the topic of Koreshanity. One reason for the reticence was that, even as late as the mid-nineteen hundreds, the Koreshans were stigmatized. Most of them had been children when they joined. They left as soon as they were old enough. Even so, outsiders kept their distance, as if being a Koreshan were contagious. Therefore, most of today's descendants grew up with only a vague idea about the most important part of their elders' lives.

The Koreshans survive in memory as a peculiar people from another time, their history evaporating in spite of the fact that they were part of one of the most important movements in America.

This book tells their story. Though parts of it seem unbelievable, it is a work of nonfiction. No detail or event was invented. Every quotation is from a written source or interview. Because all of the believers are dead, I leaned on archives, oral histories, letters, journals, meeting minutes, court testimony, photos, and a host of experts. Where possible, I sought confirmation from more than one source.

However—and this is a big however—the story depends in part on newspaper articles, most of which were written during the era of yellow journalism. In Teed's time—much like today—publishers sought to entertain more than inform. Wherever I used a newspaper as a source, I made it clear in the text or in an endnote or both.

I have done my best to write a book that is accurate and true, not only because I am a journalist but also because the overall theme of this book is belief: what we believe and why. The Koreshans' faith shaped their lives and drove them to accomplish incredible feats. Their story shows how unshakable belief can be, even when it runs counter to reality. Even when fact bleeds through, belief has the power to triumph.

Today, the Koreshans are buried in two cemeteries not far from the settlement they built. Only one of their graveyards is accessible. It lies inside a gated golf course community near a river. Records show that their bodies were placed with their heads to the west and their feet to the east, consistent with the belief that on Judgment Day, the dead will rise and face the morning sun.

Prologue

The Man in the Bathtub

On Christmas Day of 1908, Dr. Cyrus Teed was laid out lovingly in a zinc bathtub his followers had built exactly to the dimensions of his short frame. His eyes were closed, his face expressionless, his skin dark, and his swollen tongue protruded through enlarged, turned-out lips. They draped him with a white sheet from the waist down and left his torso nude. By all outward appearances, he was dead, and had been for three days, but the followers said he was in a trance—suspended animation, they called it.

Teed lay in a bedroom on the second floor of a house at the southern tip of an island now known as Fort Myers Beach, two miles off the coast of southwest Florida. The temperature was on its way to seventy-three degrees, and the windows were doubtless open to the salt air for ventilation. The placid water of the Gulf of Mexico gently washed the shore.

Two days before, doctors from Fort Myers had examined Teed and declared him "quite extinct" of natural causes, their note read. But Teed's doctor, Augustus Weimar, who was keeping notes of his own, had observed the belly rising and relaxing and had seen the arteries rebound when he pressed them. About the men who pronounced Teed dead, Weimar wrote, "If we are not disappointed, we hope to see the Doctor visit his death examiners."[1]

Cyrus Teed believed he was King Cyrus from the Old Testament, and he called himself Koresh, the Hebrew transliteration of Cyrus; his followers were the Koreshans. Today, if there were any believers left, the Koreshan Unity might be called a cult or might be referred to by the more neutral phrase "high-demand society" by people trying to get their loved ones to leave. History puts the

Koreshans with religious, communal organizations like the Shakers and Harmonists. The people in these groups believed that by removing themselves from sin and from temptation, they would be God's chosen people.

Just as Joseph Smith, in 1839, led the Mormons to build their Zion in Nauvoo, Illinois, Teed led the Koreshans to Estero, Florida, fifty-five years later, to create a utopia, enticed by weather, free land, and the need to escape persecution in Chicago. Teed was a distant cousin of Emma Hale, Joseph Smith's wife, and he was certainly a theological relative. Koreshanity had many things in common with Mormonism, Seventh-Day Adventism, and Jehovah's Witnesses—which all began as millennialist movements whose followers believe that Christ will return, establish a kingdom on earth, and reign for one thousand years, as prophesied in the Book of Revelation. The people in these groups did not worship their prophets as messiahs; instead, the leaders were divine interpreters who prepared them for the Second Coming by translating biblical scripture and messages from God. This is what Teed was doing, and those who followed him believed that there would be a big event during which he would "translate" and redeem them, and they would be among the chosen people who would begin a new immortal life on earth.

Teed preached that he was the last in a line of seed-men who included Adam, Enoch, Noah, Moses, Abraham, and Jesus—men who had received knowledge (dispensations) from God that allowed them to lead people into a new age. Teed taught his people that God had revealed to each of these men only what they were able to understand and what their people were capable of accepting. Teed said that as the seventh, he was the most evolved, and God would reveal all, making everything knowable through him so that he could usher in the age of Koreshanity—the previous ages being Judaism (Abraham) and Christianity (Jesus).

There were many people in nineteenth-century America who believed they were prophets or messiahs. And like most of them, Teed was spectacularly unsuccessful. But it was this very lack of success, this struggle, what the Koreshans saw as persecution, that made the followers believe all the more.

Dr. Weimar was a Koreshan and a doctor of osteopathy, which was a very new field and not a respected one, the first osteopathic medical school having been founded in 1892. Conventional doctors, including the ones from Fort Myers who declared Teed dead, would not have taken him seriously.

As soon as Teed's suspended animation began on December 22, Weimar began watching the body round the clock. On day two, he saw it discolor, beginning as a darkening behind the ear, on the mastoid bone, then spreading across his chest and finally to his face. That afternoon, a blood-tinged fluid oozed from the mouth and had the odor of mors (death), as Weimar phrased it in his notes.

The nurses lifted the body into the bathtub, knowing that the followers would want to view him. They came in small groups. As shock and nervousness set in, Weimar read to them from Teed's writings, which proved that their Master had predicted a "most foul matter." The followers now believed they knew what he meant by this.

It comforted them that Teed had laid everything out in his writings, and they recalled that he had spoken many times of his translation or theocrasis when he would take on the form of a woman and lead them in a great battle against evil and, upon winning the battle, would usher in the kingdom of heaven on earth. The followers had conducted their lives as if this were true; they had given up everything for it and for their leader and for the certainty that they would be immortal. To not believe during this hour of darkness was to forsake him and to forsake Koreshanity, and that was inconceivable.

The fact that he was not with them right now was a test of their faith, they agreed, a temporary one, and they would surmount it. They needed only to be patient. "All are serene and in an intense mode of waiting," Weimar wrote. "The brightest hours are before us."

But on Christmas Eve, Weimar ordered the viewing to stop. Teed's features were rapidly decomposing. "His countenance changed entirely," Weimar noted. At first, Teed had looked like Napoleon, ready for a great battle. Then Weimar watched hieroglyphics spread across his chest—most likely the marbling that happens after death when blood vessels become visible. Finally, Weimar admitted that the body had entered a "state of corruptibility." Twenty men began work on an aboveground tomb on the beach.

That night, Weimar composed a letter to the followers who were not in Estero, writing that this was a sad Christmas, that a vault of blocks was being built, and that the Master could rest there until the change came. He stayed beside the body that night.

The room where Teed rested afforded a view of the bay side of the island, where the Koreshans docked their boats, vessels they built themselves in their shipyard up the Estero River at the settlement. This house they had built for recreation, so that the followers could take a break from busy settlement life. Teed named it La Parita, which might have meant "the little couple" or might have meant "equality," or, as one follower wrote, "the appearing," or it might have meant all three, or something else entirely that Teed hadn't shared with them. Sometimes, he named things without explanation.

The settlement the Koreshans built was inland, four miles up a river with endless, lazy bends shaded by oaks, the water sifted by the roots of mangroves and inhabited by alligators. When the tide came in, the river was deep enough to ship citrus from the orchards to the bay and up the coast to Fort Myers, where it was loaded onto boxcars and carried to northerners who had the new experience of slicing into an orange and smelling the sweet mist that brought dreams of sunny skies and beaches.

The Koreshans had built a dining hall with dorms for the women upstairs; cabins for the men; a place for the children; the Founder's House, where Teed and Victoria (his earthly female equal) lived; the Planetary Court, for the seven women who managed the daily affairs; a bakery; a general store; a schoolhouse; a laundry; barns; a small zoo; a sawmill; a printing house; the boat works and concrete works; gardens where they grew their own food; and an Art Hall, where their orchestra and band played, where they performed dramas, and where Sunday services were held. Along the river were places on the banks where they could sit, read, and lose themselves in thought. Flower gardens decorated the grounds, and shell paths connected the buildings.

It took the Koreshans fifteen years to create this settlement on a patch of inhospitable scrubland, and they weren't close to done: these were temporary buildings for the shining city they would create in Estero: the Guiding Star City, they called it. Their plans included a temple at the center, surrounded by a body of water, the Crystal Sea. Spoking out from the temple would be paths that led to broad boulevards with names like Triomphia Octagonia and Victorian Way.

Weimar was the first to see the miraculous changes at 2:00 a.m. on Christmas morning. The day before, he noted that the Master's body had darkened further; it was black and shiny like polished ebony, and it had taken on the appearance of an Egyptian god—the exact image of Horus, god of the sky, of protection and war, often depicted as a man with a falcon's head. But now there was another, more dramatic change. That morning, when the men docked at the beach with concrete for the tomb, Weimar called them into La Parita excitedly.

Weimar uncovered the left arm, which was immensely swollen and filled with water, what a medical examiner would call a blister. Through the fluid, they believed they saw a new arm and a hand forming, "as soft and fresh as that of a newborn babe," one of the men later wrote. The followers also thought they detected the faint outline of a nose forming under the old one. They had waited for some sign, refused to bury him, and on Christmas Day, they were rewarded.

The tomb builders sped up the river to the settlement to tell everyone the news. They rang the bell at the dining hall, and everyone gathered and heard about the miraculous change. They boarded boats immediately and at La Parita filed up the stairs to view the body. Even the children went, though they had been promised an outing for Christmas Day to the moving picture show in Fort Myers. This trip was all the children had talked about for several days, but they found themselves here instead, and not a one of them complained, the adults noted, as they filed past the body.

He no longer looked like their Master. He had been an undersized man but was now puffed. They agreed that he was Horus, as Weimar had said: "A great big pugnacious looking fellow," one woman wrote, "black as the blackest Egyptian. I would like to look at it again and again." In fact, many of them began referring to the body as Horus. And though Weimar had warned them before they came in that Teed might seem repulsive, they didn't think so. He was beautiful to them, and the odor wasn't bad—some found it even agreeable—and they reasoned that the smell was less strong because every opening in the body had swollen to the point that his being was hermetically sealed, which they believed would allow for transformation. Amazed, they took photographs.

Teed's favorite nurse recalled a dream he had on the night after Teed passed: A large chrysalis was sitting in a chair, and its top burst open. Something protruded and rotated and, as it did so, took on the exact appearance of the Master's head. This theory of the chrysalis took hold, especially as the Koreshans inspected the body and saw the new life forming within the clear fluid of the arm.

Except for Teed's sister Emma, who said, "That thing ought to be put in the tomb," the followers didn't want to bury him.

The nurse said, "I know the Lord is in that body, and I am going to remain with it until I have seen the worms eat all of it and crawl away in different directions before I will believe otherwise."

The local paper, the *Fort Myers Press*, was the first to report the death, which it did matter-of-factly with this headline: "Dr. Cyrus Teed Dead: Has Passed Away and Is No More."[2]

The *Chicago Tribune* followed, with a sarcastic headline that Teed's rise was due on Christmas. The *New York Times* predicted that the community would disband if Teed didn't rise the day after Christmas. Two days later, the *Times* ran a follow-up: "Dr. Teed Has Not Risen." Some articles included capsules about Teed and the movement and the troubles in Chicago. There were erroneous reports that Teed had left a large estate for his followers when, in fact, there was a mountain of debt. In Estero, telegrams poured in from reporters and followers, asking about Teed's death, but the Koreshans replied to very few of them.

"The whole country round about is in a ferment," one follower wrote to another, "and this place is watched closely."

The last thing they wanted was more attention; more than anything, they wanted to be left alone, which is what they had always wanted: quiet and isolation, though they were thwarted at every turn, it seemed, even now at this sacred moment.

The *Tampa Morning Tribune* was the first to bring up the old rumors—that Teed's followers practiced free love. Other papers followed suit, dredging up scandals from years ago—Teed was a thief; he had lured wives away from their husbands; men threatened to lynch him. These allegations and threats were one of the reasons they had left Chicago for southwest Florida, hoping to live in peace.[3]

Many of the people who chose to become Koreshans grew up during a time when utopias were flourishing, when communal living and socialism didn't seem strange and, in fact, were desirable. By pooling resources and labor, the members had more time for music, art, theater, leisure, and self-improvement. In the early eighteen hundreds, so many communal utopias had blossomed that Ralph Waldo Emerson wrote to Thomas Carlyle in 1840, "We are all a little wild here with numberless projects of social reform. Not a reading man but has a draft of a new community in his waistcoat pocket."[4]

Emerson visited at least one of these utopias, Brook Farm, a transcendentalist community in Massachusetts that attracted intellectuals and social activists, including Nathaniel Hawthorne, who was a member for a short time. The founder of Brook Farm, George Ripley, wrote Emerson to persuade him to join, explaining that he was forming a society of liberal, intelligent, and cultivated people who would live simply, away from market pressures. Emerson did not enroll.

Many socialist utopias had a religious component, like Bishop Hill, founded in Illinois in 1846; the Oneida Community in 1848 in New York; and Bethel, in Missouri in 1844. These grew out of a time of religious revival. Most of the communities dissolved by the late eighteen hundreds, but idealism didn't.

The focus shifted from religion to socialism, especially as concerns about capitalism grew.

By the latter half of the century, men were creating a new America, shaping cities, creating jobs and industry, and building railroads and resorts—John D. Rockefeller and Andrew Carnegie in New York, Philip Armour and George Pullman in Chicago, Henry Flagler and Henry Plant in Florida. These men reaped extraordinary wealth and, many believed, turned working men into slaves. Mark Twain and Charles Dudley Warner dubbed this the Gilded Age, indicating that the nastiness and corruption were coated with a thin layer of gold.[5]

The more that industry advanced, the more that people, especially educated ones, mistrusted capitalism as they witnessed the mistreatment of workers, the decline in the quality of products, and the widening, merciless divide between the haves and have-nots. America had been founded on the ideal of equality, and capitalism was eroding it. As industry advanced, people became dependent on its conveniences. And land became expensive. As a result, many utopias took the form of social action—reforming the system from within, as opposed to creating literal utopias. This was not the case with many religious societies, which continued to break from the establishment, though most of them were short-lived. For the Koreshans, capitalism was of the devil, and communal living was the divine way.

Many apocalyptic cult leaders have based religious communes on the Book of Revelation and have set out to dupe the lost, the weak, and the wounded, promising them immortality in exchange for their devotion and, usually, their money. But it's impossible to tell whether Teed was deliberately duping anyone. And the Koreshans didn't seem lost or weak.

By any standard, they were well educated; they read literature and kept up with news; they had a drama troupe; many of them painted, studying the Dutch masters; they had their own school for children and a lecture series for adults. They studied horticulture—crucial knowledge for coaxing plants from southwest Florida's sandy soil.

Teed provided journalists and writers with plenty to write about, but he wasn't easy to figure out. Much of his writing and speaking was inscrutable, thanks to flowery language and made-up words; this, his believers took for brilliance, for something they could dig into intellectually. He said he had many answers and messages for them, but could not reveal them all at once. He would do so as they were ready to accept them.

Depending on whom you believe, Teed was earnest or he was a scoundrel. He was harebrained or he was forward-thinking. He was celibate or he had sex with many women or he merely kissed and fondled them. One thing is certain: he did exert an especially strong power over women, who outnumbered the men in the community by as many as three to one.

The only thing everyone agreed on, including his detractors, was that he had charisma. He looked like any other nineteenth-century clergyman, they said— black broadcloth suit, white tie, and hat. He was about five foot six and 140 pounds with a receding hairline. But when he opened his mouth and began to speak, he was so filled with conviction that people fell under a spell.

"He does not appear to realize the amount of energy he puts into his voice," one follower wrote. "He speaks as forcibly in a parlor lecture to a few persons as though he were in a large auditorium lecturing to 10,000 people."[6]

There were so many charismatic evangelists in the nineteenth and twentieth centuries that Sinclair Lewis was inspired to satirize them in a novel, *Elmer Gantry*. Gantry was a composite of the religious hypocrites who swindled people, who engaged in drunkenness and sexual debauchery, who never believed what they preached, and who scorned the people they converted. Was Teed an Elmer Gantry? As far as the media were concerned, yes.

Like Gantry, Teed did benefit financially, though not much. It was more common that he needed money. When he had it, he spent lavishly, and he kept the society in constant debt, which some followers believed he did intentionally, to build a strong bond among the followers and keep them working toward the goal of utopia.

Unlike Gantry, Teed suffered no doubts whatsoever about his faith—or, if he did, this never emerged, even in private, early letters to his closest friend, written long before he had any success. He seemed to truly love his believers, as opposed to holding them in contempt.

As for the disproportionate number of women in the Koreshan community, some of them undoubtedly felt a romantic connection to Teed, but they were also attracted by his view that men and women should have equal standing in the society. Teed believed that marriage enslaved women, and apparently the women who joined him believed it, too, as many of them left their husbands to join.

He was probably insane, certainly narcissistic—many charismatic religious leaders are—but his followers don't seem to have been crazy. They followed him willingly, and they could leave at any time, though it was difficult to do so because they gave up their resources when they joined.

Teed believed he was doing good in the world, as reflected in his writing, and he did not advocate violence—unlike Charles Manson, unlike the leader of the group that released sarin gas on the Tokyo subways, and unlike many groups whose followers believe in the end times.

Of all of today's religious apocalyptic leaders, Cyrus Teed has the most in common theologically with David Koresh, the leader of the Branch Davidians, a splinter group of the Seventh-Day Adventists in Waco, Texas. People in Estero will quickly tell you otherwise, that the Koreshans had nothing to do with "the wacko from Waco," as one local put it. But it's no coincidence that both took the name Koresh.

Each man believed he was the prophet Cyrus, hence "Koresh." Each believed himself to be divinely appointed to receive and interpret messages from God about the Second Coming as outlined in the Book of Revelation. Each believed that the Second Coming would be preceded by some sort of violent clash with society, and this clash might end their lives. Teed believed that the clash was inevitable; David Koresh, according to scholars, was looking for a way to prevent it as the FBI surrounded his Mount Carmel compound in 1993. The Koreshans and Branch Davidians both believed that when they "died," they were simply unconscious and waiting to be transported to God's kingdom. Cyrus Teed and David Koresh had very small followings. And each man felt misunderstood.

For a *New Yorker* story in 2014, Malcolm Gladwell examined the fifty-one-day standoff between the Branch Davidians and the FBI in an article that showed convincingly that the tragedy came about as a result of a colossal misunderstanding. What the FBI viewed as a hostage crisis, Koresh believed was a threat to his family and followers, who he said were anything but hostages, free to leave any time. The FBI thought that David Koresh might lead his group in a mass suicide, as the self-proclaimed prophet Jim Jones had done in the Jonestown massacre of 1978, and as Marshall Applewhite, the leader of Heaven's Gate, would do in 1997. Those who have studied the Branch Davidians say there is no evidence that David Koresh was planning a mass suicide.

As the FBI surrounded the compound, David Koresh was trying to "decode," as he phrased it, the messages of the seven seals in the Book of Revelation. He told the negotiators that once he completed this, he would come out and submit to arrest. The FBI, believing Koresh was stalling, moved in with tanks and tear gas. A fire started—its source unclear—and seventy-four people died, including Koresh.

"Because the FBI could not take the faith of the Branch Davidians seriously," Gladwell wrote, "it had no meaningful way to communicate with them."[7]

Almost no one today has heard of Teed. Yet he and his followers were covered by the *New York Times*, *Chicago Tribune*, and *San Francisco Chronicle*, often on the front pages. He had ties to Thomas Edison; Henry Ford; Marjory Stoneman Douglas; Victoria Woodhull (the first woman to run for U.S. president); Upton Sinclair; Ralph Waldo Emerson; presidents William McKinley and Theodore Roosevelt; the painter Paul Sargent; and millionaire Marshall Field. Teed's connections to these people give his story a Forrest Gump quality.

If Cyrus Teed were alive today, he might be a wealthy man, ironically, a capitalist, had he held on to the thousands of acres the Koreshan Unity accumulated during his lifetime, including much of Fort Myers Beach, now a popular destination for snowbirds, retirees, and spring breakers.

At the state historic site, where many of the buildings have been restored, docents answer questions from the few visitors. From the road, all that's visible of the settlement is an oversized building covered in stucco the color of cake batter. It was the Koreshans' general store, long closed, and said by one of the rangers to be haunted. Almost a hundred years ago, this is where the believers sold their jams, honey, citrus, "risin' bread," cereal, and other staples.

No believers are left, and the restored community is usually quiet except for the buzz of crickets. Outside the park is the uniform, Mediterranean-style town of Estero, population twenty thousand and growing, with communities named for what once was there: Estero Preserve, Marsh Landing, and Rookery Pointe. An upscale outdoor mall up the highway from the historic site features Victoria's Secret, Apple, Barnes & Noble, West Elm, Target, Best Buy, and a Regal Cinema multiplex.

Five days after Teed's death, with the county health authorities pressing in, the Koreshans carried the bathtub containing his body down the stairs of La Parita and onto the beach, where the tomb waited.

Just days before, Dr. Weimar had written to his wife about the body: "Elizabeth! Elizabeth! If I were now at the other end of the world and knew and saw what I am seeing now, I would come as quickly as steamers or railroads could carry me."[8]

But on this day, the body looked satanic and hellish, like "the man of sin," Weimar wrote. Not quite skeleton and not quite flesh. The teeth were large, and the orbits of the eyes pronounced. Weimar reasoned that the Master's old body needed to fall away and be entombed so that he could overcome and conquer. This had been the destiny all along, but he hadn't understood it until now.

The tomb had an attractive headstone, filigreed around the edges and embossed with "Cyrus, Shepherd, Stone of Israel," no birth and death dates. The Koreshans sealed it after putting this note inside:

> In compliance with the law, and *only* for such reason, the body of Cyrus R. Teed is placed in this stone vault. We, the disciples of Koresh, Shepherd, Stone of Israel, *know* that this sepulcher cannot hold his body, for he will overcome death, and in his immortal body will rise triumphant from the tomb.

The note was signed "Anastasia," which comes from the Greek word for resurrection.

The story of the Koreshans is an odd tale, which this book aims to tell, but there's more here than entertainment. The Koreshans represent a historically important time in America when people held fast to beliefs that didn't conform. There's value in what they can teach us about our own capacity to believe—and about our tendency to dismiss those who believe differently.

✳ 1 ✳

The Illumination

Has my thirst for knowledge consumed my body?

—Cyrus Teed, *The Illumination of Koresh*

Cyrus Teed's family wanted him to be a Baptist preacher like his grandfather, and he might have become one if he had grown up in a different time and place. But he was born in 1839 in New York State, at the end of America's Second Great Awakening.

The country, especially New York, was on fire with revivals. At its height, people gathered by the thousands at camp meetings—"emotional orgies," historian Robert V. Remini called them. "Wild scenes of men and women weeping and tearing their hair, vocally confessing their sins, beating their breasts, rolling on the ground, crawling on all fours like dogs, and barking at trees where they had presumably cornered the devil." The Methodists, Baptists, and Presbyterians were in a war for souls, with the Methodists and Baptists winning.[1]

Before the Awakening, most people saw God as removed from their lives, an impersonal authority above them. But in this age, Protestants sought a one-on-one connection. It wasn't unusual during that time for people to talk to God directly and to believe that he visited them through miracles, dreams, and visions.[2]

Women easily outnumbered men in religious conversions and dominated the enthusiasm. Revivals, prayer meetings, and church provided excitement in their otherwise restricted lives of sparse intellectual stimulation, stuffy rooms, and uncomfortable clothes. Women formed religious societies and pursued reform projects, and these were considered suitable activities for them. During the Awakening, the woman became the religious foundation for her family.[3]

Revivals began to level off in the late 1830s, but they got a boost when a Baptist minister named William Miller predicted the date of the Second Coming. His ideas spread rapidly. Miller and his evangelists went from town to town, speaking to congregations of all denominations and announcing that Christ would come in 1843 or 1844. The pronouncement energized people and gave reform work a new urgency. He converted fifty thousand people and keenly interested another one million. The Baptists, especially, were revitalized, and their membership shot up. Their stance, as printed in the *Baptist Register*, was that even if Miller's dates were off, it would be wise to act as if the Second Coming were imminent and to prepare for the big event regardless. Miller spoke in Utica, near where Cyrus's family lived, and throngs of people came to see him. Given his influence on Baptists, it's very likely that Cyrus's minister grandfather and his family saw Miller speak and were influenced by his predictions.

When Miller's predicted date passed without incident, he adjusted it, and that date passed, too, and the period after it became known as "the great disappointment." Miller's Adventists split into two major groups: one believed Miller's dates were wrong and that Christ had not yet appeared; the other thought Miller's last date had been correct and that there was an appearance, but on a heavenly, not an earthly, plane. Today's Seventh-Day Adventists, the largest church in Adventism, grew from this second group.

By the 1840s, evangelists had no one left to convert in western New York, the "burned-over district," where the fires of revivalism and millennialism had blazed strongest but where now many people had lost their idealism. They wanted, and even needed, new ideas. So as the Awakening wound down, there came a time of "daring social experiments" and "courageous nonconformity," as scholar Whitney Cross wrote.[4]

An influx of Europeans during this time brought new thoughts from the Old World, most notably the teachings of Emanuel Swedenborg, which rushed into America in the 1840s. Swedenborg, an eighteenth-century scientist and religious philosopher, blended the notions that a vital force flowed throughout the body, that people could be healed by the laying on of hands, that the brain was connected to consciousness, and that certain areas of the brain were responsible for particular impulses and emotions. He taught that the physical and spiritual worlds were connected through something he called "correspondences."[5]

His theories satisfied both scientists (he began his career as a scientist) and mystics (he claimed to have had a life-changing visit from Christ and to speak with angels frequently). His doctrines show up in the work and letters of many major writers, including Elizabeth Browning, Ralph Waldo Emerson, William Blake, Samuel Taylor Coleridge, and Charles Baudelaire.

Spiritualism, the belief that the living can communicate with the dead, became wildly popular in the nineteenth century, started by two sisters in a Hydesville, New York, farmhouse on April Fool's Eve, 1848. Katie and Margaretta Fox, eleven and fourteen, "discovered" how to communicate with a ghost in their cellar. As an adult, one of the girls claimed that she and her sister had fooled the public by using props and even the joints of their toes to rap out the answers from the ghost. She later recanted this statement, and it's unclear whether the girls were sincere or were pulling a prank. Regardless, the adults believed them from the beginning, and Spiritualism caught fire. Soon there were public séances in Auburn and Rochester, and before the end of the century, an estimated eight million people in the United States and Europe were Spiritualists, mostly middle and upper class, and the majority of them women.[6]

Spiritualists were early leaders in the women's rights movement, which gathered strength in 1848 thanks to two major events in New York. One was the first-ever women's rights convention, which met in Seneca Falls, where members approved a Declaration of Sentiments stating that women had inalienable rights and that any laws that ran counter to these rights, women had a duty to challenge. The declaration included strong language for men, citing "a long train of injuries and usurpations" and stating that marriage made women "civilly dead." Elizabeth Cady Stanton read the declaration, which she drafted, revisions were made, and it was adopted and signed by one hundred attendees, both women and men. That same year saw another milestone for women's rights: a law in New York was passed to allow a married woman to hold property independently of her husband. The law became a model for other states' laws.[7]

✳

Cyrus Teed was the son of Sarah Tuttle and Jesse Teed; later Cyrus would call attention to being the "root of Jesse" (as was King David). He was born in Teedville, New York, founded by his father's ancestors, who were well-off—except for Cyrus's particular branch, which was headed by a grandfather who was a "problem child," a relative later wrote. He disliked working for others, overextended himself with credit, and eventually lost everything.[8]

And so, in the economic depression that began with the panic of 1837, Cyrus's family moved to live with his mother's father, the Baptist preacher, near Utica, a boomtown thanks to the building of the Erie Canal and a Baptist stronghold. Cyrus went to church on Sundays and heard plenty of God's message in his grandfather's sermons, and he studied his Bible. His mother would have made sure of that as the daughter of a minister in Utica.

Cyrus was a charismatic speaker from the time he was quite young. In those days, speaking skill was valued as highly as athleticism is today. Going to speeches and sermons was how people educated and entertained themselves—and fed their souls. The ministry was something parents wanted for their sons, especially when those sons were Baptist or Methodist in New York State.

At age eleven, Cyrus dropped out of school and took a job on the Erie Canal, which flowed through the burned-over district. It wasn't unusual then for children to leave school to work to support their families, and his family was large: seventeen Teeds and Tuttles lived on the grandfather's property, not all of them able to work. Five of Cyrus's siblings were younger than eight, and two aunts were "idiotic," according to the U.S. census.[9]

Along with ten thousand other boys that year, Cyrus was a "hoggee," driving the animals that pulled the lines that tugged the boats along the waterway. The origin of the word "hoggee" isn't known, but some trace it to the British "hoggler," a field laborer of the lowest class. Hoggees were almost always young boys. The work day was divided into six-hour increments. Cyrus walked fifteen miles, took a break, then walked another fifteen miles. After each shift, he loaded the animals onto the boat and traveled down the canal in the bow with them.[10]

The boys were away from home for the seven months of the season, and they were treated as adults, with the exception of their pay—eight dollars a month (about $230 today), one-third of what the men earned. Most likely, Cyrus's boss—a private boat captain—was a tyrant. The captains dispensed the pay at the end of the season and so looked for reasons to fire them or make them mad enough to quit before the season ended. Some of the hoggees themselves were bullies. One large Irish boy tried to drive Cyrus off the job, and, if the official Koreshan story can be believed, Cyrus subdued him with a well-placed punch on the jaw. Working on the canal was an early lesson in capitalism, which Cyrus formed a lifelong distaste for.[11]

The canal was Cyrus's school, and by all indications he was ravenous for knowledge. He encountered a wide variety of people—not only boys like him, but passengers on the well-appointed packet boats: wealthy people and intellectuals, the pious and not-so-pious, preachers and prostitutes.

Cyrus was loose in a world of new thought and away from his pious Baptist family—though certainly not out of the grasp of itinerant preachers, who ministered to even the lowly canal boys, and other Christians, who were watching out for them and working to improve their conditions.

It's easy to imagine the slight boy, floating down the canal on his six-hour break beside his mules, his nose in his Bible, and then walking on the towpath, eavesdropping on the conversations on deck. Certainly, walking thirty miles a day gave him plenty of time to be with these new thoughts, some of which he knew his family would find distasteful, like Swedenborgianism and Spiritualism. Pseudosciences like mesmerism and phrenology, popular at the time, would have fascinated Cyrus with their promise of bridging the natural and spiritual worlds. Social and economic ideas—like communism and land reform—also traveled up and down the canal.

At twenty, when it came time to choose a career, Cyrus chose medicine, going against his family's expectations. He hoped it could teach him the mysteries of the brain and body and put him directly in touch with the body's vital life force. He wanted to uncover something hidden in the spiritual realm. He was hardly alone in this. It was a national obsession. Preaching couldn't do this, especially now, as Baptists were turning away from science and frowning on mystics. He began an apprenticeship with his uncle, a physician and surgeon in Utica.[12]

That same year, he married his second cousin Fidelia ("faithful") Rowe, who was so petite she looked more like a child than an adult. And she *was* nearly a child, only sixteen, when they married. Her family "were not a particularly strong lot—mentally or physically," a cousin later wrote. The couple had a son, Arthur, and moved to Brooklyn so Cyrus could study medicine.[13]

Teed's studies were interrupted by the Civil War. When New York called for volunteers, there was no question that he would answer the call; he and all of his brothers served. Western New York had long been anti-slavery. In 1862, he enlisted, agreeing to serve for three years, entering as a corporal. Teed's followers would later revise that title to "medic." In Koreshan lore, it is written that "Doctor Teed" treated wounded soldiers, and when he did so, he noticed that the men with faith in a higher power recovered more quickly than the ones without faith. He doesn't seem to have corrected anyone who called him a Civil War doctor.[14]

If Corporal Teed had a realization about healing and faith during the Civil War, it happened when he was a patient, not a doctor. One year into his service, in August 1863, he collapsed from sunstroke on a march near Warrenton, Virginia, and suffered partial paralysis of his left leg. He was hospitalized in Alexandria for two months—more time with his thoughts; no improvement in his condition—before being discharged, deemed unfit even for the invalid corps.

He recovered from the paralysis and returned to studying medicine, completing his degree at the Eclectic Medical College of the City of New York in 1868, in the second graduating class.[15]

Eclectic medicine was uniquely American, a formally recognized field with two dozen colleges and sixty-five journals. Eclectics—the word originates from "select" or "gather"—chose what they felt were the soundest practices from various camps of medicine, most often using homeopathic plant remedies and, when necessary, surgery. They were opposed to what they saw as depletive practices of bleeding, purging, and blistering, methods widely used by non-eclectic physicians—"regulars," eclectics called them for short. The eclectics believed that the body has a self-healing vitality and that remedies should aid that vitality. Furthermore, these remedies should be grown on American soil. The sledgehammer approach of strong medicine and drugs, many of which were imported from other countries, was undesirable. Eclectics hoped to reform medicine, in the same way that Martin Luther had sought to reform religion. They considered themselves protestants, in the "protest" sense of the word.[16]

Today, we understand how important the medical developments of the nineteenth century were—the introduction of aseptic surgery, the perfection of the hypodermic needle, vast improvements in anesthesia. But the perception then was that this new medicine was experimental and fraught with danger: surgeries could go horribly awry, patients (and doctors) became abusers of cocaine and morphine, and so on. Many patients were fearful of mainstream medicine. The eclectic doctor of medicine—the hometown, locally trained practitioner who made house calls—was comforting. People who were educated and well-to-do trusted homeopathic remedies over new medicine's drastic measures.

Eclectics and orthodox doctors scoffed at each other. The eclectics, for instance, dismissed germ theory and other important advances. Doctors on either side of the fence maintained an imperious air and a certainty that each was in the right. But the orthodox faction was winning, and eclectics were headed for failure: top hospitals were refusing to hire eclectic students as interns, and there was pressure from the American Medical Association to tighten educational standards. The bar for admission to eclectic medical college was lower than that for orthodox schools. Teed's apprenticeship with his uncle qualified him for admission—no high school or college necessary. There was also considerable infighting within the field of eclecticism. Given the threats eclectics faced, it was natural that they looked for people to blame. Teed, a licensed M.D. in the state of New York, would be among their targets.

Teed most likely loved medical college—not only for the knowledge, but also for the opportunity to hear strong speakers. Lectures and demonstrations were the main form of instruction, though students did observe surgeries, perform dissections, and attend clinics, sometimes optional. Stories abound of the colorful professors who led the lectures: those who were bombastic, those who spoke in a monotone, those who posed trick questions, who walked out of the classroom when students misbehaved, who didn't allow students to take notes, who openly insulted or embarrassed their pupils, or who avoided students altogether.

In addition to attending lectures, students were expected to write theses, which, according to one historian, "did little more than restate the conclusions and prejudices of the faculty." Based on the reams of Teed's later writings and lectures, we can assume that Teed took on heartily the task of writing a thesis, internalizing his professors' thoughts, and very likely forgetting the sources.[17]

Much later, his own style of lecturing would be professorial and dense with scientific terms, some of which he appropriated from medicine, using hyphens and suffixes as needed, as in this passage: "The alimentary canal of the alchemico-organic macrocosm is in the form of discular vacua, in which are the amalgamated mercurial disci." He sometimes used visual aids—a blackboard, a pointer, and a piece of chalk—even when his audience was a sole reporter.[18]

After graduation, he returned to Utica to work with his uncle on the second floor of Wells House, a landmark because of the Teeds' large sign—"He who deals out poison deals out death"—in letters nearly a foot wide and running the length of the building. It was a direct reference to doctors who dispensed drugs. On the first floor was a saloon whose owner took some good-natured teasing that the sign referred to his pouring poison from the taps.[19]

By now, Teed's hope that something would be revealed to him became a fixation, and this desire came to trump everything. Next door to his house, he set up a lab—a fully outfitted electro-alchemical laboratory, he called it. To imagine what it looked like, think of the illustrations and engravings of alchemists' labs from the Renaissance, then update them for the age of motors and the voltaic battery. Alchemists in Teed's day used beakers, flasks, stills, crystallization dishes, ring stands, furnaces, water baths, crucibles, mortar and pestle, tubing, funnels, spatulas, and tongs. Teed had a microscope and probably an early electromagnetic motor. He claimed to be able to taste differences between the electrical currents that corresponded to various metals, including mercury, gold, and silver.

During the day he saw clients, and at night he spent hours in the lab, experimenting and following his passions—alchemy, metaphysics, and electromagnetism. And because he was convinced he could unlock a mystery that no one ever had, he was primed for a spiritual awakening, which happened, according to him, when he was thirty.

On a midnight in late October of 1869, Teed sat alone in his laboratory, bathed in the gleam from his lantern. His wife and son were at home, probably sleeping, as he worked at his bench. This night was the pivotal experience of his life. Much later, he wrote it up and published it as *The Illumination of Koresh: Marvelous Experience of the Great Alchemist Thirty Years Ago, at Utica, N.Y.*

That night, he claimed, he turned lead into gold, something alchemists had attempted and failed to do since the beginning of alchemy, hence Teed's self-proclaimed title "the great alchemist." He didn't explain how he did it, only that polarity and spiritual substances were involved and that he tried many times with different solutions, watching for a miraculous change in his retort, a glass bulb with a downcast, tapering neck that looks like a goose searching for something on a counter. When the change occurred, he beheld "a molecular and metallic shower of marvelously lustrous particles . . . gilding the bottom of my retort." He viewed the golden dust through his microscope, ecstatic.[20]

Teed wrote that a mystic hand was at work in the lab with him—"the hand of the Alchemico-vietist . . . moved by a desire for human elevation." And so he stayed in the lab, working and waiting, sensing that there was more to come. Teed believed that the physical corresponded to the spiritual, as Swedenborg had written. And if the mystic hand had guided him to transmute physical substance, it might reveal an even more important transformation. If it was possible to turn lead into gold, perhaps disease and suffering in the body could be transformed, too—eliminated. Perhaps man could achieve victory over death. This is why he had chosen medicine. Because if there was a profession most likely to discover a cure for death, that was it. The evening was "fraught with momentous possibilities for the future of the world," he later wrote.

He took a break on his couch. As he lay there concentrating, he felt an odd sensation:

> a relaxation at the occiput or back part of the brain, and a peculiar buzzing tension at the forehead or sinciput; succeeding this was a sensation as of a Faradic battery of the softest tension, about the organs of the brain called the lyra, crura pinealis, and conarium. There gradually spread from the center of my brain to the extremities of my body, and, apparently to me, into the auric sphere of my being, miles outside of my body, a vibration so gentle, soft, and dulciferous that I was impressed to lay myself upon the bosom of this gently oscillating ocean of magnetic and spiritual ecstasy.

He reached for his body but couldn't feel anything. It had apparently dissolved. He opened his eyes but saw nothing. "Has my thirst for knowledge consumed my body?" he wondered.

He then heard "a sweet, soft murmur which sounded as if thousands of miles away." It was a female voice. But to his amazement, he was the one speaking or, as he phrased it, "The words proceed[ed] from my own natural organs of articulation."

"Fear not, my Son," the voice said. "I have seen thee as thou hast wandered through the labyrinthine coilings of time's spiral transmigrations."

The angel told him he had lived many lives and that she had been with him, waiting to help him realize a mission. In those past lives, he had died from disease, or had been too ambitious and caused his enemies to rise up against him. So she re-created him again and again ("clothed thee in another body") and waited, and she had never allowed him a glimpse of her until this moment. Tonight, the voice said, she would reveal herself. "For thou hast desired it."

A bright, dazzling light filled the laboratory, and Teed heard the angel speak—the words continuing to come from his own mouth—but still he didn't see her. "I have brought thee to this birth to sacrifice thee upon the altar of all human hopes." Her voice thrilled him "with profoundest and most intense passion of super-mundane filial felicity."

The words "super-mundane" and "filial" are important here. Teed was aware that "passion" could be misinterpreted, so he tamped the word down with "filial." Yet the writing is orgasmic. *The Illumination* plays out like a climax. "Receive now the blessing flowing from my August Motherhood," the angel said.

"I felt the supersensual vibration," he wrote, "the thrill of the touch of that regal hand as it rested softly and tenderly upon my brow. I experienced the zephyr breath . . . full of delicious fragrance as it passed over me, touching first my head and face, and then extending over me to the extremities of my being."

He fell to his knees and said, "My Mother, behold my obedience!" An aurora of purple and gold appeared. A corona, or crown, materialized, set with twelve magnificent diamonds.

Then her face emerged, "exquisitely chiseled." Her neck, shoulders, and arms were "equally exquisite in every detail of formation, to the very finger extremes, adorned with the most delicate, matchless, consummate finger nails." He described her hair as "falling in golden tresses of profusely luxuriant growth over her shoulders."

She stood on a silvery crescent, holding Mercury's caduceus—a winged staff with two serpents entwined around it. Teed's description of her matches the woman described in the Book of Revelation: "a woman clothed with the sun, and the moon under her feet, and upon her head a crown of twelve stars. . . . And she brought forth a man child, who was to rule all nations with a rod of iron."[21]

"Thou art chosen to redeem the race," the angel said. Teed would die, she told him, and his followers, the ones he would sacrifice his life for, would achieve immortality on earth.

She also promised him he would have an earthly woman to help him with his work. She would be Teed's equal; he would find her somewhere "in that surging mass of human woe." And when the time was right, the angel—the Divine Motherhood—would descend into this woman and inhabit her.

Teed asked the angel whether she was God in female form. He asked whether she was part of the Holy Trinity, just as Jesus and the Holy Ghost were. "Yes, my beloved Horos [sic], thy voice hast spoken the truth," she said through Teed's lips.

Following his illumination, Teed reflected on his beliefs and began organizing them into a set of principles that would become Koreshanity. These may have come to him all at once, full-blown, or they may have developed over time. It isn't clear, because he revealed them to his followers gradually. In developing his religion, he had plenty to work with, having lived during a time of religious fervor and popular mystical beliefs.

His religion needed to incorporate science, he knew. The physical universe was revealing itself to be a strange place, and people hungered for a faith that cured the dissonance between the known and unknown. Scientific advances and theories proliferated—the theory of evolution; the periodic table for classifying the elements; the theory of electromagnetism—and they were widely celebrated. Science was becoming less mystical.

"The scientific spirit has cast out the demons," James Garfield said in 1867, "and presented us with Nature, clothed and in her right mind. . . . It has given us, for the sorceries of the alchemist, the beautiful laws of chemistry; for the dreams of the astrologer, the sublime truths of astronomy; for the wild visions of cosmogony, the monumental records of geology; for the anarchy of diabolism, the laws of God."[22]

Though Garfield said science was revealing the laws of God, many people believed it was contradicting them. The biggest, and scariest, proposition was evolution. How could Darwin's theory be true when the Bible clearly stated that the world was created in seven days?

Yet people had great hope that science could reveal the spirit world. Given all that science was rapidly revealing about the physical world, it seemed reasonable to believe that science would one day connect us with unseen realms.

All of the pseudosciences Garfield mentioned (alchemy, astrology, cosmogony) were still very much alive in faith, especially in mysticism. Teed shared the longing to reconcile religion and science, and he would use occult techniques like alchemy to do so. "Real" science, Teed seemed to believe, would catch up, and if it didn't, it was flawed.

His religio-science was a mix of millennialism, mesmerism, the beliefs of Swedenborg, Theosophy, Spiritualism, mind healing, Buddhism, the primitive Christian church, Egyptian myth, Gnosticism, electromagnetism, and more. He wove them together, just as the eclectic doctor blended different medical techniques. He called his system Koreshanity, giving no credit to others, and he proclaimed that it contained the answers to every question.

But for all he claimed to know, Teed kept himself unknowable. For his followers, there would always be a mystery around the corner, always more to know about Koreshanity, and it would be translated through him as they became capable of understanding it.

Many dismissed Teed as a lunatic, including some of his father's family back in Teedville. His brother Wilson was unbalanced, as documented by a historian in Moravia, New York. Wilson operated the first electric lighting plant in the village. One night the town's lights kept getting brighter and brighter, with no explanation. People who called the primitive telephone in the lighting plant got no answer, and "[Wilson] Teed was found on a hill above the plant waving his arms and talking with the spirits on the wires!"[23]

The best way to understand Cyrus Teed—and maybe the only way, given how cryptic his speeches, letters, and books were—is through the God complex, a term coined by psychoanalyst Ernest Jones, a contemporary of Freud and Jung and actually Freud's biographer. Jones is still widely cited as an authority on the God complex today, though psychiatrists no longer use that term. Today's psychiatrists would diagnose Teed with mania or narcissistic personality disorder, and likely both.[24]

Everyone, Jones wrote, had some level of narcissism, but "there is a class of men with whom [the God complex] is much stronger than usual." And the complex *was* much more common in men than in women, Jones noted.[25]

Teed embodied nearly every characteristic of the complex: "excessive admiration for and confidence in one's own powers"; "claiming powers possessed by the few"; claiming to know ahead of time when something is going to happen; and talking in monologue.[26]

Someone with the complex "wrap[s] himself in an impenetrable cloud of mystery and privacy. Even the most trivial pieces of information about himself . . . are invested with a sense of high importance." This is evident in the way Teed begins *The Illumination*:[27]

"I shall devote a little time in locating, briefly if vaguely, for you the state and town in which occurred the ever memorable events. I was born in one of the middle states of the United States of America, and was reared a short distance from an inland city, numbering at the time of which I speak, about 30,000 inhabitants."

But the subtitle of *The Illumination* told the reader exactly where he lived: "Marvelous Experience of the Great Alchemist Thirty Years Ago, at Utica, N.Y."

People with the God complex often exhibit excessive, and false, modesty (after turning metal into gold, Teed said he was "the humble instrument for the exploiture of so magnitudinous a result") and use long and circuitous diction, "at times so turgid and obscure as to render it really impossible to discover what is meant," Jones wrote. They are certain that they will be let in on a secret that hasn't been revealed to anyone else. They are usually resistant to new ideas, but when they *do* accept something new, they are likely to tweak it slightly, take full credit for it, and then make a point of emphasizing the differences between their idea and the original.[28]

Finally, Jones wrote, someone with a God complex envisions grand schemes of social reform, ideal worlds, or "even the birth of a new planet."[29]

Before she left, the angel told Teed she would be invisible to him from that point, but always with him, helping him during hard times. His mission wouldn't be easy, she said. He would struggle to make others see his light. She wouldn't go into detail about this struggle, she told him, because knowing this would be too much for him to bear.

At 2:30 a.m., Teed climbed into bed beside his slumbering wife. Two hours later, he was awakened by what sounded like a hurricane. When the winds subsided, he heard the sound of "great wings flying, and then the noise as of chariot wheels."[30]

He got up and looked out the window. He heard the chariot two more times, and then a whisper. It revealed to him the mystery of immortal life.

✳ 2 ✳

Inside the Earth

New York, 1869–1886

Thou shalt go to the land of shade.

—Angel to Teed, *The Illumination of Koresh*

Alone. After that dazzling hour that filled him, he had no one to share it with except his wife, Delia, who, history indicates, dismissed it. He was also alone in his medical practice, having left his uncle and opened his own office. When patients came, he shared his revelation and his doctrines but found that they weren't receptive. He also tried to bring his message to the local Baptist church, which not only rejected his doctrines but also froze him out by boycotting his business. He became known as the crazy doctor in Utica, so he moved to Binghamton, where he established another practice and where Delia could be close to her sister.[1]

One day in a Binghamton drugstore, he met Dr. Abie Andrews, a few years older than he and much taller. They must have made quite a pair; at over six feet tall, Abie dwarfed Teed. Abie was a religious seeker, full of spiritual questions that emerged as their friendship developed. The two men spent many hours in earnest conversation, debating points of faith, and Teed seemed to have answers to Abie's questions. Sometimes they argued heatedly on points of the Bible. At least once, Abie stormed out of Teed's office after a disagreement, with Teed insisting that he was right, admonishing Abie and telling him to read his Bible. When Abie consulted his Bible, he found that Teed had been correct. He came around to Teed's way of thinking and became Teed's first follower, a lifelong financial supporter, and his best friend.[2]

Abie's wife, Jennie, was another story. She did not accept Teed's doctrines. A genteel Southern lady with a soft voice, she grew up in Virginia in a family of orthodox Methodists. She met Abie, thirteen years her senior, in Alexandria, where he served in the medical corps during the Civil War as a Union physician and surgeon.

When Abie and Jennie married and moved to Binghamton, Jennie left her parents' home in Alexandria, and by the time Teed came along, she was busy with three children—a four-year-old, a three-year-old, and an infant son, Allen, whom Teed fondly nicknamed "Allie."

Teed's medical practice in Binghamton was flagging, much as it had in Utica and for similar reasons. People in Binghamton called him a crackpot. To make a living, he began traveling from small town to small town in New York, taking Delia and their son along, as Delia's health, never excellent, began to decline. He tried practicing in his hometown and the surrounding areas, but even there, in his birthplace, "he was without honor," wrote Carl Carmer, a writer for the *New Yorker*, years later. Teed and Delia moved farther afield, to Equinunk, Pennsylvania. The kinder Koreshan accounts say that Teed's patients were slow to pay and that this forced him to keep moving in order to make money, but it's probably more accurate that when patients heard his doctrines, they didn't return.[3]

A doctor without patients and a shepherd with no flock, he often returned to stay with Abie and Virginia in Binghamton. Abie's son Allen remembers that Teed's clothes were worn to a shine but clean and neat. "Cyrus was a capable physician," Allen wrote years later. "Had he adhered strictly to his medical practice, [he] could have made a success almost anywhere with his profession, but being imbued with these new and radical ideas, could not refrain from discussion and soon talked himself out of a thriving practice."[4]

Teed and the young Allen grew fond of each other. They often took long walks on Sundays, once going so far that to get back to Binghamton they hopped on a train of empty coal cars. Allen didn't know anything about Teed's doctrines, only that he was fun to be around; on one walk, they tried to see whether they could beat George Washington's alleged broad jump record, twenty-two feet and three inches. Allen also remembered that Teed was an expert croquet player. He and Allen's father, Abie, played in the Andrews's backyard, sometimes until well after dark, when they had to tie rags on the wickets to see them.[5]

For a short time, Teed and his family lived with his parents, who made mops in Moravia, New York. But Delia's health was failing; tuberculosis had spread to her spine, and she moved to Binghamton for good, with their then-teenaged son, Arthur. Abie became her doctor as Teed kept moving, returning periodically to check in on her and stay with Abie and Jennie.

Teed settled alone in Sandy Creek, New York, near Lake Ontario, where he hoped to make a fresh start. It was the farthest from home he had ever practiced. He didn't know a soul there, which perhaps he thought would work to his advantage. The town's eclectic physician had died, and it was rumored that the old man's practice was so successful that he left his widow forty thousand dollars. It turned out that the people were alarmingly healthy, Teed wrote to Abie. Closer to the truth was that as people learned about Teed's beliefs, the old pattern repeated itself.

"Once the people of nearby Ruralhill, Pierrepont Manor, and Lorraine heard the newcomer proclaim the true religion and the true science they looked at him oddly and the next time they needed a doctor sent to Pulaski for one," Carl Carmer wrote. Abie sent Teed money to prop up his finances.[6]

From Sandy Creek, Teed wrote Abie volumes of letters, addressing him as "My beloved Doctor" or "My beloved brother," and he gave him the nickname "Abiel," an endearment that may have referred to one of King David's warriors. Abie wrote back faithfully, the two men continuing to discuss points of religion and Abie offering feedback on the circulars and prospectuses that Teed produced to attract followers. Abie seems to have been the only person Teed took criticism from—and sometimes he invited Abie's opinions—but he refuted them as often as not, as in the case of a particular circular Teed posted in Sandy Creek, which referred to some of the residents as "conical headed heathen[s], asses or peak heads." When Abie disapproved of the circular, Teed argued that he hadn't named specific people.[7]

His letters to Abie concerned his big plans—for building a utopia and for conquering Babylon, the metaphorical home of the wicked. He wrote his sister Emma as well, letters that mulled his strategy and showed his loneliness. "My Dear little Sister. Why don't you write to me and tell me what you are thinking about?"[8]

It's evident that Emma wrote him, too, because in his letters, he mentions receiving hers. But she didn't write as often as he wished she would. "I wish you would write me often," he wrote. "Don't wait for me I am very busy with my work. Great changes are hastening with great speed."[9]

Teed's strategy for spreading his religio-science was to become accepted by an established group. In Sandy Creek, Teed joined the Young Men's Christian Association to "enlarge my sphere of action and make it and the church a stepping stone to get my truth before the world," he wrote Emma. He also accepted an invitation to be with the Methodists, which, in that day, would have angered and shocked many Baptists. It definitely upset his father, which Cyrus knew. He explained himself to Emma: "I never withdrew from the Baptist church. It withdrew from me."[10]

"If I can unite with Christians and through that association gain a hearing, it is my duty to do so if I cannot get my views to the public otherwise," he wrote Emma. "When Cyrus the Persian conquered Babylon he did it by getting into Babylon by stratagem. When the modern Cyrus conquers modern Babylon he may be compelled to go into Babylon by stratagem."[11]

Perhaps Teed's grandest plans lay with the Harmony Society in Economy, Pennsylvania, north of Pittsburgh on the Ohio River, where fewer than a hundred people lived communally and practiced celibacy. Teed tracked the society closely and doubtless took ideas from them for the commune he wanted to build. Its members were industrious, producing silk, wool, cotton, wine, rye whiskey, and other products.

The Harmonists (also called Economites, after the town's name) were wealthy—so much so that it was common in the eighteen hundreds to say that a wealthy person was "as rich as an Economite." At one point, the Economites didn't even know how much money they had. The leader had burned the accounting ledgers, signifying that finances were not a concern. They ate five meals a day, it was said, and the brick streets of their town were lined with sturdy two-story houses covered with grape vines up to the gables. At the center of the village were geometric gardens with box hedges, tulips, and dahlias, and along the bluff at the edge of town, benches beneath large shade trees allowed members to sit and overlook the Ohio River. On any given day, the broad avenues were nearly deserted.[12]

"As you walk along the quiet, shady streets," one visitor wrote, "you meet only occasionally some stout, little old man, in short light-blue jacket and a tall and very broad-brimmed hat, looking amazingly like Hendrick Hudson's men in the play of Rip Van Winkle."[13]

When Teed became interested in the Economites, a new patriarch, Jacob Henrici, had taken charge, investing the money in railroads, oil, and coal, growing the wealth further. The Economites even became a banking power in Pittsburgh. As the society shrank, the money was shared among fewer people, allowing them to enjoy more leisure. This is what Teed wanted for himself and his followers, who were limited then to only Abie and Emma, though he was working to add believers in Sandy Creek.

Father Henrici was known as Santa Claus Henrici for his generosity. He freely gave money and loans to outsiders and was supportive of communal societies whose doctrines were based on the Bible, as Teed's were. In 1880, Teed and Abie wrote to Henrici. They heard back quickly—from a Mr. Wood, apparently Henrici's secretary, asking for an explanation of Teed's theory of immortal life. "Material assistance will not be lacking," Wood wrote, "when confidence is established between us."[14]

Teed and Abie paid a visit to Economy and began strategizing. Their purpose, Teed told Abie, was to appropriate Economy for their use. He and Abie would take it over, with Abie going before him to arrange matters and to become the Economites' spiritual leader. Abie would be Teed's "Elijah," he told him in one letter. They kept up the correspondence with Wood, but Teed received only one hundred dollars from the Economites, an amount that must have insulted him, because he wrote to Abie, "When I am ready to use the people of Economy for the Divine use I shall simply command not beg."[15]

In his letters, Teed rarely asked Abie what was happening in the Andrewses' lives. When Abie and Jennie had a baby in the 1870s, he congratulated them, belatedly and briefly. But in the same sentence of congratulations, Teed expressed his hope that Abie and Jennie would begin practicing celibacy. It's not clear whether they did, but if so, it didn't last. Jennie gave birth to another son five years later.

Abie rarely mentioned Jennie in his letters, and this prompted Teed to ask about her, specifically with regard to her feelings toward his doctrine. "Is she to pass through a struggle before coming within the embrace of this truth?" he wrote. Occasionally, Abie indicated that Jennie was coming around, and Teed wrote back to encourage her, saying that she had important work to do in the coming movement, and that he thought of her as a sister, or that he wanted to think of her that way, but modestly said he didn't feel himself worthy of calling her that.[16]

Isolated, lonely, and with time on his hands, he started a newspaper, *Herald of the Messenger of the New Covenant of the New Jerusalem*, and began dreaming of the community he would build from scratch—a celibate society where members shared labor and resources—a rejection of capitalism, which he considered paganistic cannibalism, with big fish swallowing smaller ones.

As with his religious doctrines, he had plenty to draw from when working out the details of his community. Many utopias had prospered and failed in the mid-nineteenth century, and he studied the successful ones. He admired the Shakers for their piety, celibacy, and simple way of life, supported by the industry of furniture making. The Shakers (led by a woman) believed that women and men should have equal standing, as did the Quakers, who practiced gender equality long before the idea became mainstream. "Among Quakers there had never been any talk of woman's rights—it was simply human rights," activist Lucretia Mott said. Swedenborg, too, whom Teed admired, had supported equal rights.[17]

For Teed, equal rights went hand in hand with celibacy. By having sex, a woman surrendered her power to a man, which made her like a slave, and marriage was an institutional form of bondage for women. (Teed never reflected on how his own marriage figured in.) Celibacy not only gave a woman control of her own body, but it also was the secret of immortality for both women and men. Teed taught that as long as humans were divided into male and female, they would be incomplete, continually coming together in a fruitless attempt to bridge the divide. But by reproducing, they would only create more human beings that were divided.

Instead, a Koreshan should redirect sexual desire toward a desire for closeness with God, specifically, toward Teed. By focusing their love on him, they would ensure their immortality on earth. Once enough followers did this, their energy would cause an electromagnetic explosion in his brain and consume the pineal gland, responsible for sexual potency. This would enable him to pass into his chosen woman and become divine, both male and female, a mother-father god. At this point, his believers would become immortal, biune beings, too, healing the division between male and female within themselves. A man would become a woman who enclosed a man; a woman would become a man who enclosed a woman, as the prophet Jeremiah foretold: "A woman shall encompass a man."[18]

Teed planned for men, women, and children to live separately and for the children to be raised by the group. The followers would avoid "the family tie" (showing favor to their biological children) and instead show equal concern for all members. They would address each other as "brother" and "sister."

Finally, Teed developed a peculiar tenet that no other community had: earth is hollow, and everyone lives inside of it. To visualize Teed's version of earth, imagine peeling the paper map off an old-fashioned school globe, slicing the globe open, then pasting the map inside the walls of the globe. At the center of the globe is the entire cosmos. Our earth—our universe—is encased by a crust one hundred miles thick with an outermost rind of gold. Outside of this is nothingness.

Teed wasn't the first to believe the earth was hollow. Edmund Halley, Sir

John Leslie, and Cotton Mather proposed hollow earth theories. But Teed seems to be the first to claim that we all live inside. John Cleves Symmes theorized that we could enter the earth through polar openings, but in Teed's version, there were no openings. None were necessary, because the universe is contained within the earth.

Earth is stationary, according to Teed's cosmogony. Our sun, half-dark and half-light, gyrates methodically to create day and night and seasons. We are held to the earth not by gravity but by "gravic rays" emitted by the sun.

It's not clear exactly when Teed developed his theory of the hollow earth. Throughout Teed's life, Symmes's work was widely discussed and reviewed in journals and popular magazines like *Harper's Magazine* and *Atlantic Monthly*. Five years before Teed's illumination, Jules Verne published his novel *Journey to the Center of the Earth*. Teed would have known about Symmes's and Verne's works, and it's almost certain that he was influenced by them. But his theory had major differences. And in keeping with the God complex, he emphasized these differences. Just as psychoanalyst Ernest Jones wrote, Teed envisioned the birth of a new planet of sorts. Copernicus, Teed taught, was a fool.

The young Allen Andrews was shocked when he heard this theory and at first thought it absurd. In school, he had learned the Copernican model. The teachers demonstrated this as fact by having one boy hold an apple and orbit around another boy, who held a small globe. "Surely, I reasoned, these teachers would not have been hired to instruct us in anything but the truth. I was later to realize the error of this conclusion." He became a strong proponent of the concave earth theory.[19]

It would be several years before Teed had the time and the men to prove his theory. But he would do it.

For a time in Sandy Creek, Teed may have believed he was realizing his goal of forming a community. He wrote Emma that he had made his home with "a splendid family father, mother and daughter who receive the doctrine and are living it." The 1880 census lists him as "boarder" in the household of a Mr. and Mrs. Moore and their eighteen-year-old daughter.[20]

But there was evidence that he was not having success. One morning, he found this note tacked to his gatepost, left there the night before: "June 17th 1879 Nine P.M. Dr. Teed: You will be allowed 24 hours to get out of town, or be helped out. By order of Committee."[21]

"They are fighting hard here to worst me," he wrote to Abie.[22]

And to Emma: "People are getting exasperated over my doctrines. Of course I shall make no move to get out of town."[23]

Cyrus loved his sister Emma deeply. She was the baby of the family, seventeen years younger. Full grown, she was very small—only four foot eight inches tall and ninety-five pounds. She had clear blue eyes, fair skin, and light brown hair. One follower later wrote that Emma reminded her of a sparrow, "the way she would dart in to give her instructions and out again before anybody could say anything, but she was goodhearted." Said to be a talented seamstress, Emma sewed for her brother, but once sent him a shirt that didn't fit. "What was the matter that you got my sleeves so short?" Teed wrote. "About two and a half inches and the wristband pretty short also."[24]

Emma often visited her various siblings, and Cyrus's letters tracked her from place to place, asking her to visit him too. She was apparently the peacemaker and family go-between. When Cyrus was annoyed with his father, Jesse, he didn't communicate directly with him. "Ask Father" such and such, he wrote to Emma. Similarly, when Jesse was frustrated with his wife, Emma's mother, he wrote to Emma, "Tell your mother . . ."

Cyrus frequently assured Emma that his work on the Lord's kingdom was progressing. He implored her to hold fast to the faith, to be patient, and not to worry about those around her who did not believe. "Let them go through the fire if they must but look to it that your own soul be not distracted by the influences that would direct your thoughts from the ultimate work of God's chosen ones."[25]

Except when he went on a discourse, his writing to Emma was clearer than his public writing—and more vulnerable. From Sandy Creek, he assured her of his big plans. "I am as yet undecided as to the best move to make. I want you to remain there [at home] for a few days till I decide where we shall go. My next move must be a successful one. Much depends upon it. We shall be able to make a successful move soon. Be patient and faithful to the end. As ever your loving Cyrus." And Emma was patient and faithful to the end, following him and believing in him all her life and saving his letters.[26]

Cyrus's father was a letter writer, too, and a jokester who was fond of rhyme. Jesse once wrote his wife, "Old Plymouth is the very spot where I am doomed some time to squat," while away for several weeks on a job. He loved fanciful metaphors and similes, as when he described his talkative wife in a letter to Emma: "Her tongue runs like a sheep, trotting on a shingle." He wrote Cyrus, too, sometimes poking fun at him, though none of these letters survive. Teed found this irksome.[27]

"Ask Father," he wrote Emma, "why he addresses my letters S. R. Teed. I don't spell Cyrus with an S." Following his sign-off (Your Loving Cyrus), he added this:

Cyrus
C R Teed C R
C.[28]

It's hard to know whether Jesse was making fun by spelling his son's name with an "S" or whether he was taking a jab. It is clear from letters and journals that Jesse was not a follower. "If I am to judge father," Cyrus once wrote, "by what he writes me I am sure he has not much confidence either in the integrity of my purpose or my desire and ability—by the Lord—to effect it."[29]

Cyrus hung on in Sandy Creek until his business failed completely. It was the summer of 1880. His parents, in Moravia, needed help with the mop factory, and they asked Cyrus to run it. Jesse may have hoped that this would compel his son to forget his mission to save humanity. But Cyrus must have seen a financial opportunity, thinking that the mop business could support a commune. After all, many communities prospered from simple work like this, Cyrus knew. The Shakers crafted beautiful furniture; the Harmonists spun silk, cotton, and wool; and the Oneida Perfectionists produced flatware that endures today. (Brides all over the world register for Oneida silverware, china, and crystal, probably unaware that the Perfectionists practiced free love, that older women introduced teenage boys to sex and older men did the same for young women, and that the community's founder was accused of statutory rape.)

When Cyrus decided to move to Moravia, he wrote Emma with big news, though he didn't disclose what the news was exactly. "I have much to say to you. Now is the best time for you to come. . . . What I have to say to you I will not attempt to do by writing. I will talk with you when we meet."[30]

By the time Cyrus took over the mop business, he had gathered a very small following, and he started his first communal home in his parents' house. He produced a newspaper, and his people directed their energies to the humble work of making mops. Abie stayed in Binghamton with his family, but he sent money to support the group and the business.

Of the people who lived there, three were not followers—Teed's mother, father, and a sister. The others included his sister Emma; Teed's brother Oliver; and three married women who had left their husbands. One of these women had brought her two daughters. Of all the women who lived in Teed's community, only two had husbands who believed.

Newspaper reporters through the years would be quick to point out that women left their husbands to join Teed. The reports insinuated that Teed was a philanderer, and they mocked the women for having small brains. But Koreshan women were far from dumb, as reflected in their public writing and journals. They felt they had more freedom than women on the outside did. Here was a place where it was all right to leave a husband or to live apart from him and be considered an equal. Household chores and child care were shared, and this meant less work.

The townspeople of Moravia didn't believe that Teed's community was celibate. It was scandalous, they gossiped, comparing them with the promiscuous Perfectionists. One woman in the Moravia community raised considerable suspicion among outsiders: Ellen Woolsey. It was said that she and Teed had an inappropriate relationship.

Meantime, Delia was living (and slowly dying) in Binghamton. They were still married, and Teed mentioned her often in his letters to Dr. Andrews, the two men discussing treatments for her.[31]

When Cyrus visited Delia, he seemed less concerned with her health and more concerned with whether she believed in him. "I have spent some little time with Delia," he wrote Emma from Binghamton, "and find that she is growing a good deal, but it seems hard for her to accept me as the shepherd while at the same time she confesses her belief in the doctrines I advocate."[32]

The mop business wasn't going well. On a sales trip to New York City, he wrote Emma that mops didn't seem to be in demand there but that he believed things would turn around. "I hope none of you will get discouraged," he wrote to his small band of followers. "I love you more than ever and am not content to be away from my little group of faithful ones." In spite of financial infusions from Abie, the business failed, and without it, the Moravian community dissolved.[33]

At this point in the official Koreshan account, there is a two-year gap seamed over as follows: "He took his group to New York City, feeling that more converts could be attracted in a less hidebound, more sophisticated area."[34]

But Teed did not go directly to New York City. He and Emma moved to Syracuse, along with one of the women from the Moravia commune, and Cyrus's brother Oliver, also an eclectic physician, joined them. Their ailing mother,

Sarah, came for an extended visit. Their father was left behind in Moravia, and he seemed relieved that Cyrus's followers were gone, especially the females. He wrote Emma:

> I have kept the house in fine running order, mutch better, than to have *She-mates* mussing *around*, And, with close fastened doors and windows have succeeded *marvelously* in keeping aloof from *She sympathizers*, of whom I have a *terable*, *dread*, especially of sutch as carry fire-arms and fire *legs* [emphasis Jesse's]. Tell your mother Mrs. Mun has just been in, to borrow some coffee (that was all) and of course I got the news.[35]

The "news" was that Ellen Woolsey was in Syracuse, too, but not living with Cyrus. "Something hadn't *worked* just *right* and [Ellen] had given that part of the program up," Jesse wrote.

Emma invited her father to come see them in Syracuse, but he hesitated because of Sarah.

"I suppose you mean, *you* want me, to come and see *you*," Jesse responded. "Your mother . . . had said to me, emphaticly, that she did not want me to 'tag her out there' hence you see there is at present a great gulph between us." He ended the letter, "Well Pet, I want to see you, but if you can't come here, you may wait until I can do so without a violation of orders."[36]

Teed and his brother opened a medical practice in the Wolf block of Onondaga Street, "one of the most aristocratic streets in the city," the *New York Times* reported. The patients were "among some of the best people." The business was successful until, quite suddenly, it wasn't.[37]

The Teeds' advertisement in the Syracuse city directory read as follows:

Syracuse Institute of Progressive Medicine,
with a special Department of
Medical Electricity.
We are giving special attention to the treatment of
Chronic Diseases.

Medical electricity was widely accepted in Teed's time. Doctors applied electrical current to various parts of the body using a power source hooked up to electrodes. They used electricity to treat most anything—mumps, rheumatism, gout, cholera, burns, and even squinting. The body's life force was much like a battery, the theory went. The nervous system sent out impulses like an electrical flow. When that flow was disturbed by disease, illness, or exhaustion, electricity could reenergize it.

This seemed physiologically sound to many people, and it also made spiritual sense—to Calvinists, Methodists, and Quakers, at least. The practice of medical electricity became a fad in New York's Hudson Valley in the early eighteen hundreds.[38]

This was also the age of hysteria, when women were thought to suffer from maladies caused by "deranged action of the reproductive organs," wrote William White, M.D., in his 1873 handbook *Medical Electricity*. White was a professor at the New York Medical College for Women.[39]

A woman might be troubled by "mental emotions, disappointed love, religious enthusiasm, or other problems" that caused "fulness in the head, confusion, with variable states of mind." Electrotherapy was the answer, White wrote, "unparalleled . . . for all derangements peculiar to that sex."[40]

A common treatment for hysteria was for the physician to stimulate the genitals of the afflicted woman until she had a hysterical paroxysm, an orgasm. Similar treatments were prescribed for other conditions, too. White's suggested treatment for chorea (convulsions) sounds quite pleasant but for the possibility of being electrocuted:

> First place the patient in a shallow warm bath with negative at the vagina, and treat with positive S.C. (secondary current), over the lumbar region, ovaries, and pubes, with brisk current for ten or fifteen minutes; then put the feet in warm water, and treat down the spine, and over the same parts down to the middle of the thighs, for ten minutes, at the same time making a few passes over the breasts.[41]

There is no evidence that Teed performed such intimate treatments, but they were standard practices. Teed was so enthusiastic about electrotherapy that he and Abie invented their own electro-therapeutic apparatus, for which they received a patent in 1883.[42]

The most successful doctors added something special: human magnetism. "In certain mental and nervous conditions," White wrote, "a word, a look, or a touch, from the healer, produces wonderful changes in the all-believing subject."[43]

By all accounts, Teed had plenty of magnetism. Descriptions of him usually mention his eyes, hazel brown and mesmerizing. One reporter described them as "implacable, unreadable, hypnotic."[44]

In June 1884, Mrs. Ezra Cobb sought treatment from Dr. Teed at the recommendation of a pastor. She was suffering from nervous prostration, a vague diagnosis that included exhaustion, depression, excitement, and in severe cases, nervous breakdown.

Teed determined that Mrs. Cobb should be home in bed. Instead of treating her in his office, he would come to her house to administer electrical treatments. After a few visits, he began telling her about his doctrines and told her that he was sent to save humanity. At first, she didn't pay much attention, but as he kept visiting and talking to her, she became interested. "The man was a wonderfully plausible person," Mrs. Cobb later told the *Syracuse Daily Journal*, "and I was prone to believe almost any ridiculous theory in my nervous condition."[45]

Over the course of several weeks, Mrs. Cobb and her mother gave Teed money—some as payment for his medical services and some to advance his cause. Cobb's son Willie, fourteen, had been saving his pennies to give to his Sunday school, but decided that Teed should have it instead. "We were all so firmly impressed with the truth of his belief," Mrs. Cobb told the *Journal*, "that we thought it best to 'give to the Lord,' as he [Teed] expressed it, our substance."

In all, Mrs. Cobb, her mother, and Willie paid him twenty dollars (more than $500 in today's money), and they pledged a ring of Mrs. Cobb's. Having received this sum, Teed felt sufficiently paid and told Mrs. Cobb he would not bill her husband, which was apparently his normal practice.

There was an additional reason he chose not to bill the husband. "I learned," Teed told the *Journal*, "that her husband's jealousy was being excited, partially through the influence of a near neighbor, and this without the slightest provocation. My patient's mother was nearly always present with her daughter when I made my visits."

One day, feeling that she wasn't getting any better, Mrs. Cobb got out of bed and visited Teed's office for treatment, taking her mother along. Once outside, she experienced a change, she told the *Journal*. "Going out in the air acted as a sort of counter-irritant, and I found my faith in Dr. Teed rapidly oozing away."

At his office, she took an electrical treatment and overheard a conversation between Teed and her mother. Was Mr. Cobb kind to his wife? Teed wanted to know. Mrs. Cobb was infuriated, she told the *Journal*, which reported the events and the conversation that followed.

"I told him in a moment that I was treated as well by my husband as any woman in America."

When she didn't show up for her next appointment, Teed went to where her son worked to ask about her. "I was met by Mr. Avery [the owner of the company]," Teed said, "who threatened me . . . with mob violence, saying, 'if you do not pack up your duds and get out of Syracuse, . . . I have men and neighbors who will help you out. Tar and feathers are too good for you.'"

Someone visited his office and tried to blackmail him, Teed claimed. This man threatened to make things hot unless Teed paid him. "Not being accustomed to mobs and blackmail," Teed told the newsman, "I refused to comply, as I preferred a more honorable way of settling my account with the husband of my patient."

The matter never went to the courts. It was covered in the Syracuse and Auburn, New York, papers. The *New York Times* reported it on the front page above the fold on a Sunday.

Sure He Is the Prophet Cyrus
A Doctor Obtaining Money on the Ground That He Is a New Messiah

The district attorney told reporters he planned to charge Teed with soliciting money under false pretenses. Teed responded that there *were* no false pretenses. He could prove he was a prophet. He wrote a letter to Mrs. Cobb, which the *Syracuse Daily Journal* acquired and printed. Teed said he would return the money if she would be honest about her motivation: that she had given her money willingly and later had a change of heart.[46]

It was never about the money, Cobb responded in the *Journal*. She had gone public with her complaint, she said, in order to warn others who might not be so lucky to recover their judgment as she had. "My mother was on the verge of selling a house and lot she owns in Camden, N.Y., and giving [the money] to him for his religious work," Mrs. Cobb told the *Journal*, "and I think I should have sold my piano for the same reason, but we are both glad we did not do so."[47]

Teed's reputation was shot. Both the *Journal* and the *New York Times* had dredged up Teed's time in Moravia, when "it was said that he had eloped with Mrs. Ellen Woolsey." And though the word "elope" has innocent meanings ("run away," "escape," and "abscond"), the citizens of Syracuse couldn't resist the less pure definition.[48]

The preacher at the First Methodist Episcopalian Church in Syracuse defended Teed, saying his "peculiar" beliefs were too advanced for today's world. A handful of sources characterized the Ellen Woolsey matter as gossip or said that Teed was honorable. This didn't help. Neither did his lecture later that month, "The Science of Immortal Life." The paper, in announcing the lecture, included Teed's back story as a "crank."[49]

The Cobb incident and resulting media coverage put an end to the medical practice in Syracuse. Teed and his siblings shuttered the Institute.

Four women went with him to New York City, including Emma and a cousin, who Cyrus had hoped would help him financially but didn't. He spent all his money on moving expenses, transportation, and one month's rent and asked Abie for a loan. A few believers he had gained from upstate sent in donations, but not enough for them to be comfortable. Mrs. Sarah Paterson, who would become one of Teed's most loyal followers, wrote Abie Andrews that winter, saying that they were hungry and had little heat in their flat.[50]

Meantime, Emma got word from Jesse that her mother was ill. There was a lot of sickness in Moravia, Jesse wrote, many deaths, "and pauperism in high places." Their tenants couldn't pay the rent. "We have to paddle against a pretty strong current to pull through the winter."[51]

Emma and Cyrus's mother died that October, as did Cyrus's wife, Delia. The followers in New York City dispersed and the little group was no more. Then a well-to-do woman invited Cyrus to live with her at East Sixty-Seventh and The Boulevard (Broadway, today) so that he could work on a book.

This woman and her friends were interested in Cyrus's doctrines—or seemed to be. "As subsequent events proved," a Koreshan biographer wrote, "they were not of a deep, permanent character."[52]

Teed's new sponsor promised she would publish his book and give him money to visit Abie in Binghamton. She gave him an allowance of fifty dollars but carefully monitored how he spent it, as well as his comings and goings. She and a friend, a Mrs. Egli, wanted to separate Teed and Abie, though it's not clear why. Mrs. Egli wrote to Abie, telling him that Teed was a philanderer and that he had taken a lover. When Abie asked Teed about these accusations, Teed protested strongly, saying that his sponsors had trapped him and that they were upset because he wouldn't make love to them.

Egli had made an especially peculiar request of Teed: sexual intercourse through the urethra. Troubled, Teed shared this with Abie in a letter in which he tried to puzzle out how urethral sex would be anatomically and spiritually impure. The sponsors even prevented Teed from sending a copy of his manuscript to Abie, saying that Abie would treat Teed's writing like the word of God and therefore not edit it. Until this point, Abie had helped Teed edit his fledgling newspaper and his manuscripts, but these women insisted on having editorial control.

Teed begged Abie to ignore the letters these women sent. They were trying to drive the two men apart, and they didn't support his doctrines. He disdainfully wrote to Abie that Egli was "an every-thingist, who wants devils and saints to live together in glee."[53]

But Teed was stuck. If he did something his sponsor didn't like, she would put him out. Worst of all, she had agreed to sponsor a woman who was also a proponent of urethral sex. The plan was to house her with Teed and finance a book she would write on this topic.

Teed's letters to Abie took on a frantic and even paranoid tone. He feared that Abie would believe these women. And if he lost Abie—his most faithful follower—he would have nothing. It's likely that Abie came to Teed's rescue, sending him the money he needed to extricate himself. He moved to another flat in the city.

For all of the closeness between Abie and Teed, there is at least one thing Teed may not have been honest about with his friend. When Allen Andrews, Abie's son, later wrote about Teed, he included the fiction that Teed had been a physician in the Civil War, rather than the truth, that he was an infantryman. It might have been an incorrect assumption on Allen's part. But just as likely, Teed had told his closest friend a lie.

It had been fifteen years since Teed's illumination. The angel had told him he would walk in the shade, and that had been true, except for the happy months in Syracuse. Having no community and only a few far-flung followers, he stayed in New York and continued to lecture about the power of the brain to heal.

A woman named Mrs. Thankful H. Hale from Chicago introduced herself after one of his lectures. She was organizing a convention of mental scientists in Chicago, and she invited him to speak. She would pay his transportation and other expenses and would arrange a place for him to stay. Teed accepted immediately.

✳ 3 ✳

It Must Be Good;
It's Made in a Church

On the evening of Monday, September 6, 1886—significant because it was Labor Day and a holiday for most workers—Cyrus Teed boarded a ferry to Jersey City to catch his train to Chicago, where he would speak at the mental science convention. The boat left the dock at sunset in an intermittent rain, the sound of its horn reverberating across the Hudson River. That day in New York City, fourteen thousand workers paraded down the streets, and people celebrated into the night. It's quite possible Teed shared the ferry with holiday revelers leaving Manhattan.[1]

Labor Day was noteworthy in 1886 because the conflict between labor and business was more tense than it had ever been. That year saw more than 1,500 strikes and lockouts. Six hundred thousand workers demanded better treatment and an eight-hour workday. As capitalists got richer from industry powered by laborers, the gap between the wealthy and the poor became wider and wider.[2]

Nowhere was the labor situation more strained than in Chicago. The city had become a symbol for labor unrest and for socialism. A few months prior, in May, eighty thousand workers had marched down Michigan Avenue, demanding a shorter workday. Chicago's mayor, Carter Harrison, sided with the workers, and defended even the anarchists. For three days after the May demonstration, strikes shut down the city. Two workers were killed at the McCormick Works, and this was followed by a rally at Haymarket Square, where someone threw dynamite into the crowd. Chaos erupted, seven policemen died, and city officials declared martial law, hauling hundreds of agitators to jail. Five anarchists were sentenced to death by hanging. There's no doubt that Teed looked forward to being in Chicago, given his belief that laborers would revolt, start a great war against the capitalists, and win.[3]

For Labor Day, the city of Chicago was ready with a sizable police presence, but the celebration was peaceful for the most part. The parade was a show of pride rather than a protest. Workers, organized by trade, marched behind colorful banners with brass bands and marshals. Blacksmiths rode the route on a wagon, banging out horseshoes with a red-hot iron, throwing off sparks as parade-goers cheered. Roofers had built a small house on wheels, and as they rolled down the street, they laid slates on the roof. Thirteen thousand marched, and many more thousands turned out to watch and to hear speeches. Look at this marvelous city, labor organizers told the crowd, gesturing to the buildings that stood as proof they had resurrected Chicago after the Great Fire of 1871. The workers had begun rebuilding even as the grain elevators still smoldered. See this wealth? the speakers said. We, the workers, built it. And we will make Chicago the best city in the world. The workers picnicked, danced, and sang until midnight.[4]

Teed missed the Chicago parade by only three days. As the celebration wrapped, he boarded B&O's "Chicago Solid" in Jersey City to start his long journey. When the train stopped in Baltimore in the wee hours, he mailed a short note to Emma in Moravia, saying he hadn't forgotten her and telling her that he was on his way to Chicago, where he'd been invited to speak.[5]

The trip took thirty-six hours. The train left Washington, D.C., pushed past Harpers Ferry, powered through the Alleghenies, and chuffed through Cumberland. Over the course of an afternoon, it passed through Wheeling, Zanesville, and Mount Vernon. As late day gave way to a second evening, the rolling hills of Ohio flattened toward prairie.[6]

The next morning Lake Michigan came into view, the body of blue water extending to the horizon, so vast it looked like a glimmering ocean. The smudge on its shore, the traveler slowly realized, was Chicago, shrouded in a yellow-gray storm cloud of smoke from the coal fires of factories, ships, and steam trains.[7]

First, the train passed a house or two, and before long, groups of homes and then suburbs. The locomotive slowed. The train's whistle sounded as it clacked past warehouses, factories, and cattle pens, and inched past Lake Park and entered the thick rail yard. It was barely rolling as it passed the enormous glass and iron Exposition Building. Passengers gathered their things and moved toward the door. The train stopped at the depot, and the brakeman threw open the door and announced their arrival.[8]

Teed stepped onto the open-air platform, where steam hissed from the chimney of the idling locomotive. The temperature was in the seventies, no rain. He emerged onto Michigan Avenue and must have felt the bewilderment of many first-time visitors. To the west was a canyon of red brick and brown stone. The sidewalks were alive with people, walking even faster than people did in New York, darting in front of cable cars with bells clanging, everyone rushing to get somewhere. The city was full of horrific grime, the air tasted like coal ash and smelled of horse dung, and it rang with the relentless sound of hammers banging as more buildings went up.[9]

On that early September morning, Teed made his way to West Lake Street, where he would stay with the mental science conference organizer, Professor Andrew J. Swarts, and his wife, Katie. They were leaders in Chicago's mental science movement. Professor Swarts was an officer of the organization Teed would address that Sunday. He edited *Mental Science Magazine*, he had founded the Mental Science Church, and he ran the Mental Science University, where people learned to heal themselves and others in twelve lessons at a price of twenty-five dollars. That summer, Swarts's university had bestowed M.S. degrees upon thirty-seven healers.[10]

On the way to the Swartses' place, Teed saw the streets the workers had swarmed three days before, lined with tall office buildings, shops, pharmacies, and department stores with enormous plate glass windows that offered views to the passerby. It was early, and the stores were dark, but it's easy to imagine Teed looking in and feeling as if he were seeing into the shadowy maws of commerce—orderly shelves of shoes and boots, racks of skirts, shirtwaists, and purses, and cases of watches and jewelry, arranged to tempt the middle and upper classes.

He had the day to rest and to see the city. The conference would begin that evening.

The old Church of the Redeemer was a two-story brick church with tall arched windows at Washington and Sangamon. People called it the "old church" because the congregation had moved to a brand-new building, and now it was a meeting hall that people rented for speeches and events. This is where the mental scientists convened.[11]

The building was also a candy factory. In the basement, Berry's Confectionary made chocolate creams, marshmallow drops, strawberry coconut bars, Klondike brittle, rose cream almonds, and other delectables. Eventually, Berry's would take over the whole building and paint a sign on the brick wall: "Berry's Candy Must Be Good—Made in a Church."[12]

In the mornings, the conventioneers had business meetings; in the afternoons, lectures; and on Friday night, live entertainment. Teed would speak on Sunday, the last day.[13]

On Friday, when the members of the association had known Teed for less than two days, they elected him president. He replaced Swarts, his own host. It's not clear how this happened so quickly, but there are signs that all had not been well in the group. During a business meeting, Swarts interrupted one doctor who he claimed had spoken for longer than his allotted time. The two men traded insults, and each one left the room by a different door.[14]

At the heart of the trouble was an identity crisis over the field of mental science. Just seven years before, Mary Baker Eddy had founded Christian Science, a movement guided by the belief that controlling one's thoughts gave access to unlimited spiritual power. Thanks to Eddy's movement, interest in mind-cure treatments had exploded among the middle class. She kept tight control over her brand and wanted nothing to do with Swarts's group of mental scientists whom she believed plagiarized her ideas. Eddy and her followers made clear their feelings for Swarts ("a slow-thoughted Westerner") and his cohorts. They said that he himself did not understand what he claimed to practice. He and his ilk were charlatans, she said, and "mind-killers" instead of mind healers.[15]

Swarts's association accepted all stripes of mental scientists: Christian Scientists, metaphysicians, and anyone who called himself a mental scientist. The differences among the groups weren't clear, but all seemed to agree on one central tenet: Disease is a mistake of the mind. Our thoughts can deceive us into believing we are sick, and once we believe we are sick, it is true. If the patient believes he is well, he will get well. Mental science practitioners believed their job was to help a patient see the mistake that caused the disease. Beyond this basic principle, the Chicago group of mental scientists splintered into camps that few on the outside could make sense of.[16]

Eddy's distaste for Swarts was unrequited. At Friday morning's business meeting, Swarts proposed that the group endorse Mary Baker Eddy and the Christian Scientists and recognize Eddy for her work, which brought positive attention to mental healing and built public acceptance for it. But Swarts's proposed resolution sparked a long, heated discussion. One woman suggested they take five minutes to use metaphysical treatment to resolve the issue. Her idea was rejected. It was decided that those who wished to do mental treatment could do so on their own time. Instead, the matter was put to a vote, and the resolution to recognize Eddy passed narrowly, 12 to 11.[17]

The members agreed that Dr. Teed, as new president, would forward the resolution to Mrs. Eddy by telegraph. He didn't, later claiming he'd been given the wrong contact information. More likely, he wanted nothing to do with Eddy.

Teed's first announcements at the convention as the group's new president seemed aimed at bridging the group's differences. Under his leadership, the association resolved that, though the members held different beliefs, all of them believed in the power of God to heal, and all of them were humanitarians. This, at least, is how Swarts recorded the resolutions when he wrote them up later. But it's unlikely that Teed's announcements were this clear, as evidenced by the news reports. He had a circuitous way of talking. Here is how the *Tribune* distilled Teed's announcements: "[He said] that they were metaphysicians; that metaphysicians were metaphysicians; that nobody but a metaphysician knew what it was to be a metaphysician." This was printed in Saturday morning's paper.[18]

In response to the coverage, the mental scientists passed another resolution on Saturday, thanking the Chicago newspapers for publicizing their convention to a half-million people. [19]

Many of the attendees were not yet healers, and they wanted to start their own mind-cure practices. The organizers, realizing this, shared success stories intended to inspire them. Teed told his story of healing a man with a severed Achilles tendon. He had held together the ends of the man's severed tendon, he said, and it healed perfectly with no inflammation. One practitioner claimed to have treated a patient who had shot himself twice, clear through his own body. The mental scientists were so confident in their abilities, one newspaper reported, that they believed they could have saved the lives of Presidents Grant and Garfield.[20]

On Saturday afternoon, people streamed into the church an hour ahead of time. There were mental scientists, medical doctors, clergymen, Spiritualists, and people who had come for the free healings offered. By the time Swarts took the stage, the church was full, with people sitting in the aisles and even on the steps of the speakers' platform. He asked those who had come to be healed to approach the front of the hall. About fifty came forward, suffering from cancer, rheumatism, paralysis, and injuries. Some were invalids. Some were in wheelchairs. Some were deaf or blind.[21]

A few of the attendees challenged the scientists; one man asked why so many metaphysicians—if they had a cure for everything—had bald heads, gray hair, and bad eyesight or hearing. The speakers explained that it is easier to heal others than to heal oneself. Reverend Swarts, who lectured on Saturday afternoon, wore eyeglasses, and he had been listening to the challengers who asked why metaphysicians couldn't cure themselves. He explained to the audience why he wore glasses. Before he became a mental scientist, he believed that he needed them. Now he knew the truth, that he didn't need them. But he had formed the habit of wearing them and now it was routine.[22]

Who wanted to be cured? Swarts asked the crowd gathered at the stage. Hands went up. He led the audience in singing hymns, followed by ten minutes of silent meditation. The aroma of almond and vanilla extract wafted through the quiet church. Downstairs, peanuts were being caramelized, Klondike brittle cooled on racks, coconut toasted in the oven, and liquid cream caramel burbled in copper wells.[23]

After the meditation, Reverend Swarts asked whether anyone felt better. No one did. More prayers. More silence. More heavenly candy smells. Swarts asked again. One woman who was suffering from nervous prostration reported a tingling in her hand, but that was all. It was apparent, Swarts told the crowd, that someone was having negative thoughts.[24]

He asked for volunteers in the audience to share their stories of healing. "A woman whose head was bandaged up and appeared like a walking hospital said she was suffering for two years from a cancer," the *Tribune* reported. After four treatments, she could now eat beefsteak and do her housework, according to the *Herald*. A woman with bad eyesight could now read the signs on streetcars. Lizzie Arnold, a sixteen-year-old girl who was violently insane, was able to sit calmly in the front row with her guardian.[25]

A donation plate was passed, and attendees were asked to give generously. This "cleared the church in quick time," the *Herald* reported. The next day's headline was "The Cure Won't Work."[26]

Finally, it was Sunday, the day Teed would deliver his lecture: "The Brain." One can imagine him getting ready in the Swartses' spare bedroom, shining his shoes, slicking back his hair, neatening his beard, tying his white lawn tie, and shouldering into his worn-to-a-shine Prince Albert coat before leaving the Swartses' house and striding purposefully along Lake Street. The weather was particularly fine. That morning, more people than usual flocked to church services.[27]

Sundays were special days of leisure in Chicago. Everyone, whether from the lower or the middle class, had the day off from work, or at least the afternoon. On Sundays, the factories stopped pumping smoke into the air, and the city on afternoons like this one was thronged with men in hats and women with parasols, strolling along the sidewalks, picnicking on the velvety lawns of parks, boating in the public lagoons, and viewing public art displays. Going to lectures was also very popular. In that day, Chicagoans were hungry for intellectual stimulation and new ideas, and Sunday delivered. Churches and lecture halls featured independent thinkers speaking about reform. Theodore Dreiser, as a young journalist in Chicago, went to lectures or sermons most every Sunday.[28]

"It was such an intense relief," he wrote, "after a week of dreary economic routine, or slavery even, to find men in pulpits . . . unshackled of dogma . . . suggesting the fullness and richness of life." For the rest of his life, when Dreiser thought of those energetic days in Chicago, he pictured those men and "their intellectual dreams of a happy, perfect world."[29]

Chicago couldn't seem to get enough of reform-minded speakers. It was a place where a forward-thinking person could get traction for his ideas. Teed must have felt sure that there were people who would want to hear him.

But that afternoon, the old church was only half full. The audience consisted mostly of women, the reporter noted—educated women from the middle and upper classes. The session began with ten minutes of silent prayer, then Teed walked onto the speakers' platform, where he stood behind a marble table, flanked by two "buxom matrons of the Margaret Fuller order," the reporter wrote, referring to the women's rights advocate.[30]

Teed looked like any other mild-mannered clergyman, a *New York Times* reporter once wrote, until he spoke. "When his small dark eyes began to shine as he talked, when he fixed his audience with an almost hypnotic stare, then it became evident that here was a man marked out from the common herd."[31]

He held up the Bible for the audience to view, and he explained that people call it the word of God. But it is not. The Bible is instead a great scientific text, he told them, and his mission was to interpret it for the scientific age. The mental scientists, who wanted to reconcile faith and the science of healing, listened intently.[32]

Teed unveiled an illustration of the brain's left hemisphere with the parts labeled, and he showed how the brain generates the forces that cure the body. He spoke ably about the brain, having been trained in anatomy and the art of the professorial lecture, and his knowledge added legitimacy to their cause, the mental scientists recognized. The doctrine that disease was a mistake in thought had not been pinned down as scientifically as Teed was doing now in his speech. Here was the illustrated brain—the organ behind thought—and here was a man who knew its parts and how they regulated the body. His theories about the mysticism of mind healing paralleled the well-respected and popular teachings of Swedenborg, which helped Teed's case.

Teed told the audience that through an understanding of the science of the brain, one could heal physical ailments. But he went much further than that, presenting a startling idea: by understanding the brain, one could achieve nothing less than victory over death. In order for this to happen, he told the crowd, science and faith must be married. Teed did not reveal to them that he was a prophet. He wanted their admiration, and by now, he knew that this declaration was a deal killer.[33]

When it was time for Teed to demonstrate his healing powers, an obese woman came to the front of the church. She was barely able to stand and could toddle only a short distance. According to Koreshan lore, Teed treated her (exactly what he did isn't documented), and she walked all the way home, which was quite some distance. Later, this woman's friend confirmed that she had been permanently healed.[34]

The conference closed with a lecture by Katie Swarts, Reverend Swarts's wife, who held a master's in mental science and offered lessons from their home. Her topic was "The Gift of Healing," focused on her successes in mental science, but she was interrupted by a question from the audience that tripped her up: if someone is poisoned, a man wanted to know, would the sickness be caused by the mind or the body? Mrs. Swarts became flustered when she tried to respond, and the group rushed to her aid, shutting down the critic. A bodyguard appeared at Mrs. Swarts's side. "Hire a hall and talk yourself out," he said to the man.[35]

The dissenting voice was squelched, but the interruption had put Mrs. Swarts out of sorts. She suggested that they sing something. After that, she tried performing a couple of healings, but without the success that Teed had earlier.[36]

A. J. Swarts ended the convention by defending his wife and denouncing the challengers. They wouldn't tolerate ridicule, he said. He wrote the convention up in the October issue of the *Mental Science Magazine*, including the announcement that Dr. Cyrus R. Teed was their new leader. Swarts called Teed "a giant in the camp." He wouldn't hold this opinion for long.[37]

As for Teed, he had accomplished the first move in his stratagem for conquering Babylon: the one he had written Emma about so many years ago in Sandy Creek—inserting himself into an existing organization and gaining a hearing. The Mental Science National Association would be his platform for spreading his beliefs and for building a community in Chicago.

Alongside Swarts's write-up praising Teed ran an article with a strong militant bent. The tone is a stark contrast to any other article in the issue, and though the writer wasn't identified, the language is Teed's. Our president will gather thousands, it said, and the members will march out of Egypt. With Chicago as the headquarters, the group will go out and organize in every state. "Some lively movements will soon be reported," the writer proclaimed. "If you have heard the call now thundering over the world to come out and be separate from mammon and the beast, you can be one of our members."[38]

The conflict between the mental science group and Christian Science continued. A few days after the convention, a prominent Christian Scientist and close friend of Mary Baker Eddy wrote a letter that appeared in the *Tribune*. Ursula Gestefeld expressed, in the kindest way possible, that the convention had caused many people to misunderstand the true nature of mental healing. Jesus never drew attention to his acts of healing as these people had, she wrote.[39]

"When Jesus healed," Teed countered, "he did not make a Millionaire of himself and call it Christian Science." This appeared as a note on the bottom of a flier for one of his lectures.[40]

It's pretty clear that Teed took mind-healing ideas from Eddy, but he claimed that his system was vastly different from hers. Christian Science espoused physical healing through prayer and closeness to God. Teed said that his system went far beyond hers. Not only could he heal the body, he could teach people to overcome death. His religio-science was nothing less than the divine science of immortal life. Also, his system was much less expensive. A degree from Teed's new College of Life cost only fifty dollars for the twelve required lessons. Eddy, who had hundreds of students, charged three hundred.

Teed moved to Chicago right away and wasted no time founding a church, a society, and a press, all of which Eddy had done. Teed's college offered courses in anatomy, physiology, gynecology, and "mental obstetrics." He trained a teaching staff of fourteen women and awarded them their "Psychic and Pneumic Therapeutic Doctorates."[41]

A *Chicago Tribune* reporter covered the founding ceremony of the college, setting the scene as follows: "Fifty women in the little hall sat and cooed and buzzed, with love for humanity in their hearts and dead birds on their bonnets."[42]

The World's College of Life was also called "The School of Koresh," and the opening ceremony was the first time Teed used the word "Koresh" publicly. The reporter asked two members of the faculty what the word meant, and they weren't sure. They had looked it up in a dictionary but hadn't found the word. It was ancient in origin, they knew, but that was all.[43]

The fact that Teed's faculty did not know the meaning of the word indicates that he still had not revealed that he was Koresh. He did this a few months later. A splashy headline in the *Chicago Tribune* proclaimed "Cyrus, The Son of Jesse." The story outlined some of Teed's philosophy and said, "Christ is already here. His other name is Cyrus R. Teed." The article detailed Teed's illumination at age thirty and stated his belief that we live on the inner shell of the earth. The interview was two hours long—"two mortal hours without a break," the reporter emphasized, saying of Teed, "He can talk more to the square inch than a book agent."[44]

He and A. J. Swarts were finished, Teed having booted Swarts from his own organization. Teed was quoted as saying that both the Mental Science National Association and the Christian Scientists were "vain fools and babblers [and] professional cranks who don't know what they are talking about."[45]

Swarts fired back, saying that he may have been "asinine or pretentious" in the past, but Teed was "the boss crank."[46]

Teed even used the letterhead of the Mental Science National Association. Until he printed new letterhead, he simply struck through the address and wrote "103 State Street," the brand-new headquarters for the Koreshan Unity, which contained the World's College of Life, a lunchroom, a women's exchange where fine lace and embroideries were made and sold, and the Guiding Star Publishing House, which published a monthly magazine called the *Guiding Star*, along with lecture announcements and promotional material.[47]

His new society, the Society Arch-Triumphant, was a secular group open to members of the community who were willing to practice sobriety, chastity, and brotherly love and to pay a two-dollar membership fee. The society was the face of the organization, the group an outsider joined as the first step toward Koreshanity. To recruit members, the Koreshans held a grand reception at Chicago's Sherman House, which three hundred people attended.[48]

Teed's sister Emma was still living in Moravia when Teed wrote to her on the Mental Science National Association stationery to share his excitement. "Darling Emma," he began. "I wish you could be here and see the enthusiasm."[49]

They were taking in three to nine members at the weekly meetings of the society, he told her, and an additional one or two per day. "Today or tomorrow, I send you your certificate of membership." He described the certificate to her. Stamped with the College of Life seal, it featured an eagle flying through clouds. The bird represented knowledge, and the clouds, divine science. At the bottom was the motto "Vincit Qui Se Vincit." He conquers who conquers himself.[50]

"Ask Father," Cyrus wrote, "if he wants a certificate of membership to our society."[51]

✳ 4 ✳

The Watchmen of Chicago

Mrs. Renew Benedict attended Dr. Teed's lectures on physiology, anatomy, and faith at Chicago's Central Music Hall every week, and she was attracted to his doctrines. Quite likely, she was also attracted to Teed, as were many women. Even Chicago's newsmen, as they ridiculed him, wrote that he was dapper and charismatic. Mrs. Benedict, who had been a religious seeker, now felt she was on the right path with his teachings, believing that science held the keys to healing and immortal life and that it was possible to effect mind cures by applying physiology to faith.

So on a Sunday evening in February 1888, when her husband, Fletcher, complained of a cold, it would have been natural for her to think of Teed. She didn't disturb the doctor that night. Her husband's condition didn't seem too terrible. Mr. Benedict was in his forties, in the prime of life, and his cold wasn't surprising, given that the temperature had dipped to eleven degrees below zero the week before. Everyone thought colds were caused by cold weather, and January had been frigid.

Mr. Benedict stayed in bed on Monday rather than reporting to his job in the piano warerooms at W. W. Kimball & Co, and that's when Mrs. Benedict called for Teed, whose office was half a mile away. Soon, there was the doctor in the flesh—a small man with a big presence. He entered the Benedicts' flat on LaSalle, shed his overcoat, and came to Fletcher's bedside, directing his kindness and his mesmerizing eyes on the two of them.[1]

Teed examined Mr. Benedict, placed his hands upon the man's body, and assured both husband and wife that Fletcher would soon be well. Teed would administer absent treatment from his downtown office, he told them, joining with metaphysicians in other places to transmit mental healing simultaneously.

Mr. Benedict had attended one or two of Teed's lectures. Some said he went just to humor his wife and that he didn't believe in the doctrines. Perhaps not, Mrs. Benedict later allowed, but her husband had the utmost confidence in Teed as a physician. He had assented to his wife's calling Teed in to minister to him.

The next day, when Benedict's throat hurt and he had a constant cough and a fever of 103 degrees, Teed returned and again laid his hands on Mr. Benedict. He made a series of passes over his body, then prescribed a bath for him and administered two homeopathic plant remedies—lobelia, as an expectorant and antispasmodic, and fluid extract of gelsemine, to slow breathing and increase perspiration. If Teed followed eclectic protocol, he diluted these significantly, as eclectics believed that infinitesimally small doses were most therapeutic.

The Benedicts' landlady, Mrs. Ray, was concerned about Benedict, and she asked whether he might have pneumonia. Teed responded no. His patient was suffering from rheumatism of the intracostal muscles, responsible for breathing, he said. This seemed odd to Mrs. Ray, and she urged Mrs. Benedict to call a doctor, a *real* doctor, but Mrs. Benedict refused vigorously. The body can heal itself, she believed. All that was necessary, Teed had told them, was to have faith.

When Benedict's condition worsened the next morning—chills, fatigue, and chest pain—Mrs. Ray applied a mustard poultice and hot turpentine, in spite of Mrs. Benedict's objections. This seemed to provide some short-lived relief, and Teed was called again. But moments before he arrived, Benedict fell quiet.

Dr. Teed arrived to the smell of turpentine fumes piercing the air in the bedroom, and he saw that things were bad. Quite bad. In fact, the man appeared to be dead. Teed ordered the meddlesome Mrs. Ray out of the room for good. He checked Benedict's pulse and felt nothing. On Tuesday, the man's resting pulse had been 130. Teed kept probing as Mrs. Benedict looked on.

"Faith," Teed said into the silent room. He prayed. Several minutes passed. Teed considered calling someone else: an eclectic doctor, Merrill Pingree, who worked in his building.[2]

But then there was a miracle in the silent flat. Teed felt a thready rhythm; a pulse working beneath the tips of his fingers. Later, the *Tribune* would report that Teed exclaimed: "He has been dead for four minutes. I have brought him to life!"[3]

But Mr. Benedict's recovery was not forthcoming. In the afternoon, Teed sent for his colleague Dr. Pingree, who examined Benedict and agreed with Mrs. Ray's remedies.

On Sunday, Teed spent the night at the Benedicts', praying with them as rain fell outside. The next morning, Benedict was delirious, crying out. Mrs. Ray heard him and called another doctor. Dr. C. W. Leigh came at 9:00 a.m., but didn't stay long. He saw that there was no hope for Benedict, so he gave him several shots of whiskey to relieve the pain. An hour later, as Teed and Mrs. Benedict sat with him, Fletcher Benedict died.

A "KORESHAN" FATALITY

MENTAL HEALING FAILS TO CURE A CASE OF

BRONCHO-PNEUMONIA

The *Chicago Daily Tribune* ran the story on the front page, calling the death suspicious. Accompanying the article was an unflattering illustration of Teed's face, his mouth obscured by a mustache and conical beard. The reporter had interviewed Dr. Leigh, the doctor who administered the whiskey. Leigh remembered walking into the Benedicts' flat, meeting Teed, and thinking it strange they hadn't met before. Medicine in Chicago was a relatively small world, so Leigh at first assumed that Teed was from another medical school, but upon hearing that he was both a physician and a minister, he became suspicious. Teed seemed dumbfounded, Leigh said, by the man's condition—throat trouble, lung, heart, and other complications—and his diagnosis was ludicrous, including all of the following: diphtheria, pleurisy, intercostal neuralgia, and heart disease. Then Leigh noticed the bottles of lobelia and gelsemine, poisons unless properly used, he said, and he didn't know what doses Teed had given. In the press, Leigh accused Teed of criminal malpractice.[4]

On the day Benedict died, the landlord, Mr. Ray, came home at noon and learned that the body had been taken to the undertaker rather quickly, within a half an hour of Benedict's death. Suspicious, Ray called the police. One of the detectives spotted the death certificate and saw that it was signed not by Teed but by Pingree, Teed's eclectic colleague. However, Pingree hadn't seen Benedict since Friday morning, when he was very much alive. The cause of death, the certificate read, was pleurisy.

An autopsy began immediately. There was no evidence of pleurisy. The left lung was greatly enlarged, an abscess had formed, and the lung tissue was badly inflamed. The right lung was slightly congested. The county physician determined that Benedict died from lack of proper treatment. "He caught a cold which settled on his lungs and was simply allowed to die," the physician said.

Teed countered that Benedict had lacked faith and that is why he died. He explained to the *Tribune* reporter that medicine isn't necessary when the psychic and pneumic forces work properly. The newspaper story didn't define these terms. Teed told the reporter that mental healing had the power to cure every condition—cancer, consumption, anything. When the reporter asked Teed whether he had used any medicine on Benedict, Teed shut him down: "These people want to make trouble for me. It is I who will make trouble for them. Now mark that, sir, mark that."

The report of the interview with Teed ended peculiarly. "Dr. Teed then smiled pleasantly at Circe, and Circe smiled pleasantly at Dr. Teed, and with this agreeable interchange of smiles the death of Mr. Benedict was wafted from the memory of both." There is no Mr. or Mrs. Circe anywhere else in the newspaper story. It was obvious that by referring to the ancient sorceress, the reporter was mocking Teed and those who believed in him.

And the incident was definitely not wafted from memory; the press made sure of it. Teed was charged with practicing medicine without a license, and a coroner's inquest was set for the following day.

It was true that Teed did not have a license to practice medicine in Illinois. He had been licensed in New York, but when he moved to Chicago, his focus had changed and he didn't deem it necessary to have a license. At the inquest, Teed knew, he would be accused of neglect for *not* dispensing medicine. However, if he had chosen to dispense medicine, he would have done so without a license, therefore breaking the law.

On top of that, doctors had different definitions of medicine. Dr. Leigh thought lobelia and gelsemine were poisons while Teed believed they were cures. And Dr. Leigh had dispensed whiskey to Benedict, which was reprehensible to Teed. Doctors like Leigh carried more than whiskey in their kits, Teed knew. They dispensed morphine, cocaine, and other potent, addictive drugs. It was easy for people to get strong medicines in the late nineteenth century. Substances that are controlled now, or illegal, were in regular circulation. Medicines included not only morphine and cocaine but also opium and laudanum, ether, nitrous oxide (laughing gas), and cannabis.

When Teed's wife, Delia, was very, very sick, near the end of her life, he allowed Abie to give her morphine. Other than this, his position on drugs had been clear from his earliest days as a doctor.

At the coroner's inquest, several of Teed's followers came to support and defend him, including the widow Renew Benedict herself. They believed he had done nothing wrong and that the coroner, the detectives, Dr. Leigh, and the others were making a grave mistake. But they also believed that Teed had no choice but to allow the mistake. This is how he cast himself to his followers: he was a martyr, as Jesus and all of the great prophets had been.

The inquest took place at Bartlett's undertaking establishment on North Clark Street a block south of the river. Mrs. Benedict was the first witness. The reporter described her as "an intelligent-appearing little woman about 43 years old. She talks rationally upon all topics except that of Koreshan Science, but upon that subject she is an enthusiast of the most radical order."[5]

Her story matched what the *Tribune* had reported the previous day, with a couple of exceptions. She claimed to be the one who administered the mustard plaster and other home remedies, not Mrs. Ray. She said that it was Mr. Benedict, not she, who made the decision to call Teed. She also mentioned that Mr. Benedict had a life insurance policy worth $2,500.

When Teed took the stand, "[he] wore an air of resignation mingled with an evident contempt for the petty officials who had him on the rack," the *Tribune* wrote. "Seventy-two thousand years of mortal existence was ahead of him, with an ultimate career as an earthly god. Shades of George Francis Train! What terrors could a Coroner's inquest have?"

The coroner asked Teed why he asked Dr. Pingree to visit Benedict, and Teed said at first that it was because he wanted a second opinion. Later, he said he had no death certificates on hand. The truth was that because Teed wasn't licensed, he couldn't sign a death certificate.

The coroner asked Teed to explain his belief system. Teed said it would take too long, but he gave the jury a taste, which the reporter recorded, along with the reaction of the people present.

"You have seen a radiometer, the little windmill inside of a vacuum. The rays of light striking the alternate dark and light sides of the fans cause it to revolve. Scientists claim that light is no substance. I declare them to be wrong. Light is a substance, and it passes through the glass and gives motion to the fans in the radiometer. Light is a substance and is communicable. Mental force is a substance and is communicable. From the cells of one person's brain this power is transmitted to the cells of another, and these cells have a reflex action upon their corresponding organ in the body. This power may act one mile or it may act 10,000 miles."

"Wonderful! Wonderful!" exclaimed the women.

"My God!" ejaculated a juror. "One more case like that and I am crazy as a bedbug myself."

Teed's speech would have horrified even his colleagues in eclectic medicine and his professors at the college. Doctors like Teed who called themselves eclectics gave "real" eclectics a bad name by adding mental and faith healing to the practice. In fact, eclectics held meetings where they discussed how to protect the profession from "cranks" like Teed.

Dr. Pingree was the last witness. He claimed never to have worked with Teed before and not to know anything about his theories. When he visited Mr. Benedict's bedside, he accepted Teed's diagnosis at face value, collected his fee of seven dollars, and left. Pingree, the *Tribune* said, "left the stand as if anxious to be finally rid of the whole affair." He did not address the matter of the death certificate.

In his instructions to the jury, the deputy coroner "hinted at quacks, imposters, and 'voodoo' doctors, and declared that the public was sick of having such frauds running at large."

The jury did not deliberate long. They determined that Teed had violated Illinois laws regulating the practice of medicine. They further recommended making the law more severe in the future, to include both imprisonment and a fine for such cases. Teed was arrested and taken to the courthouse, where one of the Koreshan women paid his three-hundred-dollar bond, and he walked out a free man.

"It's a glorious thing for the cause," Dr. Teed said, as reported by the *Tribune*.

"Glorious," echoed Teed's followers Mrs. Mary Daniels and Mrs. Lizzie Robinson.

The jury had recommended that Teed be held to a grand jury, but there's no coverage of that trial. If there was one, it doesn't appear to have changed anything for him or his followers. There is no evidence that Teed ever practiced medicine again, though he continued to hold himself out as an M.D., and his followers called him Doctor. Reporters sometimes referred to him as "Doctor" as well, but usually with quotation marks.

The Koreshans emerged from the courthouse and into the chilly February air, six women and two men. Teed must have felt more assured than ever. His people had stood with him today. Their numbers were growing and the movement was gaining momentum. Attendance at the College of Life was strong— forty pupils—and Teed led regular services every Sunday. And in just a few days, they would move to larger offices, where they would open a new lunchroom and have more space for their print shop.

It's likely that Teed got the money to lease this space from a new convert: Henry D. Silverfriend from Kaukauna, Wisconsin. Silverfriend had become interested in Teed the year before, and he was "a silver friend, indeed," one newsman later reported. He owned a dry goods business in Kaukauna but was thinking of moving to Chicago to join the community.[6]

Most important, Teed had found the woman the angel had promised him—his female equal. When the time came for Teed to be translated out of the material world, he would pass into her body—a divine receptacle, as he phrased it. She would become the divine Mother who would carry his spirit. Together, they would form a biune, mother-father god. Her body would be his temple, and he would be her guide.

She was Mrs. Annie Ordway—married, of course. Teed bestowed upon her a new name, Victoria Gratia, and a title, the Pre-Eminent of the Society Arch-Triumphant. Victoria was not beautiful. In fact, her wide jaw and down-turned mouth gave her a mannish appearance. She was several inches taller than Teed, her brown hair was set in waves, and she favored dark dresses of rich brocade, trimmed with pearls. Not much is known about her because she avoided the media—and encouraged Teed to do so, too, but to no avail. She didn't keep journals, or if she did, they no longer exist. She left behind few letters. She wrote pronouncements, speeches, and articles on the doctrines of Koreshanity, but they reveal little about her personally.

Victoria was confident and aloof, like the empress Teed believed she was, the one who would walk beside him in the face of hardship, criticism, and ridicule, just as the angel had promised. On this day, she literally walked beside him as they exited the courthouse.

The same month that Teed was investigated for the death of Mr. Benedict, Victoria was dealing with her own embarrassing mess. Her oldest son, Harry Ordway, was dragged into court by his wife, who sued him for divorce in a case so salacious it filled the courtroom on a weekday. A large bailiff stood at the entrance to turn away those "whose morals might be warped" by the proceedings, one reporter wrote, adding that the visitors apparently had no trouble talking their way in.[7]

Ida May, the wife, claimed that Harry was cruel to her, that he drank excessively, and that Victoria and her husband had plotted to ruin her character. On trial day, Harry's attorney presented the following surprise accusations: before Ida May and Harry were married, when they had known each other only two days, she slept with him; she also drank with him; she had threatened to shoot him; and she once stayed in a house of ill repute. Ida May denied all of it.

Victoria was called to the witness stand, where she answered questions with "painful distinctness," the reporter wrote. Yes, she said, she would like to know whether Ida May had been untrue to her son. Yes, someone had told her that Ida May once went to the theater with another man and asked him to stay out with her all night. During Victoria's testimony, "Ida May Ordway's eyes fairly flashed sparks."

The judge chastised Harry for springing accusations on Ida May at trial. The kind of man who would do this, he said, was likely the cruel man his wife claimed he was. "He should have defended this case in a manly, honorable way," he said, "giving due notice to his wife, and letting her have the opportunity of defending herself."

Actually, Ida May had a plan for defending herself; she had information about Victoria that could destroy her reputation, but she didn't need to use it because the judge ruled in her favor. Curiously, on the day the judge delivered his decision, the Ordways were not in the courtroom—not Victoria or her husband, and not even Harry, the now-ex-husband.

As the Koreshan community gained traction, Teed wanted his best friend, Abie Andrews, with him in Chicago. He had tried for months to persuade Abie to move his family, and he even began looking for a place where they could live. He knew Jennie was hesitant, and it's clear from his letters to Abie that he had thought through how to accommodate her. He was arranging for them to stay with some friends so that Jennie could get to know the other followers and become comfortable with them. In his letters, he stopped just short of insisting. "I hope you'll come," he wrote, but he added that he knew the time needed to be right.[8]

He also wrote Abie not to listen to the malcontents. And there *were* malcontents. Once again, detractors were writing to his friend in Binghamton. They told Abie that Teed was ruling the followers with a high hand. Worse, the people writing (Abie wouldn't give up their names) smeared Victoria, saying that she was addicted to alcohol and stimulants.

When Abie asked Teed about this, he wrote back that it was all a lie, that there were a few people with petty jealousies against Victoria. Some followers, especially women, resented her position of power in the community, he said. This letter was the first record that other Koreshans objected to Victoria, and it was the first of countless times Teed would need to defend her. He did so fiercely, writing Abie that he would stand by her even if it meant losing all of his followers. He believed she was sacred—or would become so.

Teed told his old friend that he had known Victoria for a year, and she was as upstanding as Abie and Jennie. She wasn't perfect, and, yes, she had taken whiskey—Teed had confirmed with Victoria's husband—but under a doctor's orders many years ago when she was ill. As soon as she recovered, she stopped, Teed assured Abie, and she had not touched drink in the time he had known her. The people writing to Abie were trying to bring the society down, Teed wrote, but it was on an unshakable foundation.

As an additional incentive to pull the Andrews family to Chicago, Teed proposed an idea he knew would appeal to Allen, Abie and Jennie's son and Teed's pal from the Binghamton days, when the two went for long Sunday walks. The Koreshans needed an assistant for their printing operation. "Would Allie like to come on now and go to work?" Teed asked Abie.[9]

Allen, fifteen, had a passion for printing, Teed knew, and he would be on fire for this idea. Allen had fallen in love with the work when he published a small paper with a schoolmate who had his own printing equipment. Allen himself had only a rudimentary letter press; his first project came out in reverse because he didn't know that the letters needed to be set up as mirror images. He begged his father for a better press and letters, and he canvassed the town for a print shop owner who would hire him. During his summer break from school, he found a job as an unpaid apprentice for the *Axe*, a prohibition newsletter. After four weeks, he graduated to a paid gig at the Binghamton *Daily Republican*, where he swept up the type that spilled onto the floor and worked as a printer's devil and errand boy. There was only one task he refused to do—"rushing the growler." This job, often assigned to children, entailed carrying a bucket to the nearest saloon, having it filled with beer, and bringing it back for the workers. Allen quit the *Daily Republican* when he fell behind in his schoolwork, but he never stopped dreaming of the day he could work as a printer.

So when he heard that Teed had a job for him, young Allen couldn't wait to go to Chicago, but Jennie wouldn't allow it—not until the whole family decided whether they were all going. Jennie couldn't imagine living apart from her children, as Teed made clear would happen once they had a communal house. The children would be raised by the group, a practice the Koreshans followed to avoid what Teed called the family tie, a parent's tendency to favor her biological children over the others in the commune. When people joined the Unity, they were expected to sever the tie and love everyone equally.

Jennie's misgivings weren't the only reason they hadn't moved. Abie, too, was ambivalent. Not about Teed, whom he fully accepted as the prophet, and not about the rumors from the detractors. He was satisfied with Teed's answers to their criticisms. But he was uncertain about uprooting his family and his practice, and, of course, he was conflicted about asking Jennie to do something she didn't want to do.

Her parents, living in Alexandria, were also a major consideration. They made no secret of their dislike for Teed, whom by now Abie had known for sixteen years. The more seriously Abie and Jennie considered moving, the more reasons there were not to share it with her parents. The timing, for one, was terrible. Jennie's father began having heart trouble. Shortly after that, her sister Annie Ray died. It was the second child her parents had lost; their only son had died four years before.

Jennie and Abie found themselves visiting her parents in Alexandria, grieving Annie Ray's death, and caring for Jennie's father. By then, they were nearly certain they would move to Chicago in a matter of weeks, but they couldn't bring themselves to tell her parents. Telling Jennie's ailing father, Abie later wrote, would have been medical malpractice, imperiling the life of his heart patient. And Jennie's mother, in her grief over Annie Ray's death, wouldn't be able to bear it, he wrote. So as Abie tended to the father and Jennie comforted her mother, they said nothing about their plans.

Instead, Jennie broke the news to them in a letter a few weeks after she and Abie returned to Binghamton. The letter doesn't survive, but her mother's response does. Their move to Chicago, her mother wrote, would be a calamity almost equal to her daughter's recent death. She begged Jennie to come to Alexandria with the children and suggested that Abie go ahead to Chicago to get things in order first. Perhaps she hoped to get Abie out of the way and then talk her daughter out of the decision. Jennie was too hurt by the letter to respond to her mother. Abie wrote back on their behalf, explaining his actions. "I [am] acting from a religious conviction and a sense of duty . . . but I join myself with a man who is evil spoken of, whose name is a by word and reproach, who has few friends and many enemies."[10]

Cyrus was the man sent from God, Abie wrote in his letter, just as John, Moses, and Elijah were, three men who were persecuted just as Teed was being persecuted now. Abie also shared with her that he had long been dissatisfied with the church. "The Lord taught his people to pray that his Kingdom might come here, but those who profess to believe in and serve him pour contempt and ridicule upon that idea that anyone can live the divine life here. They prefer to wait til they get 'over yonder.'"

Even though Jennie was not fully sold on the doctrines, she took a hard line with her mother and defended the Koreshans and Teed. "I feel so sure that we are not mistaken—and I wish that you would listen without prejudice."[11]

And so the Andrewses moved. Allen remembers the day they left for Chicago. Two friends came to the train station to see them off in the rain. His last image, pulling away from Binghamton, was of these two people standing at the depot under a dripping umbrella.

In Chicago, the Andrewses stayed in a wonderfully comfortable house in the suburb of River Forest with a family named Miller. The husband was Sidney C.

Miller, a successful publisher, and his wife, Jeannie, a follower of Teed. Teed hoped that if the Andrewses stayed with the Millers, Jennie would see that wealthy, smart people were receptive to joining the Koreshans.

Abie planned to divide his time between practicing medicine and helping to publish the *Guiding Star*, the Koreshans' monthly magazine. Allen was thrilled to be fulfilling his dream of working in a print shop—and by the prospect of adventure in the big city. From the Millers' place in River Forest, he took the train to the *Guiding Star* offices on Wabash, near Chicago's Printer's Row. He worked on the second floor in a cramped corner by the kitchen that served the Koreshans' busy lunchroom. Allen did two types of work: running the two foot-powered presses that produced the pamphlets, programs, and invitations, and setting type for the magazine, a much larger print job done by an outside printer. Allen hand set the type—in reverse, as he had learned to do—and carried the heavy plates to the printer for the run. It's just as well that the letters were in reverse on the plates. Allen didn't understand most of the articles.

Though he had known Dr. Teed ever since he could remember, he hadn't known about his beliefs until they moved to Chicago. There, he attended Teed's public talks on a variety of topics, including "What Made the Whale Sick," on how the parable of Jonah illustrated capitalism, and "The Great Coming Crisis, the World's Catastrophe." The lectures were free and lasted more than an hour and a half: one hour for Teed to speak, as little as five minutes for audience questions, and thirty minutes for his responses and wrap-up. "His phraseology baffled me completely—such as 'alchemico-organic,' 'anthropostic,' 'theocracy,' etc.," Allen wrote. "It was almost akin to learning a new language." One day after a lecture, an old woman asked Allen how he enjoyed the lecture, and Allen had no idea how to answer her.[12]

With the added expense of larger headquarters, it wasn't long before things became financially precarious for the Koreshans. Employees hadn't been paid. Rent was late and the landlord threatened to seize the printing equipment as payment. Henry Silverfriend, the dry goods store owner in Kaukauna, Wisconsin, saved them. He "bought" the equipment from Teed so that it couldn't be seized. They structured it to look as if it were a loan payment. Specifically, Teed had borrowed from Silverfriend sometime before and hadn't been able to pay him back. The proceeds from "selling" the printing equipment satisfied that debt and paid the back rent. A bill of sale was drawn up and Silverfriend became the official owner, though it was clear to both men that the equipment really belonged to the Unity and not Silverfriend. But in this way, a future creditor couldn't lay claim to it.

Not long after, Silverfriend sold his family's dry goods business and gave his share, $1,900, to Teed. Despite the protests of their mother and siblings, Henry and his sister Etta moved to Chicago and joined the colony.[13]

While Silverfriend was still in Kaukauna, he had a dream—Teed would hold a big convention in Chicago. Thousands of people would come from all nations. Silverfriend told Teed about his dream, and Teed assured him this would come to pass.

With the money from Silverfriend, Teed was able to pay off all of the Unity's debts and had money left, which he and Silverfriend used to sign a three-year lease on a handsome six-flat apartment building on College Place near the Old University of Chicago. College Place became the Koreshans' first communal home in Chicago. Silverfriend spent the first night in the new house. Teed's sister Emma moved in, as did his brother Oliver, whose devotion would not prove to be as constant as Emma's. Mrs. Paterson, one of Teed's early followers from the Moravia mop days, moved in, too. Ellen Woolsey, whose relationship with Teed had set tongues wagging as the mop business failed, also moved in, as did Thankful Hale, the woman who had invited Teed to speak in Chicago at the mental science convention. The Andrewses joined them, even though Jennie was still lukewarm about Teed's doctrines.

College Place was uncomfortable—many of them slept on the floor because it was unfurnished, they couldn't afford heat, and they were often hungry. But the Koreshans felt more confident than ever. They had printing offices, a successful lunchroom, a magazine, and now a communal home. Once they were settled in College Place, Silverfriend reminded Teed of his dream of the grand convention in Chicago. When shall we have it? he asked. Teed decided it would be right away. Silverfriend paid to rent Chicago's Central Music Hall, and the Koreshans advertised the convention in the newspaper. Attendance was lighter than expected, but the Koreshans gained forty converts.[14]

One of them was Jennie Andrews. She surrendered fully that day. She had been sheepish that afternoon when Teed ushered them onto the platform of the Music Hall, where they sat for the speeches. She didn't like feeling on display, but at some point that afternoon, she lost her self-consciousness. It happened when she heard Teed speak. The topic of his speech is lost to history, but we can be sure of one thing. Even the most cynical newsmen admitted that his lectures cast a spell. Central Music Hall was nationally known for its excellent acoustics, and Teed would have taken full advantage of it. The place would nearly have vibrated with conviction.

Jennie was overtaken by the belief that Teed was a man of God. *The* man of God. In trying to explain her conversion later to a friend, she said it was the most wonderful experience of her life. Had the friend been at the convention, Jennie said, she too would believe. She was now certain that this was the right place for her and her family. Her husband, Abie, spoke that evening, too, and we can surmise that this made her proud and even surer. And Victoria delivered a powerful speech in the hall: "Woman's Restoration to Her Rightful Dominion." The push for women's equality was spreading, with more women than ever working for equal rights and becoming active, visible participants in society. Jane Addams and Ellen Starr were one year away from revolutionizing Chicago by creating the Hull House to provide relief for poor immigrant workers. Women would flock there to volunteer and to advocate for a variety of reforms.

The question of women's rights, Victoria told the Koreshans and their visitors in Central Music Hall, would not go away until women were guaranteed equality. Teed's stand that women and men should be equal was popular with women, but not with many men, perhaps especially his insistence that his female followers not surrender their power to their husbands by having sex with them. His message that marriage was a form of slavery lined up with what women's rights activists were saying: that females had less power than slaves. Women thrived by being near Teed; that's clear from the journal Jennie kept. When their Master was away, the women were sad. When he came home, they felt fortified. In the newspapers, Koreshan women were dismissed as creatures who were easily led astray. But from their viewpoint, just the opposite was true. They were respected, they had governance over their own bodies and a strong sense of mission, and they had a safe place to live in a communal home where they were treated as equals to men. Without a place to go, a woman might never have the means to leave her husband. If she did, she wasn't likely to have felt safe. It was a scary time to be a single woman, especially in the city. At that very time in London, Jack the Ripper was murdering women. In Chicago, where the population was growing rapidly—it doubled in the 1880s, reaching one million—it was easy for a woman to simply get lost. Every week, young women arrived in the city with dreams of a sophisticated life. They took jobs at department stores and factories, and they lived independently, and, too often, they fell on hard times or disappeared.

Naturally, Jennie would have worried about her own daughters, especially Maggie, her strong-willed daughter who had resisted the move to Chicago. For now, Maggie lived at College Place, but how easy it would be for her to become one of those shopgirls, Jennie may have thought. Jennie confided in her own mother that she hoped Maggie would turn herself around and stay in the community, but Maggie was increasingly restless. If she left, Jennie knew, Maggie would be vulnerable but too headstrong to admit it.

As more Koreshans moved into College Place, the media paid closer attention. By all Koreshan accounts, things on the inside were calm, and they were leading pious lives. Not so, according to the papers. In 1889, the *Chicago Evening Journal* ran a front-page story to satisfy and entertain the public's curiosity.[15]

"The College of Life," the headline read, followed by a stack of subheads: "Teed . . . Exerts Strange Influence Over His Followers," "Families Broken Up by His Outrageous and Unnatural Tactics," and "Confiding Women Taken Into the Home, Robbed of Their Money and Kicked Out." It was hardly the first article about Teed and his society, but it marked the beginning of a steady watch, full of insinuation, tantalizing details, and gossip.

Knowing that readers wanted to see what lay inside the house with the odd sign, "College of Life," the reporter began his story outside the building.

"On the northwest corner of Cottage Grove avenue and College place stands a fine double, four-story brown-stone front building. . . . Here reside about fourteen men, mostly grey-headed, and about fourteen women, mostly young and good-looking. What the College of Life is, and what these twenty-eight people are after is something of a puzzle," the reporter wrote. "There is a widespread belief that they live together for anything but a holy or good purpose."

The reporter stepped inside and waited for Teed to descend the stairs and grant the promised interview. The front parlor was large and well appointed, the newsman wrote, and through an open folding door, he saw into a back parlor, where several men and women talked. They looked happy; nothing untoward seemed to be going on. In fact, nothing much of anything seemed to be going on.

Teed appeared. "His face is thin and distraught," the reporter for the *Chicago Evening Journal* wrote, "and he looks somewhat like a spiritualist medium who has been weakened by a protracted trance." He explained the College of Life to the reporter. Teed gestured to his friend Abie, indicating that he was on the faculty. When the reporter asked what Abie taught, Teed said that he "sort of" practiced medicine. In fact, Abie had been the assistant editor of the *Guiding Star*, but it had stopped publication recently, likely for financial reasons. There were no classes or recitations at the college, and no formal faculty, Teed said, and the society made money from publications and donations.

After an hour, the reporter arrived at the topic his readers most wanted to know about: Teed's beliefs about sexual intercourse. Celibacy, Teed told him, was the way to immortal life. He went into detail about male orgasm, and the reporter recorded their interview in the newspaper story. "I do not say that the secretions must be absorbed," Teed said, "but that they must not be secreted at all, but preserved in the system."

"Have you got there yet?"

"No; if I had I should be translated. But I am getting there."

How to interpret this? Did Teed mean that he did not yet have enough followers to redirect their sexual energies toward him and effect his translation? Or was he still having sex, masturbating, or practicing withdrawal? If you believe Teed's many letters to Abie on the subject decades before, he was absolutely committed to celibacy. But the Chicago public didn't have access to Teed's private thoughts. They had only the newspapers to tell the story, and here Teed seemed to be saying that he wasn't yet celibate, which cast suspicion on the entire group. It's possible that the quotes were taken out of context, and Teed rarely gave a straight answer to any question. So readers were left to form their own conclusions.

"Where is your wife?" the reporter asked him.

"I don't know," Teed answered. "She is dead, though."

The reporter asked whether the women in the house were married, and Teed said no.

"I have been accused of breaking up families," Teed told the reporter. "But the truth is that I am simply picking up those who have been divorced in the courts."

"Where are the husbands?" the reporter asked.

"I don't know," Teed said.

But the reporter apparently knew. He had no trouble finding a husband who would talk, and the story relied heavily on an interview with him, a Mr. J. S. Robinson, whose wife, Lizzie, had left him to live at College Place. Mr. Robinson called Teed a devil and a tramp who nearly made him crazy. When Teed came to Chicago, he had lived with Mr. Robinson and Lizzie rent-free; now Lizzie paid Teed's expenses and helped run the lunchroom on State Street.

Then there were the Singers, mentioned in the article, whom Teed lived with after leaving the Robinsons. Mr. Joseph Singer, a music teacher, saw that he was losing his wife to Teed. His wife recognized her folly and tried to return home, but Mr. Singer wouldn't take her back.

The list of husbands included a military general, a coal salesman, and a man at the Egyptian Preserving Company whose wife often paid Teed's notes and, when necessary, his bail. The military general cut his wife off completely, and she was forced to learn the printing business to get by, the article said. The coal man had extended credit to Teed and was now suing for payment. He lost his wife to Teed temporarily, he said, but she returned when she saw Teed's true character. A man in the silk department at Walker's told the reporter that Teed was dangerous: "He possesses strong mesmeric powers, and by exercising them on silly women breaks up homes and wrecks happy lives."

Characterizing the women as silly and suggestible helped men explain why their wives would leave. No one asked the women themselves. Perhaps they left because they were married to men who viewed them as senseless.

It was said in the newspaper story that Mrs. Paterson—the faithful Mrs. Paterson, who had been with Teed for nine years—waited on the steps of the College of Life for her savior from eleven to twelve every night. Mr. Robinson told this to the reporter and wanted to know what a character like Teed was doing prowling around town at that hour.

Some of the women were certainly sexually attracted to Teed. He was handsome and charismatic with nice eyes and a resonant voice. Marjory Stoneman Douglas described him as a "square-jawed, magnetic man." Some drawings in the newspaper show his confident bust and penetrating eyes, but others were less complimentary.[16]

"He has the appearance of an ordinary man of not the highest grade of human origin," a reporter wrote, "and his voice has a not altogether agreeable nasal tone, which completes the illusion that he is as other men."[17]

There's no hard proof that Teed was a philanderer, only accusations, and plenty of them. If he had mania, a near certainty, flirtation would have gone along with it, and this is supported by the stories women told when they left the community. Almost without exception, when a woman became disenchanted with Teed, she said he had made advances toward her or that she had witnessed him making advances toward other women.[18]

Teed defended himself in the media. "I am charged with all sorts of immoralities," he once told a reporter. "Do you suppose, if I were that kind of a man, I could hold this household here of sixty people together?"[19]

More than one woman claimed that he promised to make her his Minerva, the goddess of wisdom, and didn't make good on it, though it's hard to know how one would make good on a promise like that. There was one woman he kept such a promise to—Victoria, whom he had chosen as his Empress and supported unconditionally, even when it meant losing a follower. Thankful Hale was one of those followers. Perhaps Victoria was threatened by Hale's power, knowing that she had launched Teed's success, or perhaps Hale had stopped believing in Koreshanity, as was reported by the newspaper. For whatever reason, Victoria disliked her, so Teed ordered her to leave. Hale refused, saying he owed her money. And on a bitterly cold day in January, Teed unscrewed the hinges on her door and called a policeman to haul her away—this according to the reporter of the sensational "College of Life" story in the *Chicago Evening Journal*.

That reporter also found a spicy source in Ida May, Victoria's ex-daughter-in-law, who had kept quiet during her divorce. Now she spilled everything, revealing that during the time she and Harry lived with the Ordways, she saw a slight, well-dressed man hanging around outside their place quite often, a man she recognized as Cyrus Teed. She claimed she saw Victoria signal to Teed from the window to let him know when it was safe to come in. (Her husband was a bakery salesman who traveled frequently.) Ida May said she even saw Teed go into Victoria's room many times. Harry, Victoria's son, once told Ida May that he caught his mother and Teed in a compromising position. Ida May said, "He [Teed] is a contemptible brute. And you may print that as coming from me."[20]

What's surprising is that Harry, too, talked to the reporter. His mother was devoted to Teed, he said. "And as my father doesn't kick, I suppose it's all right." Harry said it wouldn't surprise him if Teed was guilty of "crooked work with some of those women."

The story ended with Mr. Robinson saying he planned to sue Teed for twenty-five thousand dollars for alienation of affections. The reporter speculated that Robinson wasn't likely to see any money. The college, it was rumored, was "deeply indebted to the butcher and baker and other tradesmen." Unless the Koreshans paid outstanding rent of six hundred dollars, the reporter wrote, they would be evicted from College Place in a matter of days. That was what people were saying, the story indicated, without providing a specific source.

It was true that the Koreshans were suffering. They ate a very plain diet, Allen Andrews remembered. On their second Thanksgiving at College Place, he wrote, they shivered in their coats inside unheated rooms. But the rumored eviction didn't come to pass.[21]

Reporters and editors thought little of printing hearsay in stories that were meant to entertain. Readers slurped up the gossip, sometimes attributed to no one in particular. "It is said that" or "it is believed that" accompanied claims that Teed ran a free love colony or that the Koreshans were broke.

In that time, for a story like Teed's, it was permissible for a reporter to use color or to omit facts, especially when a story was nonessential—and not much of this story was essential. Nothing was at stake unless you were a Koreshan.

"Chicago journalists knew (and if they forgot, they were reminded forcefully)

... they were writing for people who did not want wit, subtlety, compactness or logic," wrote Hugh Dalziel Duncan, a scholar of the social history of Chicago. According to Duncan, readers wanted "action, feeling, emotion and color expressed with vigor, humor, and exaggeration. Above all, [a reporter] must dramatize the news, not from the view of a dispassionate witness but from that of a participant who spits on his hands, rolls up his sleeves and jumps into the fight."[22]

The writer assigned to "The College of Life" story was from this school, inserting himself into the story. When Teed explained that he was a prophet, the reporter made this aside to the reader: "To the darkened mind of the newspaper man the Doctor seemed to say that he was the Christ and he wasn't."[23]

Story style was driven by the stiff competition among newspapers. In Chicago, there were ten major papers—five came out in the morning, and five in the evening—and hundreds of other publications, so many that "it gives you the headache merely to read the list," wrote William Stead, a British journalist who visited Chicago in the 1890s.[24]

Stead wrote that the major newspapers should be the watchmen of the city, but they did a pitiful job. In trying to cover everything, they covered nothing well, and corruption went unchecked. Newspapers had enough money to report on serious matters, he wrote, but the owners were more concerned with enriching themselves. He believed that if a newspaper chose to, it could create a utopia in Chicago by exposing corruption and uniting the city around social reform. Of course, the papers didn't want a utopia. They wanted readers.

In the 1880s, journalism became a profession. Previously, news had been written for free by friends of the editors who prided themselves on a lack of a college education, according to news historian Michael Schudson. But now reporters were paid, and paid well.[25]

The reporter on the Koreshan story was likely the new breed of reporter—young, college educated, and unmarried because the job was too consuming to allow for much of a personal life. In his off hours, a newsman (and they *were* men mostly) socialized with fellow reporters in one of a growing number of press clubs. The most famous was Chicago's Whitechapel Club, which glamorized the gritty life of the reporter—or the gritty life he fancied himself having. Situated in the back room of a bar on Newsboys' Alley, the Whitechapel was decorated in grisly irony. Human skulls sat on tables, their eye sockets lit with candles. Axes, blades, handcuffs, pistols, and ropes hung from the walls. There was a table shaped like a coffin.[26]

Reporters showed off not only for the readers, but also for each other, by telling colorful stories with a distinctive voice, which was just as important as telling the truth. And as there were no bylines with the articles, reporters weren't accountable. They weren't above resorting to antics for a good story: one newsman who interviewed Teed disguised himself as a woman seeking a new faith.[27]

If an article's purpose was to uncover corruption, readers wanted facts. If that was not the article's purpose, and if facts got in the way of the story, the story and the reporter's voice won. In the case of Teed, the facts (his doctrines) were impenetrable, and his followers kept to themselves. So the most frequent story was that things in his "heaven" were not so pure. The story was mostly entertainment.

Once, when Teed came back to the city from one of his many trips, the *Chicago Herald* announced, "Many a Chicago husband's heart will quail . . . at his return."[28]

At least one paper had a sense of humor about journalism. The *Pittsburg Dispatch* ran this sarcastic brief poking fun at the newsmen covering Teed:

A certain Dr. Cyrus Teed, of Chicago, has been telling a number of reporters that he is God Almighty. To the credit of Chicago journalism not more than one-half of the papers of that city appear to take any stock in such a story.[29]

Teed's reaction to the stories was that ridicule was a positive sign and that the more the press "pressed" him, the more valid Koreshanity looked. He referred to the coverage as advertising or, when it suited him, persecution. As Abie had pointed out to Jennie's mother, Christ had been misunderstood and persecuted, too, as had holy men throughout history.

One difference between Teed and other religious leaders is that Teed never recognized the power of a story in developing a following. Jesus had compelling stories, as did Moses and Mohammed. Newspapers weren't the only ones that lived and died by the strength of their stories; religions did too.

The Bible was filled with lore: Adam and Eve; the burning bush; the parting of the sea; Noah's ark; Job's sufferings; and the casting out of money changers, to name a few. Teed's cousin Joseph Smith had drawn thousands of followers in a very short time with his story of an angel who revealed the location of golden plates that became the Book of Mormon.

But Teed's written account of his illumination was scarcely readable, and he didn't publish it until he had been in Chicago for four years. It couldn't compete with the stories about him in the major dailies. The media told his story before he did.

Teed did have his own printing press, and he resurrected his monthly magazine. Koreshans described it, in an ad, as "depart[ing] from the usual stiff impersonality of journalism" and "the clearest search-light on the drift of current events." In it, Teed detailed his doctrines; sometimes he defended the Unity against attacks in the press, but more often, he ignored the outside world. Not surprisingly, few people read the magazine. By contrast, the public appetite for newspaper stories was insatiable. And as the Koreshans' struggles with the community escalated, those stories became juicier.[30]

✳ 5 ✳

Opportunity

Once Jennie was in Chicago, she and her mother Margaret wrote often, and their letters had a common refrain—Margaret worried that her daughter had been brainwashed by Teed and was throwing her life away; Jennie reassured her that this wasn't the case. Margaret asked about the living arrangements at the College of Life, and Jennie wrote, "I could hardly have more pleasant rooms or more pleasantly located." The College was in a quiet area, across the street from Groveland Park and in view of the tower of the old University of Chicago.[1]

Jennie looked after the children, she told her mother, and mended their clothes; Abie had a private office; and Maggie, twenty, their oldest daughter, helped in the dining room. Maggie hadn't wanted to join the Unity, but she was quite happy now, Jennie wrote; the discipline of work had been good for her, and she'd had a change of heart about Teed—somewhat. Speaking of him once, Maggie said, "I wish he was not so good & then I could hate him."

Teed's sister Emma was in charge of the house, and the women divided the duties so that no one person had a burden. There was plenty to eat, Jennie assured her mother, and, yes, they did eat meat, something her mother expressed concern about. The Koreshans were a family, Jennie wrote, and they shared everything. "Of course we have our own personal affects [sic], . . . but we all fare alike."

Jennie's mother nudged her in different ways to come home, sending news of family in Alexandria; mailing her tea, handkerchiefs, clothes, and money; and occasionally tucking a piece of disturbing cult-related literature into the package or envelope. She once sent a paper that detailed the exploits of Rev. George Jacob Schweinfurth, the head of a communal religious sect in Rockford, Illinois, ninety miles from Chicago. Outsiders believed that this cult was similar to the Koreshan Unity. Newsmen sometimes referred to Teed as Chicago's Schweinfurth, and they reported often on both groups' alleged immoralities and brushes with trouble. After a group of citizen vigilantes, the White Caps, threatened to roast Schweinfurth alive for breaking up families, Teed reported that the same group sent him a menacing letter. When Teed asked for police protection against the White Caps, the *Chicago Daily Tribune* had a bit of fun: "He is afraid somebody is going to kill him," the *Tribune* reported. "We fear Dr. Teed is not yet a soundly-converted follower of himself."[2]

Jennie explained to her mother that Teed was nothing like Schweinfurth, a false Christ, one of the many who were popping up as the last days were at hand, just as Matthew had foretold in the Bible. Time would show that Teed was for real, she wrote.

It's apparent that Jennie felt a solid sense of purpose, and being in Chicago reinforced her certainty. The city would soon learn that it had won the World's Fair, and a frenzy would ensue to clean up the streets, the pollution, and the vice, so that Chicago could proudly display itself to the world. But even before the news of the fair, major reform had started, thanks in part to a wildly popular science fiction novel, *Looking Backward—2000–1887*, by Edward Bellamy. Set in the distant future (the year 2000), the novel depicted an America without poverty, taxes, or war, where people worked shorter hours and industry was nationalized. Bellamy's book set off a massive national, and short-lived, effort to make America's economy more democratic. In Chicago, the memory of the Haymarket Riot was fresh, and the hunger for fairness and equality was pronounced. Teed, who detested capitalism, no doubt felt great satisfaction as the movement against it swelled.

Koreshans read Bellamy and even honored his work in their speeches and writings, but they were different from Bellamy's group and the other reform organizations that worked within the system to change it. Teed preached that where there was capitalism, Koreshanity couldn't function, so the Unity held itself apart from society. The members believed that by sacrificing everything to the community, they advanced the cause and helped the downtrodden, Jennie explained in her letters home. By that time, this had become a quaint idea—forming an isolated utopia as an answer to perceived corruption—and the Koreshans were especially odd to outsiders because they sequestered themselves not in a remote area, but in the midst of a ferociously growing city.

Teed did make some advances to one socialist group in Chicago, but its members weren't interested in an alliance. He also spoke to the agnostics, who "denounced [him] as an imposter that could lead his people into any-thing—Mormonism or anything else," Jennie relayed in her journal. He also approached some churches, as he had done in other towns, but was met with rejection. One Baptist minister said, from the pulpit, that he wanted to be the first to dash Teed's brains out with a rock and that he would form a mob and level the College of Life building.[3]

When Sidney Miller, the Koreshans' friend in River Forest, lost his wife to Teed, his story sounded like all the others. "He Can Do Nothing with Her," read the headline in the *Tribune*. The couple had been content, living in the elegant community of River Forest. He was handsome, with jet-black hair and a mustache, and she was pretty, voluptuous, and "considered an exceptionally bright and talented woman," the reporter wrote in mock puzzlement. Though she attended church, she never had much interest in religion until she met Dr. Cyrus Teed.[4]

Miller was tolerant of Koreshanity at first; he had allowed Abie and Jennie Andrews and their children to live with them when they moved from Bingham-ton. Then it became clear to Miller, he said, that Teed was poisoning his wife's mind, telling her to abandon sex and marriage, and asking her to turn over her worldly possessions. At some point, Sidney Miller learned that this false mes-siah promised his wife that the two of them—Teed and Mrs. Miller—would arise on October 18, 1890, not incidentally, Teed's birthday, and she would be-come his Minerva. She deserted him and their children, Miller claimed. "I have done everything I could to reclaim her," he told a reporter.[5]

But Miller was different from the other husbands, wealthier and more pow-erful, the president of the National Publishing Company in Chicago. He didn't seem to be angry at his wife ("she will not listen to reason"), but he was very angry at Teed.[6]

Another husband stood out as well, not so much for his wealth as for his apparent instability. Annie and Thomas Cole's marriage had not been happy, according to Annie's sister, Sarah Crosten, who lived with them. Crosten said they fought frequently, and Thomas often accused Annie of improper relations with her physicians, of whom there apparently were many, as Annie was often ill. Crosten said that Thomas threatened to kill Annie on several occasions and said that he would leave her with nothing.[7]

Thomas Cole himself had a very different version of the story: he told a re-porter that they had a happy marriage. "I always treated her well and gave her all my wages." But then she began receiving the Koreshans' magazine, and the women of the Unity visited her, and she abandoned him, he said, going to the College and taking their six-year-old son. Thomas wrote her and asked her to come back to him, but she refused.[8]

Cyrus Teed had yet another version. Annie did not live at the College, he said. It was unusual for him not to welcome a woman into the Unity if she was interested in his teachings, but Annie Cole was one of those unwelcome few. When she attended the public meetings, the Koreshans noticed that she seemed obsessed with Koreshanity and with Teed in particular. Teed later wrote that Annie was subject to "mental freaks," and he told her that she did not belong with them, but she continued to come to meetings, and the Koreshans tolerated her.[9]

Given Mr. Cole's suspicious nature, especially when it came to his wife's relationships with physicians, perhaps it's not surprising that he showed up on the Koreshans' front lawn one evening with a revolver. Walking past, he saw their son playing in the yard and when he stopped to talk to him, several Koreshans rushed outside, Cole said. They threatened him, he claimed, and separated him from his son. He brandished his revolver and saw his wife being ushered out of the back door of the College. They didn't allow him to talk to her, and they booted him off the property. They booted her, too, they later pointed out. But the Koreshans wouldn't get rid of Thomas—or Annie—so easily.[10]

Jennie and Abie Andrews had been in Chicago nearly three years when Abie had a stroke. It slurred his speech and confined him to bed, and he couldn't take care of himself. Jennie's mother came to Chicago to help care for him, and though the two had long disagreed over Koreshanity and his decision to take Jennie and the family to Chicago, they were family at heart, and she loved him. Margaret stayed at College Place and wrote letters to her husband back in Binghamton. She was one of the few nonbelievers who ever stayed at the Unity (the "Institution," Margaret called it). Her letters gave an account of everyday life there that contradicted the scandalous media accounts. The Koreshans treated her kindly, she told her husband.[11]

"They live very plainly," she wrote, "seldom have meat more than once a week but seem to thrive on it." She and Abie spent hours sitting together and as his speech improved, he tried to convince her that Koreshanity was the true way. Margaret wrote to her husband that Abie was anxious about her spiritual condition. "I guess he thinks I am a hardened sinner."

Jennie, too, tried to get her mother to see that Teed was the true prophet. But as far as Margaret could tell, he was quite human, she wrote to her husband.

As Christmas approached, Margaret pleaded with Jennie and Abie to come home to Alexandria for the holidays, but they said that College Place was now their home. Margaret gave up on trying to persuade them to leave Koreshanity. "Convince a man (or woman either) against their will," Margaret wrote to her husband, "and they'll be of the same opinion still. I guess this [letter] had better be burned."

Margaret's husband urged her to come home and seemed to doubt that she wanted to. He might have feared she too would be brainwashed and decide to stay at College Place. She assured him that wasn't the case. "I want to come home," she wrote, underlining each word. Money was stopping her. "[I] do not think that the RR is issuing free passes." Abie's illness had been costly, Margaret wrote. In spite of newspaper reports that Teed was enriching himself by extracting thousands from his duped converts, it doesn't appear from Margaret's letters that the community was flush. If it had been, Abie's illness wouldn't have been such a hardship.

As Abie recuperated from his stroke, Teed traveled to San Francisco, where a small following had developed, thanks in large part to a loyal disciple, Professor Royal O. Spear. Before going to San Francisco, Spear had traveled the Midwest preaching Teed's doctrines. In fact, Spear was the disciple who brought Henry Silverfriend into the fold. Recognizing Spear's charisma and talent for recruiting, Teed made Spear his front man in San Francisco and gave him the first name Royal. Spear explained the nickname to reporters: he was related to Queen Victoria, he said, and "had royal blood in his veins and a royal tongue rolling around in his mouth."

Before long in San Francisco, there were enough followers, and money, for a communal home on Noe Street, in what is now the Castro District. Teed called the home Ecclesia.[12]

The Noe Street house couldn't have been leased without several wealthy female supporters who left their husbands, men who readily talked to the media and who were from all walks of life. A nationally acclaimed geologist told a reporter that his wife had "a fever that must run its course"; a spurned carriage maker said, "Teed will sometime run against a pistol and suddenly 'disintegrate'"; and an unemployed man, reporters learned, hadn't needed a profession until recently because of his wife's considerable banking and railroad fortune.[13]

In Chicago, things were going swimmingly, too. The Koreshans' monthly magazine had a new name, the *Flaming Sword*, referring to the sword that protected the tree of knowledge in the Garden of Eden. A bigger press allowed them to print the magazine in-house. Forty of them worked in the printing operation, pumping out not only the magazine but also pamphlets, invitations, and lecture announcements that circulated throughout Chicago. A reporter who visited from the *Chicago Daily Tribune* was impressed with the operation: "They stick type, kick the press, work the paper-cutter, read proof and carry in coal for the *Flaming Sword*."[14]

When this reporter visited the print shop, the Koreshans assumed he was like all the others, there to create trouble, and one of the brothers gave him a stern warning: "You newspapers may sneer all you like, but the time's coming when you will tremble. The end of the world is at hand. Other folks fear it. We know when it will be here."

"When will it be here?" the reporter asked.

"Before you have worn out a dozen pairs of shoes."[15]

During this promising time, Abie Andrews died. He had seen the growth of the community and two successful communal homes, in Chicago and in San Francisco. He saw Teed overcome the challenges that had plagued him for so long. Everything Teed and Abie had worked toward for two decades was finally coming to pass, and his family had a meaningful role: his wife was a devoted follower, and his son Allen, a golden boy in the community. Abie had the assurance that his investment of money and energy would carry on. His life, in other words, had mattered, as evidenced by his conversations with Jennie's mother, Margaret. He died with the conviction that he would be reunited with Teed and Jennie and his family in the afterlife, if not sooner.

The new era was coming, Teed told his followers, and the World's Fair would be the battleground. The city, he said, was the true representation of Babylon—dirty, evil, and full of sin and oppression. Labor and capital would fight to the death, and the streets would run with blood.[16]

To usher in this new era, Teed would need to die a martyr's death, probably at the hands of a mob. During the Fair, Teed predicted, he would "theocratize," as he put it, dissolving, ascending, and becoming one with God, entering into his full power as the Messiah. When this happened, his people believed, they would be saved and all mysteries revealed. Just how this would happen, physically, was one more bit of entertainment for the public. A *Chicago Tribune* reporter recorded one of his conversations with a Koreshan: "Do you mean to say that you believe that Dr. Cyrus R. Teed will go shooting off into heaven like a skyrocket, perhaps from this very porch at Nos. 2 and 4 College place, Chicago?"[17]

"I do," answered the follower.

"Will you be kind enough . . . to telephone me . . . so that I and an artist may be present at his translation?"

"I will, sir, with pleasure."

The *Tribune* reporter handed over his business card.

To advance his cause and grow its numbers, Teed wanted to unite with other celibate, communal societies in the United States. He approached the two most prominent communities first—the Shakers and the Economites.

The Economites were the very society he and Abie had visited and written to when Teed lived in Sandy Creek. This was the community in Economy, Pennsylvania, that overlooked the Ohio River, the one whose leader, Father "Santa Claus" Henrici, was generous to communal religious societies and whose secretary sent Teed a mere one hundred dollars, prompting him to write Abie, "When I am ready to use the people of Economy for the Divine use I shall simply command not beg." As Teed set out for the village on the Ohio River, he would have remembered his and Abie's trip eleven years prior and the plans they made together.[18]

In San Francisco on a night in mid-October of 1891, the followers at Noe Street felt a heavy rumble like a wagon passing that rattled the city and lasted thirteen seconds. In Sonoma, people were shaken out of their beds. At the asylum in Napa, nurses struggled to calm the inmates. A few days later, before dawn, another earthquake hit, wave-like from north to south. Royal Spear and his wife felt the tremors, but not on Noe Street. They had severed ties with Teed in an angry separation and moved out of the home.[19]

The conflict started when Spear returned from a tour, preaching about Koreshanity, he told the press. He came home and learned from his wife that Teed had made a pass at her. Teed, she told her husband, tried to persuade her to "enter into relations with him." Furthermore, Teed had told her their relations would be holy because he was the king, and the king could do no wrong. After this happened, Mrs. Spear became more watchful, noticing that Teed also solicited other women in the community. Spear and Teed had a row, and Spear was not one to back down. Now that he had seen Teed's true nature, as he put it, he became bent on destroying him.[20]

There followed many splashy newspaper articles, including one in the *San Francisco Chronicle*, which sent a reporter to the Noe Street Ecclesia. He knocked on the door and asked to speak to Teed and was told by a matronly woman that the Master was out. He often spent the night with friends, she said. The reporter looked beyond the woman and into the house, where he saw a young woman, very pretty, in a negligee. This was not the only report of scantily clad "angels" in Teed's heaven. In the *Daily Inter Ocean*, an illustration showed Teed with a halo above his head and his arms around two women. The paper reported the Spears's claim that Teed kissed and caressed the attractive women and controlled their comings and goings.[21]

The same article mentioned troubles in Chicago as well, including "the sad case" of Jennie Andrews, who had come to Chicago for the sake of keeping her family together, and Jesse Teed, Cyrus's father, whom Spear described as "feeble," "silver-haired," "poorly clad," and roaming the city to sell knives and forks to make a living. Spear said that Jesse lived in the Chicago home and was mistreated because he didn't believe his son was the Messiah. This seems to have only a grain of truth. Jesse Teed did live in the communal home at around this time, but he had a job in Chicago preparing for the World's Fair. After completing his work on the fairgrounds, he left Chicago and returned to New York, writing to Emma that he didn't want to be "a block under the wheels of Zion's chariot."[22]

In San Francisco, the Spears booked the Metropolitan Hall for a lecture they promised would contain sensational revelations about Teed. The *San Francisco Chronicle* ran an advance blurb, and three hundred people showed up. Royal Spear revealed he had "caught Dr. Teed kissing women on the stairs and 'all over the plantation.'" The women Teed favored included "a widow in Sausalito; a blonde wife from over the bay, and a red-headed wife on Mission Street." Spear said his own wife would have murdered Teed years ago, but didn't want it on her conscience.[23]

Spear became so emotional in his lecture that he was "incoherent" at times, a reporter wrote. Some attendees left the hall, offended by the occasional indecency. Apparently no one in the media budged. Finally, reporters had access to two insiders, a husband and wife, with juicy details and anger in their hearts.

Then Royal Spear delivered a surprise to the audience: Teed was scheming to rob the Economites, who were rumored to have millions in their coffers. Spear said the plan had been eleven years in the making, and Teed had told him all about it when he was a trusted disciple. Two or three years earlier, Teed, as Spear claimed Teed had told him, formed an alliance with a man named John Duss, whom he sent to Economy "for the express purpose of capturing that money." Duss worked his way onto the Economites' board of trustees and had earned Father Henrici's full trust, Spear said. Meantime, Teed planted more men in Economy and was waiting for the right moment. A reporter for the

Chicago Journal wrote, "[Teed] would not appear on the scene until the fruit of this scheme was ripe for his plucking, and then he would step boldly in and gather the way-up persimmon which had been knocked down by his exceedingly long pole." Until then, Spear said, Duss was funneling money to Teed to support his travels out West and to keep the Chicago home afloat. It sounded much like the plan Teed had made with Abie, but with John Duss in Abie's role.[24]

Spear had found a partner in Chicago with plenty of time and money to contribute to the cause: Sidney Miller, the husband at the helm of the National Publishing Company. Miller had apparently been biding his time, waiting for a chance to ruin Teed, and he fixated on the alleged scheme with the Economites. He either hired a detective to go to Economy or he went there himself—there are two versions—and he tracked Teed's moves; looked for Koreshan moles; warned Father Henrici; and made enough noise that the story stayed in the papers. Miller found out who Duss's enemies in the society were and joined forces with them.

The real story is impossible to know, but it isn't likely to have been as dastardly as Spear and Miller's version, nor as innocent as Teed and Duss's. In a self-aggrandizing memoir in the 1940s, Duss laid out his relationship with the Economites and his heroic struggle to save the community. He had been associated with the society from the time he was an infant, and he left and returned many times as an adult. Duss joined the Economites at Father Henrici's invitation before he met Teed, he claimed. Duss said he didn't know Teed well at all but that he admired him and thought the Economites and Koreshans had much in common theologically. Duss did not believe Teed was the Messiah and didn't understand all of his teachings. They were broad and complex, Duss told reporters. But he defended Teed against Spear's claims, saying that anyone who wasn't able to see that Teed was earnest was a poor judge of character.

Teed readily admitted to sending people to Economy for the purpose of employment and for building an alliance between the two societies. Once his Koreshans met the one-year probationary period, they would apply for membership. Teed asserted that the confederation was for a divine commercial and industrial venture.

Teed's interactions with the Economites were closely watched because big money was believed to be at stake and because the Economites were well regarded, while Teed was anything but. As Father Henrici aged and the number of members (about forty by that point) declined, there was a gold rush on Economy. People thought this dwindling group had as much as $150 million in assets thanks to Henrici's smart investments.[25]

So Teed was hardly the only visitor to Economy, but he was the most publicized and, if the media can be believed, the most brazen. The press reported public outrage over Teed's play for the Economites' money and capitalized on the unfairness of it.

The Koreshans working in Economy included Henry Silverfriend, Teed's early financial savior, and Teed's brother Oliver, working as a machinist in the sash and blind factory. Sidney Miller, either personally or through his detective, kept a close watch on them both, waiting for a misstep, and Oliver (whose relationship with Teed was uneven at best) was the one who made it.

The Economites owned vineyards, and Oliver, the story went, as reported by the *Chicago Journal*, befriended the man in charge of the wine business. "This old gentleman one day presented the brother of the Chicago Schweinfurth with a bottle of a rare old vintage and the machinist was shortly afterward in a condition in which prudence was thrown to the winds. The outcries of a female servant quickly brought a crowd of angry men and women." The men of Economy ran Oliver out of town with horsewhips, it was said.[26]

During this time, the *Pittsburgh Leader* ran the sole positive coverage of Teed: "If Dr. Teed does not practice his teachings," the reporter wrote, "if he is seeking personal gain for personal ends, if he loves his subjects with a more earthly than platonic love, he is the most consummate, polished and best educated rogue the world ever produced."[27]

While the media attention was on him, Teed took the opportunity to share what he planned to do once the confederation among the celibate societies was complete. He would build a pneumatic, six-gauge railroad connecting the Atlantic and Pacific coasts. "[It] will carry one to San Francisco in 12 hours," the *Leader* reported. "The cars will run without wheels." The project, Teed said, would create jobs for one million people. He also told the *Leader* he had the ability, from Chicago, to set type for any newspaper in the country.[28]

The reporters couldn't make out whether the confederation with the Economites was happening or not. Some papers reported prematurely that the union between the Koreshans and the Economites was a fait accompli: "Messiah Teed Makes a Rich Haul," one headline read, while another paper reported, "The Economite Society's Millions Safe." Neither was true. When reporters asked Teed what was happening, he responded sarcastically, referring them to their own coverage. He got his information from the papers, he told them, so he would wait for the newsmen to tell him the truth.[29]

Teed had high hopes where Duss was concerned. "John is the right man in the right place," he told his followers, and Jennie recorded it in her journal. And Duss was receptive to Teed's plans to confederate the celibate societies. He noted that Teed had made inroads with the Shakers, which he saw as a positive sign. It was Teed, in fact, who introduced Duss to Shaker elder Benjamin Gates. Duss respected Gates, and he felt that he could talk to him in confidence, and he desperately needed someone to confide in.

In his new position as a trustee, Duss had learned what no other Economite knew. The society was broke. His first clue was the letters that arrived frequently for Father Henrici—collection notices from banks, calling in loans Henrici had signed without telling anyone. As Duss looked into the society's long-ignored finances, he was alarmed. To stay afloat, Economy needed nearly a million dollars, and quickly. His plan was to get a loan from some sympathetic person and use it to pay off older loans. That would free up the stocks and bonds that were collateral for those loans, and he could then sell them. But he needed to do all of this very discreetly. If the public learned that Economy was in dire straits, no creditor would come near them, and the stocks and bonds would be worthless. It was better to let people believe the society was flush. This is why the attention on Cyrus Teed was useful.

Duss met with Benjamin Gates in New York City and explained the Economites' delicate situation. "But after a long and pleasant introductory talk," Duss wrote, "he completely dashed my hopes." The Shakers were in financial trouble, too; Gates was looking for his own millionaire.[30]

Hoping to solidify his confederation with the Economites, Teed sent them a letter asking whether the society needed any of his men to serve as managers or bosses for Economy's various industries. Duss's enemies in Economy responded sharply: the Koreshans' services were not needed, and Teed should cease meddling in their affairs and consider all relations broken off. But the faction that wrote this letter was losing ground to Duss, who was already poised to lead the society once Father Henrici died.

Henrici, however, was still very much alive, and he denounced Teed in the papers. "If Dr. Teed claims he is the messiah, he is a liar and a fool," he told the *Chicago Tribune*. "The grizzled old patriarch's frame quivered with indignation" and he "seemed to forget his age for the time." Henrici assured reporters that Economy would never accept Teed as a member.[31]

The following month, the Economites held their annual feast, where they were to vote on whether to accept new members, including the handful of Koreshans who lived there. Jennie Andrews wrote that Teed had prophesized the importance of this day, calling it the beginning of the end. On the Saturday before the feast, the Northern Lights appeared in the sky, and they were especially spectacular over Economy, "reaching back to receding hills on the north and extending lengthwise as far as the eye can see," the *Pittsburg Dispatch* reported.

The *Dispatch* said the Koreshans believed the borealis was the eye of Teed in the sky, watching to see whether the Economites would admit them as members. There's no hard evidence that the Koreshans believed the borealis was the eye of Teed, but it's possible that some did. The followers often ascribed meaning to even the smallest natural phenomena, as once at College Place on the day of a funeral, the women noticed the shape of an iridescent cross in the frost on a window pane in Teed's office. As the cross faded, the shape of a spear appeared, and this transformed into the face of a man in a visor, and then into the image of a woman wearing a poke bonnet. The women believed it to be a sign and told Victoria, and it was decided that the occurrence would be written up and sent to Teed in California with the account of the funeral.[32]

On the day of the Economites' feast, the Koreshans who lived at Economy were denied membership. In fact, their names were not even brought forward for consideration. Sidney Miller took credit for this—and for busting up Teed's confederation plans with the Economites. In the *Flaming Sword*, the Koreshans thanked Miller sarcastically for giving them "exposure" in the papers and explained to readers how Mr. Miller lost Mrs. Miller. "He is a beast," the article read. "And no one knows this better than she whom he calls his wife."[33]

Fears that Teed would be killed by a mob of angry men didn't seem unreasonable to the Koreshans. Plenty of husbands and vigilantes had threatened violence, and the number of spurned husbands was growing, led by Miller and Cole. A murder would fulfill Teed's prophecy.

One Sunday morning in early January at College Place, the Koreshans were jolted awake by shrieking. Koreshan sister Loretta Lane had awoken from a nightmare in which the angry mob came for Teed and took him away. She got out of bed and dressed hurriedly, intent on finding Teed. The house was as quiet as death, she later said. Lane was a porcelain doll of a woman with snow-white hair and black brows and lashes. She had left her husband to join the Unity, tricking him by telling him she was going on vacation and taking her two children along. The husband, enraged, later accused Teed of performing some mysterious operation on his wife so horrific it was unprintable in the newspapers.[34]

Mrs. Lane stood in the cold house, spooked by the silence and firmly convinced that Teed was gone. Jennie related the incident in her journal. "They have taken away my lord," Loretta shrieked, "and I know not where they have laid him." The house came alive, and several brothers and sisters tried to settle her down. She nearly fainted, and she wasn't reassured until Teed himself appeared and told her that he was safe.

When Jennie asked Teed the meaning of Loretta's nightmare, he told her it signaled that "an influx of spirits" was coming. She recalled his words in her journal. "What would you think if a large number of Shaker[s] should come in our midst?" he asked.[35]

"Is there such a possibility?" Jennie asked, and he told her it wouldn't be strange. In fact, unbeknownst to Jennie or apparently to any of the Koreshans, Teed had become a Shaker just three weeks before, on a visit to the North Family of Shakers in New York, where he delivered two well-received lectures. He spoke to the elders first, telling them of his illumination, the Koreshan doctrines, and his plans to build an alliance with the Economites. The elders noted that the Shakers and Koreshans had much in common: both believed in gender equality and in a god who was both masculine and feminine, and both practiced communal living and celibacy. Impressed that Teed was honest and sincere, the elders initiated him into the Shakers' novitiate order—the first order, requiring a probationary period.[36]

The elders invited him to speak to the entire congregation on the Sunday he was there, and to do so as a Shaker "friend and brother," they said. He told all two hundred members of the society about his illumination and the suffering that followed—his moves from town to town and the persecution in the media. The Shakers were well aware of the bad press, and they had decided to invite him in spite of this. "If our minds had been biased by slanderous newspaper reports, the Docter [sic] would have been an unwelcome guest," they wrote in their monthly publication, the *Manifesto*. But the Shakers knew from experience that defamation happened to "those who devaite [sic] from the common course of the world."

As Jennie heard Teed talk about the Shaker influx, she thought back to a few weeks before, when the Koreshans had sung a Shaker hymn on New Year's Day, "All Together Now." And they had been singing it regularly since. Not realizing that Teed was a Shaker (and Teed didn't tell her in this conversation), she wondered whether their singing might have "generate[d] a peculiar spiritual sphere" to make way for the Shakers.

The evening after Loretta Lane's dream, they sang more Shaker tunes. When a follower began playing a march on the piano, everyone left what they were doing. Conversations stopped. The boys abandoned their game of crokinole and gathered around the piano. Teed arrived in the parlor and asked everyone to stand so that he could teach them a Shaker march. Their version of the march, he said, would be somewhat different: they should direct their palms downward rather than up, in the Shaker fashion. The reason for this, he explained, was that the Koreshan church was "distributive." It seems to be another example of Teed's taking someone else's idea and adding his own twist.

Jennie felt foolish doing the march, but as they danced past Teed, she noticed how placid and serious he looked. She had the distinct feeling he was blessing each of them. Afterward, she admitted in her journal, "there was a peculiar feeling of exhilaration, following it like electricity."

Part of the exhilaration was that the Koreshans were excited to be together with their Master, who had been traveling more and more. When Teed was away, Jennie wrote, the house seemed empty and sad. For the past two years, he had spent considerable time in Massachusetts, where he had a small following; more recently, he was in San Francisco, preparing his followers to leave Noe Street and come to Chicago; and he had been visiting celibate societies, like the Economites and Shakers, with the hope of building a confederation.

During Teed's probationary period with the Shakers, which he didn't share with his followers, Shakers did appear in their midst, and it seems that they were checking out not only Teed but the entire Koreshan community. Early one February morning, Shaker elder Benjamin Gates pulled up in front of College Place in a carriage. Teed was in San Francisco, attending to business, arranging for train tickets for the move to Chicago, and defending himself against Royal Spear's accusations, so the Koreshans welcomed Gates. The children performed the Shaker march for him, and the group sang a Koreshan hymn, followed by Shaker songs. Gates left, much impressed, saying that he felt an inner sense of their goodness. Many religious groups had visited the Shakers and spoken to them, Gates said, but Teed was something special. Jennie recalled Gates's saying, "He went down to the root of things."

Soon after Gates visited, another Shaker came—an elderly Mr. Cantrell, who had doubts about the Koreshans, having been in Chicago for a few weeks and read about them in the papers. Teed was still away. It's possible that Gates and Cantrell made a point of coming when Teed wasn't there, to see what went on when he wasn't presiding over them. The Koreshans welcomed Cantrell with a feast and singing, and he, too, came away satisfied that the reports about them were false. "I was convinced that the Lord was doing a work here for a people who would be a great people," Cantrell said.[37]

Around this time, Teed changed his look: he shaved his face clean of the beard that had hidden his lips and square jaw. It was a dramatic transformation, as evidenced by a portrait taken in a San Francisco studio. In the photo, he looks much younger than his fifty-three years. His eyes are piercing, the right one slightly larger than the left. His lips are closed in a barely perceptible smile. His jacket fits snugly at the shoulders, showing that he has put on weight. His shirt has a high, stiff collar finished with a small white blossom of a bowtie.

At the time he changed his image, he began calling himself Koresh, the transliteration of Cyrus into Hebrew, and his followers started marking the years after his birth as A.K. (Anno Koresh).

Sporting his new look, Teed went to Northern California to meet with Thomas Lake Harris, the leader of the Brotherhood of the New Life, which Harris claimed was celibate, though history leaves considerable doubt on that point. As did Teed, Harris believed that God was both male and female; Harris believed that he, too, was a prophet and that he was immortal. Interestingly, Harris, about fifteen years older than Teed, had also grown up in Utica, New York, and had established his first communal society on the shore of Lake Erie, not far from Sandy Creek, where Teed struggled to make a living twenty years later. It's a certainty that the young Teed knew of Harris. Among other things, he made national news in the 1880s when his most famous follower, the English parliamentarian Laurence Oliphant, accused him of theft.[38]

The meeting between Harris and Teed was covered comically in the media. If the two societies combined, a reporter for the *San Francisco Chronicle* asked, would having two messiahs in one organization pose a problem?[39]

"Mr. Teed groaned audibly through his gold-filled teeth," the reporter wrote, "and his eyes flashed in dangerous competition with the diamond in his collar-button."

Gold-filled teeth. A diamond in his collar button. Teed was clearly well-off, a significant change from the year before, when he was hardly able to care for Abie. The wealth, it was said, came from his new followers in San Francisco.

"Do you fear that Harris will oust you from your throne?" the reporter asked.

No, Teed answered, saying that he was unruffled by competition. He was not afraid of another messiah taking control because it simply couldn't happen.

"There is nothing on earth that can frighten me," Teed told the reporter. Not even death, he said, which he would conquer. "If the whole city stood howling at my door," he added, "I should be quite at my ease."[40]

Very soon, the city of Chicago *would* be howling at his door.

For now, though, the Koreshans at College Place were entertaining more like-minded guests. The Spiritualist George Elisha Church visited, but his visit didn't come to anything. Church wasn't a fit, though he did agree with Teed on one point: Chicago was cursed. That summer, there would be "dreadful calamities and disease," he informed them during his visit, as recorded by Jennie in her journal.[41] One Koreshan brother visited the Flying Rollers society in Michigan, and Jennie wrote that the members there received the Koreshan message well. Jennie probably did not know that the Flying Rollers practiced deflowering of virgins and treated wives as common property.

A group of celibate women came from Belton, Texas, for a visit. They had formed a society led by a woman named Martha McWhirter, who had a vision while making breakfast one morning. She was called to be sanctified, and she gathered many women—thirty-two of them—and four men. One angry husband put bullet holes in McWhirter's front door, and the male followers were taken out and whipped. These women said they felt at home at College Place with the Koreshans. They spoke to Teed about confederating for the purpose of opening a hotel for the World's Fair. Teed felt that their coming was very important: "The conjunction means an opening of another spiritual sphere," Jennie recalled his saying. But Victoria put a stop to the relationship when she and McWhirter couldn't agree on doctrines, and the ladies returned to Texas. The prospects with Harris fizzled, too, because he was egotistical, Teed told Jennie.

The Shakers, however, accepted them. In the summer of 1892, Victoria and Jennie went to Mount Lebanon, and their visit solidified a lasting bond. The only sticking point between them had been the Koreshans' hollow earth belief: "well nigh enough to turn the balance against them," Shaker elder Daniel Offord wrote. But having gone to see them in Chicago and getting to know Victoria and Jennie, the Shakers were assured of their celibate character and Christian, communal society. The Shakers planned to look into the hollow earth theory, and they trusted that whatever the truth was, it would prevail. "We have no cast-iron creed to keep the soul from growing into a more perfect knowledge of the truth continually," Offord wrote.[42]

Victoria's acceptance as a Shaker was documented by a bewildering certificate she had apparently brought with her. Drafted by the Koreshans and signed by three Shaker elders, the document not only confirmed her entry into the society, but it also approved her election as "Shepherdess of the Gynecato of the Koreshan Unity" and commissioned her to publish the "Gospel of Sexual Holiness." Accompanying this certificate was an exuberant letter from the most prominent Shaker elder, Frederick W. Evans, to "Dearly Beloved Br. Cyrus," indicating that the two groups would join forces—specifically, that Koreshanity would become a new order of the Shakers.[43]

Perhaps not surprisingly, many Shakers inquired about the arrangement. In October, the editors of the *Manifesto* published the certificate and Evans's letter in full, along with an explanation of the arrangement: "The Koreshans are not Shakers in the exact definition of the word Shaker," it read, and Teed and Victoria had not become Shaker leaders or elders. The explanation reflected the peaceful, accepting nature the Shakers were known for: "The Shakers are interested in every religious movement that comes forward for the greater peace and happiness of individuals, and for the general good of humanity."[44]

The Koreshans were more strident with their readers, publishing in the *Flaming Sword* that Koreshanity was a new evolution of the Shakers and of other old celibate bodies in the United States, which were losing influence. Koreshanity was beyond Shakerism, the article explained, "but in no way conflicts with it."[45]

The Koreshans purchased a fifteen-thousand-dollar interest in the Shakers' furnace and foundry works in Dayton, Ohio, and Teed announced to his people that the Shakers and Koreshans would exhibit together at the World's Fair, though this didn't come to pass. The Shakers weren't represented at the Fair, and it's not likely that the Koreshans were either.

The Koreshans' relationship with the Shakers aroused no interest from the outside world. "The Chicago papers are strangely silent," Jennie wrote. She guessed that the journalists were waiting to see how things went before showing antagonism. The truth seems to be that the papers didn't much care. Reporters were ignoring the Shakers and following new developments with the Economites.

Father Henrici died on Christmas Day of 1892, leaving John Duss, Teed's alleged ally, in control. The *New York Times* reported, incorrectly, that the Economites' assets were worth thirty million dollars, and the *Chicago Tribune* declared of the Koreshans, "Angels Are in Luck," reporting that the way was now clear for Teed's takeover.[46]

At Economy, Duss was keeping up appearances. Henrici had set a generous standard for entertaining guests, showing hospitality even to "tramps," as Duss called them. "Especially to tramps," he wrote in his memoir. Furthermore, "those who considered themselves of better clay expected a proportionately generous treatment, and got it—gratis of course."[47]

Such generosity had been doable when the society was flush, but now it was a burden. People who saw the Economy as "easy pickings," Duss entertained but politely deflected. The "self-deluded fanatics," he wrote in his autobiography, "tried our patience almost beyond endurance." Other visitors had worthy projects and were harder to say no to—people wanting money to support hospitals, churches, and schools—and these people usually left with some funds, granted by Economites' board, whose members were in the dark about the financial problems.[48]

As for Teed, whether he was scheming or not hardly mattered at this point;

he was Duss's smokescreen, keeping the Economites in the news and portraying them as wealthy when, in fact, they were withering. So Teed served his purpose, and Duss obtained most of the money he needed to pay off the debts; he and his wife wrapped up the affairs as best as they could, after which Duss had no need for Teed or the Koreshans. The Economites dissolved in 1905, after more than one hundred years. Duss moved to New York City and became a bandleader.

Had Teed realized his role in the Economite affair, had he not pushed for confederation with other societies, had he applied his energy instead to joining with reform groups in Chicago, the Koreshans might have been successful. They wanted many of the same things Chicago's reformers wanted, namely, the nationalization of industry and an equal distribution of resources. But what Teed wanted more than reform was separateness. And because the Koreshans closed themselves off, they were misunderstood, and they came to represent the very vice that Chicago wanted to rid itself of.

Cyrus Teed, the founder of Koreshanity, had built a following in Chicago by the time this picture was taken between 1888 and 1890. Isaac Uriah Doust, State Archives of Florida, *Florida Memory*, 255240.

By 1892 Teed had shaved his beard and begun calling himself "Koresh." The San Francisco *Morning Call* wrote, "Without his whiskers he is the most sensual-looking man one could find in a two days' walk through the city," February 17, 1872, 6. Imperial Studio, San Francisco, State Archives of Florida, *Florida Memory*, 255238.

Victoria Gratia (Annie Ordway) was the female head of the Unity. Teed believed that when he became divine he would flow into her body, and they would become a mother-father god. He commanded that the followers give her a happy life. Pictured between 1903 and 1909. Alfred Edward Rinehart, State Archives of Florida, *Florida Memory*, 256286.

The Koreshans believed the earth is hollow and that we live inside, with the continents along the inner, concave shell. The large ball represents three concentric atmospheres. The sun, not directly visible, has a light half and a dark half. It gyrates in the center of the universe, causing day (*top*) and night (*bottom*). By permission of Andy Tetlow, Koreshan State Historic Site, Estero, Florida and the Koreshan Collection. Florida Gulf Coast University Library Archives, Special Collections, and Digital Initiatives, Fort Myers.

Are Brains Necessary?

The Koreshan Unity will open Meetings, beginning Sunday Evening, July 19, 1903, to continue Every Sunday till further notice.

KORESH SPEAKS

At Corinthian Hall, 17th Floor, Masonic Temple.

Subject, July 19:—Brains the Basis of Mental Science, and How Utilized for the Healing of Disease. Opportunity will be given for Five-Minute Criticisms after the lecture.

Lecture Begins at 7:45 p. m.

COME AND BE HEALED

"Without Money and Without Price." You are free to call in your friends to the fountain of vigor and of perpetual youth. When Jesus healed he did not make a Millionaire of himself and call it Christian Science.

Complimentary. This Admits Bearer and Friend.

Cyrus Teed's breakout speech in 1886 was about the brain's power to heal. This lecture ticket from 1903 shows that the topic had staying power, perhaps due to Mary Baker Eddy's successful Christian Science movement. Note that Teed limited his critics to five minutes. Koreshan Unity Papers (record group 900000, collection N2009-3, box 319, folder 17), State Archives of Florida, Tallahassee.

Physician and surgeon A.W.K. "Abie" Andrews was Teed's first follower, best friend, and a lifelong financial supporter. When he met Teed in Binghamton, New York, Andrews was questioning his Methodist faith. State Archives of Florida, *Florida Memory*, 256323.

Jennie Andrews came to Chicago against her mother's wishes and before she converted to Koreshanity. She came to support her husband, Abie, and to keep her family together. She became one of the Unity's leading women. S. Bullock, State Archives of Florida, *Florida Memory*, 256322.

Allen Andrews, the son of Abie and Jennie, was a toddler when he met Teed. At twenty-one he volunteered to be among the first to leave Chicago for Estero, excited about the big adventure and hoping Florida's climate would help him recuperate from pneumonia. Later he was the editor of the Koreshan newspaper, the *American Eagle*. Thomas Evert Wood, State Archives of Florida, *Florida Memory*, 256267.

Koreshan Henry Silverfriend sold his family's dry goods store in Kaukauna, Wisconsin, and turned over two thousand dollars in cash to establish the communal home in Chicago. One newspaper called him "a silver friend, indeed." R. B. Alford, State Archives of Florida, *Florida Memory*, 256246.

Cyrus Teed stands in front of the Koreshans' Chicago mansion in 1898. Only eighteen Koreshans were allowed to move in at first, while the rest, including most of the children, lived in a cramped building with periodic water and heating outages. State Archives of Florida, *Florida Memory*, 257677.

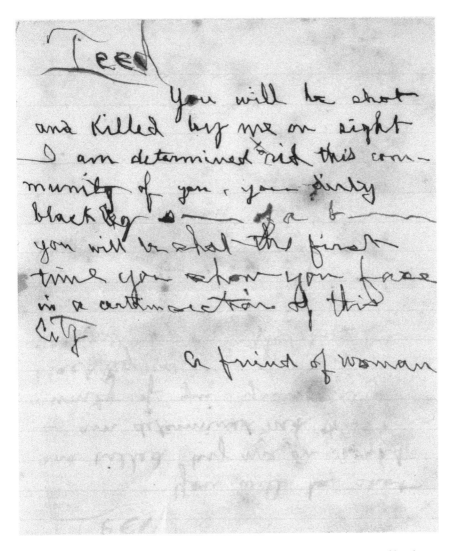

Teed

You will be shot
and killed by me on sight
— I am determined rid this community of you · your dirty
black ——— a —
you will be shot the first
time you show you face
in a certain section of this
city

A friend of woman

One of several threats Cyrus Teed received throughout his life. "If the whole city stood howling at my door," Teed once told a reporter, "I should be quite at my ease." But this letter reflects the animosity that ultimately drove the Koreshans from Chicago. Koreshan Unity Papers (record group 900000, collection N2009-3, box 229, folder 1), State Archives of Florida, Tallahassee.

✳ 6 ✳

The White City

College Place had been adequate for thirty people, but now there were sixty and more coming from San Francisco. There would be a hundred Koreshans living there once the Californians arrived, Jennie wrote, and she didn't know how they'd possibly make it work. So it should have been a relief when Teed and Victoria found a large house in Chicago's Washington Heights neighborhood, a suburb with tree-lined streets and velvety lawns in what had been farm country, a three-mile walk from the nearest streetcar. The neighborhood sat higher than the rest of the city, on a ridge formed by glaciers. Owned by Mr. Laurin P. Hilliard, who developed the area in the 1860s, the house they found sat on three acres, shaded by old trees, planted with shrubs, and surrounded by evergreens. There was a pond where the Koreshans could ice skate and plenty of space for Victoria's Persian and Angora cats to roam. In warm weather, the Koreshans could tend gardens of roses, lilacs, and lilies of the valley.[1] "It really seems too lovely," Jennie wrote in her journal the first time she saw the mansion. "I told Dr. [Teed] I was almost afraid it would be so satisfying we would stop sighing for the kingdom."[2]

But Jennie immediately noticed a problem: though the house was large, it would certainly not hold one hundred people. "It is quite a question how it can all be done," she wrote, "without any rivalry and hard feelings." Teed said he planned to build dorms on the property, and in the meantime, Jennie figured, they would share.

The Koreshans in San Francisco had waited months for Teed to call them to Chicago. Their furniture was packed, according to the *San Francisco Chronicle*, which sent a reporter to Noe Street. The newsman noted slyly that their clothing seemed to be packed as well, judging from the few clothes the young woman who answered the door was wearing.[3]

Teed had secured tickets for the San Francisco followers at thirty dollars a head, paid for by a wealthy female convert. The date was set. On April 27, 1892, they would board the train for Chicago with their belongings. One paper noted that they would not travel in a Pullman Palace car, as Teed did when he went between Chicago and San Francisco. Palace cars were decorated ornately and outfitted with leather seats, chandeliers, and table lamps, and passengers enjoyed gourmet meals in the dining car and comfortable places to sleep.[4]

Eight days before they were to leave, a 6.4 magnitude earthquake shook Northern California and half of Nevada. A night guard in Vacaville was making his usual rounds when he heard a roar, "like water which had suddenly been let loose by the bursting of huge dam gates." Most of Vacaville was destroyed. In San Francisco, the clock at the Ferry Building stopped, and glass shattered at the posh, glittering Palace Hotel.[5]

The Koreshans felt the quake—Noe Street was just three miles from the Palace Hotel—and no doubt ascribed meaning to it, given their belief that natural phenomena were acts of God. It's reasonable to assume that they believed their wise Master was removing them from San Francisco at exactly the right time. Days later, the fifty of them boarded a Central Pacific train car for the six-day trip along the southern route to Chicago.

At College Place a "For Rent" sign went up in the front window, and as Teed negotiated the terms for the mansion in Washington Heights, the media watched. One newsman climbed a tree near the new place to observe the goings-on. Another posed as a real estate agent in order to interview Teed. His reason for moving to Washington Heights was clear, reporters said: there, he would attract wealthier, more desirable women. The *Chicago Evening Journal* informed the well-heeled readers of this suburb about their new neighbor. Jennie wrote that the five-column story looked like the handiwork of Royal Spear and Sidney Miller.[6]

"It is my delight to break up homes," the *Journal* quoted Teed as saying, "and I glory in my power to do it." The reporter omitted Teed's reason for breaking up marriages: he believed the institution was a false one that enslaved women, a form of prostitution. Therefore, he was doing what he thought was right. But the writer insinuated that Teed was engaging in immoral acts with the women.[7]

As the Koreshans packed, the Washington Heights husbands and others steeled themselves for battle, meeting in secret at William Vear's neighborhood grocery store, though Vear denied this. As a storeowner in Washington Heights, he realized that welcoming one hundred Koreshans was the wise business move.

The men formed a "vigilance committee" and planned a special "reception" for Teed, the *Tribune* wrote: "If this man, this divinity with a slouch hat and gold filling in his teeth, attempts to establish his main heaven at Washington Heights he will be tarred and feathered and ridden on a rail." It was said that the women of Washington Heights were even more irate and wouldn't be satisfied with tar. The *Tribune* reporter wrote, "They hint that even lynching would be far too merciful."[8]

Most citizens of Washington Heights were far angrier at Laurin P. Hilliard—the owner of the mansion and the neighborhood's developer—than at Teed. Long before Teed entered the scene, Hilliard relocated part of the railroad line that had made their property so valuable and moved it west, where he developed more land. As a result, the older part of Washington Heights was less desirable. The fact that Hilliard was now considering selling his mansion to this crank angered them further. Jennie wrote that it was a small matter for the citizens of Washington Heights to transfer their hate to the Koreshans. The *Tribune* reporter agreed. "Every dab of tar and every feather that is administered to the sanctified being of the Messiah will have in it something of the rancor of bitterness left from defeat in the 'dummy track war.'"[9]

Several reporters covered the conflict. Some citizens encouraged welcoming the Koreshans and giving them a chance. The pastor of a nearby Lutheran church said, "If in time Teed's heaven proves to be a danger to our community, there is surely a law by which we can drive him out." But Sidney Miller, whom the Koreshans had begun calling "the devil," disagreed. The time to act was before Teed took possession, he said. Once this false messiah moved in, the neighborhood would never be rid of him. Teed could hide behind freedom of religion, Miller said, and he would be protected by the Constitution "no matter how many hearts he breaks." Miller offered to show up with fifteen men on moving day to block them if that's what the citizens of Washington Heights wanted. "If they knew Teed as I do, they would not for a moment think of tolerating him in their midst. . . . He has transformed my once lovable wife to a creature who will beg and lie in order to get money for her new master."[10]

Teed received an anonymous death threat in the mail, written in shaky handwriting:

Teed. You will be shot and killed by me on sight I am determined to rid this community of you, you dirty black leg s—— of a b—— you will be shot the first time you show your face in a certain section of this city.—A friend of woman.[11]

After Teed and Silverfriend tendered a deposit to Hilliard, indicating that the deal was going forward, a vandal painted the outside of College Place in retaliation. Teed's brother Oliver discovered the man in the act and he fled, abandoning his pail of whitewash. As harassment mounted, Jennie wrote, Teed assured his followers, quoting Christ: "Blessed are ye, when men shall revile you . . . for great is your reward in heaven."[12]

At 5:00 a.m. on the morning the San Francisco followers were to arrive, the rising bell rang at College Place, and Jennie woke with dread, knowing their group would cause a spectacle at Union Station, which would be thick with reporters. The Koreshans rode the cable car to Wabash and walked in procession to the depot, and the *Chicago Tribune* reported, "Heaven is at last united. The reunion was so touching that even the hardened gatekeepers wept until the big tears washed crooked tracks down their grimy faces and the porters groaned and sobbed." Back at College Place, Teed's followers enjoyed a generous breakfast of buckwheat cakes, ham and eggs, and pork sausage. The Koreshan home was so crowded for the celebration that many people ate outdoors. Jennie forgot her embarrassment and even found the reports amusing by the time the afternoon papers were out, and there were bigger challenges to deal with anyway.[13]

That night, at least one reporter stayed on the street, watching the house. He reported the silhouettes moving behind the curtains of the parlor—"many splendidly shaped young women" and in their midst, "the shadowy face of the self-Messiah." Through the curtains, the reporter saw Teed sitting in a big plush chair.[14]

The place in Washington Heights wasn't ready, and, in fact, the Hilliards were still living there. The followers packed into College Place, where they stayed for several days. The *Chicago Times* sent a female journalist to report on them, the headline declaring her a "daring investigator" for entering the chaos at the overcrowded College of Life. She noted that everything was packed and ready to load onto furniture wagons, and it was difficult to get into the crammed space. "It is easier to escort a camel through a needle's eye," she wrote, alluding to the Koreshans' rich furnishings, which other reporters had also noted.[15]

She included the disproportionate number of women—83 of the 110

Koreshans were female—but unlike other reporters, who normally disparaged the women, she made a jab at the men, saying that they seemed the types who do little of importance in the outside world. Teed was disappointing, she wrote—medium-sized, middle-aged, balding, tired, and apparently having made several painful visits to the dentist. One feature, she said, separated Teed from other men: "his small, piercing hazel-green eyes, a color, scientists say, never found save among those of great mental acuteness."

The most unusual thing about the article, other than the fact that a female wrote it, was that it contained the most thorough description ever recorded of Victoria Gratia. It was just a brief portrait, but it shows why there is so little detail of Victoria anywhere else.

During this reporter's interview with Teed, Victoria appeared at the parlor door. "The doctor looked nervously at a tall woman in a black gown and an enormous breastpin who stood eyeing him sternly from the doorway. It was Mrs. Ordway, the feminine president of the community, and the doctor endeavored to introduce her to the reporter, but she would have none of the scribe. She shook her mature head and gave a most un-angelic snort of disapproval. The doctor looked put out and evidently determined that his visitor ought literally to be. He may be lord and master there, but the head angel doesn't let him rest any too quietly on his throne. 'You must excuse me,'" Teed said to the newswoman, ending the interview.[16]

The sensibility of a female reporter is significant here: she didn't portray the Koreshan women as brainless, and it's interesting to speculate how a man would have described Victoria—or whether he would have included her at all. But most important, the reporter caught sight of someone else while at College Place—someone a man might not have recognized. In Chicago that week, women's rights activists from across the country were gathering for the meeting of the National American Woman Suffrage Association. One of these women was running for president of the United States—Victoria Woodhull.

And by lucky coincidence, as the *Times* reporter left the parlor, another Koreshan woman entered the room and also seemed eager for the journalist to leave. The reporter recognized her instantly: Etta Silverfriend, twenty-five, Victoria Woodhull's private secretary for her stay in Chicago. Sensing a story—a Koreshan was working with Woodhull?—the reporter made her way to the Wellington Hotel, where Woodhull and her sister, Lady Tennessee Clafin Cook, were staying and planning the campaign.

Woodhull was a controversial figure. She made a living as a Spiritualist medium early in her career, attracting the attention of Cornelius Vanderbilt, who set her and Tennessee up in business as stockbrokers on Wall Street. She became prominent in the women's suffrage movement when she petitioned the House of Representatives for a woman's right to vote. And this was not the first time Woodhull ran for president; she had done so nearly twenty years earlier. Back then, activists like Elizabeth Cady Stanton and Susan B. Anthony supported her. But in 1892, these women distanced themselves because Woodhull had supported Marxism, legalized prostitution, and free love, and had made a very public attack on preacher Henry Ward Beecher for his alleged affair with a married parishioner. So Woodhull was having trouble securing a nomination for her presidential run, and she hoped to build support at the Chicago convention.

Through a connection with Henry Silverfriend, Woodhull found and hired Etta, who she didn't know was a Koreshan. Teed, though he supported equality for women, was concerned about Etta's association with Woodhull. Two or three days after Etta took the job, Teed visited Woodhull to determine whether Etta's involvement was appropriate. He took Victoria with him to the Wellington, a point that the female reporter for the *Times* included in her story.

Woodhull told the journalist how she discovered that Etta was a Koreshan. After a short time on the job, Etta approached her with a peculiar request: "The Master wishes to speak with you."

"Master who?" Woodhull asked.

Etta led her into the corridor of the hotel, where Teed was waiting. "I saw a small, dark man," Woodhull said, "who lurked in the shadow, started at the approach of a servant, and showed a general disposition to hide in corners."

She claimed it was the first time she had met Teed; Jennie wrote that Woodhull knew him quite well but pretended not to recognize him. Woodhull told the *Times* reporter that she didn't understand what Teed wanted. He seemed to want to work with them, but she couldn't figure out what on earth he represented.

Woodhull's sister, Tennessee, on the other hand, knew a lot about Teed's doctrines. She had read the *Flaming Sword*, and she angrily told the *Times* that Teed was a plagiarist, having taken her sister's ideas about the Garden of Eden and appropriated them as his own. But Woodhull corrected her sister, which indicates that, in fact, she was familiar with Teed after all. Yes, Woodhull said, Teed had used her ideas, but their values were vastly different. He preached that women should have control over their own bodies, and Woodhull agreed. They also agreed that marriage could be a form of bondage. But Teed insisted that his followers practice celibacy, and that is where they differed. Woodhull was outspoken on the point that a woman could do whatever she liked with her body.

Teed spirited Etta away, saying that he didn't want her to be under Wood-hull's influence, Jennie wrote. But Woodhull made clear in the *Times* that *she* was the one who dismissed Etta. "I want it distinctly understood," she said, "that I despise and loathe all Jesuitical creatures who practice hypnotic quality upon neurotic organizations, and of all neurotic and hypnotized individuals commend me to the women who accompanied Dr. Teed today."[17]

The interaction shows as much about Woodhull as it does about Teed. He didn't want to be associated with her, and she couldn't afford to associate with him beyond using him as something to push against in the media as she tried to bolster her campaign.

A few days before the move to the Washington Heights mansion, a solo voice, singing a hymn, traveled through the early spring air across the Hilliard prop-erty. "No Sorrow in Heaven," the soloist, a Koreshan, sang to bless the house: "No sorrow is found in that city, no heartache and no good-bye; For all will be bright in that city of light, For there are no tears in the sky." The voice came from somewhere in the evergreens surrounding the mansion; the neighbors couldn't locate the source, but they stopped and listened. The *Chicago Tribune* wrote facetiously that every man, woman, and child in Washington Heights gathered around the Hilliard home and that people came from Fernwood, Blue Island, Morgan Park, Kensington, and Pullman.[18]

For the Hilliards, this was yet another nuisance. When the *Tribune* reporter knocked at the door of the house, an exasperated Hilliard female relative answered. "Why don't you wait until the place is sold?" she asked. The deal was nearly done. Thirty-five Koreshan trunks waited in a nearby barn to be transferred. The postmaster was holding letters for Teed addressed to the new place.[19]

The day after the hymn in the evergreens, Teed closed the sale at the Grand Pacific Hotel. As he exited, he told reporters, "Oh, we are growing and have a balance of almost $250,000 in our treasury, which, of course, is a common fund belonging to all." Jennie predicted that they would move the following week, cramming into the house somehow. Even though they would be cramped, she wrote in her journal, they would all be together, and they wouldn't need to sac-rifice for long, because Teed would build the promised outbuildings. No one knew he had other plans for the interim.[20]

One night, Teed went out and returned jubilantly to College Place, telling his followers he had a big surprise for the reporters—something far ahead of anything they had gotten ahold of so far. But he didn't divulge the surprise to the Koreshans until three days later, when he called everyone into the parlor after breakfast. The triangle rang, and they gathered to see him holding a piece of paper with a list of names. The people whose names were on the paper, he said, would move to the mansion in Washington Heights. The others would go to a building in Normal Park. It was the first any of them had heard of another place. Teed had rented an apartment building called Sunlight Flats, seven miles from the new home. "The announcement of the change of program fell as a thunder clap from a clear sky," Jennie wrote.

He read the eighteen names on the list. Jennie would live in the mansion, along with Teed's sister Emma, Lizzie Robinson, and of course Victoria. Only four of the eighteen people were men. Some children, including Jennie's, would be allowed to live in a small house at the corner of the property, called the Children's Annex. At first, no one in the parlor said anything. But as the news sank in, Jennie wrote, "many felt quite badly at the thought of being separated, especially from the Dr." They would feel worse once they saw the rental building in Normal Park. Sunlight Flats was so narrow it was more like a thick, hollow wall than a row of flats. The neighbors called it "Beck's Wall" because it blocked the view of the Normal Park School. The two-story building sat on a strip of land that was fourteen feet deep as a result of a legal battle between the owner, Dr. L. Warren Beck, and the city. Its red-brown color made it look like a "double-decked freight-car," one reporter wrote. Its fifty windows earned it the name Sunlight Flats. But the rooms were as small as closets, the *Chicago Tribune* reported, and the building "so narrow that there is scarcely room for anything but sunlight." The move happened immediately. The very night of Teed's announcement, the Koreshans slept at Sunlight Flats.[21]

The citizens of Normal Park were furious. They had never liked "Beck's Wall" and were convinced that it stood on city property and, therefore, shouldn't be there at all. Now that Beck had rented the place to Teed, they were even angrier. Just as in Washington Heights, where the citizens were primed for bitterness, so too in Normal Park.

The eighteen chosen ones arrived at the Washington Heights mansion in a steady drizzle, Jennie recalled. She was sad to leave College Place and all the memories there, being with Abie among them. But the new house and grounds enchanted her. "The place looks heavenly," she wrote, "with its great trees just budding into greenness, especially the 'Trinity Oak,' as Doctor has named the immense tree in front of the house."[22]

Teed named the home Beth-Ophrah, after the town Ophrah in the Bible, where an angel appeared to Gideon and told him he would save Israel from invasion. Once established, the Koreshans would spell out the word "Beth-Ophrah" in white stones on the sloping lawn near the street.[23]

The move to Beth-Ophrah was peaceful; Victoria had already moved in and was waiting to greet them, and the change seemed to formalize her status as queen. From here on, Jennie wrote, Victoria would be the head of the new home. Most of the women who had challenged her now lived at Sunlight Flats, where moving day had not gone well, with the Koreshans arguing over who should have which room. Meanwhile, the citizens of Normal Park mounted a fight, gathering in groups on the street and sidewalks. Some days, people knocked on the door of Sunlight Flats until police ran them away. The harassment was not as bad at Washington Heights, though schoolchildren did taunt the Koreshan children in the Annex.

The Koreshans were unpacking when Sidney Miller filed a lawsuit against Teed for alienation of affection. In his complaint, Miller claimed that Teed kept his wife "for a vile, unlawfull [sic] and wicked purpose"; that Teed misrepresented himself as a prophet; that he claimed to have "the power to give and take life, and . . . eventually [to] destroy the world"; that his wife had given Teed five thousand dollars' worth of possessions; and that Teed had promised to make her his Minerva. The most telling part of his complaint, though, was a statement that Teed had persuaded his wife "that a woman's body was her own." One scholar has said that Miller's beef with Teed was less about losing his wife and more about Teed's stance on women's rights. The amount of the suit was one hundred thousand dollars (about $2.6 million in today's dollars).[24]

Three days later, Thomas Cole, the man who had pulled a revolver on the Koreshans at College Place, filed suit for one hundred thousand dollars as well, but Cole's was a criminal case, charging unlawful intimacy. Other husbands had filed suits and created trouble, but Cole's and Miller's were the largest, and they were the most relentless in their fight against Teed, determined to chase him out of the city and joining forces with the citizens of Normal Park and Washington Heights.

When it came to Normal Park, they didn't need to work very hard. Unlike the citizens of Washington Heights, who had complained loudly about the Koreshan presence but backed off, the residents of Normal Park used legal ammunition. Two hundred citizens petitioned the court to have Teed removed on the basis that the property was not Beck's to rent. Additionally, a group of one hundred people met and formed an investigation committee to determine what

Teed was all about. When Teed heard about it, he knew Miller was behind it: "That is the devil's devil!" he said to Jennie.[25]

The writer of an opinion piece in the *Chicago Tribune* lamented that mob law was no longer acceptable; fifty years ago, that's how Teed and his ilk were dealt with, he wrote. But with mob law no longer an option, the best way to destroy the Koreshans, he said, was for husbands to make their homes so pleasant that wives wouldn't leave and for pastors to coax Teed's converts back to their churches.[26]

As the citizens went to war, reporters circulated around Normal Park at all hours, during the many protests and indignation meetings, as well as during quieter times of the day, keeping watch and giving readers whatever color they could for their stories. One reporter passing by Sunlight Flats on a peaceful night heard someone playing an organ on the women's side of the building, perhaps to accompany a worship service. And on the men's side, "someone was endeavoring to grind out Schubert's serenade on a violin."[27]

At Beth-Ophrah, a Koreshan boy discovered a bomb under the sidewalk. The *Chicago Tribune* ran a front-page story, describing the bomb in great detail, an iron cylinder loaded with dynamite, the same type used by Chicago's anarchists a few years before. It's a wonder the boy wasn't blown to atoms, the paper reported.[28]

When the *Tribune* reporter went to Beth-Ophrah to ask about the bomb, Teed was away, but there were several female "angels . . . fair and plump," calmly sunning themselves on the porch. There was no bomb, Victoria told the journalist, who offered to produce some people who had seen it, but she said that wasn't necessary. "I do not doubt," she told the reporter, "that you think you are telling the truth. If a bomb was really found the newspapers are to blame for it. They are telling all sorts of lies about us."[29]

Three male Koreshans described as "sallow and lean" stood at her side. "All the trouble in the country is caused by the newspapers," one of them said. "If there were no newspapers all wars would cease. We are not afraid of all the bombs in the country and we are happy in our religion."

On the afternoon that the bomb was discovered, Teed went to Sunlight Flats, which was surrounded by people—about four hundred of them, he estimated, in carriages, on foot, and on bicycles. He mounted the steps of the flats and addressed the crowd, and later told Jennie he got in a good many points. Though the meeting was relatively civil, he was showing signs that the outside pressure was getting to him, Jennie observed. His brother Oliver tried to cheer him up, saying, "In six months, you will take Chicago by storm." Teed disagreed.[30]

"More likely in six months," he said, "Chicago will have taken me by storm." A few months before, Teed had told a reporter he wouldn't care if the city howled at his door. But now he admitted to Jennie, his eyes welling with tears, "Sometimes my burden seems greater than I can bear."[31]

The Normal Parkers' petition to evict Teed from Sunlight Flats had been their best legal route, but it failed, and the citizens resorted to less civilized action. Upton Sinclair wrote, "The street urchins of the pork-packing metropolis threw stones at him"—literal stones that broke the glass at Sunlight Flats. Other citizens hurled insults. The media called Teed contemptible. And Jennie wrote, "Every day the papers are doing free advertising for [Teed] by misrepresenting us. I presume it will grow worse and worse until the end comes." She and the others assumed that Teed's death was imminent. And while they feared this, they also knew it meant that their immortality and the Golden Age were at hand.[32]

One day at noon, Teed and Victoria left Beth-Ophrah in a hurry to catch the Rock Island train into the city. It's possible that they had business in the city, as Teed later claimed, but it's just as likely that they had noticed two men waiting outside the house: the constable and Mr. William H. Hill, Thomas Cole's attorney. That morning, Cole had filed a warrant for Teed's arrest.

As Victoria and Teed ran for the train, the constable and attorney gave chase. The *Chicago Tribune* reported it. Teed picked up speed, sprinting so fast "you could have played marbles on the messiah's coattails," Hill later said. But Hill had longer legs and better wind, he told the reporter, so he caught up.[33]

Teed said to him, "Can't wait," breathing heavily. "I've got to go to town."

"Well, we're going to town, too," Hill said, "and I guess we'll all go on the same train."

The constable laid a hand on Teed's shoulder. "Dr. Teed, I arrest you in the name of the law."

"For what?"

"Unlawful intimacy with a married woman," the constable answered.

Teed blanched. Victoria caught up. And the four of them boarded the train for town. At 9:00 p.m., when Teed and Victoria hadn't come home, the Koreshans at Beth-Ophrah got word of his arrest. He returned late that night, having made bail of $2,500 and received a court date.

That night in Normal Park, as reporters looked on, eight hundred men gathered in a hall, clamoring for tar and feathers for Teed and shouting, "Crucify him." One man said to the crowd, "A devil has presumed to settle here. He flaunts in our faces the assertion that my wife, your wife, is immoral. What say you, men of Normal Park? Are you going to put your hands in your pockets and look to the Constitution to deal out justice to this villain, this old gray-haired wretch who was driven from New York? Shame on every man who will tolerate such a state of affairs."[34]

Sidney Miller spoke at the meeting, telling the crowd that Teed had made his hearthstone desolate and that he had sold his wife the promise of immortality for fifty dollars. "I know of fourteen people who gave $50 for immortality who are now dead," he said.[35]

Two Koreshans were spotted in the crowd, causing pandemonium. In a special dispatch, the *San Francisco Chronicle* reported that the meeting was attended by the best elements of Normal Park and Washington Heights, but that they didn't conduct themselves as such. A mob of fifty men chased one of Teed's disciples. Someone tried to throw another follower down the stairs. A rabid posse stormed Sunlight Flats but was deterred by police. Jennie remembered the scene that night at Beth-Ophrah as more peaceful, but there were men hanging around the grounds, and the Koreshans asked the police for protection.[36]

Teed's followers did not fight back or do anything to provoke the crowds; the newspaper and Koreshan accounts agree on this. But when Teed read the *Chronicle's* report about the best elements of the neighborhoods, he could no longer remain quiet. He lambasted the media in the *Flaming Sword*: "If the mob, incited to frenzy by the fabrication of sixteenth-rate asses in the form of two-legged animals saturated with fusel-oil, nicotine and sensuality is a sample of the best citizenship of Normal Park and Washington Heights, God deliver us." But he added, "We must confess, we enjoy the fight. No religious system ever did thrive without persecution and we propose to thrive."[37]

The socialists, who had dismissed Teed's overtures, stood up for him, issuing an official resolution that condemned the actions of the Chicago press and the citizens, and this made the paper, but opposition grew—one report mentioned a crowd of two thousand people at Sunlight Flats. Ultimately, the citizens decided to form a vigilance committee, volunteering as fast as the chairman could write down their names, and they established a Teed Prosecution Fund to raise money to pay Thomas Cole's legal costs. The advertisement in the paper made clear that anyone in the city, not only Normal Park and Washington Heights citizens, could send a check or cash to the treasurer of the fund, c/o Marshall Field & Co.[38]

Teed's trial date came, and thirty Koreshans accompanied him to the court-house, where Cole's attorney requested more time to gather witnesses, and the judge granted a one-week postponement. As the Koreshans exited the courthouse, the crowd made a dash to knock Teed down the stairs, but his followers protected him. Jennie noted, "Doctor's enemies looked ugly."[39]

Two days later, Teed spent a rare peaceful Sunday at Beth-Ophrah with his followers. It was warm and sunny, and the Koreshans spread themselves across the fine carpet of lawn, reveling in the beauty of the Trinity Oak and the time with their beloved Master. Jennie wrote, "I have not for months seen Dr. so apparently at leisure as he seemed today, sitting for an hour at a time without the least sign of rush and anxiety."[40]

But that evening, as the shadows gathered and the mosquitoes moved in, Teed told his followers that a plan was being concocted to charge him with murder and to imprison him. He had predicted that he would theocratize at the World's Fair, and the Fair was approaching. "I know he looks for the final blow," Jennie wrote in the same entry, but she nonetheless focused on the day at Beth-Ophrah: "I shall remember [it] as one of the perfect days. A heaven in many respects."

Teed caught a break in the Cole case. On the new trial date, Cole's side again asked for a postponement so that it could gather additional witnesses, and the judge closed the case, saying that every man was entitled to a speedy hearing.

Thus the pressure from Thomas Cole abated for the moment, but the problems with Annie Cole had begun. She lived with the Koreshans now at Sunlight Flats, having forced herself on them after a meeting, Teed claimed, by feigning illness. They allowed her to stay the night, and she never left. Further complicating things with Annie was Oliver, Teed's brother. "He has never been anything but a detriment to Cyrus," Jennie wrote. Oliver was romantically interested in Annie's sister. By year's end, they would be expelled from the house and they would get married, making Teed and Annie Cole in-laws.[41]

The more Teed traveled, attempting to expand his work, the less time he spent with his followers. "He seems to belong more to the people—more to the outside world," Jennie wrote with sadness. "Maybe others do not feel thus, but I cannot help it."[42]

The others did feel it, most painfully as his birthday approached. Every October 18, the Koreshans held a festival for Teed's birthday, and this was to be the first ever at their new heaven, Beth-Ophrah. The Koreshans were building a platform for the orchestra and preparing special souvenir programs. They would drape bunting throughout the grounds and unfurl their yellow flag.

But on October 1, Teed called them together and announced that he was going to San Francisco, and that it couldn't be helped. They needed money, and he had determined that their property on the West Coast was the best chance. It was unlikely that he would be back in time for his birthday celebration. When Jennie mentioned their sadness, he said, "You will learn how it will be to do without me after I have gone away," referring to his theocrasis.[43]

That morning, there was a tearful good-bye, in which he gave a short talk, telling them that while he was gone, they should practice tolerance and brotherly love with each other—an indication that there had been unpleasantness. When he left, the house was full of sadness, Jennie wrote, made drearier by rain, matching their mood. But then, at nightfall, they heard "the dear familiar voice." Their Master had returned. They were astonished and delighted, and their sorrow turned to rejoicing. He had been gone only a few hours, but it seemed as if he had come back from a long journey because "we had passed through all the pain of parting," Jennie wrote.[44]

There was a relatively new donor to thank for this: Berthaldine Boomer. She had known the Koreshans for a couple of years and was a member of the Society Arch-Triumphant, the club for new and prospective members, but she was not a Koreshan. Boomer and her husband, whose job selling steel to the railroads was lucrative, were religious seekers, interested in biblical prophecy and dissatisfied with the many millennialist doctrines that lacked scientific backing. They discovered Teed when a friend introduced them to the *Flaming Sword*, and his teachings appealed to them.

Mrs. Boomer provided the money to tide the Koreshans over so that Teed could postpone his trip to San Francisco, and the Koreshans busied themselves again with the birthday preparations. "The orchestra have been drilled, pianos tuned and I think everything thought of to render the day pleasant," Jennie wrote in her journal. The party was held on the evening of October 18, 1892, at Beth-Ophrah. The lawn was lit by the soft glow of lanterns. The orchestra played outdoors until it grew too cold. In the parlor, someone performed a lively reading of the chariot race scene from *Ben-Hur*, and Teed gave a talk.[45]

Jennie was especially proud of Allen, who played violin in the Koreshan orchestra that night. It was his long-held dream, Jennie told her mother in a letter that detailed each of her children's activities and successes. But she failed to mention something major: her children no longer lived at Beth-Ophrah with her. With winter approaching, all of the Koreshan children had been moved to the overcrowded Sunlight Flats in Normal Park. It isn't clear why this decision was made, but a clue comes from Jennie's journal, indicating that Teed explained the change with a prophetic statement about preparing for a battle.

"Something is ahead of us," Jennie wrote, "and it behooves us to gather up our ammunition, condense our forces and prepare for all we are worth to follow our leader on to victory. Victory and death!"[46]

Shortly after the birthday party, the World's Fair was to be unveiled in an elaborate dedication ceremony on the fairgrounds. The Koreshans considered the two celebrations related because Teed had shared with them two beliefs about the Fair: the first was that he would be murdered and translated to heaven during the Exposition, ushering in the new age; the second was that the White City was *his* idea. What the architects and designers were building was his own vision made manifest.

The Fair was transforming Chicago, even though the organizers faced terrible obstacles. In the manic rush to finish the fairgrounds and buildings in time for dedication day in October, construction flaws were ignored. A heavy June rain demolished one end of the Manufactures and Liberal Arts Building.

But the Fair employed thousands, a welcome boost to the economy and to the city's morale. Workers from all parts of the world were turning a once desolate, low-lying park into a seascape of magical white palaces at the edge of Lake Michigan, shimmering and blue. Gardeners were planting flowers and training vines to ready the grounds, even as Frederick Olmsted, the head landscape architect, was ailing. The Fair would bring international acclaim to their city, which, just twenty years before, had been in ashes after the Great Fire.

Given Teed's prophecy that he would be translated at the World's Fair, the Koreshans must have felt both thrill and dread at its approach. On the eve of the ceremony, Jennie visited the grounds and saw the decorations, writing that everything seemed to be in order for the dedication. She was most impressed by the solar eclipse, long prophesied, that occurred while she was at the fairgrounds. She asked Teed what it meant, and he told her that it marked a new era in their work.[47]

After Teed's birthday, new regulations went into effect at Beth-Ophrah and were posted around the house: any Koreshan wishing to leave the mansion needed a permit to do so and was required to complete a form stating the reason for leaving, the destination, any expense involved, and the time allowed. No one could go anywhere—not even to Sunlight Flats—without a permit from "the Empress," Jennie wrote, referring to Victoria. "It is very humiliating," Jennie said, and she fought with Teed about it to no avail. This happened following a disagreement between Victoria and Lizzie Robinson, one of Teed's earliest followers, the woman who had housed Teed for free when he came to Chicago, who had headed up the women's exchange and helped to run the lunchroom, all before Victoria supplanted her. The cause of Lizzie and Victoria's disagreement isn't known, but what is certain is that it wasn't the only such argument; several women had challenged Victoria's authority, according to Victoria. It seems most likely that the requiring of permits was a way of enforcing Victoria's control. Teed called the women together and spoke to them. They must treat her as their leader and empress, he told them, because she was divinely appointed. Jennie carefully documented the meeting in her journal.[48]

As Teed was talking, Annie Cole, by then his sister-in-law, became enraged. "You lie," she shouted, pointing her finger at him. She told them all that *she*, not Victoria, was the woman clothed with the sun and the moon at her feet. *She* was the one who would bring forth the man-child spoken of in the Book of Revelation, she said. Not Victoria. Cole acted like someone possessed until Teed took her away for a private talk, Jennie wrote. He later relayed some of his conversations with Annie in a letter.[49]

"Did I ever say to you such a thing?" he asked her.

"The internal Cyrus [did]," she responded. "The Cyrus I know and love."

When Teed and Annie returned to the room, Teed told the group that he had exorcised the devil from her and seen the horrible creature come out. After this, she was "quite melted and subdued," he said, though he didn't know how long it would last.[50]

More than a few followers were leaving the Unity at this point, notably Mrs. Benedict, the woman whose husband died under Teed's care four years earlier. She behaved disgracefully, Jennie wrote, and threatened to file suit against Teed for two thousand dollars. "Benedict!" Jennie wrote in her journal. Her name said it all; she was a reembodiment of the traitor Benedict Arnold.[51]

Undoubtedly one reason why people left was the conditions at Sunlight Flats. There was no heat that October, and the temperatures in Chicago were at freezing. Teed had ordered stoves to heat the place, but it took ten days for them to arrive. In the meantime, several of the followers caught colds, including Jennie's son Allen. She was concerned and talked at length with Teed about it. He listened patiently and kindly, she wrote, and he didn't accuse her of the family tie, as she worried he might. But on the same day that Jennie wrote in her journal that her heart ached for the people at Sunlight Flats, she wrote to her mother to say that the children would be comfortable there for the winter. A short time later, Allen's cold turned into pneumonia, which would take him more than a year to shake.

The Koreshans' plans to join forces with the Shakers, which had shown promise, unraveled, and Teed blamed Annie Cole, though evidence shows she played only a small part. Teed had been quite close to Elder Benjamin Gates—the two men had courted an investor together to shore up both groups' finances—but there was a change in the Shakers' leadership, and one elder had begun asking questions. Did Teed really believe he was the Messiah? the elder wanted to know. Additionally, at some point, it's not clear when, Teed asked the Shakers for a loan of eight thousand dollars, and they declined his request.

As for Annie Cole, who had left the Unity, Teed discovered that she had corresponded with Anna White, a Shaker eldress whom Victoria adored. When Teed received a letter from White, condemning the Koreshans, he believed it was a result of Annie Cole's lies. He responded in a venom-filled missive that revealed his protectiveness of Victoria, his hatred of Cole, and his disdain for those who didn't believe in his doctrines. When he had courted the Shakers for a possible confederation, he had been careful to say that the two religions complemented each other and that leadership could be shared, but that sentiment was gone. This correspondence showed his certainty that he was the chosen one whom other societies should follow.[52]

He answered the question about his messiahship obscurely, saying that he was the Cyrus mentioned in Isaiah. "It will make little difference whether you endorse it or not. I came to you with God's offering. Your conceit and self-righteousness has prevented you from accepting the message." Teed also said he doubted the Shakers' purity, saying that they seemed to have trouble controlling "the urges of the flesh."[53]

He informed the Shakers that Cole was trying to drive a wedge between Anna White and Victoria, and he called Cole a liar. She had claimed to be Ann Lee, the leader of the Shaker church, he wrote to the Shakers and asked them, "Does she claim it with you?" Cole had also said she was impregnated by some holy method and that she would birth a sun child. "Has she told you this?" he asked the Shakers in his letter.

"If it is your wish to nourish cockatrice eggs," he wrote, referring to Cole and her ilk, "it is your nest, not ours and you are at liberty." He continued, "If you can cast the devil out of [Cole] you are entitled to credit. I hope you the best of success." Teed's letter didn't mention the Shakers' rejection of his eight-thousand-dollar loan request, but it must have fueled his anger.[54]

Somehow, this letter and Annie Cole's actions did not destroy the friendship between all of the Shakers and Koreshans. Victoria remained devoted to White until the Shaker eldress died, and many Koreshans and Shakers remained close for years. But the hope of any formal relationship had ended. The loan request, Teed's imperious letter, and perhaps Cole's claims caused the Shakers to back away.

The year 1893 "appears to have been quiet for Koresh," scholar Howard D. Fine wrote, "apart from the usual harassments of society, including a rumor that he would be lynched." The water was turned off at Sunlight Flats because Teed refused to pay the water tax, saying that the Koreshans were a religious organization and therefore tax exempt. There was a break-in at Beth-Ophrah, and thieves took everything that could be carried away, according to the *Chicago Tribune*.[55]

More trouble among the women came to a head that winter, when Teed was out of town. Most of the women accepted Victoria's leadership, though some did so grudgingly. Others openly defied her. The question that came up at a meeting while Teed was away was a theological one: was Victoria divine? Two women believed she was—that the spirit of God had already entered her body. They were Berthaldine Boomer and Mary Mills. Boomer claimed to have had a private conversation with Teed on this very issue and that when she asked about Victoria's divinity, Teed had bowed his head and told her it was so.

But most of the women—even those who obeyed her, as Teed commanded—did not believe Victoria was divine. Teed had taught that she would not become divine until after Teed's translation or theocrasis. Jennie knew this, but she also knew that Victoria was powerful, and she had seen what happened when women defied her. Jennie diplomatically suggested that the women wait until Teed returned so that he could solve the question for them. Victoria did not want to wait.

At the next meeting of the women's mission, Victoria presided as the mission's president. One can imagine her, tall and poised in the dark Victorian clothing she favored, her wavy hair swept into a low chignon, surrounded by the more plainly dressed women. Mills and Boomer testified to her divinity. Jennie, who was expected to say something, arose and diplomatically told the group they should honor Victoria as their empress because she was appointed by Teed. At the end of the meeting they stood together and prayed; Jennie wrote that it was like a Methodist prayer meeting except that "the Lord God Almighty's name was left out and another one substituted."[56]

But after the meeting, things got ugly. Boomer and Mills insisted that the ascending spirit of the Lord Jesus was in Victoria. Jennie hadn't wanted to cause trouble, but someone needed to speak up, and it fell to her. She told Boomer and Mills that if Victoria were divine, it went against everything she had ever heard Teed teach. Mills, normally graceful and refined, became enraged. "[She] turned furiously with arms outspread and eyes blazing" and told the women that a devilish spirit was trying to defeat Victoria and eat away at their Unity. "You may eat yourselves up if you want to," she said, "but don't you dare to lay a hand on her."

The disagreement continued for two months, a crisis in their history, Jennie wrote. "It seemed to be a resistless tide that would carry all sense and reason before it . . . and if not checked would do great harm."[57]

When Teed returned, he did not answer the question of Victoria's divinity in words. Instead, there was a ceremony at Beth-Ophrah during which he crowned her with a wreath of laurels and said that her leadership represented an important era for the world: the age of womanhood and the power of women. One Koreshan read a paper she had written about the importance of obedience to Victoria.

Then, in April for Victoria's birthday, the Koreshans held a "coronation" for her at Beth-Ophrah. This was the first Lunar Festival, what became an annual celebration of Victoria's birthday, the counterpart to the annual Solar Festival held to commemorate Teed's birthday. There were music and speeches, and the Koreshan drama troupe performed the trial scene from Shakespeare's *Merchant of Venice*. Souvenir programs were printed in gold and blue, held together by gold cording. The front of the program showed a delicate crown with "coronation" printed across the headpiece.

One Koreshan described this as the most solemn and impressive occasion in the history of the movement to that point. He recorded what transpired: everyone gathered in the parlors of Beth-Ophrah to witness Teed's confirmation of Victoria's position as "Pre-Eminent." Teed explained that she was the head over all orders. He bestowed upon her a new last name, Koresh, making her official name Victoria Gratia Koresh. He also formalized the appointments of the women of "The Triangle"—Victoria, Berthaldine Boomer, and Mary Mills—and he created "The Planetary Group," seven leading women in the movement. He told these women, "Stand by Victoria at all hazards as her cabinet." He cautioned the other followers not to criticize the appointments, as they were made from the throne of Almighty God, with Teed simply as the messenger.[58]

A few months after this appointment, there was apparently more conflict surrounding Victoria, because she called a meeting of the "concilium," the governing body, on short notice. A printed white card summoned them to Beth-Ophrah, where Teed spoke. He began with the topic of jealousy, telling them in no uncertain terms that they must overcome it. People who had left the Unity did so because they were not able to overcome jealousy and because they wanted Victoria's position. He explained that Victoria was the permanent head of the Unity. Someone took minutes of this meeting, and while they don't explain what he meant by "permanent," his other writings indicate that he was referring to her eventual, spiritual permanence: that she would become the divine body he would inhabit.[59]

Throughout his life, Teed spent considerable energy enforcing Victoria's importance. In the Koreshan archives are multiple copies of a tribute he issued on one of her birthdays, emphasizing that she should be followed. Some of the copies are studied and underlined; on one is an angry marginal note about someone who refused to follow Victoria. On another occasion, Teed was traveling in Denver when he sent a letter to the women of the Unity. "My Dear Daughters of Zion in Jerusalem," it began. Victoria was unhappy, he wrote, and it was their duty to stop their fighting and honor her.[60]

"I have left in your charge a very tender plant to be cherished and nourished for the kingdom of heaven's sake; are you causing her to feel . . . that she is the apple of your eye, the hope of your empire? If not, then at once amend your purposes.

"I am afraid you are working in dangerous lines," he wrote, underlining the words. If they didn't come together to make her happy—"[to] sweeten the fountain and reservoir of the worlds [sic] final deliverance"—disaster would befall the Unity.

Financial troubles continued in Chicago, certainly made worse by a financial panic that swept the nation that year, 1893. The Koreshans were evicted from Sunlight Flats and moved to another suburb, where, again, neighbors kept close watch. The newspapers reported that there were as many as twenty Koreshan children in the new place, "bareheaded and barelegged. . . . Their brown legs and feet showed an unfamiliarity with shoes that was evidently permanent." They survived on cornmeal mush and milk, the paper reported.[61]

Berthaldine Boomer defended the Koreshans in the *Chicago Tribune* in a letter to the editor. The people of Chicago and the media should be ashamed of themselves, she said. The Koreshans were kind and pious people who had fallen on hard times. She urged religious tolerance. Boomer and her husband had continued to draw close to the Koreshans, though they didn't live with them and weren't followers. When the water had been turned off at Sunlight Flats, it was Mr. Boomer who used his influence to have the service restored. When the Koreshans incorporated that summer, Mr. Boomer was one of the six officers. Interestingly, Teed's name was not listed on the incorporation documents.[62]

Teed and Berthaldine Boomer went to the World's Fair together that summer, a visit Boomer described in her autobiography many years later. As they toured the grounds, he interpreted the statues and sculptures, telling her what the various monuments symbolized, and he rode the Ferris wheel, which represented Ezekiel's wheel, he said. From high above the Fair, she wrote, "he had a grand view of the humanity beneath."[63]

It was an insult, Boomer wrote, that the Koreshans had not been included in the World's Parliament of Religions held in connection with the Fair that fall. The Parliament was a wildly inclusive coming together of faiths that included Protestants, Catholics, Jews, Muslims, Buddhists, Hindus, Theosophists, Spiritualists, Christian Scientists, and Teed's friends the Shakers. The masses were dissatisfied with "modern, paganized Christianity," Boomer wrote, and the Parliament showed that most clearly. She pointed out what she believed was a great irony: above one entrance to the Fair was the quote "Ye shall know the truth and the truth shall make you free." But no one recognized the truth: "Under the peristyle walked the reincarnated spirit of truth of Elijah the Prophet as its promised Messenger, and the world knew him not," Boomer wrote.[64]

During this time, Teed began having visions of his own utopia—"like a thousand world's fair cities," he later told newsmen—that he and his followers would build, somewhere, from scratch. Away from the crowded city, they could lead a meaningful life, free of the forces trying to thwart them. He needed only to look to the Economites, Shakers, and Mormons to see that isolation was a key element for happiness. He had the desire and the vision, and he had confidence that his followers could manifest a great city, just as when he had desired the White City, people had created it. All he needed was a place to build.

That fall, Teed was returning to Chicago from Pittsburgh when he met a real estate man who told him about land for sale in Florida. Immediately, he was interested. Florida was sunny, fertile, and teeming with fish, and a world away from the people who were trying to bring him down. He secured three railroad passes to see the land: one for him and one each for Berthaldine Boomer and Victoria.

The chance meeting on the train would lead him, eventually, to Estero, Florida, on the southwest coast, where a German homesteader, Gustave Damkohler, had cleared some land.

* 7 *

The Homesteader

One April day in Florida in 1882, the same year Teed's mop business failed and he moved to Syracuse to practice medical electricity, a little boy named Elwin Damkohler stood on a dock in Punta Rassa. "This is the end of the world—jump right off," read the sign at the south end of the pier. The Damkohler family—Gustave, his wife, and four children all under the age of eight—had just arrived from Missouri to homestead some land.[1]

If one did jump off the dock, it was into very deep water, which made Punta Rassa ("level point") an excellent port, and a bustling one. Cattle drovers rounded up cows all over the state and herded them there to the end of the cattle trail, where the animals were led into chutes and loaded onto barges, as many as two hundred per trip, thousands each year, headed for Key West and then Cuba, where the demand for beef seemed endless. The town was rough, as one county brochure notes: "a constant bedlam of sounds from bellowing cows, the cracking of cow whips, the barking of cow dogs, the cries of the cowmen, an occasional gunshot, the shrieks from the ships' horns, and the clatter of hoofs as the cows were funneled through the chutes onto the ships. Card games and other gambling activities went on in the barracks until late at night, [and] an occasional fight broke out."[2]

When Gustave Damkohler and his family arrived, Punta Rassa was raucous. There were a couple of hotels, if you could call them that, and bars, and a telegraph office, the southernmost in the United States. The end of the world sign wasn't far off.

Homesteaders like the Damkohlers were trickling into the area, attracted by the state's new land—much of which *was* literally new, drained to get Florida out of debt. Before the drainage, the land south of Punta Rassa was "one vast plain of scrub-cypress and stunted pine," a military captain in the Seminole War wrote, "under water from three to twelve inches . . . heavy cypress swamps dotted with small islands or dry spots of cabbage tree and pine, with here and there a large dry hummock or long pine ridge."[3]

Gustave Damkohler learned about the land from an advertisement, one of many that Florida placed to let the world know there was property available for homestead. Gustave was in his fifties living in Clay Township, Missouri, a tall man, blind in one eye (it had been an evil eye anyway, he told people), well educated, fluent in German and English, and a skilled calligrapher. He had studied medicine and botany, and he had run an orphanage in Australia, where he also mined for gold (presumably how he lost his sight). He loved adventure, so the prospects in Florida must have excited him.

He chose a plot, sent in his filing fee, then uprooted his wife and children, traveling down the Mississippi River to New Orleans, where they boarded a schooner and crossed the Gulf of Mexico, eventually arriving at Punta Rassa's wharf.

The land Gustave Damkohler had selected was south of Punta Rassa, upriver from a quiet estuary, a place where his family would have peace, solitude, and acreage. Some of it was impenetrable and soggy, but there were high spots available for homesteading, and there would be more if drainage projects continued.

Damkohler's wife and children stayed in Fort Myers, near Punta Rassa, while he scouted his property. Fort Myers was still very much a cow town, so full of cows that one resident advised walking in the middle of the street at night, to "avoid stumbling over sleeping cows in store doorways." The streets were unpaved trails of deep sand bordered by weeds.[4]

Gustave and the surveyor took a rowboat to see the land. They paddled through a calm blue bay, protected by Estero Island, the barrier island now known as Fort Myers Beach. And though today the beach is densely packed with motels, ice cream huts, T-shirt shops, and restaurants with rooftop bars where snowbirds watch the sunset, it's still possible to see some of what Gustave and the surveyor passed. Much of the coastal area is a preserve of uninhabited hammock land and mangrove along a paddling route called the Great Calusa Blueway.

Gustave and the surveyor rowed past Matanzas ("massacre") Pass, where the Calusa Indians outnumbered Ponce de Leon in 1521 and shot him in the thigh with a poison arrow, leading to his death. Four miles south of the pass the two men came to a white mound where the Calusas had lived—an island of shells rising above the mangroves, thirty feet tall at the highest point and thought to have been the Calusas' ceremonial center more than two thousand years before. As they discarded their oyster shells, fish and animal bones, pottery, and other waste into kitchen middens, the mound grew, and they shaped it with water courts and ridges. After the Calusas were gone, the island provided protection for pirates who left behind gold beads, coins, crockery, and cannonballs.

The island, Mound Key, marked the mouth of the river that Gustave and the surveyor were watching for. It was easy to miss because where the river meets the bay is a delta, where shallow water spreads into the estuary through thick vegetation. The men turned the boat, paddled through the mangroves, and emerged onto a waterway about eighty feet wide. They rowed upstream against the slow current, past sabal palms and pines, and beneath oaks bearded with moss. The river narrowed, and on the banks, alligators sunned themselves, sleeping with their jaws open, ready for prey. Gustave and the surveyor made their way around, over and under fallen trees blocking the river until they came to a natural landing at a log bridge that crossed the water. They grounded the boat and climbed into a high clearing.

There's a romantic version of this arrival, passed down by the Koreshans. In their story, Gustave was alone, aimlessly looking, apparently not having planned ahead. He came upon this land, where he rested and enjoyed a meager lunch. "Here, at high noon," a Koreshan biographer wrote, "all was quiet. A light breeze played through the trees and palms, and nature's creatures sought the cool shadows." Gustave took note of the rich soil, the thickets of palmetto and scrub oak, and he wondered whether this could be the place his family would settle. "As he pondered, he was suddenly startled to hear a voice saying, 'Take and dress until the Lord comes.'"[5]

He looked around but couldn't find the voice. The breeze stopped. "Here in the deep shadows, all was utter silence . . . and he, awed and trembling, knew that here was the land he had so long sought."

The no-nonsense, and more likely, version was written by Gustave's son Elwin: his father and the surveyor located the land, selected a tent site, and then returned to Fort Myers and closed the deal. He began with 80 acres and over the next few years expanded his holdings to 320.[6]

There may be some truth in the Koreshan version as far as Gustave's awe of the land and his feeling that it had a special purpose. Elwin said that when it came to religion, his father was a bit unstable and highly suggestible. He was deeply religious and read his Bible so frequently that neighbors thought he was a crank. Gustave was a devotee of millennialist Charles Taze Russell, a pastor in Allegheny, Pennsylvania, who founded what is now known as the Bible Student movement, which spawned the Jehovah's Witnesses. Russell preached the

Second Coming of Christ and published the widely disseminated *Watch Tower and Herald of Christ's Presence.* He was one of the most famous preachers of his day.

Once the paperwork for the land was complete, the Damkohler family set out from Fort Myers with their belongings—a stove, pots and pans, dishes, utensils, and a tent. They stopped for lunch at Matanzas Pass, spent the night on Mound Key, and then reached the property, where they put up their tent and a tarpaulin, built a crude table for meals, and strung hammocks between the trees. Gustave named his place Estero, after the name of the river.

Southwest Florida in 1882 was one of the most beautiful and inhospitable places on earth. From October through April, the weather is sunny and mild, an escape from the harsh cold in the North. But the heat during the rest of the year can be brutal, and Damkohler's land had little shade, mostly longleaf pine and low scrub palmetto. At dusk and dawn, especially in the summer, the air was thick with mosquitoes. The soil was sandy, acidic, and lacked nutrients, and beneath it were limestone and clay.

But Florida enchanted four-year-old Elwin—"El-veen," as his father pronounced it. While his father and oldest brother worked, Elwin and his sisters played and wandered, seeing panthers, bobcats, and bears, and hearing bull-frogs, whooping cranes, hoot owls, eagles, and lowing cows. The alligators were so plentiful that they swarmed the river, making bathing difficult until Gustave rechanneled the water to create a safe pool. At dusk, the Damkohlers built smoky fires to keep the insects away.

Gustave planned to cultivate bees and silkworms and to grow mulberry trees for the silkworms to feed on. The bees were more successful than the silkworms, but selling the honey was tough, as the closest railroad for getting it to market was very far away. He experimented with plants that would grow in sandy soil, and he planted pineapples, but these were ruined by fires set by cattlemen who brought their herds south and burned large swaths of the new land for grazing. What wasn't burned was trampled by the cows, which pulled the pineapple sprouts from the ground and destroyed Gustave's fences. It was such a problem that Gustave sailed 125 miles to Key West, the county seat, to see what could be done. Nothing, the commissioners told him. Cattlemen were boss. Gustave wrote Florida's governor, who referred him back to Key West. So a lot of his time was taken up with fence building and repair.

The Damkohlers planted cowpeas and sweet potatoes. They had plenty of oysters, clams, crabs, and fish to eat, as well as gigantic turtles—a loggerhead could weigh more than 350 pounds. "In those cruel primitive days," Elwin wrote, "we tied a rope on the inside of its flipper and made the turtle carry one of us to its slaughtering place."[7]

According to Elwin, criminals hid in the area, including one man who kept sun-bleached human skeletons in his backyard to keep people away. To protect themselves, the Damkohlers had rifles and shotguns, a Colt revolver, and a large Cuban bloodhound.

Within two years, Alma Damkohler gave birth to a baby boy, whom they named Estero, after the place. She died two weeks later of complications from childbirth, leaving Gustave with an infant and three children to care for by himself. Elwin's older brother had left, for reasons that aren't known, and the family struggled. Gustave had spent $1,600 to settle, clear, and plant, and he needed money. Baby food was especially hard to come by, Elwin remembered, and it was expensive, requiring many trips to Punta Rassa, the nearest civilized place.

Elwin, at age six, became the oldest child. He learned to cook and sew and take care of the baby and shoot a gun so he could protect the family during Gustave's trips to Punta Rassa, which took nine days, Elwin said, because his father wasn't a sailor in those days and didn't know how to tack against the wind. Instead Gustave hugged the shoreline, poling himself through shallow water and even getting out to walk sometimes, towing the skiff behind him. Elwin was uncannily responsible for a six-year-old, and his memoir—which he wrote at age eighty-nine—is the only record of what their lives were like.

When a stranger appeared in Estero, the Damkohlers welcomed him. He took care of the children while Gustave was in Punta Rassa, cooking their meals and keeping them entertained, and he bought twenty acres from Gustave for two hundred dollars, money they desperately needed. He built a stilt house, high enough that bears, raccoons, and bobcats would leave him alone. Elwin often walked the half mile to the stranger's place to watch his progress. Nearly everything the man used came from his property. Four trees, evenly spaced, served as corner supports, and cypress trees provided the wood for the frame, walls, floor joists, and rafters. He even created a smooth floor by trimming the stems of palm trees and nailing them down, flat side up.

The Damkohlers were happy to have such an inventive and caring neighbor, until Elwin realized that he had a dastardly plan. Mr. X, as Elwin called him in the memoir, had a lady friend he encouraged Gustave to marry. Mr. X pressed Gustave to do this, and he hesitated. Then, mysteriously, the Damkohler baby, Estero, fell ill. Soon after, the rest of the children got sick, and a doctor couldn't determine what was wrong. Elwin and his father believed Mr. X had poisoned them with white lead. The baby died. Then one of the daughters died. And then the other daughter. Elwin was a walking skeleton, but he was determined to live so that Mr. X could not carry out his plan. Elwin was convinced that once his father married the lady, Mr. X would kill Elwin and Gustave so that he could take the Damkohlers' land. It was Elwin, according to Elwin's memoir, who saved the day. "When it became evident that I would live," he wrote, "'Mr. X' disappeared," and, apparently, Gustave and Elwin reclaimed his twenty acres.[8]

Gustave and Elwin, now the only ones left, cultivated vegetable gardens and orchards of pomegranates, guava, lemon, lime, orange, and sapodilla. As the years passed, the trees grew until the clearing around their cabin was nearly hidden by mango and citrus trees. Meantime, Estero was growing. The land was in such high demand that a company formed in Key West to sell Estero property. More homesteaders moved in.[9]

It seemed possible that a town would form, and if it did, Gustave's land would be at the center of it. His half square mile of property on the river lay next to the sand trail that ran between Naples and Fort Myers. The trail wasn't passable—it was a path from the Calusa days—but it was likely to be improved one day, which would make Gustave's land valuable. The trail is now U.S. Highway 41, which connects Miami to Tampa and continues all the way to Michigan.

The migration south had begun. Henry Plant bought foreclosed land and extended his railroad to Tampa. Resorts sprang up. Civil War veterans who had fought in Florida remembered the pleasant weather and came back to live. In the 1880s, Florida's population grew by more than one hundred thousand people. Railroads and development made it easier to vacation and settle in southwest Florida. Thomas Edison had built a winter home in Fort Myers.[10]

By the 1890s, the port of Punta Rassa was pleasant and civilized, nothing like the end of the world where Gustave had landed with his family. The cattle-based economy had given way to sportfishing, which meant fewer cowboys, more millionaires.

Gustave's property was not the land Teed heard about on the train from Pittsburgh to Chicago in the fall of 1893. This was the San Carlos Hotel on Pine Island, a short boat ride from Punta Rassa. In October, Teed, Victoria, and Boomer came to see it. Boomer remembers the surrey ride across the island, through weeds and swarms of insects and mosquitoes. "They settled on the back of Koresh's neck to a tormenting degree," though he hardly seemed to notice them, she wrote.[11]

The sellers wanted $150,000—far more than the Koreshans could afford, though Teed did not tell this to the newsmen in Tampa or nearby Bartow, whose *Courier-Informant* reported that he would buy not only the hotel but also all of Pine Island—seventeen miles long and two miles wide—and its hotels and cottages. There was nothing in the report about the Koreshan religion, only that the followers owned everything in common.[12]

Teed, Victoria, and Boomer stopped in Punta Rassa, likely leaving some Koreshan literature at the cable station, and they returned to Chicago, confident that Florida was the right place for their city, Boomer wrote years later, even though their trip had been unsuccessful. She felt sure that something would come of it and that things would unfold as they should.

She did not live with the Koreshans, and it was unclear whether she had signed the document agreeing to turn her property over to the Unity, though she was quite generous with her money and she wanted them to succeed. This trip had been pleasant; they met friendly people; they ate fried mullet for the first time, and guava, sliced and served with sugar and canned cream. She imagined what it would be like to live in Florida with her good friends, to follow this man she admired. In Chicago, she was a mother and a wife whose husband provided a fine living for her. She later wrote that she couldn't bear to think of leaving her husband and children, who were unlikely to join her.

One day, Gustave went to the cable station in Punta Rassa to check his mail, and he may have seen the Koreshan literature. A land agent told him about people from the North looking for property, and by this point, Gustave was thinking of selling. He estimated that the land was worth six thousand dollars, which would clear his debt and allow him to send money to C. T. Russell to support his missionary work. Gustave would keep twenty acres to pass to Elwin when he died, the twenty where his cabin was and where his wife and children were buried, and where, one day, he planned to be buried, too.[13]

So he wrote to the Koreshans in Chicago, telling them about his property and warning them away from the Pine Island land they had seen. It was overflow land, he said, not suitable for building and settling. He also poured out his tribulations—how hard he had worked and how much he had sacrificed—and asked for a copy of the *Flaming Sword*. He sealed the letter in an envelope from C. T. Russell's Zion's Watch Tower Tract Society, printed with biblical verses and proclamations about the Second Coming of Christ.

The Koreshans returned to a Chicago in shock. The mayor, Carter Harrison, had been murdered, and the World's Fair died with him—its closing ceremonies canceled, though the White City stayed brilliantly lit during the last few evenings of October, its glory diffusing into the dark sky. People visited the grounds and paid their respects.

The entire country was in dire financial shape, and Chicago was hard hit. The Fair had employed so many but no longer needed workers. Tens of thousands of people were unemployed, and the homeless slept on the floors of police stations. Mayor Harrison (murdered by a deluded man who believed Harrison had promised him a position in city government) had done his best to help, ordering the police to open their doors to the homeless. He had employed people to clean up the streets, and lobbied Congress for money to prop up the city's economy. Without funding and jobs, he said, the unemployed would riot. There were labor demonstrations, peaceful ones, but the upper class characterized them as anything but. When Harrison died, the laborers lost an important advocate. As mistrust and tension grew, violence seemed imminent. Teed's followers must have thought his prophecies were coming true: that there would be bitter fights between labor and capital, and that the streets would run with blood.

Teed, Victoria, and Berthaldine Boomer had been back for a few weeks when two letters arrived from Florida: one from an agent offering a furnished cattlemen's hotel in Punta Rassa for seven thousand dollars, the other in a curious envelope from the Zion's Watch Tower Tract Society. Boomer watched as Victoria inspected it, and she wrote, "Our sensitive Victoria Gratia said when she held it in her hand unopened that she seemed to know that it would lead us back to Florida that winter and to the right place to begin."[14]

The writer, in his impeccable handwriting, implored them not to consider any other place for their new city until they had seen his land. Teed was out of town, so Victoria wrote to him. "I feel a vein of deep sympathy go out to you, while reading of your situation, and would fain wish that you might join our religious colony." She didn't tell Gustave about their religious beliefs, but did say that they were communistic, meaning that if Gustave joined them, she said, he would be cared for, for the rest of his life. Victoria asked for a plat of his land, the price, and a list of improvements he had made. Teed followed up with a letter, also encouraging Gustave to join the Unity and asking for more information about the property.[15]

Boomer turned her attention to the other property—the cattlemen's hotel—and to how they might get seven thousand dollars to acquire it. She remembered Punta Rassa fondly—the hospitable people, the guava and fried mullet, and the certainty she felt as they returned to Chicago. She landed on an idea: some property in Connecticut that her husband might allow her to sell.

He did, and it sold for four thousand dollars, not enough to buy the hotel, but enough to give them confidence that the trip would be worth it. They wrote to the agent to let him know they were coming.

And so, on the day after Christmas, they boarded the train to Florida—Teed, Boomer, Victoria, and, this time, Mary Mills, Victoria's secretary. These women made up the Triangle, whom Teed had appointed earlier that year. It made sense that he chose them. Boomer and Mills were wealthy and they had made clear to the other women in the community their commitment to Victoria.

When Teed and the Triangle reached Punta Rassa, the agent wasn't yet there. Needing a place to stay, and knowing that the cattlemen's hotel was furnished and vacant, they somehow got inside. Victoria had brought linens for the beds; there were utensils and a cookstove, tables, and chairs. As the women cleaned the place, Teed ventured to the dock and returned with salt pork, fish, and coffee for their dinner. They ate and slept well.

Accounts diverge about whether Gustave and Teed had planned to meet in Punta Rassa. According to Koreshan lore, the meeting was divinely ordained; Elwin indicated that it was happenstance. He may not have known that his father had written Teed about the land. Elwin and Gustave had spent Christmas and New Year's in Fort Myers with a friend, the caretaker of Thomas Edison's estate. They stopped in Punta Rassa on their way home and saw an agent who knew Teed was in town. The agent took Gustave to the hotel, where Teed was standing on the porch. Gustave and Elwin later recounted the meeting. "Here is your man, Dr. Teed," the agent called to Teed.[16]

On the porch, Gustave met Victoria, Boomer, and Mills, and they talked, their conversation lasting well into the night. According to Boomer, they talked for two straight days, with Gustave recounting his struggles and loneliness. He told them, Boomer later wrote, that he had thought of leaving Florida many times, but whenever he got close to doing it, something compelled him to stay—the voice that called to him when he first saw the land: "Take and dress until the Lord comes." So he had waited.

Teed told him of his doctrines and that the Koreshans were the children of God. Boomer told him Teed was the Messenger of the New Covenant: the Messiah. She encouraged Gustave to ask Teed about his doctrines, but Gustave remembered years later, "I was so charmed by their singing and their kindness that I could find no question to ask him."

"Dr. Teed kept the whole time silent," Gustave wrote, "and staring at me with a strong look." To Elwin's dismay, his father fell under Teed's influence, becoming convinced that Teed was a holy man and that the women were the children of God. Boomer's version of Gustave's conversion is quite dramatic. "Ich habe dich lang erwartet," Gustave told Teed. *I have long expected you.* He cried tears of joy and exclaimed, "Master! Master! The Lord is in it!"[17]

Gustave couldn't sleep on the night of his conversion. He made up his mind to transfer his property to Teed, and the next afternoon, the two men negotiated the terms: Gustave would keep twenty acres and sell them the rest for two hundred dollars; he would live on the land with the Koreshans, who would take care of him for the rest of his life and take care of Elwin until he was twenty one and provide him an education. Gustave agreed to allow the Koreshans to make improvements on his twenty acres. Teed went into the hotel, discussed the arrangement with the women, and returned to the porch within five minutes. "We accept it," he said.

"You take hold of it," Gustave answered.

To prepare for the trip to Estero, Gustave, Elwin, and Teed boated to Pine Island for food and supplies. Elwin, full of mistrust for Teed, piloted the sailboat. On the way, they passed an oyster bar where several birds were feeding, and Teed took out a pistol, shot at the birds, and crippled two of them. Elwin was horrified. Years later, he wrote about the incident, the moment he began to despise Teed.

"Father and mother had taught us never to kill or harm any animal or bird unless it was needed by us." This man who claimed to be the second Christ was wounding animals for sport, Elwin saw. "Though he continued to try to win me over, he then and there lost any hypnotical, religious influence over me."[18]

Teed and the women and Gustave sang hymns as they sailed from Punta Rassa to Mound Key on their way to Estero. Victoria and Mills had both sung in choirs—Victoria, a contralto, and Mills, a soprano with a performing background. Boomer didn't have their talent, she wrote in her memoir, but she "sang naturally from the heart." Gustave piloted the boat, Boomer remembered, begging them to keep singing. His favorite song was the Sunday-school hymn "I Will Guide Thee with Mine Eye," which struck everyone as funny because he had only one good eye, and because he was guiding them, and the boat that carried them to Mound Key was called *The Guide*. "Sing, sisters. Sing again," Gustave said. "He was giddy with his new spiritual purpose," Boomer wrote, and in no time, "he seemed like one of us."[19]

At Mound Key, they built a fire on the beach, had coffee, and watched the sun set over the water before switching to a flat-bottomed rowboat to traverse the mudflats. Elwin and Gustave poled them up the Estero River.

"The water was molten silver," Boomer recalled, "filled with schools of mullet radiant with the phosphorescence." A fog lay on the water's surface, and the night sky was brilliant with stars. Most thrilling of all, she remembered, it was the first time they heard Teed sing—"Oh happy day that fixed my choice"—in a voice that was sweet and clear.[20]

It grew late, and they fell silent, rocked by the rhythms of poling through the calm water. They arrived at 10:30 p.m. Gustave built a fire, and Teed called them together around the warmth and dedicated the land in a small ceremony before they turned in for the night. Gustave and Elwin slept on the boat, using sails for their bed, while Teed and the women slept in Gustave's cabin, Teed in the attic on a cot, the women lying crosswise on the only bed. The tall Victoria rested her feet on soapboxes. They all agreed, though Elwin must have objected, that this would be the arrangement until something could be built for the Koreshans.

At dawn, Teed's party saw the land for the first time. The cabin was in a clearing surrounded by thick vegetation—lime, orange, mango, banana, camphor, and coconut palms. There is no doubt that it was a surreal experience for a Chicagoan in January: the palm trees, full shrubs, and flowers; the mild air against their skin; the land quiet except for the distant hum of Gustave's bees.

Marjory Stoneman Douglas wrote about Teed's first glimpse of the land: "The man who sailed up the Estero River with old Damkohler and looked with his brilliant glance at the lavish green growing things in the tropical light, in all that silence, felt he had found the right place at last."[21]

Teed declared the place to be "the vitellus of the cosmogonic egg," saying that it was a natural magnetic center with magical properties, Boomer recalled. Teed told Gustave it was the future location of the New Jerusalem spoken of in the Bible, Elwin later wrote. It would be laid with gold, the largest city in the world—ten times the size of New York—and within a decade, Teed said, ten million people would live there.[22]

Gustave didn't question it, and when Elwin did, Gustave told him Teed's description agreed with what the prophets proclaimed in the Book of Revelation. Before long, Teed produced an elaborate sketch of the city, showing walkways, plazas, gardens, and fountains, and telling Gustave that his cabin would be at its center, paved roads running in all directions like the streets from the Capitol in Washington, D.C.[23]

The deed for the land was transferred into Boomer's name, not to the Unity or to Teed, who Elwin wrote was not the sort of man to hold property in his own name. With this done, the Koreshans had their foothold and had barely dipped into Boomer's four thousand dollars. They bought a large sailboat and a team of horses for farming.

Quickly, Gustave went to work surveying more land for the Koreshans and writing to Tallahassee to ask what property was available. His writing was uncharacteristically messy, indicating that he was in a great rush. "I act as a friendly Agent for a big body of people of the far North of U.S. and Canada who are willing to make their home down here in earnest," he wrote. He asked the person at the land office to keep his request a secret because he feared that speculators would drive prices up.[24]

The fear was justified. Florida's population boom had begun, the editors of the *Fort Myers Press* had reported that Teed was in the county, and the public believed he had means. So if people learned that Teed had land and was growing his holdings in Estero, they might start buying property.[25]

As they settled the land, the women saw a new side of Teed. He traded his black broadcloth suit and white Regency ascot tie for shirtsleeves and a stout pair of corduroys and began grubbing the land with Gustave. One day, he walked to a neighbor's farm and returned with two razorback pigs, one under each arm, a sight that amused the women. He and Gustave built a fence for the pigs and a coop for a rooster and two hens.[26]

Many evenings at dusk, mosquitoes invaded. The women wore cheesecloth veils, and tended smoky fires, but the insects were relentless, squadrons of them feeding all night. The only relief for the women was under the nets on the mattress they shared in Gustave's cabin. In addition to mosquitoes, ticks, and other pests, there were snakes, including two large black ones that Gustave kept under his cabin for the purpose of killing rats and repelling poisonous snakes. Boomer was terrified of them—she was frightened by the Koreshans' new horses, for that matter—but Gustave refused to kill the snakes, and so Boomer endured them, along with everything else. "We had to live on high thinking," she wrote. Nightly, Teed inspired them with his talks.[27]

The Triangle cooked for the six of them, dinners of meal mush, pork, sweet potatoes, and canned goods from Pine Island and Punta Rassa. They had plenty of fish and oysters, caught by the fifteen-year-old Elwin, who later claimed that without his skills, the city folk would have gone hungry. Gustave taught them how to make bread in his Dutch oven, and they had all the bread they wanted with honey from Gustave's hives.

One night, Gustave and Elwin introduced the Koreshans to alligator tail, cut up like cutlets and cooked over the fire. Victoria declared it delicious and Boomer, wanting to please her, took a carving knife and went down to the riverbank where the dead gator lay, to see whether other parts could be used for meat. But when she poked and carved into the thick hide of the beast, she found a gelatinous, repulsive mess. It's hard to imagine the refined Boomer doing this.

In Chicago, she had her own chef. But in this new place, as Teed had told them, the Koreshans needed to experiment to survive.

Boomer made a point of spending time with Elwin—probably she missed her own children and felt that he needed mothering. He had gone without a mother for so long that his wildness was understandable, she wrote later. Closer to the truth, as evident in Elwin's memoir, he was happy being wild, and Boomer's pampering only made him angrier. One day, Boomer helped Elwin shuck oysters, the two of them sitting on a plank laid across the bow of a boat. When Boomer shifted her hefty weight, she fell into the river, and Elwin laughed at her. He had lost his own mother to this land, and now these women had moved in and taken it. Elwin saw that his father was in a state of religious delirium, under Teed's spell. "The more he influenced my father," Elwin wrote, "the more I hated him."[28]

Four more Chicago Koreshans came to help with construction. They built a rustic building for themselves, which they called a "cabbage shack" for its roof of thatched cabbage palm leaves. This done, they progressed to larger, sturdier buildings.

After a few weeks, Teed announced that he was leaving for Chicago and would arrange for more people to come. Victoria and Mills would stay behind, and they wanted Boomer to stay, too. She was "nearly unbalanced" about the decision, she later wrote. Willing to do almost anything for the Unity, she was not ready to leave her husband and children. Teed didn't try to break up her marriage, perhaps because Mr. Boomer was a supporter and a wealthy one at that. Teed once told Berthaldine Boomer not to do anything for him or for the cause until she was ready to do so from her heart. He made the Chicago decision for her, asking her to return with him, but she seemed to be coming around.[29]

Before leaving, the group made several trips to Pine Island and Punta Rassa for supplies and items to make Victoria's and Mills's shared cabin comfortable and pretty. Boomer remembered one trip in particular, which she later wrote about. Strong winds blew their boat far into the Gulf, where they became stranded for a day and a half. But she wasn't distressed, she wrote. "With the Master on board, we felt like the disciples on the Sea of Galilee with Jesus."[30]

They slept on the boat, and Boomer remembered the sound of a big drum fish booming rhythmically against the hull while she watched Teed sleep, "beyond anything natural it seemed to me," and felt complete serenity.[31]

✳ 8 ✳

Under the Canopy
of Heaven

A map of the world that does not include Utopia is not
worth even glancing at, for it leaves out the one country at which Humanity is always landing. And when
Humanity lands there, it looks out, and, seeing a better
country, sets sail. Progress is the realisation of Utopias.

—Oscar Wilde, "The Soul of Man under Socialism," 1891

Allen Andrews was one of the first to volunteer to go to Estero. He was twenty-
one, still weak from the pneumonia he had developed a year before at Sunlight
Flats, and eager to be in the tropics and out of the cold weather. It was early
February when he and sixteen others boarded the Chicago, Rock Island and
Pacific Railway near Beth-Ophrah, the first of seven trains that would take the
group to Florida. Mostly, they were young, including the teenage girls Teed
called his thunder daughters, a nickname that isn't explained in Koreshan lore,
but it's similar to "sons of thunder," which is what Jesus called James and John.[1]

Lillian Newcomb—whom Teed nicknamed Vesta—was Teed's favorite
thunder daughter. She was tall and blonde with crystalline blue-gray eyes, devoted to books and poetry, and committed to the cause. She and her mother
and brother had come to Chicago with the San Francisco colony, and she was
sixteen when she boarded the train.

The trip took a week, and Allen and Vesta remembered that it was monot-
onous until they reached Florida, when the landscape opened up into citrus
groves: "mile after mile of lush green trees heavily laden with their ripe golden
fruit," Allen wrote, about seeing them for the first time.[2]

The group spent the night in Bartow, Florida, at a rambling country hotel with no plumbing, where they washed their hands and faces in tin basins. The next morning, they woke to the noise of cackling chickens and to the news that the southbound train wouldn't leave until the afternoon. Impatient to get there, and knowing that the Koreshans' sloop, *Ada*, would be waiting for them in Punta Gorda, they boarded an open boxcar for the last leg of the trip. The train's engine burned pitch pine, spewing cinders and smoke and dusting them with ash. The train stopped periodically to take on loads of fruit; the packing-house employees emptied crates of oranges at their feet, and the Koreshans feasted on citrus, and they sang to pass the time. One of them had a harmonica and another, a guitar, and with them was a caged parrot brought by one of the girls. It's easy to imagine the squawks of the bird muted by the wind and dull ringing of metal on rails.

The boat ride from Punta Gorda to Estero was rough, Vesta remembered, and all of them were seasick. They spent the night at Mound Key, where they built a campfire and roasted oysters, which steamed and exploded in the flames like corn in a popper. The next morning, they rowed up the Estero River towing a boat loaded with their possessions. At the mouth of the river were mangroves, growing straight out of the mud and forming islands of reddish roots that filtered the estuary and stained the water the color of tea. As the group progressed upriver, the mangroves gave way to banks of land grown over with palmetto, towering pines, and coconut palms. Allen remembered there were so many fish in the shallows that the bottoms of their skiffs rumbled with them. The boats often got stuck in the mudflats, and the men used poles to push them into deeper water.

They hit bottom so many times that some got out of the boats and walked overland through the bush. Eighty years later, Vesta remembered slogging along with their belongings and the panicked parrot until they reached the ox-team trail that crossed the river, and they saw Gustave's cabin and the old German man excitedly welcoming them.

It was February, and Gustave's mango trees were in bloom, shooting out panicles of red-orange flowers. The temperature reached eighty degrees that month, warm enough for swimming. "The boys are diving, plunging, and spurting in the salt sea water like young whales," wrote one Koreshan in Florida to another in Chicago. "It is summer here, you see." They picnicked outdoors, feasting on fish and honey, sweet potatoes, grits, milk, and bread.[3]

On moonlit nights, they went for boat rides and sang to the accompaniment of violin, mandolin, and guitar, and "made the welkin ring with their songs and laughter," Allen Andrews wrote. And on nights when there was no moon, the

Koreshan brothers and sisters paddled the river to stir up the bioluminescence with their oars. Disturbing the water produced clouds of flickering blue-green plankton, an effect one follower compared to the Milky Way. Sometimes they entered the water and bathed in the phosphorescence, carrying it out on their skin.

"This all under the canopy of heaven," the letter read, making clear that they were certain they had been guided here to build God's kingdom. "Life and immortality are before us." The writer enclosed two silver scales from a tarpon.[4]

The letter writer may have sugarcoated life in Estero. Gustave's and Elwin's experiences were quite different, as was Allen Andrews's. Most of the Koreshans slept on the ground for ten months as they cleared the land. Allen remembered the difficulty of uprooting saw palmettos, a plant with stiff, sharp-edged blades and rough roots that "resembl[ed] a thousand-legged worm, hold[ing] tight until the last rootlet is severed."[5]

At night, they burned what they had grubbed, and the fires provided some relief from thirsty mosquitoes. Much worse than those, Allen remembered, were ground fleas, more tenacious, tougher to kill, and not carried away by wind or deterred by smoke. Sleeping on the ground made the men easy targets, and they found that the best remedy was to wrap themselves in blankets to trap the fleas. One morning, Allen counted forty-two of them caught in the lint.

Another pest Allen mentioned was Elwin Damkohler, whom he described as a barefoot urchin and braggart. No matter how large a fish someone caught, Allen wrote, Elwin had caught a bigger one. He claimed to have once caught a tarpon so big it pulled him off the boat, carrying him at a terrific speed through the water, under the water, and even beneath submerged logs. Elwin held on through it all, he told them, until the fish got tired and he was able to drag him ashore.

Elwin was just as exasperated by the Koreshans as they were with him. He was especially irritated by their hopeless boating skills. A man named Gus Faber was assigned as captain of *Ada,* and he was so incompetent that once, in high seas, Elwin locked him in the cabin and took over. The Koreshans, he noted, had a tendency to panic when something went wrong on the water. On one trip, a sailing mission to Punta Rassa, Faber lost control of a jib rope, which was not a big deal, Elwin wrote, but when the rope slammed against the hull of the boat, Teed and Victoria emerged from the cabin, alarmed. Teed seemed certain the boat was sinking and that they would all die. According to Elwin, Teed begged Elwin to save their lives. There was no danger at all, Elwin remembered, and the fact that the Messiah feared for his own life confirmed for Elwin that "it was time to get out of the Koreshan hell."[6]

The first substantial structure in the settlement was a two-story log cabin with a thatched roof and a floor made of lumber to keep out the fleas, Allen noted with relief. He wrote that they felt like they were living in luxury, even though "there were open spaces between the logs that you could almost throw a dog through." The breeze through the cabin kept them cool, but it brought in the rain, too. Heavy rains can turn nearly horizontal in Florida winds, and the men learned to move their beds to the center of the room to avoid having their bedding soaked. The rain brought more insects, and they slept under nets, waking to find them "black with mosquitoes prodding their bills through the cheesecloth in search of human gore," Allen remembered.[7]

In Chicago that winter, the abandoned White City caught fire. The blaze started in the casino in the Court of Honor and spread across the gateway to the Fair, destroying the peristyle, the music hall, and casino, and showering ash onto the Statue of the Republic—a sixty-five-foot gilded woman wearing a laurel crown—which looked out over charred and twisted steel, her gold plaster chipped. The ruins reflected Chicago's overall condition.[8]

British journalist William Stead recorded Chicago's descent in his 1894 book *If Christ Came to Chicago!* Arriving as the Fair closed, Stead observed the city and interviewed people in power, in poverty, and in jail. He wrote about the homeless sleeping on the floors of police stations, about the churches that weren't doing enough to help, about corruption in City Hall, and about the newspaper publishers who reported it all with sensationalism when they should have pushed for reform. *If Christ Came to Chicago!*—in spite of the title's exclamation point and the illustration of Jesus casting the moneychangers from the temple—was not hysterical, but a well-researched account from an outsider.[9]

Boomer knew about the book (it was a best seller), and she wrote that Christ *had* come to Chicago, meaning Teed, and that he had found things as Stead described. "He worked faithfully there," she wrote, "and travelled from coast to coast trying to enlighten the people of the great cities with this Science of the truth. But few welcomed the light. . . . After residing in Chicago as his headquarters, and finding it generally unripe to receive his message, His wisdom led him to determine to start the building of a new city with his handful of followers."[10]

In April 1894, four months after securing the Estero land, Teed went public in Chicago about his Florida utopia. The *Chicago Herald* ran a splashy, four-column Sunday story that included an illustration of how the streets would be laid out, a map of southern Florida, a portrait of Teed, and several inaccuracies—notably the projected population (eight million people) and the cost to build the place (two hundred million dollars). The accurate version, according to Teed, was that the city would house up to ten million people, not eight million, and it would be created without the use of "so called money." It would encompass thirty-six square miles and its avenues would be four hundred feet wide. "It is hard to believe [Teed] believes in it himself," the *Chicago Herald* reported, "but he does."[11]

The *Herald* reporter marveled that the followers believed it, too. "Dr. Teed is the absolute, immaculate and inviolate high muck-a-muck if there ever was one," the reporter wrote. "Neither his acts nor his motives are inquired into and his word is law—the only law."[12]

For their first Christmas in Estero, the Koreshans (there were twenty-two of them in Florida by that point) sailed *Ada* to an island, built a campfire on the beach, and listened as Teed addressed them. It was a moonless night, the sky sparkled with stars, and the only light came from the campfire. Just a few feet away, the Gulf waves splashed onto the beach. Offshore, *Ada* looked like a phantom in the darkness. In the distance was the light from the Sanibel lighthouse, looking like the brightest star in the sky. Teed wore his linen hat and corduroy trousers with his black dress coat, having changed out of the brown cotton jumper he often wore—one he had gotten during his visits to Economy. "The firelight played on his face," one of the Koreshans later wrote. "He looked so lovely, so good, so pure!"[13]

They had decided that this would be their last Christmas night—that they would no longer celebrate it because they believed the Messiah was with them. So Teed didn't speak about Christmas. Instead, he told them about a vision that Swedenborg had. In it, the Swedish philosopher saw a race of English-speaking people in Africa who possessed the original Word. Swedenborg had not known how to interpret this vision, but Teed knew exactly what it meant. Emmanuel Swedenborg had seen them, the Koreshans, Teed said, at the center of the sphere. They were the nucleus that would spread the Word, he told the followers that night.

To attract people to Estero, the Koreshans lectured in Chicago, while Teed toured the East Coast. They printed a pamphlet that outlined "a plan for the immediate relief of the masses." Omitting the belief that Teed was a prophet, the tract said little about the Koreshan religion except that believing in it was optional for anyone who joined them. Instead, the focus was how the city in Estero would operate, much of it reading like a reaction to how poorly Chicago functioned.[14]

"No dumping of sewage into the streams," it read, counter to Chicago's practice of emptying sewage into the Chicago River. A "movable and continuous earth closet will carry [away] the debris and offal," which would be turned into fertilizer—an idea that one-upped George Pullman's method of sewage disposal in his utopian town for workers. The streets would be laid out at different elevations to avoid collisions, as sometimes happened in Chicago's crowded streets, where a pedestrian could be struck and killed. The city would have none of Chicago's smudge or smoke, the pamphlet read, and none of the evils of capitalism, because property was owned communally. This was no mere experiment in an isolated place, the writers assured readers: the Koreshan system would establish branches in every city in the world. For now, it said, people who wished to join would need to pay their own way, but the group was raising money for a transportation fund. Money should be sent to treasurer Lucius S. Boomer, Berthaldine Boomer's husband.[15]

A section entitled "How Shall I Get There?" provided directions to Estero: Take the Florida Southern railroad from Jacksonville to the end of the line, then sail to St. James on Pine Island. There, the Koreshans will pick you up in a sloop and carry you the rest of the way.

The country needed a plan for the immediate relief for the masses. Unemployment soared as high as 18 percent in 1894. The nation was in the worst economic depression it had ever experienced, and in Chicago, things were especially bad. In May, after the Pullman Palace Car Company cut wages, 90 percent of its workers went on strike, setting off rail worker strikes across the country. Parts of the rail system completely shut down, and mail couldn't get through, prompting President Cleveland to send federal troops to Chicago to keep the mail moving and to control the rioting. The violence was so bad that in July some of the striking workers were shot by the troops. Also that month, arsonists struck the fairgrounds, burning most of its majestic buildings to the ground.

For the Koreshans in Chicago, though, it seems to have been a happy, hopeful time. Cottages had been built on the Beth-Ophrah grounds so that more followers could live there. Teed traveled to Estero occasionally to monitor progress, but Beth-Ophrah was his base, so he was with them most of the time. They received regular positive news from the settlers in Estero, and while they waited for their New Jerusalem to be ready, they went about their daily lives, educating the children, preparing the meals, and publishing the *Flaming Sword* magazine. The violence against them had subsided, as had media coverage. In fact, a four-line blurb in the *Chicago Tribune* in 1895 asked whether anyone knew what had become of Teed. The suit from Sidney Miller was dismissed for reasons that aren't known. And even the death of a follower in her thirties (consumption) at Beth-Ophrah garnered little attention. One disenchanted follower incited a flare-up that resulted in a couple of indignation meetings but came to nothing. The citizens of Chicago—though they would have preferred to see the Koreshans go—were no longer actively trying to drive them out.[16]

And the town of Fort Myers welcomed Teed and his followers. The citizens believed that he had money, and if he succeeded in building his city, it would be good for the economy. People in Fort Myers were curious about the Koreshans, but not suspicious. When Teed or one of his followers visited town, the *Fort Myers Press* reported it, saying that they were well educated and polite. "They are all workers and will make their part of the country a veritable paradise on earth, if intelligent work will accomplish it."[17]

At first, Gustave and the Koreshans worked together in farming the land, but the Koreshans—and one man in particular—had new ideas. Oscar L'Amoreaux was respected in the community because he had been a professor of Greek and Latin at Wheaton College, a fact that was trotted out to the media occasionally to give the Koreshans some credibility. Before that, he was a farmer, and soon after he arrived in Estero, he began studying and experimenting with crops and consulting with men in Fort Myers about planting.

L'Amoreaux ordered clippings from California—figs, pears, jujubes, and grapes—and planted them in the nursery with the help of Allen Andrews, who was also very curious about horticulture and wrote about it extensively through the years. "Although we tended [the plants] assiduously, they failed to respond satisfactorily and eventually died," Allen wrote.[18]

"Soon," Elwin wrote, "there were no vegetables for anyone to eat."[19]

Allen disagreed with Elwin's account. They had plenty of food, according to him. "If anyone went hungry he had but himself to blame."[20]

Ultimately, when L'Amoreaux and Gustave couldn't agree on what to grow, Gustave turned the garden over to the professor. One day, Gustave discovered L'Amoreaux setting out trees on Elwin's land, the twenty acres Gustave held back when he deeded the property to the Unity. He apparently had forgotten his agreement with the Koreshans allowing them to make improvements to his land. What he did remember and later record was his confrontation with

L'Amoreaux. Gustave approached the tall, gaunt man as he worked. "Sir, I want to call you not professor now, but ask you as a brother, do you know that this land belongs to Elwin, my son."[21]

L'Amoreaux responded, "If we want to plant an orange grove or anything, what is that to you?"

Elwin and Gustave were outnumbered, and busy. Before long, more Koreshans arrived from Chicago, meaning more work for Elwin, according to Elwin. One day the supply boat from Punta Rassa was delayed by bad weather, and the group of fifty was hungry. Elwin remembered in his memoir his conversation with Teed, who said to Elwin, "Get us some fish for these people to eat."[22]

Elwin replied, "All right, but what have you to catch them with? There are no hooks, no nets. I can't catch them with my bare hands."

"Get the fish," Teed said.

Elwin wrote that he had no choice but to cooperate and provide unless he wanted to leave without a penny. And he knew very well how to catch fish without nets on the Estero River. He and a helper took two skiffs and two lanterns to the mouth of the river and waited in the dark for the tide to come in. On Elwin's cue, they knocked their lanterns against the sides of the boats, scaring the mullet. The startled fish flew out of the water, and so many of them jumped toward the light of the lanterns that the two boats were full in no time. Elwin wrote that one heavy mullet struck his left arm and left a lump that he had for the rest of his life.

And though Elwin was prone to exaggeration, this method of fishing—known as fire fishing—was confirmed by several Koreshans, who claimed to improve on it. They constructed a basket, surrounded it with burning pine knots, and attached it to their largest boat, then tied several skiffs to the boat, waiting at the mouth of the river for the night tide to come in. When the water rose, the mullet swam upriver toward the boats. Confused by the firelight, they jumped—into the basket, onto the banks, and directly into the skiffs. The fish flew with such force that the Koreshans had to dodge them to avoid being struck. Allen remembers catching 166 fish in one night this way.

The people of Fort Myers followed the progress in Estero through the *Fort Myers Press*. At the Koreshans' invitation, the editor of the *Press* visited and toured their grounds and plantings. The editor saw that they had planted bamboo, shrubs, trees, grains, and every imaginable kind of vegetable, experimenting with what would grow best in the sandy soil. They had two cabins, one for men and one for women, and a barn for the horses. Lunch was a four- or five-course meal that the editor described in the paper as bountiful and sumptuous. He reported that he was quite impressed. "I have never known a people more highly praised by their neighbors. As for myself I never experienced a more enjoyable visit. If their enterprise succeeds, 'Koresia' will some day be the gem of the peninsula."[23]

November 29, 1894, was the first time that Thanksgiving Day was officially celebrated as a national holiday in the United States, and while others feasted, Gustave decided to commemorate it by fasting. He recorded the day in detail several months later. "I was under a heavy depression of mind," he remembered. He was headed across the property to tend to the bees when he passed the women's cabin, where Teed and Victoria sat on the porch. Teed called him over and asked him to sit, and he did. "I was in awe of Dr. Teed, believing he was the savior of the new dispensation."[24]

As the men sat together, Gustave noticed Victoria at a writing desk nearby, preoccupied with some paperwork. Teed broached the matter of the twenty acres Gustave had held back for Elwin. Teed and Victoria had been pressing him for a decision that week, and Gustave had been anguished about it, perhaps the reason he was despondent on Thanksgiving. He knew that transferring the property would be for the good of the group, but not for Elwin.

Teed reminded Gustave of a story in the book of Acts, in which Ananias and his wife, Sapphira, sell land to give money to Peter, but hold back some of the price. When Peter learns of this, he says to Ananias, "Thou hast not lied unto men, but unto God." Upon hearing the words, Ananias dies instantly, followed by his wife.[25]

Teed told Gustave that to have the Lord's blessing, he must turn everything over to the Unity. Holding anything back went against the principles of Koreshanity. Teed reminded him that he and Elwin could live on the property as long as they liked, and they would be fully cared for. Victoria, more practical, told him that the Koreshans wanted to improve the property, but didn't want to spend money doing so if the Unity didn't own it.

From where they sat on the porch, they could see the fruit trees Gustave had planted a decade before. The orange trees held green orbs that would ripen soon. Then Victoria brought over a paper, and Gustave saw what she had been working on. It was a deed, already filled out except for the signature lines. "Hadn't you better give it over to the Unity?" Teed asked.

Teed read aloud what Victoria had written, which stated that Gustave would convey the property to her, as trustee of the Unity. There was no mention of compensation, though it was listed on the deed as one dollar, which is standard even today. Gustave heard the legal description, the coordinates he was so familiar with, having done all the surveying. "The west half of the northwest quarter" and on and on. It ended, "and is the present site of the said Gustave Damkohler residence." He signed it. As for Elwin, Teed assured Gustave, they would take him to Chicago, give him a good education, and make a man of him.

"I, my father's only living child, was disinherited," Elwin wrote. A few nights later, Elwin claimed, as he and Gustave slept on the boat, he woke to the sound of his father crying "like a baby, realizing what he had done to me."[26]

In late December 1894, there was a freeze in Estero—something the Koreshans hadn't imagined possible. On the first night, the temperature was in the twenties; on the second, thirty-two. They built bonfires to keep warm and worried about what would happen to their plantings. As it turned out, because the plants were still dormant, most survived. In a happy surprise, Allen discovered that the cold air made for excellent fishing, a fact he may have learned from Elwin. The fish, numbed by the water, stayed in deep pools in the mudflats instead of swimming out with the tide. On that first cold morning, Allen set out with Elwin, and they speared jewfish, snapper, perch, and sheepshead, filling their boat.

"You may think this a large fish story," Jennie Andrews, in Chicago, wrote to her mother, Margaret, telling her that Allen had caught five hundred pounds of fish, some as large as forty pounds. Allen wrote Jennie often, and she read his letters aloud to the followers at Beth-Ophrah. In her next letter to her mother, she told the fish story again. "I wonder if I shall be repeating myself," she wrote, and then repeated the catch of five hundred pounds.[27]

"He is a general favorite," she told her mother about Allen. In Estero, he was still practicing his violin, she wrote, and he played with the small Koreshan orchestra there. He might become the postmaster of Estero, she wrote, if the Koreshans were granted the post office they had requested from Washington, D.C.[28]

Doubtless, Margaret was against the move to Estero, and not only because it would take her daughter and grandchildren farther away. She believed, as evidenced by her letters, that Jennie had fallen under the influence of a crazy, perhaps dangerous man. Being isolated in Florida would only make things worse and would mean that Margaret had truly lost her. But she knew that if her letters focused exclusively on Jennie's belief in Koreshanity, it would drive them apart. So mostly she included news from home—births and illnesses and deaths, visits from her other children and grandchildren, a new rail extension that brought the train right past their door. That Christmas, Margaret sent Jennie money, asking that she spend it on herself, not the children. She used it to fill some cavities. "So I carry the evidence of your kindness with me always, as I see the fillings," Jennie wrote.[29]

Unless her mother brought it up, and she did from time to time, never abandoning hope that her daughter would leave, Jennie avoided the topic of Koreshanity. In February, there was a beautiful snow at Beth-Ophrah, which she described to her mother: "Every pine needle was covered separately as though with white plush. Every evergreen—spruce, fir, pine and arbor vitae were a mass of white lace work and tassels, to stand under them and look up into their branches made one think of a fairy grotto or an ice palace."[30]

In this same letter, Jennie responded to a newspaper clipping Margaret had sent concerning a cult called the Sanctified Band, whose believers lived in floating arks off the coast of Virginia, Maryland, and North Carolina and practiced bigamy and a form of worship that involved shouting and leaping. Members of the cult were required to cut all ties with nonmembers, perhaps what Margaret feared most when it came to Jennie. They were in the news at the time, defending themselves against charges of breaking up marriages (many of the members had left spouses to join the Band) and being a nuisance to the community. The trial was widely reported.

The fact that her mother sent her a story about the Sanctified Band upset Jennie greatly. "If you do not know your own child better," she wrote, "if you do not have any more regard for Dr. Andrews and the purity of his life than to believe this . . . it is both an insult to me and an insult to his memory." Jennie missed Abie terribly, as evidenced by her journal entries, but she also believed that the work meant that the two of them would be together again in the afterlife. Her faith in Teed comforted her.[31]

"I cannot help but feel," Jennie wrote to her mother, "that He is the Cyrus that shall deliver the children of Israel." And if it weren't the case, she added, "one must come yet whose name is Cyrus . . . or else the Lord's words are without meaning."[32]

In the last letter that survives between Jennie and Margaret, Jennie wrote, "My dear Mother, I cannot bear to have you feel as you do about us. I love you and I want you to see things differently." She kept the letter for two days before sending it. In the envelope, she placed a Japanese persimmon seed from Florida, describing the fruit as "large as an orange and very luscious."[33]

Shortly after the first freeze, another, harsher one hit—and it became known throughout the state as the Great Freeze. Crops in Estero survived for the most part, but farther north, the effects were disastrous. Citrus groves were decimated. Orange and grapefruit trees that survived the first freeze were killed by the second—stripped of their leaves, many of them toppling under the weight of their frozen fruit. What had been vast, thriving grove land was reduced to row upon row of dead and fallen trees with brittle branches.

But in Lee County, the citrus trees survived, and the fruit sold for high prices. Quickly, there was a land boom in Lee. Growers in central Florida who could afford to start over bought large swaths of property in Fort Myers and Estero, where land was still plentiful and cheap. One Montana millionaire who came to Lee County intending to raise cattle switched to citrus and planted a large grove upriver from the Koreshans, as did smaller growers. The citrus boom was coming, and the Koreshans would be ready to profit, with a general store, a post office, machine shop, and boat works.

Their settlement was growing, thanks to a sawmill they bought, dismantled, and moved to the southern end of Estero Island. With the lumber, they built several new buildings, and they profited by selling the boards to outsiders. Demand was strong—theirs was the only sawmill within one hundred miles—and the water around the island was deep enough that schooners could pull up and load. Around the sawmill, the Koreshans added a dormitory for the mill workers, a dining hall, a shed, their machine shop, and boat works. By the end of the year, they established Estero's first post office there. The island became a satellite location for the inland settlement.[34]

However, there was a problem with the island land: the Koreshans didn't own it. Though Teed had placed a squatter on the property with the idea of homesteading, he had not applied for homestead, and another man, a non-Koreshan, claimed that the territory was his. Gustave—by this time a near expert at property claims, surveys, and land deals—wrote to the land office and tried several strategies to get the land for the Koreshans. His letters, at first circumspect, became more emotional: "The sawmill is needed here to saw our lumber for building our City, the New Jerusalem!" When his efforts were thwarted, he believed there had been a conspiracy, and he accused the land lawyers. It's very likely, according to one scholar, that the man Gustave blamed was F. A. "Berry" Hendry, the patriarch of the Hendry clan, the most powerful family in Fort Myers. If someone wanted something done in Fort Myers, there was no getting around the Hendrys, and Gustave had not gotten around them. He wrote to the land commissioner: "I know the whole transaction, the deal was all played." Regardless, the Koreshans kept the sawmill right where it was.[35]

Inland, at the main settlement, the Koreshans added houses, barns, sheds, and a three-story dining hall/dormitory, which one Koreshan said was the largest building in Lee County. If the Fort Myers newspaper can be believed, the settlement had become a paradise. The editor who visited described its broad walks, large trees, and views of the water. "A succession of terraces rise one above the other, planted with palms and shade trees," he wrote without a hint of sarcasm. "Settees are scattered around, and here, amid the hum of the bees and the breath of the poppy, one can drowsily nod, imagining himself in the Acadia Longfellow has made immortal in 'Evangeline.'"[36]

The worship hall was filled with the balsamic smells of palmetto, flowers, and pine, the editor reported. The Koreshan orchestra and choir were excellent. The people were happy and contented, with clear complexions and bright eyes, he noted. Happy chickens pecked through the poultry yard—Barred Plymouth Rocks, Brahmas, White Plymouth Rocks, Indian Game chickens, and Buff Leghorns. "There may yet come a time, and that not so very far distant," wrote the editor, "when the people of Lee county will point with pride to the Koreshan Unity."[37]

The plan, once they were established, was to build a grand temple surrounded by a circular sea, the Crystal Sea, three hundred feet wide, fed by water from the Estero River and the bay. The temple would be at the center of the city, and its dome would rise three hundred feet into the sky. The Koreshans drove a post into the ground to mark where the temple would be. Gustave surely noticed his cabin was nowhere near it.[38]

Elwin's dissatisfaction grew. The Koreshans had promised him an education, and they assigned a boy to teach him to read and write. But Elwin didn't like his teacher. "I could not stand the humiliation of studying under this boy whom I considered somewhat less than intelligent."[39]

Allen Andrews wrote of Elwin, "He seemed to imagine that education was something to be acquired through having it poured into one's head with a funnel, without any conscious effort." Elwin was especially annoyed with the Koreshans' belief that they lived inside the earth. Anyone with common sense, he later wrote, could see this wasn't true.[40]

The Koreshans bought Elwin new clothes and even took him to Chicago to see the big city. "But nothing pleased him," Allen wrote. "The skyscraper buildings were not as tall as he had imagined; the elephant at the zoo was not big enough."[41]

Elwin was thoroughly disgusted with Teed and the Koreshans—for taking their land, for duping his father, and for ordering the two of them around. He decided to leave, permanently. He asked for his father's blessing, telling him he intended to go to Fort Myers, get a job, and finish school. Elwin later recorded what his father said: "I will not stand in your way. I have made such a mess of our own home affairs, go with God's blessing." Elwin, seventeen, packed a few clothes and some food and walked up the sand trail to Fort Myers, sixteen miles away.[42]

✳ 9 ✳

Our Cosmic Egg

Teed knew that the world was hollow, but he wanted to prove it. The facts were these, he said: Earth is an enclosed sphere that contains the entire universe, and there is nothing beyond it; we live on the inner shell, looking *in* on everything God has created, rather than out into infinite, unknowable space.

This was central to Koreshanity, which held that the cosmos is knowable and that we have a special place in it—at its boundary, to be exact—as opposed to being insignificant specks in a vast mystery. Teed's proof for this was simple and comforting: God would not create a world we couldn't understand. To be a Koreshan and to know that we live inside is to know God, he said. "To believe in the earth's convexity is to deny him and all his works," Teed wrote. Therefore, those who accepted Copernicus's ideas suffered under a dangerous delusion.[1]

Teed lectured about the hollow earth and spoke to reporters, but no one took him seriously. A handful of newspaper stories did explain the theory and include illustrations of how it worked, but mostly it was met with derision. One news brief read, "Possibly Dr. Teed does his thinking with a hollow skull." It was another bit of entertainment for the public, but, unlike the accusations of swindling people and stealing wives, the earth belief didn't impact anyone, so readers were only mildly curious. Most troubling to Teed, as reflected in his writing, was that scientists didn't deign to respond to his idea. So for all of these reasons, he was driven to produce hard evidence and, in doing so, he would revolutionize the world of science, and everyone would have to listen.[2]

To back up other facets of his religion, he had used science, and he would do the same with this, only better. His other theories—like the brain as battery, and the invisible life forces—relied on what many people called pseudoscience. But to prove his earth theory, Teed planned to use physics.

A particular question in Isaiah confirmed for him that the world was hollow, measurable, and comprehensible. "Who hath measured the waters in the hollow of his hand, and meted out heaven with the span, and comprehended the dust of the earth in a measure, and weighed the mountains in scales, and the hills in a balance?" The answer, of course, was God. And Teed decided that he would measure the earth as well—or he would shepherd his people to do so.[3]

In 1895, in Allegheny, Pennsylvania, there lived a man who believed that the earth was flat. His name was Ulysses Grant Morrow, thirty-one, and he spent all of his spare time investigating his theory, measuring, drawing meticulous charts and diagrams, and keeping careful notes. He had become fascinated with astronomy when he studied it in school at age fourteen, and as an adult, he started a monthly paper about religion and astronomy. He had a day job and worked on his theories on weekends and nights, sometimes all night. His wife, Rosa, said this obsession was her only rival for his affections.[4]

Ulysses wore owlish eyeglasses with thick frames and had a moustache and Van Dyke goatee. His PhD, it was said, was from Chicago's College of Higher Science, which is where he met Teed, though nothing is known about that institution. He made his living as a shorthand expert and stenographer, he taught courses on shorthand and business, and for a time he was the principal of the Corning School of Shorthand. He also published a pamphlet on phonetic shorthand and offered his services teaching this skill through the mail. Ulysses was a good writer and a fast typist. "Professor Morrow was the first person I ever saw using a typewriter," a Koreshan later wrote, "and it seemed impossible that he could hit the keys so fast and know what he was doing." A trademark of his typing was that he always used purple ink, not black.

Before he met Teed, Ulysses was a seeker; he followed the teachings of Charles Taze Russell, the minister in Pennsylvania who founded Zion's Watch Tower Tract Society, the same man Damkohler had followed before he met Teed. In the mid-1890s, Teed visited Allegheny to debate Russell and converted a few of his adherents.

By the time Ulysses learned of Teed's concave earth theory, he had poured years into his flat earth theorems and didn't want to let them go. But he became infatuated with what Teed called the cellular cosmogony, and he tried integrating their two theories. Teed critiqued Ulysses's experiments in the *Flaming Sword,* and he must have been persuasive because Ulysses disavowed his flat earth research. "The skeleton I had erected has now crumbled before your cutting arguments," he wrote to Teed, "and I am free to examine Koreshan Science with my mind void of preconceived opinions."[5]

Within a year, he and his wife converted to Koreshanity and led a small community of about thirty in Allegheny, holding meetings at their house. Ulysses became determined to help Teed prove that we live inside, and Teed appointed him as the leader of the newly formed Koreshan Geodetic Staff, giving him the title of astronomer and geodesist.

The staff's first project was to tackle the most common question about the concave earth: if the earth curves upward, critics asked, why does a ship disappear over the horizon? The Koreshans set out to prove that this was a mirage. They gathered opera glasses, a telescope, sketch pads, and various tools and took a rowboat to the Michigan and Illinois canal, choosing it because the water was calm and boat traffic was light. They drove a stake into the bottom of the canal and placed a target on top—black, white, and red like a bull's eye, so that they could easily see it from a distance and take measurements against its concentric circles. Once the target was placed, three men rowed precisely three miles. Anchoring their boat, they viewed the disc and saw that all of it was visible. They rowed another two miles and were pleased to see the full target again. Throughout, they took precise measurements and drew sketches.[6]

They then tested it in the opposite direction, using a white, reflective target this time and rowing five miles. The bottom of the target disappeared; however, they could see it clearly through a telescope, which they held at various documented heights above the water. They continued their experiments on a pier at Lake Michigan, where they watched yachts, steamers, and schooners and noticed that, indeed, the vessels appeared to vanish slowly over the bulge of the horizon, which they estimated was twelve miles away. The hulls could not be seen with the naked eye, or with opera glasses, but a telescope with a 50-power lens rendered the ships' hulls clearly visible.

Their visual tests were complete and proved that the earth was concave, they believed. "It seems strange," Ulysses wrote, "that a matter so easily observed as this should have so long escaped even the most casual observer—to say nothing of the scientist." But scientists ignored them.[7]

Ulysses and Teed realized that to be taken seriously, they needed to go beyond mere visual tests and use mechanical methods instead. Because we live inside the earth, they reasoned, the ground curves upward. By projecting a horizontal line at a constant height, Teed and Ulysses could show this upward curve. Their horizontal line would travel a certain distance and meet back up with the ground, whereas if we lived on the outside of the earth, as almost everyone believed, the line would travel into space indefinitely and never meet up with the surface. Ulysses and Teed had calculated that the earth was twenty-five thousand miles around, had a diameter of eight thousand miles, and curved upward at a rate of eight inches per mile.[8]

Teed and Ulysses planned to create their horizontal line next to a large body of water so that, in addition to measuring the vertical distance between the line and the land, they could make sight lines from the line out into the water at varying distances.

This couldn't be done in Chicago, but Florida was ideal, with its stretches of empty shoreline along the Gulf and its mild weather. Furthermore, the Gulf was part of the ocean, and their visual tests had been on inland waters. They imagined that this was one reason scientists had ignored them. Perhaps, they reasoned, their critics believed that inland waters did not conform to the earth's contour, though there is no evidence that anyone lodged a complaint like this. Being on the Gulf would eliminate this criticism because, Ulysses wrote, "no sane mind" could question that it followed the contour of the earth.[9]

The Koreshans learned of a man who owned nearly all of Naples, a few miles south of Estero, and he was willing to let them camp on the beach and conduct their experiment. As luck would have it, the man co-owned the Louisville, Kentucky, *Courier-Journal*, and it's likely that Teed and Ulysses saw an opportunity for coverage. Funding for the project came from Berthaldine Boomer's husband, though he was not a Koreshan. Not incidentally, Teed and Ulysses appointed the Boomers' older son, Lucius Messenger Boomer, to direct the project; his name appeared beneath Ulysses's on the expedition letterhead, which read, "The Civil Engineering, Scientific and Geodetic Staff of the Koreshan Unity." The plan was in place. Their geodetic team would go to Florida, led by Ulysses Grant Morrow, and measure the curvature of the earth.

Before they could begin, they needed a way to run a perfectly level horizontal line over land, an apparatus that could maintain a constant right angle, and do so with unimpeachable precision. Ulysses, who had a talent for useful inventions, got to work drawing sketches for a giant ruler of sorts: a Geodetic Rectilineator, they called it. There were at least four identical parts. Each one looked like a section of fence for a horse corral, except that the posts were very tall. In effect, each structure was a double-T square held in place by cross planks and made rigid by diagonal tension rods to ensure that it maintained a right angle. The fence sections were designed to be bolted together. To ensure perfect alignment of the sections, brass plates on either end were etched with precise calibrations. To keep the rectilineator level as the earth curved away from it, the team would put supports of varying heights beneath it.[10]

Expert mechanics spent four weeks building the rectilineator to Ulysses's specifications. It was made of mahogany that had been seasoned for twelve years inside the shops of Pullman's Palace Car Company. In September 1896, the rectilineator was complete and ready for unveiling, and the Koreshans threw a party at the old Town Hall in Washington Heights, circulating a densely worded event announcement. The *Chicago Tribune* wrote that those who received the invitation must have felt tremendous relief. "The residents of that suburb, some of them at least, have been greatly worried for years as to whether they were living on a flat or spherical planet, or whether the earth might not be a parallellopiped [*sic*] or a lune. Some of them, it is said, have lain awake nights." The reporter continued, "It is hinted that science is trembling on the verge of a great discovery."[11]

There was literary and musical entertainment, and the Geodetic Rectilineator was unveiled. Ulysses explained how it worked, giving special attention to the brass facings that would ensure the proper alignment of the sections. Within two months, the team was packing its surveying equipment to go to Florida: telescopes, a level, protractor, etc.—instruments "of the kind used by sane men," the *New York Times* marveled. "And the most amazing feature of the case is that they understand these instruments and know how to use them."[12]

In late 1896, the geodetic team took the train from Chicago to the end of the Florida rail line, then sailed to Estero Island, where they stored the rectilineator and other equipment in a shed near the sawmill—the one the Koreshans had built on land that wasn't theirs. Having unloaded, they boated up the Estero River to the settlement and reunited with the pioneering brothers and sisters they hadn't seen in three years. They spent several days catching up, recruited members for the geodetic team, and, after a few days of rest, they returned to the island, unloaded the shed, and transferred the equipment to *Ada* for the trip to Naples Beach.

It's lucky they removed everything from the island when they did. Days later, on a Friday night, a fire ravaged the sawmill, machine shop, and boat works, and it nearly killed Gustave. It's hard not to believe that someone deliberately set the fire to get rid of the buildings, especially given the timing: Gustave was there when the fire happened; his angry letter to the land commissioner, just three months prior, reflected animosity between the Koreshans and the community; and it's highly unlikely that a natural fire would ignite in December on the beach, let alone in the evening.

Another curious thing happened in December a few days after the sawmill fire. On the last day of the year, Teed and Gustave had a disagreement, their first ever. Gustave had been devoted to Teed from nearly the moment they met two years earlier, as evidenced by his dramatic conversion; by his giving up his land and even the acreage he had planned to save for Elwin; and by his waging an emotional battle for ownership of the beach property. The cause of their fight isn't known, but it's reasonable to assume that Teed was disappointed over how the land deal had gone in spite of Gustave's best efforts, and he may have expressed this disappointment. Given Teed's alleged demands on Elwin ("Get the fish"), one wonders whether he was similarly demanding with Gustave, who was emotionally vulnerable at this point in his life, he later said. He had nearly died in the fire, and his only son had left the community, disgusted with Teed. It's telling that, in spite of Gustave's considerable land surveying experience, he did not participate in the geodetic experiment on Naples Beach, not even as a witness. He said later that he had begun to question his faith in Koreshanity.[13]

The destruction of the sawmill was a blow to the Unity. It was their first industry and a source of significant income. Ulysses, who saw symbolism in even the most mundane occurrences, wrote that the fire was a sign that the devil was at work trying to thwart the geodetic project.[14]

In late December, the Koreshans set up tents on Naples Beach and built a headquarters, a shack with a thatched-palm roof that would come to be known, fondly, as Starvation Camp on Desolation Avenue. The plan was to run the rectilineator four miles down the beach, beginning at an elevated point and keeping a constant height by using supports beneath it. To advance the rectilineator, the team would fasten the sections together end to end, verify that they had achieved a right angle, and then move the backmost section to the front and so on.[15]

Ulysses dug a straight line down the beach to guide in placement of the rectilineator and then tested the apparatus with practice measurements, finding that it was out of whack, which he had expected, given that it had rattled 1,300 miles in a series of freight cars from Chicago. Furthermore, it was exposed to sand, rain, wind, and salt air. The special cover he had ordered for it had not arrived, so at night, they covered it as best as they could with a tent. Another challenge was maintaining the guideline Ulysses had dug in the sand, as the wind was constantly disturbing it.[16]

More devilish than any of this was that a man on the team was stirring up trouble. A Mr. Jaffray had learned that Ulysses's test measurements were off, and he proclaimed to anyone in Estero who would listen that the rectilineator was flawed, incapable of projecting a straight horizontal line. In the camp on

Naples Beach, he told the men on the team that the project would fail and that they shouldn't associate themselves with it. Fearing that Jaffray would tamper with the rectilineator, the Koreshans installed watchmen around the clock.

Ulysses believed that Jaffray was the new form the devil had taken to stop their work, and Teed believed this as well. He was accustomed to ridicule from the outside world, but he would not tolerate it from within, he told his followers. Teed defended Ulysses and the rectilineator, writing, "We would prefer a thousand enemies outside the camp to one inside." Ulysses stayed quiet, planning to let the rectilineator do the talking. Once the team saw how accurate it was, he was confident that they would believe, he wrote to a friend. He bent to his work, adjusting the cross arms and tension lines, but Jaffray was having an influence. The Boomer's younger son, Harry, walked off the project, "fully impregnated with Jaffray's foolishness and disgust for Koreshanity," Ulysses wrote. More alarming, Lucius, his general manager, resigned, too.[17]

Ulysses regularly updated Evelyn Bubbett, a Koreshan living at Beth-Ophrah who managed the publishing house and put out the *Flaming Sword*. Evelyn was an early follower of Teed's, converting after she saw him speak at the mental science convention at the candy factory church in Chicago. Fair-skinned with blue eyes, she was five foot seven and had light brown hair and always dressed well. She was one of the few women whose husband joined with her. They lived in the first communal home on College Place, took the vow of celibacy, and broke the "family tie," promising to love all Koreshans equally rather than to show favor to their own family. They devoted their whole lives to the Koreshan Unity.

Ulysses sent Evelyn articles and illustrations for publication in the *Sword* and for sale to newspapers throughout the country. With his material, he included letters to her confiding the problems on the project and his determination to overcome them. About Jaffray, Ulysses wrote to Evelyn, "I am here for the purpose of performing the work I was commissioned and sent to do and WILL DO IT."[18]

After breakfast one morning, he came into the dining room to find Jaffray leading a meeting with the men, and he could no longer remain quiet. "I exposed the whole scheme," he wrote to Evelyn, and told the men to show some "manliness." The next day, Jaffray packed up and left. To Ulysses's relief, Lucius Boomer rejoined the geodetic team as director. Harry did not return to the project.[19]

One night that week, a fat possum wandered into Ulysses's tent as he and Allen Andrews sat talking. (Allen was one of the three night watchmen for the rectilineator.) Ulysses wrote to Evelyn asking what she thought the possum symbolized, and he described the incident to Evelyn.[20]

He stroked the animal's back and said to it, "Hello, sir. Where did you come from?"

"Better get him by the neck," said Allen, who had been in Florida much longer and knew easy food when he saw it. Allen and Ulysses trapped the animal in a barrel until morning and had a feast the next day, which Ulysses regretted, he told Evelyn. The animal had looked so innocent, gentle, and wise. He wanted to believe it represented his triumph over Jaffray, he wrote, but he knew that possums were deceptive. Perhaps it was a sign of more trouble to come.

And it did, this time in the form of bad weather. In February, Gus Faber, the hapless boat captain who had so exasperated Elwin, wrecked one of their boats on a trip from Estero, where he had gone to pick up their laundry and items that the Chicagoans had sent them. Faber returned to Naples in a terrible storm, and heavy surf and strong winds battered the boat and scattered the Koreshans' clothing along the beach. Allen Andrews remembered that his valise was swept into the Gulf, along with one new shoe and most of his clean washing. That night, he slept in damp bedding.[21]

Soon after this was another boat wreck. This time, one of the men had gone to Doctor's Pass for clams. He collected so many of them that his boat sank and overturned, one thousand feet from shore. He didn't know how to swim, so he sat on top (or rather bottom) to wait for his rescuers. Luckily, the boat stayed afloat, and he survived, but "there was excitement enough in the camp . . . to do us for a month!" Ulysses wrote Evelyn. On top of this, Ulysses's typewriter broke, the keys piling up on each other when he tried to type. He took it to pieces at midnight one night and put it back together.

The storms continued, making it impossible to start the work. "The devil is certainly against us, but I hope he may grow tired of sending storms and rains," Ulysses wrote.[22]

Finally the weather cleared. The men adjusted the rectilineator, moving the sections down the shore to test the line, then backing them up to the starting point to compare measurements. At last, they were satisfied that the line was perfectly horizontal, and they could begin. Ulysses wrote to the followers at Beth-Ophrah that everything was finally ready. It was March, nearly three months after they had arrived on the beach.

Ulysses was so enthusiastic that he considered applying for a Nobel Prize, he told Evelyn, though the prize had not yet been established. Swedish chemist and inventor Alfred Nobel had died in December and bequeathed money to establish the prizes, but Nobel's family was contesting the will. Ulysses must have expected that all would be worked out within the year, because he wrote that if he applied ahead of time, the committee could send the prize money without delay once the Koreshans proved the earth's concavity.

The team worked its way down the beach with a chest of equipment, which Ulysses catalogued—"a thermometer, microscope, calipers, rulers, compass, spirit level, triangles, protractor, telescope, thumb bolts, adjusting gauges, celluloid test card . . . and the books of the Staff." A few days after they began the experiment, tragedy struck. Mr. Boomer, Berthaldine's husband and the project's funder, died. Lucius, the director of the expedition, moved back to Chicago to settle his father's affairs and didn't return. Ulysses pressed on without him.[23]

Each time they moved a section from the back of the rectilineator to the front, they took painstaking measurements to line up the calibrations on the brass plates. While the alignments were being done, the sections were held together with small setscrews. One person was in charge of the top screw and another in charge of the bottom. They checked the alignment first with the naked eye and next with a microscope. For additional verification, they dropped a plumb line and spirit level ("the finest and most sensitive obtainable," Ulysses wrote) from the rectilineator. "The plumb and level invariably tell the truth," Ulysses wrote. "They are silent witnesses . . . which man cannot bribe nor change to suit a theory."[24]

Once the team was satisfied that the sections were aligned, the alignment was noted in a record book, and each staff member initialed the entry. The plates were clamped together and then fastened with bolts, and the gap between the sections was tightened and tested, first with a Bristol board feeler gauge of .015", then with a more precise celluloid card of .001". The investigating committee, which included Victoria, checked the alignment and issued a signed statement to the staff, and this statement was added to the records. The team then unbolted the rearmost section and brought it to the front.

After a prescribed distance, they backed up, taking the sections one by one in the opposite direction and repeating their measurements until they reached the original starting point. This was done to confirm that the alignment was true. This technique was the Castle System of Reversals, invented by Koreshan sister Eleanor Castle, the only woman on the geodetic team. Eleanor was well educated—a former professor of languages at the University of Chicago. She had joined the Koreshans in Chicago, leaving her husband, who told the newspapers that she and their son went to the World's Fair one day and simply disappeared.[25]

Every eighth of a mile, the team projected an air line from the rectilineator to the water, using mean tide for all of their measurements and a special mercurial geodetic level that Ulysses had invented for the expedition. Every item of adjustment, test, observation, and measurement was written in the daily record book and signed by the operators and witnesses, including tourists who were looking on and whose names and cities were noted. At night, the rectilineator was covered, and men took shifts guarding it. The watchmen signed statements about the precautions they took.

Things went fairly smoothly, except for a couple of violent storms that required a frenzy of sandbagging to protect the line they had marked to guide the path of the rectilineator. The line was very important to them, and symbolic to Ulysses, who wrote, "This white line is the actual mark we have made in the world, our path to success, the route of demonstration."[26]

The rectilineator stopped at Gordon's Pass, an inlet of water two and a half miles from the beginning point. They couldn't march the rectilineator across the water. And even if they could, the coastline turned east at the pass. So the level line they had spent weeks forming with the rectilineator continued as an air line that went well offshore and stopped at a boat anchored at the four-mile endpoint. They finished the work with a telescope and a series of complex diagrams. This is highly curious—because the existence of Gordon's Pass was no surprise. Perhaps they never planned to run the rectilineator the entire four miles that Ulysses and Teed determined was necessary. At any rate, the air line hit the water at the point they expected it to. They were done.

Success. The earth did, in fact, curve upward at the rate they had posited. They had triumphed. It was July, and after months of fieldwork and countless challenges, they had accomplished their goal. The Koreshans had irrefutable proof that they—that everyone—lived inside the earth. Ulysses would continue to work on the inner earth theory for the rest of his life, perfecting and tweaking it and discovering new things, but he clearly viewed this as a huge achievement.

Ulysses stopped in Louisville on his return to Chicago and granted a thorough interview to the *Courier-Journal*, the paper co-owned by the man whose beachfront property they used in Naples. In Chicago, Ulysses spoke to a reporter for the *Times-Herald*, telling him, "Nothing can now impede the progress of the Koreshan System; it is invincible." Teed and Ulysses even issued a public challenge to scientists, encouraging them to contest their proof. Teed told the *Fort Myers Press* he would re-create the experiment anywhere for anyone to witness. Some reports, which seem to be erroneous, said Teed offered a ten-thousand-dollar reward to anyone who found fault in their calculations.[27]

According to Teed, the discovery was widely covered in the media, and the news reached millions of people: "The startling information . . . flashed from city to city, and from continent to continent, reverberating around the world." The Koreshans said they had heard from people in all parts of the English-speaking world and from France, Germany, India, and Mexico. Actually, the coverage was not as extensive as the Koreshans claimed; the truth seems to be that there were only a handful of news reports, many of them quite brief.[28]

The following year, Ulysses and Teed published their findings in a two-hundred-page book titled *The Cellular Cosmogony*, which they advertised for sale in the *Flaming Sword* and elsewhere. Much of the writing, especially the part written by Teed, was impenetrable. He and Ulysses devoted several pages to "irrational objections" raised by "chagrined critics." The men had heard of two main objections: the first was a claim that the rectilineator was not accurate. Teed and Ulysses responded as follows: they had taken extra precautions to ensure that it was accurate; critics who said the apparatus was flawed had never seen it; and the time spent building the rectilineator (four weeks) had not been for nothing. The second criticism was that the Koreshans intentionally tilted the first section of the rectilineator upon beginning their experiment. Teed and Ulysses assured these detractors that they had not done so, adding that the critics should have been brave enough to participate in the geodetic expedition themselves. Teed challenged anyone to repeat the experiment and disprove the measurements.[29]

Ulysses and Teed did not name their critics, who were probably not in the least chagrined and instead were people making dismissive, offhand remarks. There is no record that anyone sent in a written objection and no evidence that a scientist rose to Teed's challenge. The truth is that no one much seemed to care.

Nevertheless, *The Cellular Cosmogony* became an important piece of literature for the Koreshans, and the success of their experiment gave heft, they felt, to their marketing slogan, "We Live Inside! Drop In and See Us." This was printed in literature and on tickets to lectures and even on a lapel pin that the Koreshans produced and advertised in the *Flaming Sword*. The round button featured an illustration of the hollow globe, opened to show the continents in the inside shell. In the center was a ball representing the heavens, on which was printed, "We Live Inside."

Certainly, the concave earth theory distinguished Koreshanity from every other religion. It insulated the believers, united them spiritually, and comforted them with scientific proof that they lived in a finite world they could understand. And soon their entire group would live physically apart and insulated in their Jerusalem in Florida, where like-minded people would flock and where they could know peace. Until the city was finished, the job of the followers in Chicago was to be patient and to help outsiders see the truth.

It's not clear how many people were persuaded to join by the proof that the earth was concave, but the Koreshans did continue to pull in followers. In auditoriums and on the streets and in the *Flaming Sword*, they proselytized using their slogan, which inspired at least one man. Lou Staton, who would take a leadership position in the Unity years later, remembered the encounter that changed his life.

> I was barbering in the Sherman Hotel in Chicago. I left my room for a walk down State Street. The nineteen-hundred elections were going on. Speakers were hollering about that on one corner and on the other the Salvation Army was holding a meeting, but I wasn't paying anybody any mind. Then I saw a fellow speaking beside a post that had a sign on it—WE LIVE INSIDE. What he said made sense, and I stopped to listen. I bought a copy of the Flaming Sword from a man standing beside the speaker. It was 3 cents but I gave him a nickel and said, "Keep the change." I read it in bed that night. Before I went to sleep I was inside.[30]

Gustave Damkohler homesteaded the land in Estero, Florida, that became the Koreshan settlement. He gave Teed the land for a pittance but later claimed he did so in a religious mania. Teed nicknamed him "Damfooler." This picture was taken in 1902, after he left Florida. Michael A. Wesner, State Archives of Florida, *Florida Memory*, 256305.

Gustave Damkohler's old cottage on the Estero River, 1946. The Koreshans moved it to this location to make way for their city. State Archives of Florida, *Florida Memory*, 256195.

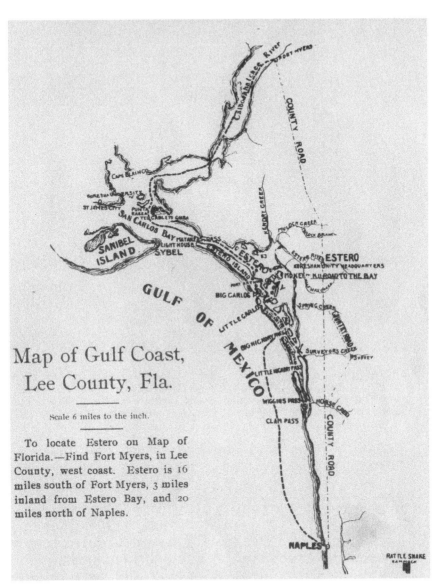

Southwest Florida, ca. 1905. The county road from Estero to Fort Myers (*top*) was deep sand, sometimes impassable, which made traveling by boat more practical. In Herbert and Reeves, *Koreshan Unity Settlement*, 24.

Berthaldine Boomer wrote that she was "nearly unbalanced" over whether to move to Estero, reluctant to leave her family life in Chicago, which included a personal chef. She financed the successful scouting trip to Florida and became one of the Unity's leading women. Harvey, State Archives of Florida, *Florida Memory*, 256270.

Loggerhead turtles, which average 275 pounds, were plentiful and provided meat and eggs for the Koreshans. Emma Norton, Cyrus Teed's sister, is on the left. State Archives of Florida, *Florida Memory*, 257970.

Teed's New Jerusalem would be home to ten million people. The inset at bottom right (see enlargement below) shows the temple at the center of the city, surrounded by the Crystal Sea. By permission of Andy Tetlow, Koreshan State Historic Site, Estero, Florida and the Koreshan Collection. Florida Gulf Coast University Library Archives, Special Collections, and Digital Initiatives, Fort Myers.

Cyrus Teed strolls beside the Estero River. State Archives of Florida, *Florida Memory,* 255231.

Ulysses Grant Morrow invented the rectilineator and led the 1897 expedition to Naples Beach to prove the earth's concavity. He was so obsessed
with his geodetic research that his wife once said his hobby was her only
rival. State Archives of Florida, *Florida Memory*, 256288.

THE RECTILINEATOR

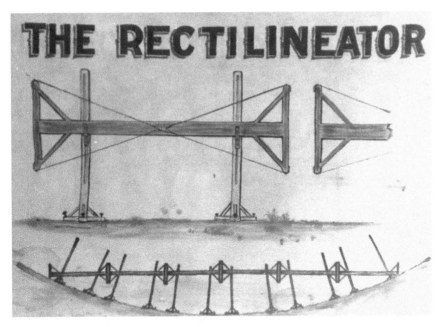

Ulysses Morrow's invention was a double-T square of mahogany designed to make a constant right angle. Its sections were clamped together and advanced down the beach during the geodetic survey. The bottom figure shows the straight line meeting the surface of the concave earth. State Archives of Florida, *Florida Memory*, 257846.

Koreshan Geodetic Survey near Naples, FL - 1897.

The geodetic team poses beside the rectilineator on Naples Beach during the geodetic survey in 1897. In the center the short man in black with the creased hat is Ulysses Morrow. The woman next to him is his wife, Rosa, and in front are their two children. Koreshan Unity Papers (record group 900000, collection N2009-3, box 16, folder 1), State Archives of Florida, Tallahassee.

Cyrus Teed, Victoria Gratia (*center*), and Eleanor Castle exhibited at the Pan American Exposition in Buffalo, New York, in 1901. This booth and the model of the globe have been restored and are in the Art Hall at the Koreshan State Historic Site. State Archives of Florida, *Florida Memory*, 255343.

The Koreshans' general store was the main commercial link with the non-Koreshan community. At the intersection of the Estero River and the county road to Fort Myers, the store sold staples like cereal, along with jams and "risin'" bread from the Koreshan bakery. State Archives of Florida, *Florida Memory*, 257373.

Most of the Koreshan women in Estero lived in dorms like this one, upstairs from the dining hall, pictured between 1905 and 1910. Sheets divided the rooms. Furniture and other comforts of home filled fifteen boxcars when the group moved from Chicago in 1903. State Archives of Florida, *Florida Memory*, 257181.

Koreshan students and teachers pose outside the schoolhouse sometime between 1909 and 1924. Girls and boys were separated. Both studied reading, writing, and arithmetic. In addition, the girls learned sewing, baking, printing, and dressmaking while the boys learned agriculture, beekeeping, and boatbuilding. State Archives of Florida, *Florida Memory*, 256836.

Meals in Estero were formal affairs with tablecloths, china, and crystal. These women sat at the first sisters table. *Left to right*: Emma Norton, Virginia Andrews, Christine Hamilton, Esther Stotler, Evelyn Bubbett, and Etta Silverfriend. State Archives of Florida, *Florida Memory*, 256912.

Koreshans pose in Estero in front of the Planetary Court, where the leading women lived. *First row*: Lou Staton, Evelyn Bubbett, Cyrus Teed (Koresh), Annie Ordway (Victoria), Emma Norton, Andrew Howard. *Second row*: Virginia Andrews, Christine Hamilton, Berthaldine Boomer, Etta Silverfriend, Elizabeth Robinson, Esther Stotler, Addison Graves. *Third row*: Rollin Grey, George Hunt, Henry Silverfriend, Samuel Armour, James H. Bubbett, John Sargent. *Fourth row*: Charles Hunt, George Hussey, Thomas Gay, Ross Wallace, Moses Weaver. State Archives of Florida, *Florida Memory*, 256916.

✳ 10 ✳

In the Outside World

There are souls who are always reaching out, seeking
something more ideal than life as a rule seems to offer.

—Marie McCready McConnell, "Growing-Up Days
in a Celibate Community," 1976

In the spring of 1897, while most of the Koreshans were consumed with the
survey on Naples Beach, Gustave left Estero, walking down the same trail Elwin
took less than a year before. One can imagine the tall sixty-four-year-old with
the bushy beard and one good eye, struggling through the deep sand alone, carrying a few possessions, some matches, and food, and walking away from what
no longer belonged to him—good land in a promising location where a river
crossed a trail. His family had endured many hardships: the cattlemen setting
fires on his property each year; the cows trampling the fences and uprooting
the pineapple buds; the deaths of his wife and children; and his separation from
Elwin, who recorded years later in his memoir adventures of the kind that happen only in Florida. There was the time he and his father hunted turtle eggs at
night and came upon what they thought was a bear, which made them freeze
with fear until they realized the bear was simply a bush blowing in the wind.
They had close brushes with bobcats and panthers. Once devilfish surrounded
Gustave's boat and nearly capsized it, an incident that spooked him so badly
that the family referred to it as "Father's Terrible Experience."[1]

Then came Teed. Gustave had believed him completely—that for the rest
of his life he would be cared for, that Elwin would be educated, and that his
cabin would be at the center of a large city. But now even that cabin belonged
to the Koreshans. He had nothing to show for the work he put into the land. He
wanted it back—all of it.

As soon as he reached Fort Myers, he found the most powerful attorney in town, Louis A. Hendry, and filed suit against the Unity and Teed, demanding the return of his land. In a great irony, his new attorney was the son of Berry Hendry, the man Gustave likely blamed for blocking the Koreshans from getting the beach land where the sawmill was. In other words, one year before, Gustave had raged against a Hendry on behalf of the Koreshans, and now he was fighting the Koreshans with the help of another Hendry.

In the lawsuit, Gustave claimed the Koreshans had defrauded him. When he met them, he stated, he was despondent, verging on insanity. "I was in such a condition of mind," Gustave said in his testimony, "that if you wanted to cut my throat I could not say no."[2]

He testified that they took advantage of his emotional state and pressured him to convert, even before they met. He produced the first letters he received from Victoria and Teed, in which they encouraged him to join the Unity. Teed and his "women sorcerers" had hypnotized him and charmed him with their sweet singing on the porch in Punta Rassa and on the boat trip to Estero, he told the court. He had believed that Teed was the Messiah, that these people were the children of God, and that he was giving his land over to the Kingdom.

Several witnesses in the case supported Gustave's instability. Two doctors and a woman who had deserted the Unity testified in their depositions that Gustave was unbalanced when it came to religion. One of the doctors had known Gustave for ten years and testified that he suffered from religious mania. The female deserter recalled for the court that Teed, Victoria, Boomer, and Mills pressured him for three nights to turn over the twenty acres that were Elwin's. She remembered his words as he roamed the Unity grounds, "screaming and hollering out, 'My God. My God, will I give my son's property away?'"[3]

Gustave testified that Teed was the prince of all great liars—"an imposter, the man of sin, the prophetic person of Anti-Christ . . . a Judas Iscariot because before the deed was written, he crawled out of his bed in the night, kissed me 3 times, when already in his mind was decided how to defraud me and my son." Gustave also testified that Teed made people commit perjury to get land from the government, a direct reference to his own efforts, no doubt.[4]

In their answer to the complaint, the Koreshans denied telling Gustave they were the children of God or that Teed was the messenger of the covenant. They produced the contract that all members were required to sign when they joined the Unity, agreeing to give up all possessions to the group, but Gustave said he never signed it. Furthermore, Gustave claimed that his land was worth six thousand dollars when he surrendered it to them, but the Koreshans contested this, saying it was nearly valueless when they saw it the first time, that he had cleared only an acre and built a log cabin and a shed. Records show that this wasn't true: Gustave had planted trees and crops and had a thriving apiary. He had improved the boat landing, rerouted water to create a dam to trap fish, and created a pool for bathing to keep his family safe from the alligators—all before the Koreshans arrived.[5]

During the Damkohler lawsuit, which Teed referred to as the "Damfooler" case, there was good news in another legal action against Teed. The Thomas Cole trial finally went to court, after many delays. This was the one-hundred-thousand-dollar criminal suit filed in Chicago by the man who charged Teed with alienating the affections of his wife, Annie. At the trial, the most damaging testimony was about the Coles' own marriage and not Teed's interference. Thomas accused Annie of striking him with a knife during a quarrel. And Cole's case was ruined by the revelation that he was seeing another woman. The *Chicago Journal* pointed out the hypocrisy: "While Mr. Cole values his wife's affections at such a high figure, his own affections have been transferred . . . to a second helpmeet."[6]

Teed's attorney moved for a judgment of nonsuit, and it was granted, thus ending one of the many lawsuits Teed faced. The Damkohler case dragged out for a year before the judge delivered a decision: he awarded half of the land to the Koreshans and half to Gustave. But the big winner was Louis A. Hendry, Gustave's attorney, who received eighty acres as payment for his services, leaving Elwin and Gustave with eighty, which they sold to pay off debts and start new lives. Elwin finished high school in Fort Myers and eventually became a sportfishing boat captain in Punta Rassa. Gustave moved back to Missouri, and then to Los Angeles, attracted by the prospect of gold, but found that other prospectors had beaten him to the fortune. He moved to Alaska, also for the gold, and died in Juneau at age eighty. It's not clear what Louis Hendry did with his land, but the Koreshans continued to increase their holdings.[7]

During Gustave's lawsuit, the citizens of Fort Myers began viewing the Koreshans differently—negatively. The revelations in his suit were a likely influence, but there was something else: a comprehensive investigation in the *Pittsburgh Daily News* that found its way to the editors of the *Fort Myers Press*. Headlined "Misery in Estero," the Pittsburgh story went inside the Florida settlement and gave a radically different picture from the one Fort Myers readers had seen just a few months before, portraying the Koreshans as a harmonious, happy bunch. "Misery" was the first public indication of unhappiness inside the camp.[8]

Malnourished Koreshan deserters were showing up in Fort Myers, the

Pittsburgh story said, having walked sixteen miles from Estero. Two men, weak from hunger and barely able to speak English, came into a store asking for meat, according to the storekeeper. He gave them uncooked salt bacon, the paper reported, and the men devoured it. Over the past two years, there had been dozens of deserters, the reporter wrote. Some made it home because their families sent money for train fare, but others were stuck in Fort Myers indefinitely. Those who were strong enough to work took jobs and saved money. Women who had left their husbands to join the community were in dire straits. One of these women, Harriet Wright, was not mentioned in the story, but she left during this time, to Teed's great relief. She had caused considerable trouble for him, he indicated in a letter to a follower in Estero. She had been trying to free other followers, she wrote in a letter to the editor of the *Fort Myers Press*. A year after she left, Teed indicated that he was still trying to fight the "devils" she created in the camp—followers who were dissatisfied and trying to take him down. Wright returned to Denver, Colorado, where she had been an artist before meeting Teed, but now was homeless and destitute, and it was Teed's doing, she wrote.[9]

It's curious that the story was covered by a Pittsburgh reporter rather than by the *Fort Myers Press*, which reprinted it three months after it appeared, but there were reasons for this. Some of the deserters were from Pittsburgh and had returned, disenchanted. Teed had a small following around Pittsburgh. Ulysses Morrow and his wife, for example, had come from Allegheny City. Also, not long before, Pittsburgh readers had followed Teed's exploits in Economy, Pennsylvania, when he was accused of attempting to take over the Economites. This gave the story a "where is he now?" appeal. Unlike the editors in Fort Myers, Pittsburgh editors knew there was a sure story because they knew Teed's background. So the *Daily News* had sent a reporter and an illustrator.

Merchants in Fort Myers told the reporter they were suing Teed for nonpayment of bills. He had taken out credit with several stores when he arrived, but he was slow to pay, they said. Gustave gave similar testimony: "He has a method of creating debts that he is not willing to pay." Shopkeepers cut off his credit, forcing him to take his business elsewhere.

Throughout the years, scores of newspaper stories about Teed and the Koreshans were inaccurate, sometimes wildly so, but this one was on the mark, especially as it concerned Teed's financial troubles. His letters in the archives through the years include instructions to the Koreshan who handled the Unity's business affairs, directing him to pay small amounts to creditors who were making the biggest fuss.[10]

The Pittsburgh reporter and the illustrator ate dinner at the settlement and described the meal as worse than one would get at a boardinghouse—tomato gravy, light bread, boiled fish, and pennyroyal tea devoid of nutrition. The property, on the other hand, was lush and beautiful, the reporter noted, lifting a paragraph of text from the positive *Fort Myers Press* story written the year before, about the terraces leading up from the river, and settees where Koreshans could nap under shade trees and palms; he also used the comparison with Longfellow's Acadia in *Evangeline*.[11]

Yet, he concluded, "the colony dwells in poverty and deprivation, building some of the most remarkable air castles ever heard of." The people were wretches. Converts continued to arrive, replacing those who left, and the reporter attributed this to Teed's magnetism and to false advertising. "Teed is . . . a hustler and a boomer. He was cut out for a land agent, but seems to have missed his calling. He is presenting Estero as a paradise."[12]

Teed himself was not going hungry, the reporter said. He was fed by pretty maidens and ate better fare than the others. He and Victoria spent so much time together that, were they not the leaders of a celibate society, the journalist wrote, "they might be mistaken for lovers." There was also a note that Teed liked Lee County because not many people lived there, and he hoped to gain a political foothold. This information was buried in the middle of the long story.

In Chicago, recent deserters revived Anti-Teedism. One woman in particular, Mattie Watson, who had lived at Beth-Ophrah, catalogued Teed's transgressions and provided an alarmingly long list of deaths at Beth-Ophrah: a man had died of consumption in an unheated room in the middle of winter; a young girl had fallen in love but was confined and, as a result, died of a broken heart; a woman starved to death while she was sick; a girl sharing a cramped room with four others died because her mother was too hypnotized by Teed to save her.[13]

Posters bearing flames alerted people to mass indignation meetings where they could hear stories from "liberated victims" and others. There were two such meetings in Washington Heights, where Mrs. Watson and others spoke and where people demanded Teed's removal. The accusations were the same. Teed was a false messiah, a home wrecker, and a thief. His followers in Chicago survived on watery carrot soup and mush, according to Mrs. Watson, and they wandered the railroad tracks looking for coal to keep warm, the *New York World* reported. Meantime, Victoria and Teed were bedecked in silk and diamonds, it was said. Teed had even presented Victoria with a special birthday present, the *New York Times* and another paper reported—a sword of gold, melted down from several Koreshans' wristwatches.[14]

In response to the indignation gatherings, Teed held his own public meeting—oddly, he brought the Koreshan orchestra with him. It's not clear whether they played for the crowd of four hundred. He denied every charge, saying emphatically that his followers would stay in Washington Heights. This was the plan until the Florida colony was ready and everyone could move.[15]

For whatever reason—perhaps because everything was hearsay, perhaps because the papers had other stories to cover—the flare-up died and, once again, the Chicago Koreshans were left in relative peace.

Marie McCready was thirteen when she and her family moved to Chicago. They had been living in Freedom, Pennsylvania, very close to Economy, when Marie's father, William, heard that Teed was lecturing in nearby Beaver Falls. In spite of controversy, Teed had continued developing a following around Pittsburgh.[16]

William McCready, serious, quiet, and deeply religious, took his entire family to the series of lectures. To Marie, they were tiresome, but she enjoyed the streetcar rides to and from the hall. She and her sister Lovelle entertained themselves by memorizing the advertisements posted inside the streetcars, reading them on the way to the lectures and rehearsing them, silently, while Teed spoke. Many years later, when Marie was in her eighties, she wrote a memoir about her family's experiences in the Unity, and she could still recall the verses for Heinz baked beans and Sapolio soap.

About her father, Marie wrote, "There are souls who are always reaching out, seeking something more ideal than life as a rule seems to offer, even though their own lives might seem . . . to approach as ideal an existence as mortals should expect. Father was one of these." He had investigated many different creeds, she wrote, but none had completely satisfied him until then.[17]

When Teed wrapped up his stint in Beaver Falls, William McCready arranged for him to speak in their town, and he took care of everything, reserving the hall, printing the posters to advertise, and inviting Teed to stay at their house. Marie remembered that her parents sat up with him and talked late into the evening and soon after made plans to move the family to Chicago. It's not clear what McCready saw in Teed, but Teed saw a man running a successful printing business in a small town, no easy feat. He was good at selling ads, Marie wrote. William had also managed a post office, he had been a telegraph operator, and, in his spare time, he liked to weave rugs. In Chicago, Teed would put him to work selling ads for the *Flaming Sword* and proofreading copy. William also liked the outdoors, a promising trait for the life of a Florida settler. Abigail McCready did not want to move to Chicago—she even suggested to William that he go without her—but her desire to keep the family together won out.

The expansion of Beth-Ophrah was not complete when the McCreadys arrived in Chicago, so Marie and her sisters were sent to live in Englewood with the other children and the workers at the printing plant, and her parents lived at Beth-Ophrah. This didn't last long, because Marie's mother protested. She insisted that her daughters live at Beth-Ophrah with her, and Teed accommodated her, though the matron and assistant matron at the mansion were not happy about it. In her memoir, Marie recorded an exchange her mother had related to her. Two women in the living room at Beth-Ophrah were talking about the McCreadys when one said to the other, "I don't know what Doctor was thinking about, bringing in that sickly woman and all those children. She'll die and then we will have the children on our hands."[18]

There's no evidence that Abigail McCready was sickly, though she had suffered a devastating tragedy years before, losing a six-year-old daughter, Margaret. Marie remembered Margaret's long blonde hair, which glinted in the sunlight as her mother braided it or combed it out for Sunday school. One day, the girls were playing when Margaret slipped and fell, hurting her back. Within a few days, she died from her injuries. Losing Margaret might have been a reason Abigail wanted her girls with her at Beth-Ophrah, though Marie and her sister Lovelle were not full-fledged citizens, Marie remembered. She wrote down something the matron's assistant once told her and Lovelle: "Children and dogs are all right in their place, but their place is not in the house." This indeed applied to Duke, the tan mastiff who belonged to the Koreshans. He stayed outdoors, didn't get baths, and was fed kitchen scraps. But there was another dog at Beth-Ophrah, a Great Dane, who got the opposite treatment. Queenie belonged to two wealthy sisters, and she was kept indoors and given regular baths, meals, and walks.[19]

Marie and Lovelle loved the adventure of being in Chicago. Too young to work, they enjoyed great freedom, riding their bikes all over the neighborhood. On the weekends, they biked with their father, who had never ridden a bike before they came to Chicago, but he learned how especially for them, so that he could go with them on longer Sunday rides.

The only time of the week Marie didn't enjoy was the Sunday sermon. Teed never spoke for less than two hours, and he was no easier to understand than he had been in Beaver Falls. Sometimes to occupy herself, Marie mentally diagrammed the grammar of his winding sentences to practice for English class, or she thought about a book she was reading, or she planned new dresses she wanted to sew. She wished she could get out of going to the sermons, she wrote. "But they were a must, so we all went."[20]

Even so, she was very fond of Teed, as many children were, with the notable exception of Elwin Damkohler. Teed was kind to Marie and Lovelle. As he had done with Allen Andrews all those years ago in Binghamton, he took time to talk to them and expressed interest in what they did. Some afternoons, Marie and Lovelle waited for him to come home, and they would run across the lawn at Beth-Ophrah to greet him with hugs. He slung an arm around each of them, and they walked across the grounds together to the mansion. Sometimes Victoria was with him, and, Marie recalled, she wasn't the hugging type. "Standoff-ish" and "finished" were the words Marie used to describe her. Victoria showed more affection to her Persian and Angora cats than to people. She seemed irritated by the younger girls and frequently corrected their speech and table manners. She did like the older girls, who were better behaved and who took classes from her in drawing, painting, embroidery, and singing. Marie's oldest sister, Catharine, was Victoria's best voice pupil and therefore a favorite.[21]

Marie and Lovelle were made to sit on the porch while dinner was prepared, not allowed inside the house until the second dinner bell was sounded. One day, the two sisters were shivering outside when Teed happened along. Marie recorded their conversation in her memoir. "Why aren't you girls inside where it is warm?" Teed asked.[22]

The girls explained to him that they were not allowed in the house. "Well, I know where you are allowed," he said. "Come with me." He took them into his study, where there was a bright fire and a certain brown mastiff dog: "Stretched out in luxurious comfort lay Duke, doggy smell and all," Marie wrote. And after this incident, Teed instructed the matron to allow Marie and Lovelle into the house at any time.[23]

One day, an exciting guest arrived at Beth-Ophrah, an ample woman in an elegant black dress that gathered at the neck. Her two scarves—one orchid, one white—flowed nearly to her waist, and her bleached hair was pinned neatly back, revealing a mysterious scar that ran beneath one eye and upward to her temple.[24]

Madame Diss Debar, as she called herself, was a friend of Berthaldine Boomer. She was invited to live at Beth-Ophrah and given the "red carpet treatment," Marie remembered. Madame held court in her room, regaling the older girls with her tales of traveling the world, her time in India, and her many supernatural experiences. She was a princess, a baroness, a countess, and the godchild of Pope Pius IX, she claimed at different points in her life.[25]

Diss Debar was none of these things; she was an Irish woman from Kentucky and one of Chicago's most notorious confidence women. By the time she met Teed, she had been imprisoned twice for fraud—serving two years in Joliet Prison and six months in the penitentiary on Blackwell's Island. The latter was for defrauding an elderly man and getting his Madison Avenue townhouse in New York.

The Koreshans knew about her past, but she was repentant when she appeared on the steps of Beth-Ophrah, a follower later wrote in the *Flaming Sword*. According to this account, Diss Debar poured out her confessions and begged to be let in. "She declared that she had never been honest in her life, but that now she was honest and desired to be saved." The Koreshans were willing to save her, they said, and they took her in out of pity.[26]

Just as likely, they took her in because she announced her intention to give the Unity a large sum of money. Apparently, Teed was not bothered that Madame might not have come by the money honestly.

Teed probably found Diss Debar spiritually compatible. She practiced Theosophy, which is a mix of mysticism, Buddhism, Zoroastrianism, Swedenborgism, and others. Part of Theosophy's appeal was that it promised access to unknowable worlds, and it didn't require that followers abandon existing beliefs. Teed had drawn from (or outright plagiarized) Theosophy in developing his doctrines, and Victoria had been a Theosophist before meeting Teed. The Theosophical Society was cofounded in 1875 by a Russian woman named Madame Helena Petrovna Blavatsky. Among Madame Diss Debar's many claims was that she was the reincarnation of Blavatsky and, as such, carried Blavatsky's astral essence.[27]

Marie's older sister, Catharine, was one of the girls who visited Madame in her room at Beth-Ophrah. When the McCreadys heard what Catharine was doing, they warned her to stay away, and they were right to be concerned. Marie wrote that Diss Debar pressured Catharine and another girl to leave the Unity and go into the city with her. When Teed learned of this, he was enraged.[28]

Things turned sour quickly. The Koreshans caught Diss Debar stealing a gold necklace and a diamond ring, which she pawned, and they had the pawn ticket to prove it. One day, Marie and Lovelle were playing outside when there was a ruckus; Madame came crashing down the kitchen stairs, screaming and crying. Her orchid and white scarves were missing, Marie noticed, and her yellow hair fell around her ruddy face in short wisps. She was drunk.[29]

"The next morning, she was hustled away, not to return," Marie wrote.[30]

In the fall of 1898, the *Fort Myers Press* reported that another colony might come to Lee County—the Order of the Crystal Sea, to be located next door to the

Edison estate on seven thousand acres. The divine city would be home to a people known as Fruitarians, who subsisted on fruit and nuts and practiced celibacy. Their leader was Princess Editha Loleta, who claimed to be the daughter of King Ludwig of Bavaria and his mistress, Lola Montez, the dancer thought to have inspired the saying "Whatever Lola wants, Lola gets."

Loleta was none other than Madame Diss Debar, who had left Beth-Ophrah six months before and reinvented herself again, dropping the name Diss Debar from her long list and marrying a man named Frank Jackson, the alleged owner of the property next to Edison's. The papers reported that Loleta met Jackson in Chicago at her attorney's office while settling the estate of one of her late husbands. Jackson was eleven years younger than she and one-third of her weight, tipping the scales at 112 pounds, one paper reported, compared with her 300, calling to mind the nursery rhyme about Jack Sprat and his wife.[31]

The *New York Herald* covered their marriage in New Orleans—a celibate marriage, Loleta assured reporters—and the plans for the Order of the Crystal Sea in Florida. The reporter noted the same scarves Marie McCready remembered so clearly, putting them right in the story's lead: "[Loleta] shrugged her fat shoulders under their draperies of white and purple," as she explained the plans for her new colony, which would revolutionize the world. Her theology was suspiciously close to Teed's: God is biune; modern-day marriage is prostitution; and immortality is possible ("I will never die," she said).[32]

She and Jackson were going to Fort Myers to prepare for the arrival of their Fruitarians, after which they would continue to India to perfect "an anthropostic battery, through the instrumentality of which we propose to materialize the personality of the Diety."[33]

This idea, too, appears to have been Teed's. He had informed his followers that their energy would create a friction that would cause the battery in his head to explode, at which point he would flow into Victoria.

The princess and her diminutive husband arrived in Fort Myers with a New Orleans millionaire, and the three of them settled downtown. It soon became clear that Loleta hadn't come to Fort Myers to plan a colony. Instead, she was there to warn the people of Fort Myers about Cyrus Teed. "Silence on my part would be little less than compounding a felony," she told the *Fort Myers Press*, which printed her every allegation—at least, the allegations that were fit for print.[34]

Soon after she had moved into Beth-Ophrah, Loleta claimed, a young Koreshan girl alerted her that Teed was mistreating the girl. When Loleta began paying closer attention to his activities, she observed all manner of heinous doings, she told the *Press*—abortion, self-pollution, and growths on the young

Koreshans' necks due to Teed's medical experiments. Several of the Koreshan women shoplifted, she said, in order to supply Victoria Gratia with finery. Teed had murdered Berthaldine Boomer's husband in order to collect his insurance money. This, Loleta said, she had heard directly from Mrs. Boomer.

In Estero, Loleta had learned, the followers' health was deteriorating, and the young people were like wild animals, chasing each other for sex. The Estero post office was being used for fraudulent purposes. She urged the county commission to investigate Teed. "Prudence demands . . . the extirpation of this modern octopus from your midst," she said.[35]

Teed fired back in the paper, explaining why Editha Loleta and her husband were attacking him: in New Orleans, they had lured the millionaire they were now traveling with by misrepresenting themselves as Koreshans and offering to take him to Estero. This man intended to become a Koreshan, Teed said, but Loleta and Jackson intended instead to spirit him away to India, along with one of the attractive Koreshan girls. Teed remembered that in Chicago, Diss Debar attempted to take Catharine McCready and another girl into the city, with impure intentions.

"Their little game was blocked," Teed wrote. So Princess Loleta and her husband now sought revenge, he said. The Koreshans told the *Press* about Princess Loleta's crimes and her incarcerations in Joliet State Prison and on Blackwell's Island.[36]

This was one of the liveliest stories the young newspaper had seen. The coverage prompted the disgruntled Harriet Wright, the artist from Denver, to write to the editor a second time. When she lived at Beth-Ophrah and in Estero, she wrote, she saw Teed fondling and kissing the women and abusing them at his pleasure. Beth-Ophrah was a harem, she said, and Teed was an "oily-tongued monster." She had heard him say that "he must have 'friction' to help get up his 'Biological Battery.'"[37]

Princess Loleta's next step was to go before the Lee County commission, where she accused Teed of crimes that weren't printable, the *Press* reported. Lending weight to her claims was a Mrs. Catherine West, an ex-Koreshan who testified against Teed in the Damkohler trial. She corroborated Loleta's accusations and told commissioners that Teed had been living a double life since he arrived in Estero. Early on, West said, Teed told the Koreshans not to reveal to the people of Lee County that he was posing as the Lord Jesus. He also announced to them his plans to bring enough men to Estero to outvote the people of Lee. To the citizens of Fort Myers, this probably seemed as likely as the tales of growths on the Koreshans' necks.[38]

But even if one-tenth of Loleta's claims were true, the *Press* reported, "he ought to have been in the clutches of the law, long ago." The paper concluded the story by expressing indignation over the possibility that Teed was deceiving people and marring the good name of Lee County. But there's no evidence that the county commission took any action.[39]

Getting no satisfaction, Loleta moved on and, before long, made news in London, where she and her husband, who had taken the names Swami Laura Horos and Theodore Horos, were jailed for fraud. During their trial, inspectors found that the couple had marked up several pamphlets from the Koreshan Unity and readied them for printing in order to promote their beliefs and organization, the Theocratic Unity. Doubtless, Teed felt vindicated. After all the times he had been accused of taking others' ideas, someone was getting her comeuppance for stealing his.

One last note: Teed may have been telling the truth about the millionaire Loleta brought to Fort Myers. There's evidence he supported Koreshanity, at least for a short time. The year after the Loleta ruckus, he paid Teed's travel for a visit to New Orleans.[40]

✳ 11 ✳

At Last

Teed's main man in Estero was George Hunt, who was among the very first Koreshans to come to Florida from Chicago. George and his brother, Charlie, had grown up in Oregon, which is where they were living when they somehow learned about Teed. George was tall and had blue eyes and tightly curly, thinning hair, and he dressed neatly in khakis and boots. He clerked at the general store, worked as a boat captain, relieved Allen in the post office, and hunted. He played the organ and sang tenor in the quartet, appreciated a good joke, and knew how to handle emergencies. In short, he held Estero together during the early years.

Teed's gratitude was evident; he addressed him as "My Dear George, Good and Faithful" and told him, "You have accomplished a great work and one that will be known through the ages." Teed often told George to encourage the followers and keep their spirits up.[1]

In 1899, when there were about thirty followers in Estero, Teed wrote George that he expected an influx soon and that they had received applications from people all over the country, but he was hesitant to allow them in until he was sure they understood the Koreshans' purpose. Also, he didn't want to send a large group to Estero until he could be there himself. And he was impatient to be there.[2]

Stopping him was a stubborn lawsuit, filed by a female doctor in Boston demanding repayment of a $3,500 loan, which was part of the money Teed used to build Estero—one hundred thousand in today's currency. Dr. Vienna Parsons produced promissory notes that Teed had signed, which gave the suit more validity than others where Teed claimed that people willingly gave over their money. Teed said he signed Parsons's notes under duress and imprisonment.

The suit dragged on, taking considerable time and energy. Adding to Teed's frustration was that it kept him from traveling for lectures, because he could be summoned in the case on short notice.

There were business troubles in Estero, too, which George was trying to manage—someone was suing Teed for two thousand dollars over a boat, and another suit was looming. But Teed always seemed confident that things would work out; it's clear in his letters to George. He mentioned that a wealthy family was about to join the Unity and that two current followers were settling an estate and that he would be able to send money to Estero before long. Until then, George would need to do his best. Teed told George frequently that he trusted his judgment.

Business and financial trouble seemed more of an inconvenience for Teed than a cause for alarm. "The Master betrayed no concern whatsoever over the needs of the morrow," one follower wrote. When Teed had money, he spent it. When he didn't, he thought nothing of running up credit. Teed's spendthrift ways mystified and likely frustrated many followers, but Henry Silverfriend, Teed's longtime friend and financier, felt certain that Teed had a strategy. Henry believed Teed kept the society in debt so that the followers would rise to the challenge of one day surmounting it.[3]

The Fort Myers paper reported that Teed had moved assets around in the past to avoid paying debts. It's true that he had done this previously, but at this particular time, as the Koreshans were settling Estero, his letters to George indicate that there weren't assets to move.[4]

Teed told George he was contemplating bankruptcy protection—"which will place [a creditor] just where he ought to be"—though there's no evidence that he ever filed. Teed had also applied to the government to receive a pension for his service in the Civil War, claiming disability from the paralysis caused by heat stroke during the march in Virginia in 1863. Records indicate that the government rejected his request.[5]

When the Parsons case was finally settled and the sheriff in Chicago came to collect the $2,200 judgment, Teed declared that he owned little more than his clothes—no cash or receivables.[6]

It's clear from Teed's letters that he trusted George more than he trusted anyone, even Victoria, in spite of the fact that she was the appointed Pre-Eminent of the Unity and presumably the person who would be his stand-in. The only other person he had trusted so much was his late friend Abie Andrews. But his relationship with George was very different from his friendship with Abie. The letters to Abie, decades before, were best friend letters, in which he wrote about his uncertainties, worked out his tenets, shared the smallest daily troubles, and showed insecurity, like his worry over whether Abie's wife, Jennie, was committed to the movement. The letters to George show the evolution of Teed as a confident prophet. He did not discuss his personal life. Even when Teed's father, Jesse, died—at Beth-Ophrah at age eighty-four of natural causes—there's no record that he mentioned it to George. While Teed acknowledged the troubles in the community and expressed concern, he didn't ask George's advice and didn't show uncertainty. Instead, he gave direction and solutions, though sometimes the "solution" was that he trusted George to make the right decision.[7]

By 1900, the followers in Estero were grumbling that George and Emma were too strict. This complaint made its way to Teed, who also learned that two colonists were plotting to start their own group based on Teed's doctrines. He wrote George, telling him and Emma to be less rigid and to include the others in the Unity's decisions. "We cannot force people to do what is not in their hearts to do," Teed wrote. "Hold the society together by the spirit of liberty and love," he wrote. "There is no other way."[8]

In Chicago, the colonists were sacrificing as they waited to move to Estero. Allen Andrews, who went back to the city for a while, noted that the Koreshans spent all their money on coal and on doctor bills to treat winter illnesses. "Until one has lived in Florida several years," Allen wrote, "he never realizes under what unhealthful . . . conditions northern people live during the long winter months."[9]

Accustomed to the peacefulness of Florida, Allen had forgotten how noisy Chicago was. He recalled arriving at Polk Street Station and feeling the bracing air and hearing the screeching of the elevated train. The city was bleak, loud, and stuffy, he wrote.[10]

The Koreshans had to leave Beth-Ophrah, unable to afford it any longer. They rented smaller quarters in an old opera house in Englewood, and they kept a fire burning in the printing composition room to keep from freezing, Allen remembered. They still faced sporadic opposition from Chicago's citizens. In one instance, Koreshans were pelted with eggs while preaching on a street corner.

The Chicago followers were eager to get to Florida, where the reports from the settlers were positive. Unlike in Chicago, where money was required for everything, much of the food in Florida was free. There was meat, thanks in part to George and Charlie Hunt. True to their last name, the brothers were expert hunters, and they trained the young boys to bring home wild turkeys, deer, duck, and razorback hogs. Loggerhead turtles were excellent sources of meat and eggs, but harder to catch than one might think. "They have such powerful jaws that I have known one to snap a one-inch plank into slivers," Allen Andrews wrote.[11]

The Koreshans' gardens flourished. The *Fort Myers Press* reported "thrifty buds" in the ground, pineapples, sweet potatoes, guinea grass, and a nice field of sugar cane, which they made into syrup, using a horse-powered grinder, and boiled for various uses, including peanut brittle. At cooking "bees," the women sat around the tables in the dining hall and pared potatoes, deseeded guavas, and shelled peas.[12]

But even though food was plentiful, it was a hard living, and the Koreshans changed the tone of the recruitment literature around that time. In the early years, they had promised followers a paradise in Florida. But now, the literature was more honest: "People coming to us in Estero come to a 'simon pure' pioneer life, one of strenuosity and sacrifice . . . we have not yet reduced labor to a luxury, for our people are performing some drudgery."[13]

In 1900, Marie McCready and her sisters Lovelle and Catharine came to Estero with a group from Chicago. Their parents stayed behind, planning to join them later. By now, Marie and Catharine were in their late teens; Lovelle was only eleven, but the McCreadys trusted the larger Koreshan family to take care of her. Before the girls left, their mother, Abigail, took them shopping in the city to prepare for the trip. She bought them new washcloths and towels, and each of them got a brush, comb, and mirror set. Marie remembered hers years later. They were adorned with little turquoise-blue china hearts set in a silver filigree ornament—a small reminder of the city life she left to come to Estero.[14]

It was most likely autumn when they boarded the train for Florida with several other Koreshans. The girls had been thrilled about the adventure of going to Estero, but when their mother took them to the station, Marie and her sisters were struck with last-minute dread, wanting to back out and stay in Chicago. Abigail promised she would follow soon, and they got on the train, weeping as it pulled out of the station.

They traveled in coach for the three-night trip, not able to afford sleeper cars. Most of the Koreshans in the group were young, Marie wrote, so they didn't mind sleeping sitting up. They sang to pass the time. They ate picnic style. When the train stopped for long enough, they toured the towns. Marie's mood had improved by the time they reached Florida. She was enthralled by the fruit trees and palms and warmer weather.

At the end of the rail line, they boarded a boat for the night trip to Estero

Island. It was Marie's first time on a sailboat. "The soft flapping of the big white sails, the full moon above and its long reflection on the rippling water made it all seem to be part of a story instead of something that was happening to us." Adding to the dream quality, Teed had joined them for the trip up the river the next day. She later wrote about the experience.[15]

He exclaimed, "Isn't it beautiful?" But Marie didn't think so. Not completely. Certain things about the place, she wrote, were beautiful. The sky was a brilliant blue with wispy clouds, very different from gray Chicago. The air was salty and clean. But she was disappointed in how plain everything was. The mangrove islands that others had talked about were just clusters of roots clutching the mud. She had expected actual islands, but these were good for nothing but snakes, she wrote.[16]

She remembered that the pine trees were pretty and that the eucalyptus trunks appeared to have been rubbed to a smooth finish. There were palm trees of all different kinds, clumps of bamboo that looked to her like ostrich plumes, and umbrella trees. But after years of hearing how wonderful the city at Estero would be, she arrived to find that there was no city. The buildings, most of them, were "ugly, black, unfinished shells," she recalled. The contrast of manmade ugliness and natural beauty was pronounced, she wrote.[17]

But the natural beauty overwhelmed her at times. There was a freeze during Marie's first winter in Florida. It was nowhere near as severe as the Great Freeze that ruined the groves in central Florida, but the men weren't taking chances. They worked through the night to protect the groves, lighting fires in the rows to keep the young trees warm. Marie watched from her third-floor dorm room, seeing the men move along the rows, pink clouds of smoke rising above the groves. It was too beautiful, she said, to sleep.[18]

She and her older sister, Catharine, lived upstairs in the dining hall, which Marie wrote was the only presentable, finished building. Lovelle, whom she was much closer to than Catharine, was sent to live in the children's cottage. Upstairs, instead of walls separating the rooms, sheets hung from the ceiling between the beds. Marie and Catharine took down the sheet between their rooms to make one big room. They slept on mattresses stuffed with pine needles, which gave the beds a woodsy smell, but which needed fluffing each morning. This was done by reaching into a hole in the ticking. The needles poked their hands and wrists, producing measle-like bumps.

The beds were draped with cheesecloth suspended from a light wooden frame. Often, she woke to find mosquitoes and sand flies clinging to the cloth, and more than once, a bat hanging onto the outside.

Every room had a rocking "chair," made from barrels cut in half, which didn't allow for full rocking. "[We] had always been in the habit of really rocking in the chairs we had known before, but were not long in learning that this would land us on the floor." They had to settle for the "little mincing motions the barrels would allow." Many of the women painted their barrels for decoration.[19]

Breakfast was at 7:00 a.m.; dinner at noon; and supper at 6:00 p.m. Someone rang the bell outside the hall to call everyone to meals. Then each table was called separately—"first sisters," "second sisters," and so on, followed by the men's tables. Brothers and sisters were segregated for meals, except for Victoria and Teed, who sat together at the main table when they were in town. Marie worked in the dining hall, cleaning up after dinner. The linen tablecloths needed to be shaken out and laundered, the silverware polished, the plates and glasses cleaned and put away.

She had happy memories of her first year in Florida. The young Koreshans spent most of their time outdoors, collecting wild huckleberries and mushrooms. They picnicked together, always with a chaperone. At the dock, they took off their shoes and dangled their feet in the water, clear enough for them to see the large gar and sheepshead, which Marie described as looking like convicts in striped suits, and jackfish, whose yellow bodies caught the sun.

Being from Chicago, most of the Koreshans didn't know how to swim, and they learned once they came to Florida. The girls made their own swimsuits—knee-length dresses requiring seven to ten yards of wool or flannel. Marie made hers from a red blanket. It had short sleeves, bloomers that covered her knees, and a skirt she buttoned around her waist when she wasn't in the water. She was proud of it because she patterned it so that the sleeves and skirt were trimmed in black using the stripes at either end of the blanket.

The men swam on separate days, and didn't wear swimsuits. Sometimes, the girls would slip out of their suits once they got into the river, with one girl standing on the bank to keep watch. Marie later wrote about the joy she felt shooting through the water without clothes weighing her down.

They rowed in the river, sometimes in the early morning when the river was misty and dew dripped from the trees. Alligators often slid into the river and glided past, close enough that the animals' wakes gently rocked the boat. In the evenings, a boy who played cornet brought his instrument along and played for them on the water. On moonless nights, they fire fished, using the technique Allen learned from Elwin years before.

In pictures from this time, the young people look happy and carefree. Photos show young girls costumed for a drama, band members in crisp uniforms, teenagers posed on the beach. They are smiling for the camera. "Their faces are not those of religious fanatics," one scholar wrote. And most of the children were *not* religious fanatics. They hadn't chosen to be Koreshans. They volunteered to go to Estero for the weather and for the adventure, as opposed to their beliefs.[20]

By contrast, the adults have serious expressions. They are posed in rows, a few of them staring at the camera inquisitively, their heads slightly tilted. They are neatly dressed, the men in laundered white shirts and jackets with ties. The women wear white or light-colored long skirts and shirtwaists with long sleeves to protect them from the sun, and their hair is pinned into buns. Teed and Victoria stand with them, in the center of the front row.

Even if Victoria weren't at the center of most group pictures beside Teed, she would be easy to identify. All of the women except for her wore lightweight fabrics with a loose weave, suited for the outdoors in Florida. Victoria's dresses were made of richer fabrics and were more fashionable—puffed sleeves, lace collars. Her hair framed her forehead, rather than being pulled away from her face. She wasn't dressed for hoeing a garden or even for setting a table in the dining hall.

Victoria spent more and more time in Estero, and as she did, a few followers questioned why she was not the one running the settlement and overseeing George and Emma. These followers reminded her of her speech about a woman's rightful dominion years ago and of her coronation at the first Lunar Festival, where Teed said that she was the leader. They counseled her to replace George as the manager, and to replace Emma, Teed's sister, who was the matron.

Teed heard about this and wrote to George that these followers were filling Victoria's head with rot. "There is a dense ignorance," Teed wrote, "of the whole purport of the Koreshan system." Teed told George he had not given Victoria absolute power. "Every person on the face of the earth shall depend upon the baptism from the Messenger before there can be any exercise of authority not subject to the mandate of Cyrus." He added, "No man nor woman is compelled to accept my authority. None need follow me if not awake to the importance and character of my mission." As a postscript, he added that George should read the letter to the whole community if he saw fit.[21]

Teed never said a negative word about Victoria. Instead, he was angry at the people who were trying to take advantage of her and wrest control for themselves, as he saw it. He defended her fiercely, reflecting his devout belief that he and Victoria, as a mother-father deity, would redeem the followers.

His biggest frustration seems to have been getting the followers to respect and obey Victoria. Many times, he lashed out at the members who opposed her or who tried to use her. Though the Koreshans followed him willingly, most of them didn't have the same respect for Victoria. They loved him, worshipped him, but not her. Some of the Koreshans even mistrusted her; in one apocry-phal account, she was fated to murder him.

Teed spoiled her, and, as a result, some followers—and many reporters—believed they were lovers. There's no conclusive evidence for this. Victoria did leave her husband to join Teed, but she kept in touch with her husband for a while. There's a record of her visiting him and caring for him once when he was sick. But ultimately Victoria and her husband divorced.

She didn't keep journals, or if she did, they don't survive. If there were let-ters between her and Teed, they no longer exist. She wrote pronouncements, speeches, and articles, but these are focused on the doctrines of Koreshanity and reveal little about her personally.

There is one tantalizing letter. It's undated, incomplete, and written by Victo-ria, who was by then in Estero, to a Koreshan woman at Beth-Ophrah. Victoria enclosed a letter from Teed, which doesn't survive, and referred to it when she wrote the following: "I am heartbroken. I gave up all for him, and what have I will I have not got him. What I shall do I don't know." Victoria begged for a train ticket to Chicago.[22]

Her language could be romantic attachment, but it could also reflect reli-gious devotion. At any rate, the trouble was soon healed, apparently, as Victoria stayed on. George Hunt wrote much later that Victoria was a great trial to Teed and that those who were close to Teed knew it. "He was not ignorant of her frailties and short-comings; but he knew enough about mortality to make al-lowance for her weaknesses as well as ours."[23]

Most of 1902 was especially rough for the Koreshans. In Chicago, Mr. Hilliard, the millionaire who sold them Beth-Ophrah, was on the verge of suing Teed, and had hired someone in Fort Myers to track Teed down. Teed gave George a specific message for this man: "Say to him that I do not owe Hilliard one cent."[24]

In Estero, the Koreshans were suffering from the hard work of beating back the wilderness. Some were tired to the point of exhaustion and suffering from headaches. A few of them had festering warts, which they referred to as Florida sores for lack of a better name. The sores looked like mosquito bites, but they grew and spread.

The Koreshans lost their dentist, Charles Addison Graves, who left the Unity and showed up in Fort Myers accusing Teed of some unspecified injustice, tell-ing anyone who would listen that he had cut all ties to the Koreshans and was moving to Cuba. Before long, some of the followers had tooth trouble. Teed wrote to George, "Tell the folks who want their teeth fixed that I think an arrangement will be completed soon for its accomplishment."[25]

Teed heard that the colonists were complaining about George. "I want to caution you," Teed wrote him, "to be on the watch of yourself regarding the utmost consideration for all the wants of our people. Hear them particularly and give ample explanations why all wants are not met. Give the people all to understand that we will meet all their wants always when we can. Do not be impatient nor seemingly unkind nor neglectful."[26]

He closed the letter, "How are the sick? Write me at once."[27]

When Teed spoke in Fort Myers, he didn't let on that anything was amiss. The very same week that Teed instructed George to go to the bank immediately and deposit funds to cover some checks he had written, Teed boasted to the people of Fort Myers that he would bring thousands of people to Estero. The *Fort Myers Press* responded that the county commission should make him an immigration agent for Lee County. The town of Fort Myers couldn't compete with Teed's claims of a New Jerusalem the editors of the *Press* wrote snarkily, adding that Fort Myers's best enticement for newcomers was that grapefruit yields were two hundred dollars per tree. The *Press*'s editors wrote that the promise of big grapefruit yields was "a flea bite" compared to owning a share of utopia.[28]

For several days, Marie had no energy. As she swept around her assigned tables in the dining room after dinner, she felt so weak she could only drag the broom, and one sister fussed at her. There couldn't be anything wrong with someone who had such rosy cheeks, she said.[29]

"Mother would have noticed at once that all was not well," Marie wrote. But her mother was still in Chicago. Marie wanted to be with her, but Teed was making plans for the Chicagoans to move to Estero as soon as possible, so it didn't make sense financially to send her back. What she longed for, more than Chicago, was to be in Pennsylvania with her grandmother in the house she remembered fondly, where the cookie jar was always full. As she felt worse and worse, she thought of her grandmother more often, knowing she would be taken in and well cared for. So Marie wrote her and asked for a train ticket home. She knew her grandmother had saved a little money for them for emergencies after she visited Chicago and saw that they didn't always have what they needed.[30]

One day, climbing the two flights of stairs from the kitchen to her room, Marie needed to take breaks to rest. The next day, reaching for dishes to reset her tables, she fainted. She woke up in her bed, surrounded by several girls watching her fearfully.

Typhoid. Five other girls in the dorm came down with it too. With more people in Estero and a dry spell, the cisterns had gone dry. A new well was dug, but it wasn't deep enough, and the water was contaminated, leading to the outbreak.

Teed's sister Emma took care of Marie. She had learned eclectic medicine long ago in Syracuse when she and Teed practiced together, and in Estero, she grew herbs outside of her cabin. Marie didn't like Emma because she was strict. "She seemed always to be telling us that we could not do something we wanted to do or giving us some job we did not want to do," Marie wrote.

Emma's treatments were anything but gentle. She gave Marie an emetic, followed by ginger water, and then stayed to be sure Marie took the medicine. "She stood there, tiny and mild looking, but uncompromising in her will."

Two girls with typhoid went into a delirium right away. They were strong girls, Marie remembered—Nora, a big laughing Irish girl, and Minna, who was Marie's age but much larger and husky. Two or three women stayed by Nora's bed all of the time, because she constantly tried to get up, and she had tremendous strength. Both girls cried out constantly, Nora singing "Home Sweet Home" at the top of her lungs—so loud, Marie said, it rang in her brain when she closed her eyes. Both Nora and Minna died of the fever.

Marie kept her eyes open, willing herself to stay sane. Someone sat with her around the clock. Her sister Catharine whistled to her to pass the time; she was a good whistler, but Marie had a hard time enduring the noise. Another woman kept her entertained with stories, but they were gruesome, part of a long serial about men and women who were captured by Turkish bandits who beat or killed their victims. Marie was grateful for the company, so she listened.

Summer came and when the weather turned hot, Marie was tormented by enormous horseflies. Her attendants spent hours waving them away from her bed with the mosquito switches the Koreshans wove from shredded palm or palmetto leaves. These had a loop for hanging around the wrist so they could be carried all the time. When the insects were especially bad, the attendants let down the cheesecloth and tucked it underneath Marie's mattress, which made her unbearably hot.

With the heat came afternoon rains. One day, while Marie was confined to bed, lightning struck the building. A violet light shot right past her bed, she remembered, and exited through the window. It started a fire. The men brought pails of water, and, helped by the heavy rain, they extinguished it. From that point on, Marie was terrified of even the lightest rain.

Marie's sister Catharine wired their mother and told her to come immediately. Abigail boarded the train for the three-day trip, and then the boat to Fort Myers. There was a woman on the boat with her child. Making conversation, the woman asked Marie's mother where she was headed, and when she answered Estero, the woman was alarmed. Abigail related their conversation to Marie, who recorded it.

"Why, that is where that terrible community is," the young woman said.

"In what way are they terrible?" Marie's mother asked. "I have lived with the community in Illinois for almost four years and have never found anything wrong with them."

"The young woman stared at her a minute," Marie wrote. "Then, clutching the child to her as if to shield it from something evil, moved to the other side of the boat, refusing to even look in Mother's direction the remainder of the trip.

"The captain of the launch, a kindly, weather-beaten old man, who had listened to the conversation without taking part, now remarked comfortingly, 'Don't mind her, Ma'am; some folks just talk.'

"But are the Unity folks disliked by their neighbors and people in Fort Myers?" asked Mother.

"Well, ma'am, I figure it this way. The Unity folks mind their own business, which is more that [sic] some others do. I only know the men who meet my boat to send or get cargo or transfer passengers, but they always seemed all right to me. I figure there are two kinds of people who talk against the Unity. One is the politicians who don't get elected. You know the Unity is making itself felt in politics now because they all vote, and they seem to vote the same way. Then there is the young men. The Doctor has some danged pretty girls down there and he won't let the young men come to see them, and that makes the young men mad."

Abigail stayed at Marie's side except to go downstairs for meals. Marie dreamed of Pennsylvania and fought delirium. She heard voices in the dining hall and "the rattle of pots, pans and dishes in the kitchen and dining room, and the calls of the cooks and servers at meal times: 'first sisters,' 'third sisters,' 'seventh brothers'; the first and second bells ringing; the prayer being read before each meal. People walking, walking, walking on the three bare floors of the building and the constant murmur of voices, people calling to each other outside . . . and the continual striking of clocks." Each sister in the dorm had a clock—striking on the hour and half hour and some on the quarter hour—none of them in sync. Marie and her mother moved to a small cottage so that Marie could have peace.

Twelve weeks after she fainted in the kitchen, she sat up in bed for the first time, propped by pillows. After that, she got steadily better, but she still wanted to go home to Pennsylvania, even though it would mean leaving her parents and sisters.

A booming citrus harvest turned things around in Estero in late 1902 and early 1903. Teed arranged for a drilling crew and boring equipment, and soon, there were deep artesian wells that brought uncontaminated water to the surface. It smelled like rotten eggs, but it was good water, and they got used to the taste. The followers compared it with eating onions; the more you ate, the less you noticed the taste. And they found that letting the water aerate made it better.

Upstream, the non-Koreshan growers who had planted after the Great Freeze now had fruit-bearing trees, and there was plenty of demand in the North. The Koreshans' citrus packinghouse was busy, men and women loading crates with ripe fruit. The colony, as planned, was ready to profit. They had their own fruit to sell, and a boat works for repairing boats, and their first "power boat," a wood-burning paddlewheel steamer they christened *Victoria*, captained by George Hunt. Some of the outside growers hired them to ship citrus down the Estero River and up the coast to market.

There had been trouble in Estero between the Koreshans and non-Koreshans, but it seemed to be over by this point. The squabble concerned the post office, which had been on Koreshan land since 1895. The non-Koreshans petitioned Washington to have it moved off of the settlement, saying it had been obtained by fraud, perhaps referring to the contested beach land. The non-Koreshans got their wish, and the post office moved. It irked the Koreshans, and it enraged Teed. But with the citrus harvest going strong, everyone needed to work together.

In addition to income from citrus, there were infusions from new members and from an inheritance that two followers received and turned over to the Unity. By the beginning of 1903, Teed decided it was finally time for all of the Chicagoans to move to Estero. In preparation, the settlers beautified the grounds, hiring a crew to help, digging sunken gardens and mounds and planting more shrubs and flowers and widening the walkways. The children moved out of the cottage, and it was converted to the Founder's House, where Teed and Victoria would live permanently—in separate quarters on either end of the house. With them would be Emma and also Vesta, now twenty-four and Victoria's personal maid.

In Chicago, the Koreshans had a huge packing job—Victorian sideboards, beds, tables, and other furniture, books, china, paintings, a piano and other musical instruments, trunks of clothing, the equipment from their printing plant, including heavy type, a wood-burning boiler, a steam engine, and machinery for the laundry. It took fifteen boxcars to carry it all to Florida.

On a windy, overcast Tuesday in November 1903, the last of the Koreshans boarded a train at the Englewood station and left Chicago. Three days later, they arrived in Florida to temperatures in the low seventies. The high in Chicago that day was twenty-four degrees. The Fort Myers paper ran a brief about their arrival, reporting that there were more Koreshans in Estero than ever.[31]

An enormous barge carrying their possessions arrived after they did. They staged it at the southern tip of Estero Island, which by then they apparently owned outright, having settled the dispute. The belongings were shipped upriver on a small barge that made so many trips Allen Andrews wrote that he lost count. It took months before everything was in place.

The nine-year wait was over. All two hundred of them were together in their peaceful, beautiful utopia—far away from Chicago, able to live free of rent and without the need for coal, free of winter illness and harassment. In December 1903, Teed made his last trip from Chicago to Estero and settled there permanently, to the delight of his devoted followers. They worshipped him:

> Our Glorious Sun of Righteousness, we behold in you the climax of all that toward which the race should reach in its aspirations for God. We know that in your life of lives there may be found every attribute of the perfect man, every function of the essences of regenerative life, by which regeneration and redemption are wrought. We behold in you the biunity of those sex forces in which the universe is renewed and perpetuated. Make us grow into your likeness and image, that in being like our God, we may regard ourselves his offspring. Feed us with the Bread of Life, and thus enable us to perform your service in our devotion to the neighbor. We are grateful for everything which may be effectual in rounding the character and constituting us men. Bring us into fellowship and into the states of mind and body that will insure to us our full redemption. Amen![32]

This was their Wednesday breakfast prayer, one of the many in the book of *Koreshan Daily Graces*. Before each meal, they sang a hymn and prayed to the mother-father God. Each Sunday at 11:00 a.m., there was a worship service— much like Protestant church services, with hymns, prayers, litany, solos, and a sermon. These were held in the dining hall at first, but the Koreshans began work on an Art Hall for worship services, theater, and musical entertainment.

At last, they were together with their Master, who united them. Now that

Teed was there to guide them, conflicts over Victoria's power seem to have quelled. They were able to focus their energies on him, which was the divine way. By all indications, they felt secure and inspired to build their city.[33]

The Koreshan Unity became a corporation under New Jersey laws and modeled after Standard Oil's structure, an interesting move considering that Teed called Rockefeller a national danger who represented everything he opposed—capitalism and the almighty dollar. Presumably, the corporation would make it more difficult for creditors and plaintiffs to sue the Koreshans and reach their assets.[34]

A two-story printing building went up, the printing press from Chicago was assembled, and Allen Andrews headed up the operation. The Koreshans printed announcements, bulletins, invitations, and booklets, both for the Unity and for outside clients. They had the technology for color printing, a rarity in those days. Their bakery turned out as many as five hundred to six hundred loaves per day of "risin' bread," made with yeast. The bread sold well because leavened bread was scarce. The general store was fully stocked with fruit grown on the Unity grounds—oranges, pineapples, melons, coconuts, strawberries, tomatoes, and more—along with honey, molasses, jams, and cookies.

The settlement was alive with work during the day and entertainment at night. Every evening, the Koreshans gathered in the dining hall to listen to music on the phonograph. One of the women had brought a collection of two hundred records into the Unity. They played cards and sometimes they danced. The women paired up for polka, two-step, and waltz, and the men joined in for the Virginia Reel or square dancing, Marie's favorite, because the boys asked the girls, very formally, whether they would like to dance. Years later, Marie remembered the voice of the square dance caller, Ross Wallace. He had used his strong, persuasive voice on the street corners of Chicago to bring new converts to Koreshanity.

The square dancing made a vivid impression on Marie because it was the only time the girls and boys were allowed to pair off. Marie explained in her memoir that the teens had the same attraction to the opposite sex as any other young people did. They often gathered in secret, but according to Marie, they respected their elders by staying in groups, not pairs. When the older folks were occupied, the younger ones gathered in the kitchen to make fudge, or at the laundry, where they fried frankfurters over the laundry stove, or in the bake room, which was abandoned after supper was over and the chores were done—any excuse to be together.

At the Koreshan school, the children learned the usual subjects, along with trades, like beekeeping and surveying for the boys and sewing and laundry for the girls. Teed insisted that the Koreshans stay informed, Marie remembers, and there were newspapers from all over the country. Someone read the headlines aloud at dinner. And there was plenty of reading material in their library, in the corner of the dining hall: books by Shakespeare, Robert Burns, Emerson, Longfellow, Gibbon, Goethe, Tolstoy, Dickens, and James Fenimore Cooper.

For the adults, Teed taught anatomy, physiology, chemistry, physiology of the brain and nervous system, astrobiology, and metaphysics. There was even a class on Esperanto and lectures on dentistry, given by Dr. Graves, who had reconciled with Teed and moved back to the settlement, where he lived in the Founder's House with Teed, Victoria, Emma, and Vesta.

In April, five months after the Chicago contingent came, the Koreshans celebrated the annual Lunar Festival for Victoria's birthday. Under the trees, they set up refreshment booths; they decorated the dining hall with palm leaves, pine boughs, potted plants, and flower centerpieces; and in the evening, they lit the grounds with torches and Japanese lanterns. Marie remembered that the girls got new dresses for the occasion, and everyone enjoyed a lavish meal. A formal ceremony included speeches, readings, singing, and music from the band or orchestra. There was a four-page program, printed on the Koreshans' own press, the cover page in color, bearing emblems and flourishes and the year, A.K. 64.

By the time of the Lunar Festival, the Koreshans were fully settled, all of their furnishings in place, and by all accounts, they were happy and self-sufficient. They decided to incorporate the town of Estero.

Perhaps the single most important event in the history of Fort Myers happened in 1904, when the railroad reached downtown. Shortly after 11:00 a.m. on Saturday, February 20, the railroad men pulled the last rail from the flat car and threw it into place at Monroe Street, where a platform was ready for a new depot. The women of the town festooned the engine with flowers and brought sandwiches, cookies, and candy to the railroad workers. The businessmen supplied a box of five hundred oranges and cigars for everyone. Mrs. James E. Hendry was escorted to the tracks and given a sledgehammer, and she drove in the last spike, connecting Fort Myers to the rest of the country. Citizens climbed aboard the engine and sounded its bells and whistles. Colonel Edward Lewis "E. L." Evans fired his cannon in a salute.[35]

The railroad made it easier to get citrus and vegetables to market, which benefited the Koreshans and other growers. But the biggest effect of the railroad was that it started the commercial fishing industry in Fort Myers. Fishermen loaded their catch onto refrigerated cars bound for northern markets. The railroad also brought traveling shows and circuses to town, and these were a wildly popular form of entertainment.

But Fort Myers was still a cow town, quite literally—cows wandered the streets of downtown, uprooting and trampling gardens, in spite of an ordinance requiring people to keep them penned. The animals roamed free, protected by the cattle barons. The Spanish-American War had renewed the Cuban demand for beef, and Punta Rassa was once again a major cattle shipping port.

The railroad inspired the people to build the outpost into a real town, though there wasn't much money to do it. Soon Fort Myers faced a conflict over how money should be raised and how it should be spent. Many citizens were against taxation and opposed to issuing bonds.

As a result, when the businessmen wanted to pave First Street, they paid for it themselves, bringing in shells from the mounds created by Calusa Indians hundreds of years before. The citizens hadn't wanted to pay for something that benefited only the merchants. They wanted to spend money on a school, a water works, and sewers instead.

Progress in Fort Myers was as slow as the cows that meandered the newly paved First Street. The town did get a fire department, a volunteer one. And it had telephone service, which was rough in those early days, requiring that the talker shout or repeat himself to be understood over the static.

While people in Fort Myers were preoccupied with their town's progress—or lack thereof—the Koreshans built support for Estero's incorporation. They found an unlikely ally in Philip Isaacs, the editor and co-owner of the *Fort Myers Press*, which had printed several disparaging, suspicious stories about them. "Misery in Estero," the reprint from Pittsburgh, told of Koreshan deserters coming to town, starving and unable to afford to move home. There was the Princess Loleta flap. And the dismissive report about Teed claiming he would bring thousands to Estero and take over politics in Lee County. There were smaller stories, too. In a story that had every reason to be positive, the reporter included a dig. When the Koreshans' paddlewheel steamer took first prize in a race at the town's first regatta, the newsman wrote that they had been given too great of a handicap head start.[36]

Isaacs was running for Lee County judge, and he needed votes in the fall 1904 election. By then, there were more than fifty Koreshan men of voting age, and they could be counted on to vote as a bloc. In a county of eight hundred voters, fifty was a big number. Isaacs sent one of his men to Estero to court the

Koreshans, and Teed saw an opportunity he never would have had in a bigger city. For years, Teed had been powerless against nameless, big-city editors. But in a town this small, people knew the editor. On visits to Fort Myers, Koreshans bumped into Isaacs in front of Gilliam's grocery and, once, at a party where their orchestra entertained. The two men struck a deal: Teed would instruct his followers to vote for Isaacs if the editor would stop the bad stories in the *Press*. Isaacs not only agreed to do that, he also gave the Koreshans their own weekly column in the *Press*.

Teed must have seen the Estero column as a vehicle for growing the settlement and building support to incorporate the town. In order to grow, they needed people to join. Now that the Koreshans were consolidated in Estero, the industry developed apace. Their commercial printing business was successful. They sold their fruit and vegetables. And they produced products for their own needs—mattresses, shoes, clothing, hats, baskets, and tinware—which they planned to sell to outsiders once they had more people and could boost production.

The Koreshans became known for their concrete manufacturing, not only blocks for construction but also ornamental medallions and flourishes for urns, fountains, and columns. They made busts and statues in their sculpting department.

Teed had the perfect writer for the new column in the *Press*: Ulysses Grant Morrow, who had led the geodetic expedition. He was detail oriented and completely committed to the Koreshan cause, and he knew how to write—he typed many articles for the *Flaming Sword* about the expedition as it was happening—and he met deadlines in spite of storms, a broken typewriter, and a devil in the camp.

Ulysses wrote the Estero column throughout the summer of 1904. He published it under the pen name "Veritas." His real name, Ulysses Grant, would not have been well received; Lee County was named for Robert E. Lee. Each week, Ulysses focused on a different way that Estero was wonderful. It was truly a planned city, he wrote; because they had started from nothing, they were designing it in an orderly way, unlike most cities, where there was continual tearing down and rebuilding. He expounded on the city's inevitable growth, the Koreshan industries, the citrus, the boat works, and so on. More and more people would come down, he wrote, and Estero would be a model.

With the printing press up and running, the *Flaming Sword* resumed production that summer, meaning more coverage of Estero, though the readership was dramatically different from, and smaller than, that of the *Fort Myers Press*. The *Sword* told Koreshans and potential converts the deeper meaning of things—world events and local ones, including stories about why Estero was important.

It was prophecy, the editor of the *Sword* wrote, that the Koreshans had come to Florida. Teed had worked out that Estero was the safest place on earth to be for the coming apocalypse. It was the cosmic center of things, and it would grow into a great civilization. They had escaped the hells of capitalism. Their exodus from Chicago represented a new epoch in the movement.[37]

In the *Press*, Veritas/Ulysses laid out the Koreshans' plans for "a beehive of industries" in Estero, making everything from shawls to concrete. His articles formed the basis of a prospectus the Koreshans issued three years later to attract workers. This pamphlet, issued in 1907, gives the best picture of how determined the Koreshans were to make their socialist colony successful. Some of the industries built on what they were already doing, and others were completely new ventures.[38]

By 1907, the Koreshans produced their own concrete and would soon have new pressure molding machines to produce blocks in many different sizes. They had the technology to make sidewalks, steps, and pavers—desirable in Fort Myers, which had resisted paved streets not long before. By the time the prospectus was issued, their business was so dominant that they were awarded the contract from Lee County to provide concrete for the Machinery Hall and Council Building, under construction in Fort Myers.

In the tin shop, the Koreshans made galvanized wares, gutters and water pipes. They produced wagons for their own use and planned to market these to outsiders once they had the production capacity. They developed patterns for producing both steam- and gas-powered engines, and were working to perfect a marine gas engine, which would also become a commercial product.

They planned to put a packinghouse on Mound Key, right on the bay, to make it faster and easier to get crops to market. They were pursuing commercial fishing and would build more boats for this purpose, as well as an icehouse at the southern tip of Estero Island. It would keep fish fresh and be big enough that they could rent space in it to outside fishermen.

The plans were grand, as one might expect. And not limited to Florida. In Bristol, Tennessee, they had an interest in a furniture plant. By some accounts, they owned the entire plant. There was a foundry for casting machines and engines, pulleys, hangers, bending forms, and parts for chairs, the factory's specialty. The Bristol company held eleven different patents—for woodworking, dowel-making, and chairs—with rocking chairs being the most highly touted products. The specialty was a bentwood chair with four legs and a patented base that supported a rocking mechanism—a sort of early glider, and a big improvement on the precarious split barrel rockers Marie remembered in her memoir years later. The chairs were available directly to the public on the installment plan, the prospectus said, and half a million had already sold.[39]

Business prospects in Honduras looked promising for the Koreshans, too. According to the pamphlet, the Unity was negotiating with the Honduran government for a land concession on the north coast. The property was on either side of a river, and the soil supported a variety of crops, including sugar cane, rubber, and bananas. The Koreshans already raised cane for syrup in Estero, so they knew how to grow and process it. Rubber production was soaring, driven by demand from the auto industry, and though the Koreshans didn't have experience growing rubber, they had researched it, showing in their prospectus figures from *India Rubber World*, which projected generous income beginning in the eighth year and climbing. Bananas were big business, too.

On the surface, a Koreshan venture in Honduras seems outlandish, but given what was happening at the time, it's somewhat plausible. The Honduran government, seeing profit in bananas, was offering deals to companies that agreed to develop the land for agriculture. Many of the concessions went to U.S. companies because they had the capital to invest.

What doesn't seem plausible is the quantity of land the Koreshans claimed to be negotiating for—two hundred thousand acres. Such a deal with Honduras might have been one of Teed's manic dreams. Or it's possible that the Koreshans were dealing with a Honduran official who was negotiating as if he spoke for the country. Either way, mania seemed to be a factor. And irony. The Koreshans were planning a communal society in Honduras, which had become known as a banana republic, where wealth was concentrated in the hands of a few and where the government and companies colluded for profit.[40]

Nevertheless, they expected to start several colonies there and grow crops, raise cattle, and produce lumber. They would build a city with a harbor and shipping facilities to allow them to ship goods to the United States. The operation, the prospectus said, would be managed by a society of well-off people from Italy and Poland. It is not clear why they chose people from these countries—whether they had a connection there or whether this was one of Teed's eccentric ideas. Plans with Honduras never materialized. The pamphlet also mentioned Koreshan business interests in Cuba, but it didn't specify what these were.

The prospectus, *The Solution of Industrial Problems*, explained how the Koreshan cooperative worked: All income went into a common treasury that paid the expenses. Workers owned shares in the corporation and therefore reaped the rewards of their labor directly, thereby avoiding wage slavery and the tension caused by labor unions. Everyone shared in a society that ran smoothly and took care of its children and elderly. The prospectus explained that they were not a charity and could not provide a home for someone who was not able to work.

A person who came into the Unity with money would buy shares in the corporation and be provided with what he needed to operate in his chosen industry. For example, someone who wished to set up a fishing operation would buy shares, and Unity would provide him with boats, nets, and tools—along with everything he needed to live, including food, clothing, a place to stay, and an education for his children. The proceeds from his fishing would go into the Unity, and the member would collect dividends based on the Unity's overall success.

If someone without money wanted to join the cooperative, he would be given stock and then work to "earn" that stock until he was on an equal basis with someone who had come in with money. People could also purchase shares with land rather than cash; the Koreshans would take over the property and sell it on his behalf, or manage it, if the person wished to stay on the land.

The pamphlet was illustrated with photos that showed the Koreshans sewing, baking, making concrete, and more. There was a photo of the brass band, pictures of the hogs and chickens and even Teddy the black bear cub, behind bars in the Koreshan zoo on the Grand Promenade near Bamboo Landing. The factory in Tennessee was pictured, along with photos of the rocking chairs.

The prospectus did not detail the Koreshans' religious beliefs, but it did say the Unity was not trying to convert readers to Koreshanity. Instead, the prospectus outlined the social, industrial, and commercial activities. They accepted Methodists, Baptists, Catholics, Presbyterians, or people who had no religious beliefs. Joining the cooperative was open to anyone seeking to better themselves, it said.

At the very back of the pamphlet, past photographs of shells, the pineapple shed, the hunters' camp, mounted fish and birds, a map of Estero, and subscription information for the *American Eagle*, there were two pages that would have puzzled someone who had never heard of the Unity. These explained that Koreshanity had several orders, from the external cooperative order to the central order of the church. "The Door of entrance into our Homes and Orders is through the Society Arch-Triumphant." The prospectus did not go into detail about the different orders of Koreshanity, but, in short, the Koreshan structure accommodated people who did not wish to become celibate or practice the

Koreshan religion. Only the innermost order of Koreshans was celibate; these followers lived in the settlement and were promised immortality because they broke the family tie, lived separately from their spouses, redirected their sexual potency, and focused all of their love on their Master. People in the outer, cooperative order were not required to be celibate, but they could share in resources if they surrendered their own possessions and worked for the Unity.

The final page of the booklet gave instructions for ordering literature. "Send us One Dollar," the ad read, and in return the publishing house would send a packet of literature and the book *The Cellular Cosmogony*.

The Koreshans seemed confident, one scholar noted, that success was inevitable for their star-shaped New Jerusalem. "Estero, they firmly believed, would certainly soon become the world center of commerce, culture, and the Koreshan commonwealth."[41]

In 1904, when Ulysses was writing for the *Press*, the Koreshans were already realizing many of these plans as they proceeded with their plan to incorporate Estero.

"The City of the New Jerusalem to Be Incorporated," the *Fort Myers Press* ran above the fold on the front page in early August 1904, pushing down a story about a hanging to take place in nearby Arcadia that day. Estero would become famous, the sarcastic story read, one of the greatest cities of the continent, attracting tens of millions of people.[42]

"You think this is a joke?" the reporter wrote. "Well, hardly." Under Florida law, twenty-five voters could take steps to incorporate a town, the writer informed readers. The Koreshans had put legal notices in the post office, giving notice of an incorporation meeting less than one month away. The citizens of Estero "are stirred as they have never been before," he reported.

The orange growers bitterly opposed the incorporation, but they were vastly outnumbered by the Koreshans, who owned merely one-eighth of the land they proposed to incorporate. "Those who live on the outside," as they identified themselves, didn't want to be part of a town run by such peculiar people. And they especially didn't want to pay taxes to support the Jerusalem—which was nothing but air castles anyway, the growers said. Rumors spread that the Koreshans would build three-hundred-foot-wide avenues right through their groves. The growers stopped doing business with the Koreshans, and they wrote frequent letters to the editor of the *Fort Myers Press*, which reported every detail of the growing tension.

Ulysses, who still had a weekly column in the *Press*, used it to fight back. He argued that the Koreshans' plans were quite real—not air castles. If the growers didn't believe the city would materialize, why were they fighting it? "People rarely oppose a myth," Ulysses wrote. His words echoed what Teed had said many times: that opposition made the cause valid. Ulysses kept up the marketing tone, but added a spiteful element. Incorporating Estero would cultivate public spirit, he wrote, which was more important than cultivating orange trees.

The growers described for Fort Myers readers the suffering they endured during the Great Freeze of 1895 and how it had forced many of them to move and start over. "Many of us are poor men," they wrote in a letter to the editor. Some of them had worked full time at established groves so that they could make enough money to cultivate their own land. And now that they were just getting on their feet and enjoying good harvests, they were to be burdened with taxes? No. They were indignant.

Furthermore, *they* were the ones who built Estero, not the Koreshans. What have the Koreshans done? they asked the readers of the *Fort Myers Press*. Come and see. "Take a look all around the whole country," the growers wrote, "and then judge for yourself who you think deserves the credit."[43]

Ulysses kept up his descriptions of the town's amenities in the *Press*, and he announced that they were building a new university, renovating the San Carlos Hotel on Pine Island, where they would offer free education for all. But anti-Koreshans would be excluded from this opportunity, he wrote.[44]

"Let them build whatever they will," the anti-Koreshans responded. "We will be contented to be led up on the highest hill and be allowed to look down on their City of the New Jerusalem and be forbidden to enter its gates."[45]

Ultimately, the Koreshans had little choice but to give in. They would limit the incorporated town to their property only. However, they announced their intention to charge tolls for shipping citrus down the Estero River. The non-Koreshans made more jabs, writing that Teed was anything but Christ-like. They called him boisterous, vindictive, and easily riled.

On the appointed date, the Koreshans gathered at the Koreshan general store and held a vote that, not surprisingly, approved the incorporation. Officers were elected, all of them Koreshans: Dr. Charles Addison Graves, mayor; Henry Silverfriend, clerk; and George Hunt, one of nine aldermen. Teed did not hold an official office, perhaps because he knew it could hurt their relationships with outsiders, who would say that it proved he was the town's dictator.

The Koreshans owned 110 square miles of Lee County. The town, Ulysses bragged, was twice the size of Washington, D.C. But a quarter of the land was actually water, as the town's limits extended into Estero Bay. Teed's explanation was that he planned to dredge the bay and build up the islands, and he believed that the state of Florida would do further drainage of the Everglades, creating more land. Finally, as Dr. Graves told one visitor, there would be a great upheaval of the earth when Teed theocratized, making more land to build on. So by including the water, Teed would argue, he was thinking ahead.[46]

The Koreshans created a town seal: a sun rising over a waterscape with a swan floating in the water. Surrounding this was a laurel wreath and at the top, a six-pointed star. Estero's new motto, "The Guiding Star City," was written between the star and sun.

On the day of incorporation, two stories ran on the editorial page of the *Press*. The first was a letter from Estero's anti-Koreshans, who wrote that they were relieved to be left out of the incorporation, but that they would fight the Koreshans' threats to block their use of the river and bay. The second editorial was by Ulysses (as Veritas), saying that all talk of powder and bullets would subside in time, that the public would see that the Koreshans ran a clean city, and that their rights were protected under the Constitution.[47]

In the news section, Isaacs reprinted a story from the *Palatka News* that called the Koreshans "a party of cranks" and ended sarcastically: "Those who desire corner lots in the New Jerusalem, Lee County, Florida, should speak for 'em early and avoid the rush."[48]

Teed could remain silent no longer. He had stayed out of the newspaper battle all summer, allowing Ulysses to be his front man. But after the incorporation, he wrote a letter to the editor, refuting the anti-Koreshans' claims, point by point. He began by thanking the *Press* for its fair coverage, and he congratulated himself for staying out of the fray. Then he launched into a kitchen-sink tirade that included the Koreshans' past business dealings with the growers. He assured readers that the Koreshans were doing well financially, in spite of the growers' claims to the contrary. He brought up the matter of the post office fight, long since settled. He knew, he wrote, who was responsible for taking it away. These men had "poured a tissue of lies into the Postoffice Department at Washington." He also responded to their comment that he was not kind, affectionate, lowly, or meek like Christ. He was not aware that this was a requirement for public service, he wrote.[49]

The anti-Koreshans got the last word in the *Press*, writing that Teed's irate letter made them glad they weren't part of Estero. They could now go back to their orange growing—alone. They were happy to stand aside and watch the city grow.

Which it did. Marjory Stoneman Douglas wrote about the settlement in

Everglades: River of Grass: "Huge brown board buildings were rising among oleanders, eucalyptus, date palms, and bamboos." Ulysses continued his column. His first article after the incorporation focused on how very healthy the environment of Florida was. In the next, he rhapsodized about the Unity grounds. Eucalyptus swayed in the breeze, the bamboo stalks waved, and a hundred shades of green greeted the eye. A carpet of soft grass, which many said wasn't possible in the sandy soil, was just as fine as the lawn in a city park. The Koreshans were planning a terraced river landing shaded by the feathery leaves and scarlet flowers of their large royal Poinciana. At the top would be a large bed of French canna lilies bordered by zinnias. It would look like the steps in Egypt that ran from the palace to the Nile, he wrote.[50]

The incorporation fight didn't damage the relationship between the Koreshans and the rest of Lee County. Coming up was the South Florida Fair in Tampa, held to encourage more people to move to Florida and make it their home. The fair boasted the largest Ferris wheel ever seen in the South, a carousel, and exhibits that included an erupting volcano, a Wild West show that was claimed to rival Buffalo Bill's show, an exhibit called Mysterious Asia, and a high-diving horse named Ben Hur.

The Koreshans had a spot in the Lee County exhibit booth. They brought more than one ton of grapefruit from their grove and stacked it into a pyramid, six feet tall and nine feet around at the base. They had constructed an electric automation of the universe for the Pan-American Exposition in Buffalo three years earlier, and they displayed this in Tampa. Their marching band won a prize for its performance at the fair.

Once home, the Koreshans put on their own festival, a miniature World's Fair that the Koreshans claimed was better than the Pike, the carnival arcade at the Louisiana Purchase Exposition in St. Louis. The Koreshan version included a Cave of Wisdom, where someone in Oriental costume told fortunes. There was a wigwam exhibit with a fortune-telling squaw. Music played from a "Victor talking-machine" brought from Chicago by one of the women. In one pavilion was an exhibit of spirit photographs, and in another, an eruption of Mount Pelée. A flotilla of three launches decorated with red lights came down the river, with the Koreshan orchestra playing on one of them. Ulysses detailed all of it in the *Press*, saying that he counted three fairies in the flotilla.[51]

The winter of 1904 saw a record-breaking crop in Lee County. Growers filled thousands of boxes with oranges and grapefruit, and a special orange train rolled out of Fort Myers every other night, headed north. Teed did not carry through on his threats to block growers' access down the river, probably realizing that he didn't have a case.

In 1905, the Art Hall was complete. Construction had progressed rapidly with two hundred colonists. At the hall, their Sunday services were more formal than the dining hall services had been. The leaders of the Unity sat on the stage on platforms of varied elevations—Teed and Victoria were on the highest plane, while the women of the Planetary Court were on another, then the men of the Stellar Chamber and the men and women of the Signet Chamber.[52]

The Art Hall was also home to their concerts and dramas, for which they built their own sets and made costumes. The hall became a center of culture for the surrounding community. Everyone was invited to the Koreshans' concerts, where the orchestra performed works by Wagner, Grieg, Verdi, Gounod, Beethoven, and operettists Victor Herbert and Franz Lehár.

The Koreshans held a grand opening for the Art Hall in May 1905, and three dozen people from Fort Myers came to the celebration and toured the grounds. A first-time visitor, whom the *Flaming Sword* described as "a prominent Fort Myers lady," wrote about the event for the *Fort Myers Press*. She was marvelously impressed by how clean the place and the people were. "They all looked as if they had just emerged from a bath." Their clothes were immaculately laundered and their houses arranged artistically, she noticed, and she was charmed by how gentle and deferential they were to each other and to the guests. At lunch, there was food for two hundred people, the tables were laid with linen, and the orchestra played while they ate. The print shop wowed everyone. "I doubt if there is one so well equipped in the South," the prominent lady wrote, mentioning the presses, the folding machine, the liner and binder. "Not a scrap of paper nor even a cobweb on the unfinished walls."[53]

There was an especially surprising guest at the Art Hall celebration: Arthur Teed, Cyrus's son, now in his forties. He had become an artist of some renown—a romantic impressionist who worked in oil, egg tempera, charcoal, and ink. When Arthur was fairly young, he had found a sponsor in New York who paid for him to study at the best schools in Europe. For the party at the Koreshan Art Hall, thirty of his works were on exhibit, including one he painted as a gift for Victoria's birthday. There were landscapes, studies, and scenes, like the vividly colored *Triumph of Death*, which the visitor described as styled after the Old Masters. The collection was eclectic, including a sunset in Estero, a Dutch hut, and a study entitled *Combat between Egyptian and Assyrian Kings*. Arthur's work was the first permanent exhibit in the hall.[54]

Teed had purchased some of his son's paintings—or that was Arthur's understanding, though he had not been paid; Teed might have thought the paintings were gifts. There had been ugliness between them several years before, perhaps related to Teed's abandoning Arthur and his dying mother in Binghamton, but it's apparent that by 1905, they had moved past this. In fact, Arthur was full of admiration for his father. For Teed's sixty-sixth birthday, Arthur dedicated a poem to him, one he had written in Rome. It was printed in a small booklet bound with a woven cord. On the dedication page, Arthur had written, "A son takes pleasure in dedicating this little fancy to his father, Dr. Cyrus R. Teed (Koresh), . . . with a wish for the continued felicities of a ripe age and great work done."[55]

Perhaps the most beautiful building on the grounds was the house where the seven leading women of the community lived. Teed called them the sisters of the Planetary Court, and they included Jennie Andrews, Etta Silverfriend, Lizzie Robinson, Evelyn Bubbett, and others who had been with Teed since the early days. Berthaldine Boomer was one of them. She joined the Unity fully once her husband died. These sisters were said to manage the affairs of the community, though it's clear that George Hunt did most of the managing, so it's possible that their positions were more ceremonial than anything. Their Victorian-style house, also called the Planetary Court, was two stories with a balconied cupola, a wrap-around porch, and large windows.

That summer, the Koreshans began work on their promised university by renovating the long-idle San Carlos Hotel in St. James City. This was the hotel Teed had seen in 1893 but couldn't afford, the place Berthaldine Boomer remembered riding to in a surrey through tall weeds, and seeing squadrons of insects, some of which settled on the Master's neck.

Summer was a terrible time for working on the hotel, given the heat, heavy rains, and bugs. Vesta called the place Hotel de Swamp. The workers burned smudge pots around the clock to keep the mosquitoes away. One night, a worker left a smudge pot burning, and a fire started, racing through the empty three-story frame building and burning it to the ground, forcing the Koreshans to abandon the plans for their university.[56]

As the fire burned, Marie McCready packed her things. Her mother and her sisters helped; her father, who opposed her move, didn't. William was more committed to the Unity than ever. He took care of the bees, Gustave's old job; he proofread the magazine and other literature; and he was even a justice of the peace, though he knew very little about law. Wanting to do an excellent job, he taught himself by studying law books.[57]

Over the next five years, William watched his daughters leave the Unity one by one. Marie had been dissatisfied for a long time, she later wrote, and never felt completely healthy after the typhoid. She went to live with her grandmother and, once she felt completely healed, took a job in Washington, D.C. Three years later, Marie's sister Lovelle left and found a job that put to use the skills she learned at the Unity in bookkeeping and stenography. Catharine left a year after Lovelle. All three of them married. As did many young members who came into the Unity as children, the McCready sisters, now grown, wanted to begin independent lives.

✳ 12 ✳

Fight

Fort Myers's ruling family was the Hendrys. Nearly everyone in a position of power in the town was a Hendry, married to a Hendry, or worked for one. Philip Isaacs, the editor of the *Fort Myers Press*, was in the last category. The Hendrys brought him to town as a hired gun to start a newspaper and drive out the existing one, run by a staunch Republican. Fort Myers was a town of Democrats, as were Lee County and all of Florida.[1]

Given the political leanings of the town and the fact that the Hendrys bankrolled Isaacs, it was an easy matter to drive the Republican paper out of business, though first there was a vicious, but short-lived, press fight. A few years after the Hendrys started their paper, in a move that seemed preordained, the county commissioners stepped in and forced the two weeklies to merge. It was called a merger, but it was really a takeover. Isaacs even took over the paper's name, and the *Fort Myers Press* became an organ for the Democratic Party.

Philip Isaacs had plenty of news to cover. When Fort Myers got the railroad, he was the editor. When the first automobile came to Fort Myers and raced along the newly paved streets at eighteen miles per hour, Isaacs's paper covered it. His biggest story was Thomas Edison's decision to spend his winters in Fort Myers. And when the inventor announced his plans for a storage battery, he gave the scoop to Isaacs, who promptly wired the news to the major dailies, where it made front-page headlines. Isaacs also ran frequent stories on Edison's fishing and hunting excursions and on his social life.

Philip Isaacs agreed with the Hendrys on every issue except one: taxes, which he was staunchly opposed to. Isaacs was one of the businessmen who paid personally to pave First Street, and he was one of the town's volunteer firefighters. But the ruling family wanted taxes and bond issues to fund city improvements. In 1904, the town had a dirty, littered wharf, and it needed sewers, water works, and a seawall.[2]

The mayor was Louis A. Hendry, the same man who represented Damkohler and walked away with half of his land. He was accustomed to getting what he wanted, and he wanted a bond issue. When he proposed it, Isaacs fought it in the *Press*. The editor's strongest argument, he must have thought at the time, was that the town didn't have the authority to issue bonds.

Mayor Hendry responded by taking a group to the governor's office, where they camped on the front steps, presented the problems, and returned victorious, with the governor's permission to issue bonds. Isaacs was apparently a sore loser; he reported this news in a manner so vague the average reader couldn't have understood what happened.

Though Hendry won the bond battle, he lost the mayorship soon after, replaced by an anti-taxation man whom Isaacs supported in the *Press*. In that same election, Isaacs won the office of Lee County judge, thanks in part to the Koreshans' support. Isaacs's power was growing, and he was posing challenges for the Family Tree of Lee, as the Hendrys were known, no longer their puppet. He had the favor of the new mayor, a judge's seat, and the power of the press.

During this time, Teed received an anonymous letter. It was hardly the first hate mail of his career, but it was by far the most detailed and specific that survives, an eight-page screed that named names. As opposed to the physical threats he received in Chicago, this one was written by someone who wanted to destroy Teed's reputation. "I am watching your movements," the person wrote, "and will expose your fraudulent business whenever an opportunity presents its self."[3]

Based on the contents of the letter, the writer had been intimately connected with the Koreshans, and it seems likely that he was a follower at one point, though he was too proud and too angry to admit it. He wrote that he had lived in the colony, but as a "private detective" for the purpose of infiltrating it.

Where are the men who did all the work to settle the land? the writer asked. Gone except for four of them. The rest left in disgust, he claimed, and some of them are keeping body and soul together by trying to sell firewood in Fort Myers. He claimed to have overheard two Koreshan men talking after one of Teed's sermons: "He is a lunatic. I would get out of this if I had $5.00." The other said, "I would get out if I had $2.00."

Furthermore, the writer claimed, Teed and Victoria had been found in a compromising position. Teed had kissed a lot of women, in fact, and the writer had it on good authority (from Mrs. Wright, the artist from Denver) that his breath was terrible. "Mrs. W. says that when you kissed her she smelled your foul catarrhal breath and she wonders how 'Old Vic' [Victoria] could stand so much of it."

"You have robbed widows of their money and character and then turned against them," he wrote. "You are a Liar," he put in thick red ink. "Where are the 'Thunder Daughters'?" he asked, listing the names of the six young, pretty women who came to Estero in the early days. The answer was that only Vesta remained.

The most surprising thing the writer mentioned is something that was airbrushed from Koreshan history: Victoria's son impregnated one of the thunder daughters, and they had a son out of wedlock.

The writer boasted that *he* was the one responsible for removing the post office from Koreshan land and that he had exposed the fraud. Teed forced his female followers to lie for him, the writer accused. "Are you in the 'Napoleon' role now?" he asked. "A runt like you with this face could pose better as 'Punch,'" referring to the self-satisfied, often aggressive puppet with a protruding nose and chin. Besides that, the letter writer drew a caricature in profile of Teed. It is an amazing likeness of both Teed and Punch. The writer had collected information on Teed for many years, and he was waiting for the right time to air it.

He signed the letter "Your Hater," and beneath that, he added a cryptic phrase in an old Spanish dialect: "I vow that your land will go up in flames."

By the time the 1906 election arrived, Isaacs was the chair of the Democratic executive committee. Seats were open for county commissioners, the tax assessor, the tax collector, and the treasurer. Though the election would be held in November, the Democratic primary in May would decide everything.[4]

The Koreshans, Democrats, planned to vote in the primary and to throw their considerable bloc vote behind candidates Isaacs did not like—pro-tax people. At the heart of the matter was this: now that Estero was an incorporated town, it was entitled to county tax funds, and the Koreshans wanted officials who would send funds their way.

As the chair of the Democratic executive committee, Isaacs arrived at a way to stop them. He and his committee decided to require Democrats to sign a pledge before they could vote in the primary. The pledge affirmed that the voter had supported Democrats across the board in 1904; it was widely known that the Koreshans had voted for Republican Theodore Roosevelt for president. They liked Roosevelt because he broke up monopolies and resolved labor disputes. Though he was part of the capitalist structure they despised—and supported by railroad barons and steel magnates—he knew how to bargain with the devil to accomplish social reform.

But other than voting for Roosevelt, the Koreshans voted entirely for Democrats in 1904. Even so, they didn't qualify to vote in the 1906 primary under Isaacs's rules. The Koreshans showed up to vote anyway. The poll workers handed each man a copy of the Democratic pledge. Koreshan Ross Wallace—street preacher turned square dance caller and now a candidate for county commissioner—was the first in line. He took the piece of paper, crossed out the crucial clause, signed the pledge, and returned it to the election official, who allowed him to vote. One by one, each of the fifty-five Koreshan men did the same, striking through the words that disqualified him, signing the document, and casting a vote.

Four days later, Isaacs and the Democratic executive committee revoked the Koreshans' votes. The decision was unanimous, and the state of Florida supported it. By voting, Isaacs said, the Koreshans had committed a misdemeanor punishable by three months in jail.

Throwing out the votes affected the primary results for only one minor office. But it made some margins so thin that a few candidates won by single digits. Teed had said a long time ago that the Koreshans would outvote the citizens of Lee County, and they had come uncomfortably close.

But now they were disenfranchised, and they had no say over how the county's money would be spent, even though they paid property tax, and at a higher rate than several of their neighbors did, they discovered. Speculators paid a lower rate.

They wanted to protest, but Philip Isaacs gave them no room in his paper to do so.

Allen Andrews, thirty-one, worked at a rolltop desk on the second floor of the new Koreshan printing house, a frame building made of heart pine and one of the tallest in the community. From the second story, Allen could see the houses, barns, cabins, and boat works of the settlement. It was quite a change from his view of the cramped alley behind Montgomery Ward in Chicago when he was a teenager. His view showed how far the Koreshans had come since the days in Binghamton, when Teed's only follower was Allen's father, Abie.

"Guiding Star Publishing House" was painted in white on the water tank that supplied the water for the steam that ran the rumbling presses. Inside, the shop was filled with natural light from tall windows, and there were three cylinder presses, three job presses, two power paper cutters, two folders, a wire stitcher, a numbering machine, a bundling press, and a roller-casting outfit. It was one of the most sophisticated print shops in the country, and with everything in its place, as the prominent lady from Fort Myers had noted during the Art Hall celebration the previous year. Allen loved working there. Printing was what he had wanted to do since he was fifteen.[5]

He never wanted to be the editor of a newspaper, however, or so he claimed when he heard the idea. Immediately after Isaacs threw out the Koreshans' votes, Teed called an indignation meeting, saying it was essential that they strike back. They would start a weekly newspaper right away, he decided, and the group determined that Allen would be the editor. Though he wasn't a journalist, he knew all the steps involved in publishing. Allen must also have known that this was a nearly impossible task on short notice. But being familiar with Teed's grandiose schemes, he knew that Teed wouldn't be dissuaded. There wasn't time to mull, and Teed wasn't someone to say no to. So the *American Eagle* was born, with Allen Andrews as its editor and main writer.

The first issue, four pages, appeared an impressive two weeks after the Koreshans' votes were torn up. The main editorial, "Our Initial Scream," began as follows:

> From out of the heat of the recent Lee County political strife has been hatched THE AMERICAN EAGLE, full-fledged and strong of beak. His flight is lofty,—no place, though high, escapes his keen, far-seeing eye.[6]

The biggest news, on the front page, was that the Koreshans planned to form a new political party: the Progressive Liberty Party, which stood for public ownership of utilities, equal distribution of wealth, and open government.

The *Eagle* came out every Thursday, the same day the *Fort Myers Press* was published. No accident. It was more attractive visually than the *Press*. The Koreshans used book-quality paper rather than newspaper stock, and their typography was more advanced than that of any of Florida's metro newspapers. All of the type was hand set, and the craftsmanship was masterful. The front page was in color.

Though Allen claimed to be timid, someone who would sooner run than fight, his articles show otherwise. He had abruptly become the leader of a political battle, and he seemed to take well to it and even to have fun. On the front page, he mocked the pledge that Isaacs forced all Democrats to sign.

> New Resident.—I wish to vote in this primary.
> Judge of Election.—Are you a Democrat?
> N.R.—Yes.

Judge.—Did you vote for Andrew Jackson?

N.R.—Why (er-r) yes, I believe that was his name.

Judge.—Did your grandmother vote for Thomas Jefferson?

N.R.—No! Of course not.

Judge.—Well, why didn't she, and if she was alive do you think she would do it now?

N.R.—I'm sure I don't know.

Judge.—Was your great-grandmother a hoot owl . . . ?

N.R.—I don't see what that has to do with politics.

Judge.—Everything in the world! See Section 586½ of Chapter 45,382, Revised Statutes.[7]

Nearly every issue of the *Eagle* featured an editorial cartoon starring "the little judge," one of the Koreshans' many nicknames for Isaacs. He was easy to caricature—a small man, he had a large nose and often wore a hat, which covered his mostly bald head. One cartoon showed him training a trick donkey, which he wouldn't allow anyone else to ride. Years later, Allen reflected, "There is nothing more cruel than to ridicule a little guy who takes himself so seriously."[8]

Judge Isaacs objected to the Koreshans' voting as a unit, but he hadn't objected two years before when they had voted for him for Lee County judge, the *Eagle* pointed out. Allen wrote that the "little editor fellow in Fort Myers . . . has since managed to warm an infinitesimal section of the County Judge's bench."[9]

The Koreshans called for Isaacs to resign as Lee County judge on the basis that he could not be impartial if he also chaired the Democratic committee and ran the *Press*. Furthermore, if Isaacs thought the Koreshans had committed a misdemeanor, why wasn't he prosecuting? Isaacs wrote that the Koreshans wanted to make Rome howl just so they could advertise themselves. They responded that Isaacs had mixed up his geography. It was Jerusalem, not Rome, they were making howl.

For several weeks, there was no response from Isaacs. He had explained to his readers that he refused to give the Koreshans any more "ads." After that, he went silent, no articles about them. The battering from the Koreshans continued. In one weekly cartoon, Isaacs was depicted as a baby in a frilly gown, drinking from a bottle labeled "power." "Recent Events Would Indicate That He Is Losing It," the caption read. A hand reached into the second panel of the cartoon and took the bottle away, leaving the judge kicking and crying. It must have been hard for Isaacs to remain silent. The Koreshans were clearly baiting him.

The cartoon was true, though Isaacs might not have realized it. His power was slipping because of a stance he had taken against the Hendrys. In August, just as this cartoon appeared, a Hendry had taken back the mayoral office, replacing Isaacs's ally. The new mayor proposed another bond issue—for sewers and water works—which would be on the ballot in November. Isaacs came out against it in an editorial, displeasing the Hendrys.[10]

Though the *Press* was quiet on the matter of the Koreshans, Fort Myers's citizens weren't. The Koreshans received a letter signed by several people, saying that men were coming for them and they should ready their guns.

"Our guns are ready and primed," one Koreshan responded in the *Eagle*, but said that their guns were "loaded with facts" rather than bullets. Some of the men at the settlement *did* arm themselves to guard the place and prevent anyone from setting fire to the buildings.[11]

Meanwhile, the Koreshans' Progressive Liberty Party grew, attracting voters who felt that Lee County politics had become corrupt. Republicans, Socialists, and even some Democrats joined the party, protesting the control that Fort Myers had over county funds and the fact that resident landowners paid higher taxes than speculators. The men in power were not addressing this.

Isaacs kept his silence in the *Press* for four months. A writer in The *American Eagle* wrote, "Constant dripping will wear away a stone." And it did. Isaacs finally spoke. He encouraged readers not to join the Progressive Liberty Party. It is the party of just one man, he wrote: Koresh, "posing as a supernatural being." It was time to expose him, Isaacs wrote. "From now until [the] election we intend to remind Koresh of some of his past history, and show to the people the pretty little game he is now playing."[12]

"The Sphinx Has Spoken," the Koreshans wrote fearlessly in the *Eagle*. "It is rumored that the little judge-editor is to issue a special Asbestos Issue of the Organ. We await its advent with interest."[13]

For a little while longer, Isaacs held onto whatever it was he claimed to know. Meantime, Teed wrote in the *Eagle* that Isaacs had long targeted him, once printing that Teed had been arrested for forging a draft of one thousand dollars. It was true that Teed had been arrested, but it was a mistake, the sheriff determined, and Isaacs never ran a correction. Isaacs also printed that Teed attempted to buy favors from him early on, once trying to give him five dollars for a notice in the paper that cost fifty cents. Teed said it never happened.

While readers waited for Isaacs to publish what he had promised, something big happened. It started with a mix-up on the telephone. A friend of the

Koreshans was coming to Estero and planned to stay overnight in Fort Myers at the Florida House hotel, owned by the Sellers family.[14]

On the day the guest was expected, one of the Koreshans telephoned the hotel from Estero to see whether he had arrived. The *American Eagle* later reported the telephone exchange. A Mrs. Sellers had answered the phone, looked for the guest, returned to the phone, and said, "He's not here." Shortly after that, the guest arrived, and Mrs. Sellers rang the Koreshans to let them know.

"I thought you told me no one by that name was stopping there," the Koreshan said. It should have been insignificant, but tensions were very high between the citizens of Fort Myers and the Koreshans. When Mrs. Sellers mentioned the conversation to her husband, he got mad. Erroneously, he believed that the person on the other end of the phone was Koreshan Ross Wallace, the candidate for county commissioner on the Progressive Liberty Party ticket. Mr. Sellers decided that during the phone conversation, Wallace had accused his wife of lying.

In fact, the person on the phone had been Richard Jentsch, a young, muscular man whose job it was to protect Teed. The situation between the Koreshans and the citizens of Fort Myers had become so tense that Teed traveled with a bodyguard.

As it happened, Wallace came to Fort Myers on business a few days after the phone conversation. He saw Sellers on the street and stopped to say hello. Wallace thought they were exchanging pleasantries, he later swore in an affidavit, but Sellers suddenly grabbed him by the collar and punched him. And he kept punching. Wallace guarded his face and did his best to dodge Sellers's swings. He demanded an explanation. He was able to make out that Sellers believed Wallace had called his wife a liar, but Wallace had no idea what the man was talking about.

Sellers picked up a heavy piece of wood to strike Wallace, and Wallace fled to the courthouse. Behind the building, he found the mayor and begged him for protection, but the mayor did nothing. Wallace returned to Estero, planning to come back in a day or two to talk to Sellers when he was not in such a passion.

On the day Wallace returned to Fort Myers to make peace with Sellers, a group of Koreshans—including Teed and his bodyguard, Jentsch—happened to be in Fort Myers meeting friends who were arriving on the train. Wallace found the town marshal and asked him to go with him to meet Sellers. The marshal told him to let it go, but Wallace persuaded him that the three men should talk.

Wallace and the marshal found Sellers in front of Gilliam's grocery store, where Wallace explained that Sellers was mistaken about the phone call. He had not talked to Sellers's wife, he said, and he certainly had not called her a liar. No Koreshan would ever do so, he assured Sellers.

Cyrus Teed, on his way to the train with his people, saw Wallace, Sellers, and the marshal talking in front of the grocery store. Knowing about the dispute, he thought he might help, he later swore. He directed his people to go ahead to the train station to meet their visitors and then approached the three men. He was in his usual attire, wearing his black broadcloth suit, black hat, and white ascot, out of place in Fort Myers.

In Isaacs's version of the incident, Teed walked up just as the marshal had brokered peace between Wallace and Sellers. Though Isaacs wasn't there, he described Teed in his story: "His eyes were flashing fire and his chin was elevated as he accosted Mr. Sellers and opened the old sore by defiantly stating that no one had insulted his wife. Dr. Teed boldly call[ed] Mr. Sellers a liar."[15]

Teed's version differed from Isaacs's. He told Sellers that telephone conversations were easily misconstrued. Poor connections often made it difficult to hear. Why, even courts didn't accept telephone testimony, Teed said. But Sellers got hot. Both Teed and Ross Wallace recounted the exchange later in their affidavits.

"Don't call me a liar," Sellers yelled at Teed. He swung at him and struck him in the face. He swung again, getting in two more solid blows. And so started a brawl that was equal to anything Fort Myers had seen in the cowboy days, the *Fort Myers Press* reported. Sellers pounded Teed's head with his fists. Witnesses later said that Teed struck Sellers, but Teed claimed that he moved in closer to protect himself and raised his arms to block his face.[16]

When Teed looked to the marshal for protection, he got none. Instead, the marshal stepped forward and slapped Teed so hard that his spectacles fell to the ground. By now, forty or fifty men had gathered, and some jumped into the chaos, either to break it up or to get their shot at a Koreshan, it was probably hard to tell which.

Richard Jentsch arrived—"a trained pugilist," Isaacs later wrote, "with the duck and the side step, the upper cut and all the other punches and tricks of the professional bruiser." Isaacs reported that Teed had come to Fort Myers with his prizefighter specifically to stir up trouble. Isaacs also made a point of mentioning that Sellers was sixty-five years old, but didn't include Teed's age, sixty-seven.

Richard Jentsch slugged Sellers and then the marshal. Six men jumped on Jentsch and knocked him to the pavement, and the marshal beat him with his billy club. "You hit me again and I will kill you," the marshal said, according to Wallace.[17]

This is when Teed's group from Baltimore, which included two young boys, exited the train and saw what was happening in front of the store. Someone in the crowd asked one of the boys whether he was a Koreshan. When the boy answered yes, the man struck him in the face, and another man pushed him, grabbed his valise, and flung it into the street. The other boy was grabbed, struck, and knocked into the crowd. Another of Teed's guests from the train jumped into the fight and came out spitting blood. The marshal arrested Teed, Jentsch, and a third Koreshan and took them to jail, where they each paid a ten-dollar bond. They forfeited the money rather than return for the court appearance the next week.

The *American Eagle* claimed that the fight was a put-up job. The townspeople made a plan two years ago to kill Teed, the *Eagle* reported, and this plan was specific. "A respected gentleman, and by the way an official of Myers . . . remarked, 'I can lay my hand within ten feet of where "Teed" would have fallen.'"[18]

On the Thursday after the fight, Isaacs let loose in the *Press* with what he knew. His paper produced two editions that day. Curiously, news of the fight did not appear on the front page. Instead, it was inside the paper: "Teed Starts a Street Fight!" Readers expecting front-page coverage of the fight would have been puzzled to find a leisurely story about Teed, lounging in a Chicago mansion in a maroon silk dressing gown, patent leather slippers, and a white lawn tie, digging his feet into a fur rug and answering reporters' questions about a bomb found under the steps at Beth-Ophrah. The headline was "Teed Poses as Martyr." It was a reprint of an old story in the *Chicago Times*.[19]

Isaacs ran seven Koreshan-related articles that day, three of them written years earlier at the height of the Chicago mess, showing Chicago's citizens in all their rage. Isaacs didn't run dates on any of the Chicago stories, so a casual reader might have thought they were quite recent. Buried in Isaacs's lengthy editorial was the explanation that the stories were old.[20]

The only voice of reason in the paper that day was a letter to the editor from a reader who encouraged the citizens of Lee County to forget the flap with Teed and to focus on the election issues. This was dwarfed by the scare headlines. "For the Price of a Wife" told the story of Sidney Miller's one-hundred-thousand-dollar suit against Teed for alienation of affections when his wife joined Teed's "harem." The Miller case had long since been settled out of court. Another story from Chicago included a report of one of the indignation meetings in Normal Park, during which one man, seventy-seven, said he "would take a shot gun and give Teed a through-rate ticket to hades if Teed ever lured one of his female relatives into his heaven."[21]

In the *American Eagle*, the Koreshans dismissed the articles as old news, long since settled or proven false. But the following week, Isaacs assured readers, "We have interviews SECURED WITHIN THE PAST FEW WEEKS." The capitalization is his and shows his rising hysteria. Isaacs never used all caps within the text of a story. "We had known but very little about this fiend in the garb of a gentleman," Isaacs wrote. "We have made it our business to look into his past life."[22]

In his editorial, Isaacs apologized to readers for having to print these articles, which he would roll out over a series of editions. Parts of them were too indecent to print in the *Press*, he added, and those he would omit. But readers deserved to know about this man, he said, who had designs on taking over Lee County. Isaacs ran quotes from Koreshan deserters who had come out strongly against Teed. These were fresh names—people who hadn't made the pages of the Chicago papers. Isaacs had done extensive reporting, or more likely, Teed's hater had done so and was feeding him the information for this attack. The collection of people quoted was so broad it could have come only from someone who had been on the inside, observing Teed for decades. This information was the result of a long, intimate study of Teed's past.

It's not likely that Isaacs himself was the hater. That writer had claimed to be in the Estero community near its beginning, and Isaacs had not arrived until after the Koreshans settled there. Also, the grammar in the letter is not that of a professional editor. The hater might have been Elwin Damkohler. There are plenty of clues it was not Gustave, though the writer mentioned Gustave as a source for some of the information. Ultimately, it's impossible to know who the hater was (Teed had too many enemies to narrow it down), but one thing is clear: he and Isaacs had found each other.

Isaacs closed one of his impassioned editorials by evoking the name of Robert E. Lee, for whom Lee County was named. Isaacs exhorted his readers to hold true to Robert E. Lee's principles. "Down with Teedism in Lee County forever."[23]

In the *Flaming Sword*, whose readers were sympathetic to Koreshan beliefs, Ulysses Morrow wrote that the Koreshans were being persecuted yet again, just as they had been many times in the past. The fight could only make them stronger, as the movement thrived on opposition. The people of Fort Myers didn't realize that they can't defeat the Koreshans, the article said. They hadn't expected Richard the Lionhearted to come to Teed's defense, Ulysses wrote, referring to Teed's bodyguard, Richard Jentsch. Ominously, Ulysses added: "There are forms of redress of which the unthinking may not be aware."[24]

This seems to refer to the coming martyrdom, Teed's theocrasis, which the Koreshans believed would set things straight. The wicked would be judged.

But in the *American Eagle*, Teed demanded more immediate forms of redress: the town should dismiss the marshal, investigate the mayor, who watched the fight and did nothing, clear the arrest records of Teed and his two men, and return the thirty dollars' bond money. He also wanted reimbursement for the repair of his spectacles. Teed's appeal in the *Eagle* began logically enough, but swelled to his characteristic mania. He would call on President Roosevelt, he wrote, to investigate the matter. "We will give Fort Myers the greatest lesson of its existence." He closed by threatening to take Koreshan business away from Fort Myers, resulting in a loss of hundreds of thousands of dollars to the town's economy.[25]

Isaacs ate it up. He responded in a colorful article five days before the election. "Have pitty [*sic*] on us, O Koresh! Do not wreck vengeance on a poor, defenseless people." Isaacs added that citizens should expect Florida's governor to send troops to Fort Myers and that Roosevelt would call Congress into a special session to determine the matter of whether Fort Myers should reimburse Teed for his broken glasses. Isaacs wrote that Teed was either fit for a lunatic asylum or he was the greatest charlatan and humbug of the twentieth century. If this was a performance from Teed, comic opera stars needed to step up their game, he wrote. Finally, he said sarcastically, the Fort Myers economy would be in shambles without business from the Koreshans. Prosperous shops would soon have "to let" signs in the windows.[26]

In reality, the town wouldn't lose much if the Koreshans boycotted it. But Teed didn't see things that way. His followers began work on a gasoline launch so that they could do their shopping in Tampa, more than one hundred miles away.

The election happened, and the Koreshans' Progressive Liberty Party made a respectable showing, though none of its candidates were elected. Teed proudly wrote that day that he was proud his party had run a clean campaign in the face of opposition. Even some Democrats had voted with them, indicating that they wanted to distance themselves from what Teed called "the ravings of a venomous calumniator" (i.e., Isaacs). On election night, Teed was hung in effigy from a telegraph pole in Fort Myers. The dummy was left there overnight until town officers cut it down the next morning.[27]

The street fight aged Teed dramatically. A picture of him with his followers a year before the fight shows him looking distinguished, his posture erect, standing in his customary place at the center of the bottom row. But in a photo taken with the group after the fight and just before the election, he sits off to the side in a carriage, his right arm draped on the arm of the coach, his left drooping alongside his knee. He is so close to the edge of the photo that the corner of his right elbow isn't shown. His face has changed shape and color, appearing pale and turtle-like, the chin no longer prominent. He is alert, looking at the camera, but the piercing gaze isn't there. He has lost weight. Though he normally wore a hat, he doesn't in this picture. His bare head reveals that what little hair he has is white.

The fight nearly unhinged Isaacs, who must have believed that if he ousted the Koreshans from Lee County, he would be a hero, and that it would make up for his disagreements with his patrons, the Hendrys. But they continued to be frustrated by Isaacs. During the election, Mayor Hendry's bond issue was defeated, in part because of the newspaper opposition.

The war of words between the *Eagle* and the *Press* didn't stop after the election. Through the winter, as Teed worked on a novel, the Koreshans kept pressure on Isaacs. He was not fit to be a judge, they wrote in the *American Eagle*, and they planned to trip him up as much as possible for his remaining time in office.

Then Estero's town officers—all of them Koreshans—petitioned Lee County for half of its road tax funds. Passions flared, and Isaacs took action. The county commissioners petitioned the state to revoke Estero's incorporation. Isaacs contacted his colleague at the Tallahassee *Sun* for help, and the editor sent a reporter to Estero to investigate. The resulting story in the *Sun* took up two full pages. It quoted detractors and dredged up stories of spurned husbands, duped wives, and indignation in Chicago. The editor called Teed "religious fungi" and his community, a mushroom cult. Some mushrooms are harmless, he wrote. Teed's was poisonous.[28]

The article in the *Sun* was well timed, priming Tallahassee legislators to address the issue of Estero's incorporation. The county commissioners proposed two solutions. At the very least, the town of Estero was too big. Much of the land was under water—where it would stay, they said, in spite of Teed's prediction that the earth would heave up around the New Jerusalem. Reducing the size of the town to its land area only, one could see that Estero was not entitled to half of the road taxes, the commissioners asserted.

The second proposal, the one county commissioners really wanted, was for legislators to revoke Estero's incorporation altogether. The *Sun* supported this in a second story: "Teed is not the first rascal who has made religion a cloak for his designs against the property and personal liberty of others. But he is the only one now allowed to do business in the State."[29]

After the story appeared, Isaacs wrote with satisfaction that Koresh's days were numbered and that the *Press* would no longer respond to the "hysterical screechings" of the *American Eagle*. "Set yourself up as a little god," Isaacs wrote.

"Make your followers think they are living on the inside of the earth. If you will agree to keep on your own side of the fence, the *Press* will forget that you are living."[30]

In May, Tallahassee revoked Estero's charter, and abruptly the town was no more. Isaacs penned a gleeful editorial: "'Old Cy's' Pet Scheme Knocked Out!: Florida Legislature by a Unanimous Vote Abolishes the Sham Town of the Old Pretender: All that is left of the 'New Jerusalem' on Estero Creek is a few large barns to house the fanatics."[31]

The decision to revoke Estero's township was later determined to be unconstitutional, and Estero became a town again, but for the moment, the disincorporation was a triumph for Fort Myers and for Isaacs.

But Isaacs's editorial would be his last jab at the Koreshans. That spring, he had sealed his doom with the Hendrys. They had introduced yet another bond issue, this time to improve Fort Myers's unsightly wharf and build a seawall. Isaacs came out against it in the *Press*. And within six months, he was writing his good-bye column. A week later, he resigned his position as judge. Then he left town for good. In "The Story of Fort Myers," a definitive history of the town, there is a "Who's Who" section. Philip Isaacs doesn't warrant a mention.[32]

There is one last detail. During the first week of October—the same week that Isaacs's valedictory column ran in the *Fort Myers Press*—there was a large fire at the Koreshan settlement. The blaze destroyed two livestock barns. The animals escaped and weren't harmed. Was it the work of Isaacs? Or the work of the hater, who had vowed in his eight-page letter that Teed's land would go up in flames? Or both?

The *American Eagle* printed a good-bye to Isaacs.

> The Judge, soaring upon the pinions of fame, flushed with success . . . attempted still higher flight, but in so doing he also ran up against a warm proposition, the wax fastening of his wings melted, and he fell with a dull, sickening splash into the sea of oblivion.[33]

Though it was the Hendrys who forced Isaacs out, the Koreshans took considerable credit. In turn, Isaacs could take credit for Teed's injuries, even though another man delivered the physical blows. The editor built the tension that led to the attack. Both men lost the fight. Isaacs had believed he was invincible; Teed believed he was immortal. Those turned out to be illusions.

✳ 13 ✳

City of the Blessed

There is a coming world-wide catastrophe.

—Cyrus Teed as Lord Chester, *The Great Red Dragon;*
or, the Flaming Devil of the Orient

It's impossible to know when Teed's suffering began. The Koreshans said it started the moment Sellers struck him in the face, at 1:45 p.m. on October 13, 1906. They believed that their Master never had a pain-free day after the fight. That fits neatly into the martyr narrative, but there are other possibilities.

At some point in the year after the fight, the headaches began, along with pain on his left side, shooting down his arm. Doctors called it neuritis, a catch-all term for nerve pain. Today, a neurologist would diagnose him with nerve root injury, specifically, radiculopathy because the pain radiated. This pain can be severe, stubborn, excruciating, electric, and burning. It can develop slowly or come on suddenly. Based on Teed's symptoms, he might have had a pinched nerve, a herniated disc, or arthritis. Trauma to his head during the fight could have caused sudden nerve damage, as when lifting something heavy causes a herniated disc. Or it could have aggravated some existing condition like arthritis.[1]

After the fight, in the fall of 1906, Teed retreated to the beach house, La Parita, to nurse his wounds and write his novel. There, on the south end of Estero Island, he had solitude and peace; this was where the Koreshans came for picnics and beach parties—a large, two-story, wood-frame house near coconut palm groves, papayas, mangoes, and pineapples. With the windows open, he could hear the soft surf and feel the salt-air breeze through the pine and buttonwood.

Teed's novel is an apocalyptic story in which Japanese and Chinese forces invade the United States and bring about Armageddon. In the book, thousands of people come together in Florida on the Gulf of Mexico in the City of the Blest (Estero). The people are building one thousand mysterious machines. They don't know what they are building or preparing for.

In the novel, Asian invaders close in on Florida, and things look grim for the city. Then the author reveals the purpose of the machines: the people have created radio-directed flying machines or, as Teed calls them in his book, non-gravo-wireless-power-aerial navigators. Teed wrote his book during the golden age of the airship. The commander of the fleet of airships is called the Princess Admiral. There's no mistake that this is Victoria. From these airships, they drop exploding balls onto the invaders. Other mysterious dirigibles appear and rain fire onto their enemies. The people in the city are safe.

Then their "Messenger" theocratizes by "pass[ing] into his receptacle, [which was] the arch-natural Womanhood of the new dispensation" (Victoria's character). Once he passes into the woman, she has divine wisdom and dominion over the world. The people of the city dematerialize and reappear in a new form, each one both male and female.[2]

He titled his book *The Great Red Dragon; or, The Flaming Devil of the Orient* and wrote it under the nom de plume Lord Chester. The title refers to the great red dragon from a story in the Book of Revelation in which a woman appears, clothed in the sun and standing on a crescent moon, and wearing a crown with twelve stars—exactly the woman from Teed's illumination. In the Book of Revelation, she is giving birth to a man-child who will rule all nations, when a dragon comes, ready to devour the child. There is a war in heaven, and the dragon is cast out.

Though Teed called his work a novel, the story described the end of the world as he told it to his followers. In fact, in his author's note, he said that everything in the story would come to pass. He began reading his manuscript to his followers in the fall of 1907, and he told one Koreshan he had been commanded to write it.[3]

Futuristic invasion novels were popular when Teed wrote his, and it was common that the invaders were Chinese or Japanese, because this was a time when Americans feared mass immigration from China and Japan. This fear was called "the yellow peril," a term William Randolph Hearst made popular. Books in the genre shared common themes, but Teed's novel had uncanny similarities to H. G. Wells's novel *The War in the Air*—the Chinese and Japanese invade the United States, upstate New York is devastated, and airships are prominent. Wells's book ran as a serial in the *Pall Mall Magazine* in 1908. Teed's book was published in 1909.[4]

Lest a reader think that Teed had gotten his ideas from Wells, the Koreshans added a publisher's note to *The Great Red Dragon*. This book, it said, was written in the winters of 1906 and 1907 and sent to several prominent publishers, who rejected it, "but not before they note[d] the main points. These points have since been incorporated in other stories that have been published in leading papers and magazines." In other words, the Koreshans believed it possible that H. G. Wells took ideas from Teed, indirectly through his publisher.[5]

While writing his novel, Teed corresponded with his son, Arthur, who seemed not to know his father was suffering. Arthur had asked his father to pay him for the art that hung in the Art Hall, and now he stepped up the pressure, claiming he was owed $7,500. When he didn't receive any money, Arthur sought other forms of payment, ordering some groceries from a Fort Myers store to be delivered to him in Winter Park, Florida, and charging the goods to Teed's account. It worked once; he received the order, though most of the contents were damaged. But when he tried contacting the grocery store about the damage, the owner ignored him. It's probable that Teed hadn't paid his account with the grocer.[6]

Arthur wrote his father with a proposed settlement for $2,500. If Teed didn't have the money, Arthur said he would accept a few things he had seen at the Unity when he visited: the Studebaker canopy two-seated bicycle carriage; a first-class sewing machine; and a grand piano. He wanted to make things easy for his father, he wrote, and didn't want to file suit. He said he was willing to treat this as a transaction between friends.

Yet it's clear that Arthur's old anger had flared up. The letters between Teed and Arthur in 1906 and 1907 are the best window into their past relationship. Arthur's impatience with his father was long standing, as reflected by cruel letters he sent Teed when the Koreshans lived at College Place in Chicago in 1892, Jennie Andrews recalled. Arthur had written letters to Jennie as well. She had, after all, been part of his life when he was a child. Jennie and Abie lived in Binghamton, where Arthur and his mother, Delia, moved when Delia was too sick to keep traveling with Teed. Abie doctored Delia while Teed went through New York, working out his religio-science and practicing medicine, or trying to.

During the College Place years, at least one of Arthur's letters was so terrible that Jennie remembers Teed saying he wouldn't show it to the devil. Jennie threw another of Arthur's letters into the fire. And all these years later, as Arthur asked for payment for his paintings and claimed that he wanted to settle the matter in a friendly way, he mentioned thirty letters Teed had apparently written him since 1899, indicating that they—and Teed—were crazy. Arthur quoted from a letter Teed wrote him in 1900, asking him to join in a gold and copper venture. Teed explained that he owned seven million dollars in gold and copper mines and wanted to make Arthur the vice president of his Gold Producing Corporation Union. (Perhaps the "producing" part of the company name refers to Teed's claim that he could create gold from base metal.) According to Arthur, Teed said there were $250,000 worth of claims set aside for his son. Arthur had an attorney check on this, and there was no evidence of these claims and no evidence that Teed owned any mines.[7]

Arthur evidently had held onto his resentment over Teed's treatment of his mother, too. When he wrote his father asking to be paid for the art, he included a stinging passage about why he needed the money: he had taken on debt to buy and furnish a house for his wife.

"I wished to feel that I have made some return to my wife for her own disappointments in life." This seems to be a veiled reference to Delia's sacrifices and disappointments, which Arthur apparently felt his father had done little to rectify.[8]

He filed suit against Teed in August 1907.

Teed stayed at the beach house the rest of that summer and fall, finishing his novel. It was unusual for him to be in one place for such a long period. While building the community in New York, in Chicago, and then Estero, he traveled frequently and was never with his followers for very long before leaving to take care of some business. Though he was in Estero now, he was removed, visiting the settlement sometimes, but staying on the island. It's possible that he had nerve pain by then and wanted to hide it. Or that removing himself was part of his narcissistic personality disorder—he wanted his followers to long for him and then to celebrate his return. Another possibility is that Teed was bipolar and that he experienced periods of depression in addition to his mania.[9]

Whatever the reason he withdrew, there were early signs that his absence was affecting the community. Henry Silverfriend was the first to notice. The Koreshans were proceeding with their plans to expand industry in Estero and in Bristol, Tennessee, and Henry was there helping manage the furniture plant. When not in Bristol, Henry traveled, especially to expositions—there were many of them in that day. He set up a booth in each town where he sold chairs and spread the Koreshan doctrine, or attempted to.

If his Master was suffering, Henry didn't know it. He wrote Teed from the Jamestown Exposition in 1907 about the opportunities there, asking Teed to come in person to deliver a full course of lectures. There was a beautiful auditorium, and Henry had made connections that would benefit the Unity. "Answer soon," he wrote at the bottom of his letter, underlining it. Four months later, still in Jamestown and having difficulty building an audience for Koreshanity, Henry wrote, "Why do you not answer my letters? Your devoted Henry."[10]

At the Estero settlement in the winter of 1908, the air was filled with the smell of boiling molasses and the whirring of the sugar cane mill. It was the season for turning cane into syrup. Steam-powered machines crushed the plants and extracted the juice, which the Koreshans poured into vats and reduced to syrup, the aroma reminding some of the northerners of sugaring off maple syrup back home. The Koreshans had planted more sugar cane than they ever had, in four varieties.

In the early months of 1908, they built two livestock barns to replace the ones destroyed by fire. They finished the icehouse, which promised to increase their profits from fishing, and they completed the packinghouse for fruit and vegetables. They had their new pressure molding machines, too, which gave them the ability to produce a variety of stone shapes from concrete. Their plans for economic expansion were moving ahead, though they still needed workers. The Bristol furniture was selling well. The prospectus was done and ready for the public. But where was it? Henry wanted to know.

He was exasperated with Teed. He wrote to his Master from the Florida Mid-Winter International Exposition—"a greater opportunity than we have ever had before." Tens of thousands of people were there, crowding around exhibits like Madam Van's Educated Horses and Turner's Educated Fleas, an Iggorote Village, Sanford's Celery Exhibit, and a new invention called an infant incubator.[11]

Henry built one of the most conspicuous booths at the fair, with a platform and a canopy. His chairs were selling, he told Teed, but he was having trouble making converts. He didn't understand why Teed wasn't coming. A friend who had been in Estero came through Jacksonville and told Henry that the colony and the master were doing well. Teed *did* write Henry during this time to let him know he was coming through central Florida but that he would not be stopping in Jacksonville. He didn't explain why. It made no sense to Henry.[12]

Henry might have been the first to see that without Teed's magnetism and charisma, they couldn't survive. Having him at the expos would fix things, Henry knew, but apparently it wasn't going to happen.

He asked Teed to send the globe, maps, and photos of the colony, along with Koreshan literature, which he had ordered three times. "You seem to overlook a great part of my letters," Henry wrote. He must have known that the new prospectus would be perfect, and no doubt he was frustrated that they had gone to the trouble to make such a book if they weren't circulating it in Jacksonville, their best chance to reach people in Florida. "To start a thing and then throw it down is what we have been doing long enough," Henry wrote Teed. He ended with a P.S.: "Please read this letter carefully."[13]

A few days after Henry wrote to Teed, something historic occurred at the Jacksonville Expo: Lincoln J. Beachey, a twenty-year-old pilot and daredevil, made the first motorized airship flight in Florida. In the late afternoon, Beachey's propeller started, kicking sand in every direction. He released the anchor, and the enormous dirigible—a cigar-shaped bag filled with gas—lifted off the ground. Thousands watched. The dashing young Beachey, in a suit and tie, sat strapped to the bamboo frame beneath the blimp steering it. The flight lasted twelve minutes, and the *Florida Times-Union* reported admiringly, "Beachey has won his way to the clouds and rides whithersoever his fancy may dictate."[14]

If Henry saw the flight—and there's every reason to believe he did—he might have wished for Teed, knowing his Master's fascination with the giant dirigibles.

When Teed reemerged in February 1908, his followers could see he was suffering. Having finished his novel, he began lecturing again locally. He gave Sunday sermons in the Art Hall, attended some events and lectures, and went to Fort Myers to conduct business. Now sixty-eight, he applied to the government a second time for pension benefits, and it appears that he received them this time.[15]

He resumed traveling, on a punishing schedule. But instead of going to the expositions where the crowds were and where Henry wanted him to be, he followed his old strategy of hitting the big cities, staying in a hotel, hiring a lecture hall, and putting a notice in the paper.

In May, he settled in Washington, D.C., and decided to start a colony nearby. He stayed in a three-story house four blocks from the White House. A follower named Mrs. Bellingham found the house, signed the lease, and paid rent of fifty dollars a month. The gossip in Estero was that Mrs. Bellingham lived in the house with Teed, but he denied it. "I am keeping house all by my lonesome," he wrote George Hunt.[16]

In the mornings, Teed walked to the park in front of the White House and fed peanuts to the squirrels. They climbed onto his hand to take the nuts and sat beside him to eat, piercing the shells and digging out the insides. He came to think of the squirrels as little pets, and he wrote about them to longtime follower

Evelyn Bubbett, the same woman who had been the editor of the *Flaming Sword* and whom Ulysses Morrow had confided in during his time on Naples Beach, sharing his dreams and daily annoyances. Evelyn was the treasurer of the Unity for a time and a member of the Planetary Court.[17]

Teed chronicled his Washington life in a series of private letters to Evelyn, whom he addressed as "My Dear Evelyn Queen," and signed off, "Ever your own King and You my Queen." Teed had always called Victoria his queen, so this was an odd way to address Evelyn. He obviously cared deeply for her. He told her he wanted to bring her to D.C. that summer.[18]

"If you want something to fill your mind," he wrote to her, "keep me in mind. Let nothing detract from your love for me for if I should lose that or any part of it it would be a more serious matter than I could bear. Don't go away and forget me, my darling angel." Though this sounds romantic, it isn't likely that he and Evelyn had a romance, given her marriage to a trusted follower and her vow of celibacy. More likely, Teed valued her as a model follower; she had focused her love on him as he had directed all Koreshans to do in order to bring about his theocrasis and ensure their immortality. Not everyone did so, and Teed couldn't abide "halfway Koreshans," he once wrote to a woman who was following both Koreshanity and the teachings of Swedenborg.[19]

Mrs. Bellingham had rented a lecture hall for him, and he had it fixed up with paint, pictures, and charts, and named it Universology Hall. In the *Washington Post*, he advertised his lectures: every weekday night and a service each Sunday. The hall seated 125 people, but attendance was nowhere near that. He told Evelyn he wasn't discouraged. He detailed for her his plans for the colony near D.C.—on a farm eighteen miles east of the city on the Patuxent River and along the Washington and Chesapeake Railroad. He called it Hollyrood ("the holy cross"). He had secured three hundred acres already, he wrote to Evelyn, and sent a team of men and horses to begin work. He had met with two men about building a boulevard from the planned town to Annapolis. When Evelyn asked who was paying for it, he responded that he was backing himself "without anything but cheek."[20]

He assured Evelyn that, in spite of the gossip, Martha Bellingham did not live with him and never had. He also disputed a claim about yet another woman who was said to be a frequent visitor. It was nonsense, he said, a rumor started by a woman in Estero who wanted to irk Victoria. Apparently, the rumor worked. Victoria joined Teed in Washington, where they spent the summer together. With Victoria and Teed away from Estero, the Koreshans began renovating the Founder's House into a stone fortress.

Gossip made its way to Teed frequently. Notably, he got word that Ulysses

Morrow in Estero was grumbling. Teed wrote Evelyn, "Have you heard of Professer's [sic] disaffections?"[21]

Ulysses had never stopped working on the theory of the concave earth. As far as Teed was concerned, the experiments were complete, the book was published, and the matter was shut. There was nothing left to discover. The followers believed it absolutely—it was at the center of their faith—but they didn't dwell on it, and it wasn't part of daily life.

But to Ulysses, it was everything. In his off hours, when he wasn't editing the *Flaming Sword*, he studied the earth's curvature, made measurements, consulted charts, and drew diagrams. And he discovered what he believed was a flaw.

The overall idea was still sound, Ulysses thought. The earth was indeed concave, and everyone lived inside. But his recent calculations were at odds with what he and Teed had documented. There were improvements to be made. Exactly what they were isn't clear from his writings. He wrote vaguely about a problem of "squaring the circle" and some work he was doing with angle trisection.

When he suggested the improvements, Teed had waved them away, and this caused Ulysses serious concern. It might not have worried him quite so much, had he not noticed other things about Teed, too. Lately, Teed's morals seemed to be slipping, Ulysses noted. He recorded this many years later in a letter.

"[Teed] had, at first, at least, a high conception of the elements of righteousness," Ulysses wrote, "and exerted a good influence upon his following. But . . . he was losing that high conception, and was failing in various ways."[22]

Checking his calculations multiple times, Ulysses believed that the truth was plain. There was an error Teed was unwilling to see. If the cellular cosmogony—the foundation of Teed's entire religion—had a defect, how could Ulysses be sure that Koreshanity itself was true?

He couldn't. That was what he arrived at that summer. Worse, he reflected much later, Koreshanity might be an outright lie. If Teed was too egotistical to admit his mistake, he was hardly a god.

From D.C., Teed wrote to Evelyn, disparaging Ulysses. "Professer [sic] forgets that he is not highly illuminated."[23]

The other men in Estero were excited about their new project of renovating the Founder's House for their Master while he was away. They planned to transform it from a wood-frame house to a stone building by veneering it with artificial stone created with their new concrete pressure molders. The whole house would be faux brownstone, the first floor surrounded by a colonnaded wall and the second story having Corinthian columns. To the west, a cylindrical tower would rise two and a half stories. The house would be different from every other building on the property. Sturdier. Permanent looking.

By July, Teed was in terrible pain that wouldn't let up. He couldn't sleep nights at all and couldn't lie flat in a bed, so he napped sitting up in a chair. The headaches were debilitating and the shooting pains more frequent. He believed he had suffered a brain hemorrhage as a result of the street fight. He saw many doctors—some of the best in the country, a Koreshan later wrote—but there was little they could do for him.[24]

He gave up his lecture hall and pared down to one lecture per week rather than six. He wrote his followers in Estero with a schedule of how he spent his time in Washington: During the day, he saw visitors and he tried to work, and this distracted him from the pain. At 10:00 p.m., someone rubbed his left shoulder and arm for two hours. He took a hot bath, slept in his chair for twenty minutes and then walked ten blocks to a Turkish bath for treatments. "My pain is excruciating," he wrote, telling them that he dripped sweat from his right side while his left side was "as dry as a powder horn."[25]

"Notwithstanding all this, I am attempting to promote the building of a city," he wrote to his followers, referring to Hollyrood. He was also trying to establish a bank and many other enterprises—"on the financial basis of about twenty-five cents," he wrote.[26]

This is what was keeping him from Estero, he explained. He wanted more than anything to be with them, he said. Something would happen very soon, he added: "The time is ripe for a rapidfire system to be inaugurated. The breath of God will go like a whirlwind when the hour arrives." This seems to refer to the end of the world, because he follows it with, "None will come permanently who are not marked for the fold."[27]

In Estero at sunset in early October, a group of Koreshan brothers stood on the porch of the general store in the gathering twilight waiting for the mail wagon. A double-seated surrey came into view, moving slowly as it approached the wooden bridge and crossed the river. The men watched, hearing the clop of hooves on boards and the grit under the carriage wheels. When the surrey pulled past the store, they saw through the dim light who was inside: the Master and Victoria with three attendants.[28]

One of the brothers ran to unlatch the front gate for them and then went to the dining hall, where the sisters were cleaning up after dinner. He told Sister

Emma the news, and she announced Teed and Victoria's arrival. The carriage proceeded without ceremony to the Founder's House, where Teed and Victoria exited, greeted the followers briefly, and then went inside.

The Koreshans, knowing that Teed was not well, were delighted that he had come home so that they could take care of him, and they were confident that he would rebound with some rest. His birthday was approaching, and they began making preparations for a big festival. They decided to invite the public.

For a while, the Koreshans continued the improvements to the Founder's House even though Teed and Victoria were living inside. Teed often pulled a chair outside and talked to the men as they worked. One day, he told Ross Wallace, the brother in charge of construction, that he would like a little house of concrete stone, just for himself. Wallace told Teed they would try to design something worthy of him. He didn't think much of it at the time. William Mc-Cready remembered the conversation.

"I shall only want a small one," Teed said, "square, just room for one."[29]

Hundreds attended the two-day Solar Festival that year to celebrate Teed's birthday, including outsiders from Fort Myers and Estero. One witness recorded the first evening in great detail. The grass terraces on either side of Bamboo Landing were decorated with white stars. As night fell, the orchestra played an overture, and fifteen young Koreshans dressed as Athenian guards in shining helmets and shields descended the steps to the river. They performed a sword drill, then faced the audience and recited in unison a stanza of *Armageddon*, a work by Teed.

Then Koreshan girls appeared, dressed as bees and flowers. Others acted out a woodland scene. Three clowns in pantaloons performed stunts and danced. Perhaps most memorable was an enormous dragon, which represented the yellow peril. It was 110 feet long, "with an enormous head and terrible flaming eyes," one guest wrote, "fire and smoke issuing from its nostrils." Several people in the crowd screamed as the dragon weaved across the landing and through the trees and out of sight. Then a large white float came up the river, carrying boatmen dressed in white with red sashes and seven beautiful maidens, each dressed in a different color of the rainbow for the "Dance of the Rainbow Nymphs." For the final vocal number, all of the performers assembled on the stage and sang the "Soldiers' Chorus" from Gounod's opera *Faust*.[30]

That evening, Victoria led a prayer for Teed; it was the first admission to the outer community that he was sick. The following day, his birthday, Teed preached as forcefully as ever, according to Lizzie Robinson, who wrote about the festival in the *Flaming Sword*. Teed read from the Book of Revelation and other parts of the Bible that related to the coming of God's messenger. "Blessed are they that do his commandments that they may have right to the Tree of Life, and may enter in through the gates into the city."[31]

He beseeched his followers to be kind to each other, an indication that some of them had not been. Teed's son, Arthur, was there for the celebration, and he didn't seem worried about his father's health, as reflected in a letter he wrote shortly after he visited. He began it by saying briefly that he was sorry Cyrus was ill, but he continued for four pages about the urgency of settling the $7,500 suit. Ultimately Teed and Arthur settled their business, with Arthur accepting four hundred dollars, plus the return of the poignantly titled painting *The Penitents*, which Arthur had made clear was important to him.[32]

After his birthday, Teed spent more time inside, continuing to live in the Founder's House. The Koreshans stopped the renovation to give him some peace. The bottom floor was done, veneered in stone and with a wall of arched columns. The top, where Teed lived, was exposed wood siding with a shingle roof. The overall effect was unattractive: an enormous unpainted shanty appearing to rise out of a Tuscan villa. The tower beside the house sat squat and unfinished, collecting rain.

From the odd, unfinished second story of his house, he had a view of the citrus trees with their hard green globes two months from ripening. Beyond the trees was the Estero River. His sister Emma stayed by his side, perhaps creating herbal remedies from the garden outside her cottage, as she was known to do. She had never seen her brother so ill. Late that month, there was a heavy downpour, two and a half inches of rain. One can imagine that from his spot over the river, with Emma tending to him, Teed would have heard a piercing chorus of oak toads cheeping like baby chicks. And the plaintive bleating of narrow-mouth frogs.

Henry Silverfriend gave up—not on the community and his devotion to Teed, but on trying to run the Tennessee furniture plant and on carrying out Teed's wishes. He resigned in a letter. Things at the plant were a disaster, he wrote, and he couldn't continue without more men and money. "Have begged for this aid until now we are up against the real thing. Promises will not answer now."[33]

Not only did he resign from Bristol, he told Teed he wouldn't help with Hollyrood. He didn't understand the plan, he wrote, and when he asked for clarification, he had gotten none. Henry apparently didn't know that Teed's condition was serious. He devoted just a few words to Teed's health in his letter: "I hope you are feeling well again." He signed off, "With much love, I am as ever your devoted disciple, Henry D. Silverfriend."[34]

The Koreshans did not appear to be alarmed about Teed's health, because when Victoria returned to Washington, D.C., at the end of October, no one thought it strange. She needed to carry on Teed's work to build Hollyrood while he recuperated. And he felt well enough to see her off. They took the boat together to Fort Myers, where she boarded the train.

It's possible, given the way nerve root injury manifests, that Teed had good days and bad and that Victoria's departure happened on a good day. On bad days, he stayed in the house and hid his condition from all but those who were close to him.

A week after Victoria left, he was much worse, his pain more severe, and he went with his nurse Gus Faber to La Parita. Faber gave him salt baths and electrotherapeutic treatments, using a machine Faber invented.

One day, some of the band members visited the island to play for him. Rather than come into the house, they sat on the pier nearby and played. One of the musicians remembers that not far from where they sat was the Koreshan boat *Success*, half sunk and full of sand. It was a cloudy day, and the temperature was in the low sixties, cold by Florida standards. Teed sat in his room, the windows thrown open so that he could listen and watch. Someone handed him a pair of binoculars. "He directed his eye to each one of us," the band member wrote, "calling our names as he did so. This was the last I ever saw him alive."[35]

In December, Teed became so weak that he couldn't move in and out of the salt baths on his own and needed to be lifted. He now had two male nurses, and they put him in the bathtub and washed him very carefully to avoid causing him pain. As the men helped him into the tub and washed him, he winced, but he joked that they were performing jujitsu on him. They were heartened that he had his sense of humor.

He began getting messages from the spiritual world, his followers believed. He told Ross Wallace that there would be a great influx of people, asking him to repair several of the boats in order to be able to carry the people when the time came. "It is evident," one follower wrote, "that he now sees what is going on, both in the spiritual and natural world, and it is very probable that as his mind comes in closer contact with the interior, they are directed what to do there."[36]

"It's coming," Teed said, according to a follower who heard him. "I see them." This same night, Teed asked his nurse for medicine. There's no record of what kind of medicine he took, but it was strong enough that the nurse resisted giving it to him at first, indicating that it was strong and that Teed was bending his own rules about drugs.[37]

Teed instructed Victoria to stay in D.C. "The present strain here would be too much for you to bear," he managed to dictate to a follower, "and my desire is that you keep yourself in tranquility."[38]

Emma said it was Teed who couldn't stand the strain of Victoria's being there. She would agitate him. Emma assigned one person to be the sole communicator with Victoria, writing to her daily and casting Teed's condition in the brightest possible terms.[39]

Teed had a paroxysm that lasted sixteen hours, the hardest he had ever had. One Koreshan remembered that he cried out in agony, "Jerusalem come take me, come!"[40]

After the pain passed, he said to Emma, "I must pass through the shaddow [sic] of the valley of death, and I dread it."

"But you have nothing to fear," she said.

"I dread it."

As Teed's condition worsened, the followers were careful about their correspondence with those outside of Estero, fearing that the Fort Myers post office would intercept and open their letters and learn about his illness. From Chicago, one follower sent Concord grapes and a glass urinal, both of which Teed had requested, and she sent them directly to the island rather than to the settlement, to avoid having the package go through the Fort Myers post office.

After the long attack, he was pain free for two days. He could move his arms over his head, which he hadn't been able to do for eleven months. His followers rejoiced. This was the turning point, they concluded. Sister Esther wrote Victoria with the good news, and Victoria wrote back right away, a letter "to my people." In Washington, D.C., she said, it had rained for three days, but on the morning before she received Esther's happy letter, the sun had come out, and she felt that it was a benediction. Even the quarrelsome sparrows in the trees outside her window were singing. She rejoiced upon reading the letter, understanding that the weather was a reflection of this blessing. She wished she could be with them in Estero, she explained.[41]

"But he [has] willed it differently, and I believe he knows best," she wrote in her letter. Her tone became lofty in the last half of her seven-page letter as she gave them guidance.[42]

"Do not allow yourselves to be pessimistic, but hopeful. Do not be penurious, but generous. Accept God's blessing to you through your afflictions and serve the Lord with Joy and with Gladness and come before his presence with thanksgiving, and into his courts with praise. The land will soon resound with the news of commemoration of the birth of Christ."[43]

By the time her letter reached them, their Master was dead.

On the morning of December 22, at 8:30, Teed asked for a teaspoon of salt. The nurse, Brother Gay, recalled this last hour and recorded it: "Every sacrifice should be seasoned with salt," Teed said. "It is thus partly purified." The salt was brought, and he wet his fingers, touched it, and placed it on his tongue three times. Thirty minutes later, he asked what time it was. Thirty minutes after that, his head dropped to one side. He was gone.

"Said he was comfortable about 2 minutes before the end," Brother Gay wrote. "End was very quiet, hardly noticeable. Simply ceased."[44]

Then came the Fort Myers doctors who declared him "quite extinct." The followers waited for the body to revive. On the second day, when discoloration set in, Jennie wrote, "But we could not, would not believe it until we were forced to recede inch by inch from the strong assurance behind which we had fortified ourselves."[45]

Emma sent Victoria a telegram: "Animation suspended, can you come?" Twenty men began work on the tomb. Jennie wrote, "We are waiting in faith and patience for we know not what, but we are sure everything will be all right and the apparently inexplicable will become clear to our understanding."[46]

In Washington, D.C., Victoria received the telegram and held it unopened for a moment. Martha Bellingham was with her, and Victoria said, "Now I am going to tell you what I heard before I open this. Shortly before this, I heard the Master's voice and he said in a very natural tone of voice, 'I have passed out.'"[47]

She began the three-day journey to Estero, arriving the day after Christmas, but she didn't go to the island immediately. She retreated to the Founder's House instead and stayed there until lunch the following day. She ate very little.[48]

"She is softened and very lovely," one follower wrote. "She feels [her] place with dignity as well as humility and we are proud and thankful to have her here." Victoria spoke to the group after lunch, the follower recalled, telling them that what had happened was not yet theocrasis. He will return, she said, and shake hands with every one of us, and do his work before the theocrasis. Only then would Victoria be endowed with power. "We need to wait," she said. "And bide our time."[49]

And then Victoria shook hands with each person there. She and the Planetary Court boarded Brother Addison Graves's new boat, and he took them to the island. It was five days since Teed died. By the time she arrived, the stone vault was waiting. Presumably, she viewed Teed's body, which by then looked hellish, Weimar wrote, like Satan. Emma had said they needed to bury him, and the followers were resigned to it. Victoria agreed that it was time to put him in the tomb.[50]

A few days after Teed was entombed, one follower wrote, "He is the great alchemist—has now entered the crucible and become the sacrifice by which the world is to be transformed. He has taken the first and most awful leap—and he certainly will not stop there."[51]

Philip Isaacs was the editor of the *Fort Myers Press*, which bought ink by
the barrel and used it unsparingly against Teed. Isaacs's inflammatory articles fueled anger that culminated in a street fight. State Archives of Florida,
Florida Memory, 140473.

FORT MYERS PRESS.

"No Stormy Winter Enters Here, 'Tis Joyous Spring Throughout the Year"

VOL. XXII.   PORT MYERS, LEE OO., FLORIDA, THURSDAY, OCTOBER 18, 1906.   NUMBER 44·

OR THE PRICE OF A WIFE

. Teed, the False "Christ," Sued
for One Hundred Thousand
Dollars Damages.

**HE PLAINTIFF IS SIDNEY C. MILLER,
WHOSE YOUNG WIFE OLD "KOR-
ESH" INDUCED TO ENTER HIS
HAREM.**

he Suit Only the First of a Series and
the Self-Styled "Messiah" Will Also
Be Prosecuted Criminally--In-
dignation Meeting to Be
Held the in Auditor-
ium Soon.

(FROM THE CHICAGO TIMES.)

One hundred thousand dollars is the emand made on "Dr." Cyrus R. Teed, he false "Christ," of the College of .ife, by Sidney C. Miller, whose young .ife old "Koresh" had persuaded to nter his earthly harem. Teed, like

Stomp, E. S. Metcalf. The meeting was attended by about one hundred citizens and was determined in its expression to rid the community of the Teed nuisance.

There were a number of Dr. Teed's devotees present, and excited groups of citizens gathered about four or five of them and eagerly propounded questions in regard to Teed, his peculiar doctrine, and the manner of life which was led by the community. Prof. Lummery, who seems to be in charge of the Normal Park branch, had the most to say. He was bold and defiant in his attitude, and protested that Dr. Teed was a moral man and had the same right to live up to his convictions that was accorded to other people. "Dr. Teed is divine," he said. "He possesses a thorough knowledge of the Hebrew language, although he has never studied it at all."

When the Koreshanites had been heard for about an hour the meeting of citizens was called to order on the station platform, and W. C. Shaw was made chairman. He stated that the object of the meeting was to ascertain

POWERS OF STATE DRAINAGE BOARD.

Albert H. Roberts, of St. Petersburg,
Argues that Powers will not be
Excessive.

The statement is frequently made that the Board of Drainage Commissioners, in addition to being granted extraordinary powers, are not responsible to the legislature or anybody else for their actions. This is an error, arising generally from ignorance doubtless, but an error all the same. It is true that the amendment does not specify that the Commissioners shall make reports to the legislature, but there are ample provisions for this in the State constitution, which is not set aside by the amendment; for while the amendment creates a board and confers upon it certain powers, is does not relieve the individuals composing is of their duties under the constitution and laws of the State. Back of all stands the power of the legislature to impeach and remove from office any man on that board for misfeasance (or malfeasance) in office, even though a

posed board of drainage commissioners a responsible body, responsible to the courts, responsible to the people, responsible to the legislature, then what in the name of common sense do we need to make them a "responsible body?" We anxiously await suggestions.   ALBERT H. ROBERTS.
In Tampa Tribune.

Sixty-Three Engines for the Coast Line.

Sixty-three new locomotives will be delivered to the Atlantic Coast Line Railway company this month direct from the Baldwin Locomotive works.

They will be passenger engines, freight engines and switch engines, all of the latest types. Thirty of these locomotives will be delivered direct to this division of the road and they will be pressed into service immediately upon their arrival.

These new locomotives will greatly benefit the operating department of this great railroad system.

The Atlantic Coast Line railway is now preparing to handle the great rush of tourist travel which has already turned southward and are arriving in Jacksonville daily.

With the Koreshans' new political party threatening to sway the 1906 election, Philip Isaacs undertook a campaign to prove "Teed's rascality," reprinting articles from the Unity's Chicago days. Article printed in the *Chicago Times*, c. 1892, and reprinted in the *Fort Myers Press*, October 18, 1906.

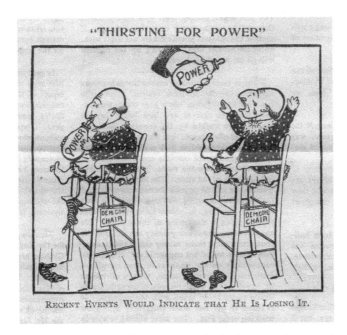

"THIRSTING FOR POWER"

RECENT EVENTS WOULD INDICATE THAT HE IS LOSING IT.

In their political paper, the *American Eagle*, the Koreshans lampooned Philip Isaacs, editor of the *Fort Myers Press* and chair of the Democratic committee, after he destroyed their ballots in the 1906 primary. Koreshan Unity Papers (record group 900000, collection N2009-3, box 296, folder 2), State Archives of Florida, Tallahassee.

This rare panoramic photograph of the community, taken in the early nineteen-hundreds, shows the general store at *front right*, Damkohler's cottage behind the store, the three-story dining hall (tallest), and the Founder's House in front of the hall. Courtesy of Koreshan State Historic Site and the Koreshan Collection. Florida Gulf Coast University Library Archives, Special Collections, and Digital Initiatives, Fort Myers.

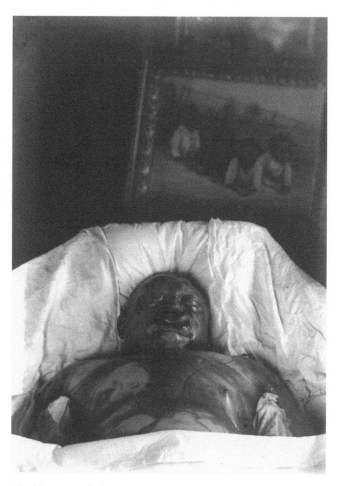

The followers took this picture on Christmas Day 1908, three days after Teed died. His body lies in a zinc bathtub made especially for him. The Koreshans watched the body for five days, until county health officials forced his burial. Koreshan Unity Papers (record group 900000, collection N2009-3, box 7, folder 15), State Archives of Florida, Tallahassee.

Before he died, Teed asked for a house of concrete stone. "I shall only want a small one," he said, "just room for one." His tomb sat on what is now Fort Myers Beach until a hurricane destroyed it in 1921. State Archives of Florida, *Florida Memory*, 255347.

A Koreshan woman thought to be Teed's sister Emma sits at the ruins of Cyrus Teed's mausoleum after the October 1921 hurricane. State Archives of Florida, *Florida Memory*, 258140.

Hedwig Michel fled Nazi Germany in 1940 and came to Estero when only thirty-five followers were left and the settlement was crumbling. She became the Unity's president, revived the general store, and donated the land that is now the state historic site. State Archives of Florida, *Florida Memory*, 256563.

This picture was taken the day after Hedwig Michel donated the settlement land to the state. She sits (*center*) with the last three original Koreshans. Note the contrasting expressions of Michel and Conrad Schlender (*left*), who did not get along. Vesta Newcomb and Alfred Christensen are on the right. A note accompanying the photo reads, "Final Four," though many descendants do not consider Michel a Koreshan. State Archives of Florida, *Florida Memory*, 257192.

Fifty-seven Koreshans are buried in this cemetery inside a gated golf course community in Estero. Cemetery #1, on a bend in the Estero River, is inaccessible. Courtesy of Nathan Hill.

✳ 14 ✳

After Koresh

Most of us fear death. Most of us yearn to comprehend
how we got here, and why—which is to say, most of us
ache to know the love of our creator. And we will no
doubt feel that ache, most of us, for as long as we happen
to be alive.

—Jon Krakauer, *Under the Banner of Heaven*

For a time, there was hopefulness, confidence that something would be made
clear, as Jennie Andrews had written to a follower. The Koreshans studied their
Master's writings for clues—and discovered many things they hadn't noticed
before. His teachings, the only tangible thing they still had of his, strengthened
their faith.

By reading, they discovered they must have been wrong about how things
would transpire. The Koreshans had assumed that Teed would die and theocratize in the same moment or at least in quick succession. He provided great
detail about theocrasis: he would *de*materialize, pass into Victoria's body, and,
once inside of her, he (they) would become a biune god. At that time, the followers, too, would become immortal, biune beings. But though Teed had predicted his own death—at the hands of a mob of Christians—and his translation, he didn't reveal the dates and never prophesied that these two events,
his death and theocrasis, would necessarily happen at the same time. So they
waited.[1]

Three major natural events that happened in conjunction with Teed's
death also strengthened their beliefs. He had taught the principle of "corre-
spondential analogy": when something happens in the spiritual world, there

are corresponding events in the human and physical worlds. Teed died on the winter solstice, the day that the sun appears to stand still in the sky, just as Teed became still. The day after his death, there was a total solar eclipse, visible in South America and southern Africa. "An eclipse," Teed wrote, "is the opening of the circuit of the great physical magneto-electrical battery." This had meaning for a Koreshan. Teed taught that when he theocratized, an electromagnetic explosion would happen in his brain, allowing him to pass into the spiritual world. For a Koreshan, the opening of this circuit could provide a way to make the explosion possible. Finally, on the day they entombed him, an earthquake of 7.5 magnitude struck between Sicily and Italy's mainland, causing a tsunami and killing more than one hundred thousand people. Teed had predicted this in a lecture in Chicago many years before. He said, "Coordinating and contemporaneous with the dissolution of the physical form of the Shepherd, the Stone of Israel, there will be earthquake shocks and tidal waves, devastating life and property to an extent hitherto unknown in this age."[2]

So his writings gave them great comfort, at least in the short term. "Our faith in the Messenger remains unwavering," a follower wrote in the *Flaming Sword* in 1909, two months after Teed's death.[3]

The group was less sure about who should lead them. Teed left no uncertainty about Victoria's spiritual role. Fifteen years before, after her coronation, he declared her the permanent head of the Unity. But did that mean she was their leader now? Or did it mean that she was the *eventual* leader—after he passed into the receptacle of her divine Motherhood?

She seemed quite human to them, at least for now. And not everyone liked her. And Teed wasn't there to defend and protect her. Very few of them believed she was their leader and instead chose to believe that Teed was coming back.

That spring, four months after Teed died, the Koreshans celebrated Victoria's birthday with the Lunar Festival in April, their tradition for many years. The day was more subdued than usual, and the public was not invited. In the morning, a bugle call cut through a light rain, calling everyone to breakfast. Victoria, sixty-five, was escorted into the dining hall by several of the younger women. The Koreshan dentist, Dr. Addison Graves, with whom Victoria had become very close, gave the greeting address. The Koreshan orchestra played during breakfast. Victoria spoke about the early life of the movement, read her Imperial Edict, a message to the Koreshan people, and unveiled a plaster bust of Teed. All day and evening, there was entertainment, including a drama, a musical fantasy, and a parody of a scene from *The Merry Widow*.[4]

Four months later, Victoria was gone. She and Addison Graves moved to central Florida and married. A handful of followers went with them, but the larger community shunned her. Her marriage proved to them that she was not the woman Teed thought she was. The accusations began. One Koreshan wrote about a time he took a trip with Victoria and she encouraged him to shoplift. Another Koreshan, who visited Victoria in her new home, noted that she appeared to be Catholic, that her ivory rosary beads were well worn, and that two Catholic priests often visited. Pictures of the Virgin Mary hung on the walls. The follower also said that Victoria never relinquished "the family tie." When she died in 1923, she left her son all assets, some of which, the followers claimed, the community paid for.[5]

In the early years after Teed's death, most of the Koreshans continued to believe in him, and they stayed in the settlement. But their numbers dwindled as time passed. Some of them stayed and believed for the rest of their lives, among them, Evelyn Bubbett and her husband and children, Jennie Andrews and her son Allen, Berthaldine Boomer, Henry and Etta Silverfriend, William and Abigail McCready, George Hunt, and Vesta Newcomb.

Some of those who left tried to form new communities. One small group, calling themselves progressive Koreshans, moved to Fort Myers and formed the Order of Theocracy. They issued a periodical called the *Double-Edged Sword* and opened what became the largest laundry business in town. This group included Ross Wallace, the man who ran for county commissioner on the Koreshan ticket in 1906, and Thomas Gay, Teed's favorite nurse, the one who said he would remain with Teed's body until he saw the worms eat all of it and crawl away in different directions.

A few of the Koreshans tried to take over the movement. Teed's nurse Gus Faber claimed to be the Koreshans' new leader, the Supreme Counselor of Koreshanity, whom Teed anointed on his deathbed, but Faber did not gain any followers. The strangest person who claimed to be Teed's successor was Edgar Peissart, who had belonged to the Unity all of one month before Teed died. He too claimed that Teed, on his deathbed, passed many spirits to him. Edgar printed religious fliers showing his own face superimposed over Teed's. This was a pattern for him. Edgar joined at least a dozen fringe groups in his lifetime, and he pops up in history here and there as a minor character, usually trying to wrest control from one messiah or another. At one point he claimed to be the projection of Shaker leader Ann Lee, and he created posters to indicate this, too.[6]

Ulysses Morrow, who left the Unity a few days after Teed died, moved to New Orleans with his wife, Rosa, and took a day job as a linotype operator. On nights and weekends, he continued working on the inside earth theory, which he called Field Theory. One Koreshan in Estero, convinced that Ulysses was the new savior, pleaded for him to return. He claimed not only that Ulysses had surpassed Teed in the cosmogony work but also that Teed had passed the mantle of messiahship to Ulysses. He believed Ulysses could complete the work Teed couldn't have, even if he had lived. "He started many things," the follower wrote Ulysses about Teed, "all in the most rough and crude way. Not a one did he ever finish in a workmanlike manner. Nothing was ever whipped into shape."[7]

Ulysses told the follower he wasn't interested. He had come to believe in a personal relationship with God, as opposed to one that required an intermediary. "I will follow no man," he wrote, "nor will I ask any man to follow me." And Teed had definitely been a man, Ulysses wrote to the follower, not a god.[8]

When Allen Andrews came across an article about Ulysses's work in a New Orleans paper, he was enraged. He wrote to the paper's editor and accused Ulysses of plagiarism, but the editor did not run his letter. In fact, it was Teed, posthumously, who had plagiarized Ulysses. In 1922, the Guiding Star Publishing House issued a new edition of *The Cellular Cosmogony*, which omitted Ulysses's name completely, along with the credit for his invention of the rectilineator. The sections Ulysses wrote, which amounted to half of the book, appeared word for word in the new edition, but Teed was the sole author. Gone was the introduction in which Teed praised Ulysses to the heavens, saying he was the man Teed spent twenty-seven years looking for—someone capable, honest, efficient, and knowledgeable.[9]

Two years after Teed's death, the *New York Times* followed up on a rumor that two Koreshan men tried to unseal Teed's tomb to see whether he had risen. Both men immediately became raving maniacs when they touched the stone, and they died soon after, the *Times* reported.

The journalist summarized Teed's and the Koreshans' activities—changing metal into gold, practicing celibacy, measuring the earth to prove its concavity, keeping vigil at the bathtub. "A more singular combination of sense and fantasy has not been shown since Joseph Smith 'dug up' his tablets and made himself the leader of the Mormons," he wrote.[10]

Henry Silverfriend was interviewed for the story. He was in Bristol at the furniture factory sorting out the finances; the plant had left the group with a debt of about twenty thousand dollars. Henry told the reporter that there had been disagreements among the followers over matters of theology, and that these had divided the Unity, but even so, "nearly everyone believes that in due time the tomb will open of itself and that Dr. Teed will come forth and do what he taught he would."

The *New York Times* got many details wrong in the story—it inflated the number of followers, reported that the Bristol plant was profitable, contained the assertion that a rich German gave Teed the land in Estero, and characterized the Koreshans as uneducated. Inaccuracies in the media about the Koreshans were nothing new, and there were many reasons for this. Sometimes reporters didn't interview the Koreshans for stories. Other times, the Koreshans refused to talk to reporters who, they judged, would distort the story. Or there were interviews, but Teed and his followers spoke in riddles, the reporters thought. Many reporters suited the facts to popular beliefs rather than reporting. Because who could pin down whether Teed had affairs with his followers or what he believed about himself? Did he think he was a messiah, or did he know he was a con man?

There was a reason the public felt the way it did about the Koreshans. And there was a reason the Koreshans believed what they believed. Those reasons were largely the same. Koreshanity gave its followers concrete facts, even if those facts couldn't be proven. So did the media.

Though the *Times* story about the lunatics at the tomb missed the details, it captured the truth absolutely, saying that Teed had enormous power because he came along at a particular moment in history. "He availed himself of the social unrest and of popular interest in science. He only repeated the guesses of men through many centuries, but he repeated them at a singularly lucky moment, and no doubt by reason of this good fortune acquired much merit in his followers' eyes."

How long would they believe? the reporter asked. How long would they wait for him to rise? He closed the story: "A few scientists should go down to Estero, study this singular situation, and report to the world on the working of that strangest of all things, the human mind."

In 1921, on October 25, the week after Teed's birthday, a hurricane hit the Gulf Coast of Florida. William McCready rode it out alone on the beach in a cottage a few steps from the tomb. He was one of two men who lived and worked on the island and kept watch over the tomb to protect it, if necessary, from raiders or vandals.[11]

On the morning of the hurricane, at about 6:30, the winds had strengthened and water began washing into the cottage. William opened the doors to let the water flow through, the only hope of saving the little house (and him) from being carried away. At about 7:00 a.m., the water rushed in, in volumes, and William saw an immense wave strike the tomb. The storm was too rough for him to assess the damage. He fought for nearly six hours to keep the door to the cottage open, and the water rose to his armpits before receding, at around noon, when the winds finally subsided.

The vault was open. Waves and wind had demolished it, and the concrete blocks had collapsed into a pile. Several Koreshans gathered on the island and cleared debris from the site. There was no trace of Teed's zinc bathtub that had functioned as a coffin, though the plank it had rested on was intact. The marble headstone survived: "Cyrus, Shepherd, Stone of Israel."

Evelyn wrote her children with the news. She had always believed, she said, that the tomb would be opened by nature in some major upheaval, and this confirmed her belief. For days, they cleaned up the mess on the beach and looked for signs. There are pictures of them around the wreckage, including one of Emma sitting on a broken concrete block, dressed completely in white and looking downward. There are also pictures of them sharing lunch on the island after the storm.

By then, there were fewer than a hundred Koreshans left. A few days after the hurricane, fourteen of them went to the beach. Combing the sand, they found several bones and his skull. "You can imagine how we felt," Evelyn wrote to her daughter. But Evelyn was reassured by something Emma said that Teed once told her: he didn't know whether his bones would dissolve. "So," Evelyn wrote, "we know that what happened is all right." They put the bones in the Estero post office, which was in the settlement, so that they would be safe.[12]

Perhaps this had been the theocrasis and he had risen, they thought. Or perhaps it hadn't. The board met and decided to be patient and to trust. "He will manifest himself in his own good time & manner," Evelyn wrote. "No amount of speculation will help matters."[13]

Life went on. Thomas Edison, who had a winter estate in Fort Myers, visited the forward-thinking Koreshans and became friendly with them. He and his wife, Mina, attended dramas in the Koreshan Art Hall. On the fiftieth anniversary of the incandescent bulb, the couple was stranded at the Unity when a heavy storm interrupted their trip to Fort Myers. The Koreshans took them in and fed them, ironically by candlelight, because the storm had knocked out the power. Edison's wife often visited the Koreshans' Rustic Tea Garden, one of her favorite places to have lunch. The painter Paul Sargent, son of longtime Koreshan John Sargent, visited and gave the Koreshans several of his paintings to hang in the Art Hall.[14]

Henry Ford, who also had a winter home in Fort Myers, had an especially keen interest in the Koreshans. He had established his own utopia, Fordlandia, in Brazil, and he visited the Koreshans five times during the winter of 1931. He was interested in their washing machine, their electricity, their beliefs in reincarnation, and, oddly, their papayas. Ford was seeking the ultimate food—one that would cause children to develop equally. He bought a supply of papayas and some canned foods from the Koreshans for the experiments in his Dearborn, Michigan, lab.[15]

The number of Koreshans declined steadily, and by the early 1930s only fifty-five believers were left. Allen Andrews was the president of the Koreshan Unity, the for-profit corporation Teed established in New Jersey in 1903. He was the boy from Binghamton whom Teed nicknamed Allie; the son of Teed's very first believer, Abie Andrews, and Jennie; the one who joined Teed for Sunday walks down the railroad tracks and who watched him play croquet in the twilight with his father. He was one of the first to come to Estero, welcoming the adventure and hoping the Florida climate would help him recover from the pneumonia he developed while living at Sunlight Flats. He had also led the war with Isaacs of the *Fort Myers Press* by becoming the editor of the *American Eagle*.

In 1930, a crew from Fox Movietone News came to the settlement, apparently to do a story on the Koreshans' inside earth belief. In a rare clip of raw film, there is Allen—silver haired, wearing a suit with a bow tie—looking directly into the camera and explaining the science of Koreshan Universology. He stands in the woods beside a working model of the globe, hinged in the back so that it can be opened to reveal the cosmos, represented by a ball that spins on an axis. The globe sits atop a platform with a sign beneath it: "We Inhabit the Concave Earth." Allen speaks matter-of-factly about the geodetic survey on Naples Beach thirty years before and how the Koreshans proved the theory conclusively. The hinge creaks when he opens the model. When he turns the ball, the axis squeaks.[16]

He delivers the speech as if he has done it many times, except that the producers apparently rushed him at the end. He speeds up as he tells us that China is not beneath our feet but instead, above us. There's no evidence that the Fox story ever aired.

Though Allen believed in Koreshanity, he had developed other interests since Teed's death. In 1916, he bought his first automobile, a used "Tin Lizzie" (a Ford Model T), which gave him access to places he had never seen, even though driving the sand roads was difficult on the skinny, high-pressure tires. In his memoir years later, he remembered getting stalled in the sand and sunk in mudholes many times and having to jack up the rear of the car and place palmetto leaves under the wheels to get going again. In the 1920s, Allen joined a group called the Trail Blazers, the first men to drive cars across the swamp and muck lands of the Everglades to lobby for a highway connecting the east and west coasts of Florida.

The Model T opened up his world, and he found that he loved to travel. He also loved tropical plants, thrilled by them ever since he had glimpsed the orange groves from the train in 1894 when he traveled from Chicago to Estero with the other young Koreshans. Now free to explore, he visited banana farms and mango orchards, where he learned about varieties of fiberless mangos. He talked to growers all over south Florida and discovered new plants to try in the nursery in Estero. He grafted tangelos, a hybrid of grapefruit and tangerine, and planted Chinese peaches, lychees, plums, figs, and strawberries. A botanical gardener in Miami gave him orchids, crotons, and acalyphas, which he transplanted to Estero, along with nearly sixty varieties of hibiscus in an array of reds, pinks, oranges, and yellows.

Allen looked for a solution to what many saw as the problem of swampland, where nothing economically valuable would grow, and he learned of a tree that was doing well in Australia on similar land: the melaleuca. He ordered seeds from Melbourne, planted them, and was delighted that the melaleuca thrived, rapidly seeding itself and forming dense evergreen stands.[17]

Allen turned the *American Eagle* into a horticultural review, and he published articles about his travels and plant discoveries; shared advice for preventing root knot, nematode, and all manner of disease; wrote about how to plant various tropicals for maximum yield; and ran interviews with nursery owners and botanists. The acclaimed horticulturist Henry Nehrling contributed stories regularly. The *American Eagle* became a respected journal—and Allen, a respected horticulturalist. The number of subscribers rose, and for the first time, the paper broke even financially, Allen claimed.

Meantime, he remained president of the Unity. Buildings were falling into decay, the small group of Koreshans was shrinking, and the orchestra disbanded. Koreshan Claude Rahn, who spent most of his time in Philadelphia, wrote about his reluctance to return to Estero for visits. The food, he wrote, was insufficient and always had been. The place was depressing, the people isolated, and the trouble, "strangely enough," he wrote, centered on Allen. The followers tolerated Allen, and no one would stand up to him. "Morally, he is clean, socially, he is a bore," Rahn wrote, adding that his hearing was poor and his eyesight defective. Allen made daily trips to Fort Myers and elsewhere and came to Estero only to sleep, according to Rahn. Allen ate dinner with the members only twice a week, one of those days being Thursday, when he had to be in Estero to put out the *American Eagle*. Otherwise, Rahn wrote, Allen ate in restaurants wherever his jaunts took him, and showed little concern for the followers, who worried about their next meal. At five foot eleven and 210 pounds, Allen was "the fattest and best fed member of our Unity," Rahn wrote. How was he able to pay for meals and incidentals and upkeep of his car? Subscription and advertising money from the *American Eagle*, Rahn wrote, answering his own question.[18]

The followers' faith in Koresh was still strong: "The Master, though unseen, is surely sustaining his 'little flock' and bestowing his blessing," a Koreshan wrote in the *Flaming Sword* in 1936 as the group prepared to celebrate Teed's birthday. Even when the post office burned down, incinerating Teed's skull and several bones, their belief didn't seem to waver.[19]

But many of them suffered from physical and emotional pain. There's a poignant example of this in Franklin Jacke, the hunchbacked keeper of the general store. He came to Estero with the big group in 1903 and took pride in his job, keeping the store well stocked and arranged. When the new store opened in the mid-1920s, he sent his mother a postcard photo of it, writing her that tourists and northerners often remarked that it was the best-kept store they had seen. But over the years, Jacke's eyesight failed, and the store faced financial trouble. By the 1930s, during the time Rahn wrote about, Jacke was in a deep depression. He struggled until he could do it no more. At age sixty-one, he committed suicide.

"Dear Folks: I am about blind, cannot see to do my work today. With all the business cares which no one knows, I am unable to stand this. I have gone to the river. Look for my hat on the point. I am so blind cannot see people in the store; just a dim outline."[20]

A few Koreshan brothers waded into the river and found the body. The deputy who examined Jacke found deep scratches on his face. It appeared that either before or after jumping into the water, he had tried to claw out his own eyes. George Hunt found the hat and, nearby, Jacke's coat, pocket watch, and handkerchief neatly folded on the bank.[21]

In 1940, when only thirty-five Koreshans remained, a curious thing happened. A Jewish woman escaping Nazi Germany arrived at the settlement. Hedwig

Michel (pronounced "Mitchell") had been the headmistress of a boarding school, operated from her own home in Frankfurt. A teacher at the school chanced upon a copy of Teed's *The Cellular Cosmogony* in a library and began writing to the Koreshans. He shared the book with Michel, and she read it with interest. When she needed to flee Germany and had nowhere to go, the teacher wrote to the Unity, and the Koreshans invited her to Estero.

When Michel arrived, she found that weeds were reclaiming the settlement and the buildings were in bad shape. The Planetary Court, where the leading women had lived, had become known as "the dead house" because it was in such disrepair. When it rained, the water came in. She surveyed the place, saw possibilities, and determined that Allen needed to go.

Allen had been the president of the Unity for nearly twenty years when Michel began a campaign to oust him in the late 1940s. She claimed that Allen had veered from the work of the Unity, that he traveled too much, and that he ate well while the other Koreshans went hungry. She found an ally in Laurence "Laurie" Bubbett, the son of Evelyn Bubbett, who had died in 1935. With Michel's help, Laurie Bubbett wrested control from Allen.

Allen's and Laurie's families had been important members of the Unity; their mothers, Jennie and Evelyn, had been on the Planetary Court; and their families traveled together. It's likely that the two men had been friends at one point, but now they were enemies. Allen filed a lawsuit, charging Michel and Bubbett with embezzlement and attempting to take the Unity's five hundred thousand dollars in assets for their own use. He wrote articles in the *American Eagle* and letters to the editor in the *News-Press*, detailing what he thought was their abuse of power. He claimed that they were mistreating one of the elderly Koreshans, denying him food and medical care. The judge dismissed Allen's case, finding no grounds for the accusations. Following this, Allen wrote to Hearst Publications in New York and tried persuading the company to report on the drama that was playing out, saying that Hearst's thousands of readers would find it interesting. The publisher, apparently, ignored his letter.[22]

Allen was senile, Michel and Bubbett declared in a list they drew up to catalogue the remaining Koreshans and their physical and mental conditions. It's interesting to note that Henry Silverfriend is not on this list, though he was still living. Henry had been declared mentally incompetent and was committed to the state hospital, relieved of all his duties at the Unity and of all rights or benefits, according to the legal documents, which were signed by Laurence Bubbett.[23]

Bubbett took over not only the presidency of the Unity but also the *American Eagle*, Allen's life's work. According to Allen, Bubbett ran it into the ground within ten months. Within a year of Allen's ousting, a fire destroyed the printing house; it burned for a week and turned the once-grand building to a pile of ashes and warped and twisted machinery.[24]

The fight between Allen and Michel and Bubbett didn't end there. In 1950, Bubbett charged Allen with physical assault, and Michel accused him of threatening to smash her house. Allen took an ax and destroyed a nursery plant stand, something Allen confirmed, saying that the stand did not belong in the nursery. Bubbett and Michel had him arrested.[25]

When Allen had a car accident, Michel and Bubbett wrote the state, asking that his driver's license be revoked. The state denied the request and a squabble ensued, in which Bubbett and Michel found witnesses who claimed that Allen's driver's license required him to have mirrors on either side of the car and that he was not allowed to drive at night, which he was doing. Allen was subjected to a driver's exam, which he failed, and his license was revoked.

By the time Allen published his memoir in 1950, he was bitter. The last chapter, filled with vitriol, is titled "How the American Eagle Was Wrecked." The following year, he wrote his will, in which he explained that he had devoted his life's work to the Unity and that the directors had taken his rightful share of the assets. He wrote that upon his death, his membership in the Unity would terminate. "I owe them nothing," he concluded. He died that year.[26]

Bubbett as president and Michel as secretary revived the community economically. Michel did most of the work, according to the official Koreshan history, *The Koreshan Story*: She reopened the general store, installing refrigeration for food storage. She sectioned off a part of the store and created a restaurant that served fresh fish and hush puppies. The official story credits her with adding a gas station, Standard Oil, though this was there long before she arrived. She restored the Planetary Court and made it her home. When she received reparations money from the German government, she donated it to the Unity to keep it going. The official history also says that she was a healer, using herbal remedies to keep the elderly Koreshans healthy, that she sewed dresses for the three oldest members, and that she cared for Etta Silverfriend during her terminal battle with breast cancer.[27]

But this sunny view of Michel wasn't the whole story. She was controversial. Though the official Koreshan story holds that Michel was the group's spiritual leader, there's no indication that she believed in Teed. In her later years, she was called "the last Koreshan," but at least one of today's descendants doesn't accept that title. Bill Grace, a retired Fort Myers attorney whose grandmother and great-grandparents were Koreshans, said Michel was not one. "Let me tell you something about Hedwig Michel," Grace said. "She was an interloper."[28]

Grace believes, as Allen did, that Michel mistreated the elderly Koreshans, and there's one record of an argument Michel had with one of the elderly Koreshans, Conrad Schlender, who wrote about a fight they had when he was seventy-two. According to Schlender's account, Michel picked the fight with him after dinner, accusing him of complaining about the food. "If you're not careful," Michel told him, "you'll go down there (pointing towards the cemetary [sic])," Schlender wrote.[29]

Mimi Straub, the founder of the Estero Historical Society, knew Michel and said they didn't get along. Straub described Michel as self-assured and dominant, and said that she knew how to make money and to use people. Bill Grace mentioned that Michel lived an extravagant lifestyle—that while the elderly followers suffered, she took trips to Europe. Pictures survive that show her on cruises with Laurence Bubbett. She wrote letters to Claude Rahn during a European vacation that she and Laurie took together—Paris, London, Zurich, Germany, and Italy to name a few. A neighbor observed that Michel drove a Cadillac that was too long for the carport she had added behind the Planetary Court.

But descendant Scott Ritter remembered that Michel was absolutely committed to the Koreshans, including the belief in the hollow earth. Ritter recalled his father asking Michel in 1960 whether Sputnik, the first manmade satellite to orbit earth, changed her belief in the cellular cosmogony. She said no, adding that if "the men" were here, they would be able to explain it. Ritter believed she was referring to Koreshan men who had studied and proved the theory.[30]

In the early winter of 1979, while Ritter was staying in Estero, he and Michel had many discussions about the Koreshans. Michel wanted there to be a fourth generation of Koreshans that would somehow revive the group. She wasn't referring to bringing their beliefs back, Ritter said—Michel was well aware that those had died. Rather, she wanted this new generation to host educational programs, though she didn't provide specifics.[31]

Ritter believed Michel wanted something to show for the forty years she had worked there. "She was afraid of people seeing the Koreshans' legacy as being a bunch of wackos," he said. "She wanted the world to know that the Koreshans were well-educated people with high standards and that they were important, somehow." She didn't reveal her entire vision for accomplishing this. But he is sure it was grand. He didn't ask her for more information because he couldn't take on the responsibility. "I was twenty-five and trying to make a living," he joked.

He remembered that Michel and one of the older Koreshans didn't get along, but he doesn't believe Michel would have mistreated her. "That doesn't sit well with me," he said. A scholar who met Michel in the 1970s also has positive impressions of her. She was naturally suspicious and careful, he said, but cooperative.[32]

Without exception, everyone, even her detractors, said she was a shrewd businesswoman who worked very hard, who saved the Unity economically, and who did more than anyone else to preserve the Koreshan legacy. She is the reason that the settlement exists, Bob Ritter, Scott's father, said. Without her, "it would have been a Hyatt or something."

In 1948, in the midst of the war between Allen and Bubbett and Michel, a writer for the *New Yorker*, Carl Carmer, came to Estero to write about the Koreshans. He interviewed Michel and Bubbett, who showed him around—and successfully hid from him the conflict with Allen, as reflected by Carmer's resulting peaceful story in his collection *Dark Trees to the Wind*. There were twelve Koreshans left, six women and six men, most of them elderly. The brothers and sisters continued to dine at separate tables, as they always had. Meals began with the Koreshan Daily Graces composed by Cyrus Teed. Carmer interviewed Teed's sister Emma, ninety-three, but she said she didn't remember much about the old days.

Michel and Bubbett had no plans to add members. "We're worried by dimwits," Bubbett told Carmer. "Why, we could keep this place filled with crackpots who couldn't possibly get along together!"[33]

Anyone who joined wasn't likely to be a sincere believer, Bubbett said, given the landholdings and the stock. "Many shiftless people would like to join us just to live out their days in idleness."[34]

Bubbett told Carmer that after the death of Koresh, people lost their drive. He said he expected that the Unity would die with its last members—but only on the material plane. There would be a corresponding gain in the spiritual world, he told Carmer.

And the theory of living inside the world would live on, Michel said: "It is a great truth and it will someday sweep across the world."[35]

On the morning Carmer was leaving, Michel and Bubbett took him to see the cemetery where many of the Koreshans were buried. The three of them climbed into a high-bodied station wagon and drove through tall trees on a path so poor that they had to get out of the car a few times to look for the trail. They reached a point where the trees ended at a flat expanse of scrub oak and palmetto. This was it—a few modest gravestones bordered by a rectangle of rocks and shells. Carmer read the names on the markers: Peter Blem, John Sargent, Gustav Faber, and others. "Wind was blowing across the wild low level of green leaves," Carmer wrote. "There was no other sound."[36]

"This is where the twelve old folks will probably rest," Bubbett told Carmer. He and Michel said they planned to improve the road to the cemetery and to weed the site and make it look nice.[37]

Bubbett died in 1960, and Michel took over as the president of the Unity. She began plans to preserve the settlement and to educate outsiders about the hollow earth belief. She arrived at two ways of doing this. She would arrange for the Unity to donate three hundred acres of land to Florida with the understanding that the settlement would become a state historic site. She would also form a nonprofit foundation whose primary purpose was to bring the truth of Koreshan Universology—the universe according to Teed, including the hollow earth theory—to the world, enlightening people who were "so deeply in ignorance," as Claude Rahn wrote. He was helping her to plan. They discussed the possibility of offering scholarships related to this work and encouraging scientists to repeat the measurements.[38]

Michel and Rahn mapped out the intent for the foundation, and she wrote, "We will not be a museum piece, dead, though of interest as an historical epoch in the development of the country." As she saw it, the purpose of the state park was to preserve the history, and the purpose of the foundation was to keep the Koreshans relevant—"as much of the future as [they are] a creation of the past, fully living after we are gone."[39]

In 1961, Michel carried out her plan to give three hundred acres of land, along with the Koreshans' furnishings, personal effects, and archives, to the state so that the property could be turned into a historic settlement. Michel and the three elderly Koreshans would live on the property until their deaths, at which point the state would have all rights to the land, and it could become a park.

Vesta Newcomb was by then in her seventies and one of the three remaining survivors. She was Teed's faithful thunder daughter who had left her family at age sixteen to be among the first to settle Estero, carrying the squawking parrot from Chicago, sleeping on the ground for ten months, and surviving on peanuts one winter. She had worked many jobs at the Unity—as Victoria's maid, a teacher at the Koreshan school, a laundress, and a clerk at the general store.

Once statuesque, Vesta was now stooped, her eyes bright blue as ever. She never married.[40]

"I am an old maid," she joked with an interviewer when she was in her eighties or nineties. "You see, I had a sharp ear (still do) and I often heard things I wasn't supposed to. Although all of the [Koreshan] women were celibate, some had been married and widowed, and they would be talking over their marriage experiences. Being young and impressionable, I wanted none of that."[41]

By 1969, Vesta was the only original Koreshan living. She stopped believing in the hollow earth theory on July 20, 1969. "The boys landed on the moon," she said in an interview. "When that happened, I knew it couldn't possibly be true." She was ninety. She and Michel were the last ones living in the park—Vesta in a cottage and Michel in the Planetary Court—and they rarely spoke, descendant Scott Ritter said. Vesta had nowhere to go and no money. Occasionally, she left the settlement on foot. One neighbor in Estero remembered Vesta coming to see her, asking for money to buy food. The neighbor, unable to help, returned her to the settlement each time. Vesta also visited a cousin in Fort Myers, where the story was the same.[42]

There was property left after Michel donated the land to the state, a few hundred acres—a fraction of what the Koreshans had owned: between 5,700 and 7,500 acres in southwest Florida. It's impossible to get an exact figure, because some of the property was held by individual members, a precaution Teed took to protect assets from creditors and lawsuits, and it's doubtful that everyone who held a deed surrendered it altruistically to the Unity.[43]

After Teed's death, the land that *did* legally belong to the Koreshans dwindled. Much of it was lost to squatters in the early years. The rest was sold, little by little, in dozens of transactions to individual buyers. The money from sales kept the community going or helped pay off debt and settle lawsuits. The sales ran through Cyrus Teed's old corporation, a for-profit enterprise, subject to property and capital gains taxes. In 1972, Michel created the private nonprofit foundation she had considered for more than a decade, so that the organization could be exempt from federal income tax and property tax.

In 1974, Vesta died and was the last to be buried in the derelict Koreshan cemetery, leaving Michel alone at the settlement, living in the Planetary Court. She began giving public tours in 1979.

That year, Michel also built a headquarters for the foundation on land belonging to the Unity, directly across U.S. Highway 41, which in Teed's day was the heavy sand road to Fort Myers. When he was alive, the trip took five or six hours, depending on whether a traveler had a team of oxen or "a thin enemic [*sic*] skeptical horse," one Koreshan wrote. By the late seventies, the trip was possible in well under an hour.[44]

The building Michel commissioned was odd, not particularly well suited to Florida's climate, because it was constructed of wood even though by then sturdier materials were available. Its shape was especially strange: its footprint was a nautilus shell. The building's outer wall was a spiral; it circled outward, wrapped around, and overlapped itself near the front door. Another strange thing about the design was that, in addition to office space, an apartment, and a library and reading room, there was a large open room where the Koreshans' furnishings, artifacts, literature, and documents could be displayed. This, in spite of the fact that the Koreshans had agreed in 1961 to give these to the state to be exhibited at the settlement. In the seventies, it became clear that Michel had changed her mind.

When the headquarters building was completed, she—and perhaps other members of the Unity board—removed many items from the settlement: Victorian furniture; musical instruments; an extensive library of books, paintings, and miscellany like the leather shin guards Teed wore as protection from snakes when he walked through the woods; a woman's palmetto wrist fan for swatting at horseflies and mosquitoes; several typewriters; and on and on. Many of the artifacts stayed at the state park. There were, after all, plenty of furnishings and effects to go around. It had taken fifteen boxcars to bring it all from Chicago in 1903.

The archives were a different story. Michel took the bulk of them: histories of the families, Teed's letters to Abie Andrews and to his sister Emma, Jennie Andrews's journal and letters, hundreds of photographs, tickets to Teed's lectures, programs for Lunar and Solar Festivals, organizational records, and even recipes and sheet music. The state park's archives paled in comparison to what Michel possessed.

It isn't clear why she moved these things. Perhaps she had a change of heart after promising many of these objects to the state. Perhaps they had sentimental value to her; certainly, they had financial value as collectibles and antiques. It might have been her intention to start a museum. She moved more than enough material to the headquarters to do so, and the design of the building was suited to it. Based on what she named the building, her aims included making the archives available to scholars: the Koreshan University Headquarters/Pioneer Research Library.

One theory about why Michel removed items from the settlement is that she had become bitter: she had expected that the state would move faster and donate more time and energy to restoring the settlement and building the park. When the state did not meet her expectations, she transferred items to the new foundation building.

Minutes of board meetings reflect that Michel was otherwise cooperating with the state to actively preserve the legacy and to educate the public. And she felt a deep attachment to the settlement. When the air-conditioned apartment in the headquarters building was finished, everyone expected that she would move in, but she remained in the Planetary Court, saying that she wanted to live in what she called "her garden." That's where she stayed until she died, at which point she was buried on the settlement just a few steps away from the house. Wrought-iron bars form a small box around her grave. It's ironic that Michel is buried in the settlement when none of the original Koreshans were. Even more ironic is that Teed's tombstone sat across the street inside the College of Life building rather than in the park.[45]

Michel's tombstone reads, "Be ashamed to die until you have won some victory for humanity." In a short pamphlet, "A Gift to the People," she made clear that her victory was donating the settlement land and buildings to Florida.

It would make sense for the state park and the foundation Michel started to work together, but this didn't happen. As Estero grew, and as U.S. Highway 41 widened, so did the gap in Teed's legacy. On the west side of the road was where the Koreshans had lived, under the control of the state. On the east side were the best of their furnishings, personal articles, and most of the photos, letters, ledgers, and documents they left—controlled by a foundation that owned what remained of their land, a few hundred acres becoming more valuable.

And this was the 1980s, when Florida was shifting from sunny paradise to bizarro world, as depicted by writers like Dave Barry, Tim Dorsey, Carl Hiaasen, and others. "A lost utopia," historian Gary R. Mormino wrote, "a dystopian, overdeveloped land overrun by corporate theme parks, rapacious developers, and crazed drug lords."[46]

✴ 15 ✴

Florida Forever

A Marriott resort stands on the flat point of land where Damkohler and his family arrived in 1882 and where Teed and his Triangle of Women stayed while scouting property. Over the bridge from Punta Rassa is Sanibel, an island for vacationers and millionaires, its main road smooth and lined with black, ribbon-like bike paths—very different from the "goshawful washboard" Allen Andrews traveled in the 1840s.[1]

Though the land has been heavily developed, it's possible to get a sense of the natural world the Koreshans saw more than a hundred years ago on their boat trips between Punta Rassa and Estero. It's best done from the water, on the paddling trail that meanders through the bays of Pine Island, Captiva, Sanibel, and Estero. Mullet leap from the water and slap the surface. Dolphins come up for air, sometimes so close to your kayak that you hear them inhale. Hundreds of squawking pelicans and egrets weight the trees of uninhabited islands, which appear to be land but are clusters of mangroves growing out of the underwater muck. Good for nothing but snakes, Marie McCready once wrote. And the mosquito problem hasn't changed. Go outside on a warm night after a rain and they will find you instantly.[2]

The trip from Punta Rassa to Estero takes you past Estero Island, which follows the coast inward. At its northwest tip is Fort Myers Beach, a riot of bright shops, restaurants, bars, and crowds, with a pier jutting into the Gulf where fishermen reel in silvery fish. On the south end, where Teed died and where the Koreshans' first sawmill and post office stood, development thins to a few timeshares and hotels. South across the estuary is Mound Key, where the Calusa lived two thousand years ago and where the Koreshans roasted oysters, camped out overnight, and waited for the tide to rise so they could row home up the tea-colored river shaded with oaks.

On the land where the Koreshans settled, many of the major buildings have been restored—to the extent the state's budget, outside donations, and grants have allowed. In a clearing, the dinner bell hangs from a post, marking the spot where the dining hall and women's dorm once stood. Near the river is Gustave Damkohler's cabin, Florida wood-frame vernacular, one of the first houses built in Lee County. Inside his shack are a bed, desk and chair, a doctor's bag, and a wooden trunk. Near the cabin, the graves of Damkohler's wife and three of their children are marked with large rocks. No one knew where the bodies were until recently, when a dog trained to detect human remains identified them. A few yards from the graves is a bamboo forest that began as a planting from Thomas Edison's estate. The trees are so dense that the stems rub each other in even the lightest breeze, groaning like the hinges on heavy doors.

On the porch of the Planetary Court, painted a muted yellow, visitors can rest in large rocking chairs. Outside, a placard shows pictures of Jennie Andrews, Etta Silverfriend, Berthaldine Boomer, Evelyn Bubbett, and the other women who lived there. In the Founder's House, where Teed and Victoria lived, a television plays a looping video about the Koreshans, including a reenactment of Teed's street fight in Fort Myers. In the restored Art Hall are a stage, paintings by Arthur Teed, and a section of Ulysses Morrow's rectilineator.

The people who created the exhibits paid careful attention to detail. In Vesta Newcomb's sitting room, her original birdcage holds a fake white dove. In her bedroom, a parrot perches atop a wire planter. Whoever furnished the cottage knew that Vesta carried a parrot all the way from Chicago to Estero, a detail she dropped in an unpublished interview.

Guided tours are frequent during the tourist season, and there are docents in the buildings. What's lacking is an interpretive center, meaning that visitors who don't take a tour may come and go without understanding the community. They enter the settlement from a small parking lot, pick up a pamphlet from an unattended box, walk down a path, and arrive beside the Art Hall. Detailed kiosks tell the story of the Koreshans, which the visitor pieces together by walking from building to building on the shell paths.

Every winter, there are nighttime ghost walks at the settlement, where actors play the parts of various Koreshans: in the Art Hall, a wife and her reluctant husband are joining the Unity, while on the porch of the Planetary Court the community's leading women grieve Teed's death. Gustave Damkohler stands outside, shaking his fist and airing his grievances to the crowd. He is mostly blind, heavily bearded, and frozen in time—on the verge of leaving, having realized that Teed stole his land. At the bakery, Koreshan men in smocks distribute hermit cookies.

The park also hosts a concert series, afternoon teas, a taste of history luncheon, an antique engine show, and a farmers market. But usually the grounds are quiet. On the fringes of the settlement, gopher tortoises lumber across prairies of palmetto; armadillos forage in the dirt for grubs; and snakes weave along the ground—black racers, the occasional diamondback rattler, and, rarely, the endangered indigo. Most of the park—the once-wild grounds tamed by Gustave Damkohler and then the Koreshans—is a wilderness of pine, eucalyptus, cabbage palm, and live oak grown over with resurrection fern, whose fronds, in dry weather, are brown and shriveled and, by all appearances, dead. After a rain, they unfurl, carpeting the branches green.

The most unusual tree is the monkey puzzle, an evergreen with twisted, spiral leaves on its arms and lethal cones "about twice the size of hand grenades," horticulturalist Michael Dirr wrote.[3]

Outside the park is the growing village of Estero, which looks Mediterranean because, in the early 2000s, Estero's planners decided that would be the preferred architecture for new buildings. The malls and housing developments are earth-toned buildings with low-pitched tile roofs, arched windows, balconies, towers, turrets, and colonnades. Much of the town has succumbed, as have other lost Florida places, to a "paradise" of gated-community living and ahistorical culture.

Across the highway from the state park, the flimsy wooden nautilus-shaped building still stands, the structure Hedwig Michel built and where she brought many Koreshan artifacts and the voluminous archives. From the road, all that's visible is a glimpse of parking lot. Bushes and vines have claimed the cyclone fence that surrounds the property, which is for sale.

For thirty years, what went on in this hidden building was largely a mystery. Few people went in or knew that it housed hundreds of important Koreshan artifacts and nearly all of the archives. In 2001, the foundation's name changed to College of Life, for the "college" Teed started in Chicago in the 1880s and where he awarded psychic and pneumic therapeutic doctorates for fifty dollars. It was an obscure connection that almost no one knew. As a result, the relationship between the College of Life and the Koreshans was not apparent.

The foundation's purpose, according to its organizational documents, was to preserve the Koreshan legacy and to educate visitors about it, but there had long been questions about whether the foundation was doing this—and questions about exactly what the foundation *was* doing. For decades the people at the Koreshan State Historic Site and the people running the foundation rarely spoke. They were just across the road, but their missions were miles apart. How that came to be, and how the two came back together, is a strange story.

The legacies of the celibate communities with which Teed wanted to confederate—the Shakers and the Economites (or Harmonists)—have fared well. In New Lebanon, where Victoria and Jennie Andrews became novitiate Shakers in the summer of 1892, the Great Stone Barn is being restored. There's a museum and library with two hundred years of artifacts, photos, and records. Its exhibits connect Shaker culture to today. Last year's big benefit centered on an art film, *Rock My Religion*, which tied Mother Ann Lee and ecstatic religious practices to the development of rock music and youth culture in America. A past exhibit juxtaposed Shaker furniture and modern sculpture. Another demonstrated the Shakers' sophisticated system for circulating water through the settlement.

At Old Economy Village, where Teed courted Father Henrici and then John Duss, there is a six-acre village and a museum where tourists and scholars can interpret the history of the Harmonists in their original setting. A guided tour includes six original buildings, and the museum provides changing exhibits. Resources for educators include a field trip to the site, where students can visit a one-room schoolhouse, learn to write with a slate and stylus, sing songs, and milk a cow. A recent Autumnfest featured trade demonstrations that show how the Harmonists smoked meat and made rope. There's an interactive area where people can play games from the era. In the Harmony Society gardens stands a statue of the Greek goddess Harmonia, sheltered by a pavilion and surrounded by a circular pond.

In central Florida, Spiritualism lives on—at Cassadaga, a Spiritualist camp founded in 1894, the same year Teed discovered Estero. Cassadaga is an active religious community as opposed to a preserved village. Some of the people who live there are descendants of the Spiritualists who founded the camp. Many of the residents are working mediums or spiritual healers. Visitors come for psychic readings, healing, or communication with loved ones who have died. The town has had every reason to become a tourist trap, except that the residents don't want that. The place is original, old Florida with a Stephen King vibe.

Other utopian communities, though influential, have fallen into neglect. In Dickson County, Tennessee, in the 1890s, a group of socialists formed a colony on Yellow Creek near a large natural cave. They named it Ruskin, after the British social critic John Ruskin, and they were influenced by some of the same ideas that influenced Teed—communal living, an escape from what they called wage slavery, and the desire to better themselves intellectually and culturally—though the Ruskin colony didn't have a religious component. The colonists grew their own food, which they canned and stored in the cave. They manufactured and sold leather suspenders, chewing gum, and cereal coffee, and they published a socialist paper, the *Coming Nation*. They used their own currency based on work hours.

At its peak, Ruskin had 250 colonists, but the community collapsed in 1899, driven apart by ideological differences. Of the original buildings only one remains, boarded up. The cave is available for corporate events, family reunions, and weddings. Ruskin's legacy is forgotten, even though it provided a model for twentieth-century kibbutzim in Israel and co-ops promoted by the U.S. Farm Security Administration in the 1930s.[4]

After Hedwig Michel died, the secretary of the Koreshan Unity Foundation, Jo Bigelow, took over. Bigelow's only connection to the Koreshans was her relationship with Michel. Her previous jobs included editing features for the *Fort Myers News-Press* and running a ranch. As head of the foundation, Bigelow led a board of twenty-five members but rarely accepted their help. People volunteered their services to organize and preserve the Koreshan archives, give legal counsel, restore the artifacts, and raise money, but Bigelow refused these offers. Her attorney told a reporter that Bigelow was offended once when he brought up the subject of grants.[5]

Koreshan descendant Bill Grace joined the foundation because he wanted to help and because Bigelow seemed to need it, he said. As far as he could tell, she didn't have a budget, a mission statement, any of the things he thought were necessary to operate properly. "I thought perhaps the only thing she needed was education," he said.[6]

Grace tried to persuade Bigelow to offer educational programs, to have the Koreshans' documents organized into professional archives, and to restore the cemetery, but he said she wasn't interested in doing any of these things. Grace saw things that troubled him. The foundation owned a house on the beach, and the board members had agreed it would be rented to provide some income. Instead, one of the foundation's officers lived there for free. Bigelow took some of the Koreshan furniture and put it in her own house.

Grace decided Bigelow needed to go, but he knew she wouldn't leave voluntarily. He persuaded three people to join the foundation as members, including one with experience in historic preservation and another with an advanced degree in applied anthropology. The plan was to vote Bigelow out, but she preempted it by changing the articles of incorporation and bylaws: under her new rules, the members would no longer elect the board; the board would elect the board. She made this change without a vote from the members, Grace said.

Grace left, calling the foundation a sham and putting his efforts instead into a different foundation, now called Friends of Koreshan State Historic Site. The group raised money to restore the Art Hall, the Planetary Court, and the Founder's House. The rift between Grace and Bigelow ended any cooperation between the Friends group and the foundation. The two groups were suspicious of each other.

Bigelow didn't trust the state park employees, once telling a reporter that people who had been trained by Parks and Recreation didn't have the knowledge to protect the archives or oversee the land. It was like she was holding on to family treasures, said Kate Zajanc, the former museum curator at the historic site. The people at the park didn't know what objects and files the foundation had.[7]

"Getting anything from Jo was like pulling teeth," a former ranger at the park said. A part-time archivist at the historical site saw the foundation archives once in his twenty-one years with the park, and it was from the doorway to the archives only—a fireproof vault Bigelow had built.[8]

The most likely explanation as to why she closed off the archives is that she wanted to be their sole interpreter, even if it meant refusing offers to have them professionally preserved and organized.

"The archives belong to the foundation, which is a private corporation," Bigelow told a reporter for *Gulfshore Life* magazine in 1995. "I don't have to open them to anyone."[9]

Bill Grace said he doesn't understand why Bigelow was so secretive and why she wouldn't let scholars in to study the archives. "I never, to this day, I don't know what that woman was thinking of. I don't think that she was really seeking wealth or influence."[10]

A *Gulfshore Life* reporter wrote, "What drives this widow with intense eyes is the belief that she knows what's best for the Koreshan legacy." She didn't want "hordes of people" in the building, Bigelow told the writer. Her operations officer, the man who was living rent-free on the beach, agreed. "The communal system was a personal system and we'd like to keep it that way," he said. "We feel that by continuing to grow and doing our job . . . we will attract the individual and the attention we want to attract. We're not here to protect the archives and protect the heritage so someone could misinterpret it."[11]

In the late 1980s, an IRS audit revealed that the foundation was not making its required distributions to charity, and officials claimed they hadn't understood the specifics of this law. The foundation sold some land for four hundred thousand dollars to make it right. That year, the foundation was down to its last twenty thousand dollars.[12]

Bigelow, on behalf of the foundation, then sold most of the remaining Koreshan land for $5.1 million to a developer that built Pelican Sound Golf & River Club, an upscale residential community. She did not sell the Koreshan cemetery, which now sits in the middle of Pelican Sound. This is the graveyard Michel and Bubbett took *New Yorker* writer Carl Carmer to see in the 1940s. Though the foundation, under Bigelow, kept the land, it did nothing to maintain the gravesites.[13]

The $5.1 million sale upset descendants and other community members, who felt they should have some say over what the foundation could do. Grace, who objected to selling the land, told a reporter that soon there wouldn't be anything left to preserve. Bigelow said that this particular land didn't have historic value for the Koreshans. The foundation was within its rights to sell the land; the founding documents allowed it to sell land and use the proceeds to support its charitable activities. But there was the question. Was the foundation fulfilling its charitable purposes? Reporters began asking because the land sale was big news.

One such reporter was Lee Melsek, now retired, but then an investigative reporter for the *Fort Myers News-Press*, the same paper Philip Isaacs edited when he waged war on Teed, prompting the Koreshans to start the *American Eagle*. When Melsek asked to review the foundation's tax returns, Bigelow refused until her attorney told her she was required to produce them.

When Melsek asked Bigelow why she had Koreshan furniture in her house, she said there wasn't room in the headquarters to store it. When he asked the operations officer how his living at the beach house rent-free benefited the foundation's charitable purpose, the officer responded, "You ask some tough questions."

The *News-Press* devoted considerable space in its hefty Sunday edition to Melsek's coverage, and it ran an editorial recommending that the foundation be disbanded, that profits from land sales be placed into a trust, and that all holdings be turned over to the state. Bigelow had not directed any of the money from the $5.1 million sale to the Friends of Koreshan State Historic Site for restoration.[14]

During Bigelow's time as president, there *were* some successes. The foundation briefly sponsored the Solar and Lunar Festivals; the *American Eagle* came out twice a year; and Bigelow commissioned *The Koreshan Story*, a seventy-page book about the Koreshans, an idealistic account that contains several errors. At the end of her term, she donated thousands of artifacts to the park, items already on the park grounds. No one knows why she decided to do this.

Bigelow was sixty-seven when she became the president of the foundation, and she worked until she was eighty-six. She wouldn't retire, she told a reporter, until she found the right person to take over. "When I have somebody who really feels as responsible as I do, I'll retire." The person she found was Naples real estate agent Charles Dauray.[15]

The narrative of the foundation under Dauray's leadership falls into three distinct acts: hopefulness, mistrust, and recovery. Most of the story comes from newspaper and magazine articles and from public records rather than directly from Dauray, who is an extremely private person and who, as Cyrus Teed did, has a tense relationship with the media.[16]

The *News-Press* ran an upbeat profile of Dauray when he became the foundation's administrator. In the story's lead, the reporter and Dauray strolled the land behind the nautilus building and walked out to the Estero River, crunching over leaves and twigs. Dauray wore a khaki suit with a crisp white handkerchief in the breast pocket and a straw hat.[17]

"I've always been drawn, intuitively, to this property," he told the reporter, saying it was a dream job. Dauray had lived in southwest Florida for decades and had a proven commitment to preserving local history. He was also involved in politics, having run, unsuccessfully, for Naples City Council.

In his early months at the foundation, he shared his vision at a civic association meeting: keeping the Koreshan lands as natural as possible. "I want to create a place for our children and grandchildren to enjoy forever. Some orchids, some plants, some serenity, some muck." He said he hoped to restore the Koreshan furniture and to work with the nearby university to create a "living historical classroom."[18]

After Dauray took over, communication between the park and the foundation improved. The manager of the park said she and Dauray were talking about ways they could work together. One of the ideas was to bring back the Solar and Lunar Festivals, which had been discontinued. "We understand each other," the park manager, speaking of Dauray, told *Naples Daily News*, adding that Dauray seemed open to a relationship.[19]

But Dauray made a move that drew ire from descendants and others with a connection to the Koreshans. Immediately upon becoming president, he reduced the board to only three people—himself, a secretary, and an attorney, all of whom were officers. He was within the rules under the articles of incorporation, which Bigelow had revised so that no vote was necessary. Critics said there was no oversight. The officers could elect themselves and set their own salaries.

The IRS was effectively the only oversight. Dauray told a reporter he did this to make the foundation more efficient.[20]

George Horne, who had worked for the foundation as a handyman for nearly fifty years, told the media that Dauray sent him a memo telling him not to discuss the foundation's activities with anyone. Horne quit.[21]

On behalf of the foundation, Dauray bought blocks of land along the Estero River and planned to build Riverplace, a development of homes, retail shops, a conference retreat center, a hotel, a low-intensity marina, and nature trails. Dauray indicated to a reporter that Riverplace would be a campus for education and that it would host religious, environmental, educational, and history groups. Nearly half of the development would be open space, and plans called for wide buffers on either side of the river and for preserving the historic resources on the property, which included two turn-of-last-century buildings, a one-room schoolhouse, and a 1904 cottage. Most of the land to be developed was not original Koreshan property, but some was.[22]

People in Estero were cautiously optimistic about Riverplace. "If it's a sheep in sheep's clothing, it's wonderful," a member of the Estero Civic Association told the *Naples Daily News*. "If it's a wolf in sheep's clothing, that's different.[23]

Critics accused Dauray of running a real estate development company, not a foundation. Chad Gillis, then a reporter for the *Naples Daily News* and *Bonita Daily News*, wrote a series about the foundation. Mimi Straub, founder of the Estero Historical Society, told Gillis, "I don't think they [the foundation] give a hoot [about historical preservation or education]. They're strictly interested in M-O-N-E-Y."[24]

Dauray countered in the press that his critics were jealous and wanted to take over the assets of the foundation. He defended the Riverplace development: "What we are doing here is the fulfillment of what the Koreshans ultimately wanted to do," he told Gillis, noting that the Koreshans envisioned Estero as a large city.[25]

Before Riverplace could go forward, the land needed to be rezoned; Dauray had applied for rezoning in 2000. He amended and resubmitted the application many times, revising the plans, likely in an attempt to satisfy the county and critics. But the idea of *any* development on the river rankled many people in the community. The Estero Civic Association gathered two thousand signatures on a petition calling for the government to purchase the property. Dauray responded with an offer to sell eighteen acres (the original Koreshan land piece) for seven million dollars, but the county turned it down. As the state considered buying it, Dauray delayed the rezoning hearing to give it time, according to the *Naples Daily News*.[26]

As opposition to Riverplace grew, there were echoes of the conflict Teed had with the citizens of Chicago. Dauray said he was accused of ridiculous things, like selling off Koreshan artifacts at flea markets. His life was even threatened in 2002, he said. There were two phone calls, which he thinks were from the same person, after nine one night. "After 9 o'clock in Estero, if you're not asleep, you're probably not sober," he said.[27]

In 2003, Dauray was surprised to learn that a state committee had voted to evaluate purchasing the property as a Florida Forever acquisition. But he had not offered the property for such a purchase, he told a *Bonita Daily News* reporter, and no one had called him to discuss it.[28]

"I imagine it's some of our friends who like to offer property they don't own for sale without discussing it with the foundation," Dauray told the reporter. He indicated that the foundation board would meet to decide whether to go ahead with the next rezoning hearing.[29]

"These things get expensive," he said. "When they hold meetings and we're not invited it makes one a little less willing to prolong the agony."[30]

That was in March 2003. By September, the rezoning request had been withdrawn, and that was the end of Riverplace.

Given the community's stated commitment to preserving the Koreshan legacy, something it did in 2004 is odd. One of the main roads in Estero was Koreshan Parkway. As development boomed and the parkway became a major corridor, the chamber of commerce and the civic association requested that the name be changed to Estero Parkway. Landowners and developers unanimously supported it. The street signs for Koreshan Parkway were replaced without ceremony.

For a long while, the land intended for Riverplace sat idle, growing in value. People wondered what would happen to the two historic buildings on the property—the schoolhouse and cottage. Dauray told a reporter for the *News-Press*, "You can't save everything. All of the money in the world can't resurrect the past into today's reality." But he made a quick turnabout, agreeing that the foundation would give the buildings to the Estero Historical Society.[31]

In 2007, the foundation sold the land to a developer, Village Partners— eighty-five acres for $11.4 million. In a move that came back to bite the foundation, it financed a chunk of the sale.

Soon, a new development was drawn up, Estero on the River, to be built by Village Partners. It would include a theater, 530 residences, retail space, a boutique hotel, and a greenway. Interestingly, Estero citizens were more receptive to this development than they had been to Riverplace.[32]

Dauray made good on the foundation's promise to donate the historic buildings—and then some. The foundation donated one hundred thousand dollars to have the buildings moved to a community park and to cover the cost of plans for their renovation. It remains one of the largest donations the foundation has ever made, and it went a long way toward healing the relationship between the foundation and the community. The people in the historical society were delighted to have headquarters in the 1904 cottage in Estero Community Park.

Estero on the River was never developed. It was kept on hold for a while, awaiting the widening of U.S. Highway 41. And then the real estate market crashed. Suddenly the value of the land was nowhere near the $11.4 million Village Partners paid for it. The foundation took a hit, writing down the value of the note it had extended to Village Partners. Eventually Village Partners abandoned the plans.

The media left the foundation alone for a long time, and it fell back into obscurity. Most people in Estero didn't know what the College of Life Foundation did, and even descendants weren't sure any more. "I've wondered for years," Bill Grace said in 2009. Scott Ritter, the descendant whom Michel talked to about the fourth generation, said in 2010 that he was never in touch with the College of Life. "Nobody is." He said there was no purpose for the foundation anymore. That year, Dauray drew a salary of nearly two hundred thousand dollars.[33]

In 2009, the foundation donated the Koreshan letters, journals, photos, and records to the State Archives in Tallahassee. The archivists who organized the collection arrived at the College of Life in 2008 to find "a state of near-chaos," they wrote on their blog. "Hundreds of boxes of disorganized, mislabeled files."[34]

Curiously, the foundation's tax returns listed a single direct charitable activity: operating a museum and presenting one hundred years of records and artifacts. But there was no sign indicating a museum, no advertising or outreach letting the community know about a museum, no posted hours, admission charges, exhibitions, or special events. Tours were by appointment. A foundation spokesperson said that Dauray chose not to keep the museum open regular hours because it would compete with the state park. He wanted the competition between the foundation and the park to stop, the spokesperson said, and he saw this as an olive branch.[35]

Under Dauray's leadership, the foundation made donations that furthered the legacy of the Koreshans and other pioneers in southwest Florida. It underwrote the documentary about the Koreshans that plays in the Founder's House at the park. It donated artifacts and money to the site. But other donations did not directly benefit the Koreshans. The foundation supported a children's museum, a literacy foundation, and countless causes related to art, culture, the environment, education, history, and community initiatives. When asked about these donations, Dauray said that they supported aims the Koreshans valued.[36]

By 2010, the archives were gone and the artifacts were still sitting. What was happening inside the odd building with the College of Life sign out front? It echoed an earlier place and time, Chicago 1888, when citizens wondered what went on in a place called the College of Life.

The front office of the wooden building was a bare-bones place with a linoleum floor and '70s-era office furniture, except for Dauray's desk, a Koreshan piece. Against one wall was the white lollipop scale that once stood in the Koreshan general store.

Most of the artifacts were in the back of the building, in the room that formed the outer, sweeping curve of the nautilus. Floor-to-ceiling windows offered a view of the trees and, beyond them, flashes of cars speeding by on Highway 41. The curtains on the upper windows were white with gold and purple trim, representing the brilliant mist out of which Cyrus's angel emerged during the 1869 illumination that started it all. They were Dauray's idea.

On a wooden table sat a model of Teed's globe—two halves opened to reveal the continents laid out along the shell and a cobalt-blue ball at the center representing the heavens. Teed's headstone, which withstood the 1921 hurricane, hung on a wall above a nightlight. A baby grand piano, built in 1877 and brought by boxcar from Chicago, sat beneath the Koreshan flag, yellow with a geometric design, the flag they unfurled at Beth-Ophrah for Teed's birthday, when the grounds were draped with white bunting, the orchestra played until the insects chased everyone inside, and the drama troupe performed a scene from *Ben-Hur*. Behind the piano was Teed's Murphy bed.

In another room was a headless mannequin torso wearing Teed's white vest, his eagle claw stickpin, and his cravat, tied in the loose bow style he favored. Dauray said it would soon tour Lee County's libraries. There were several pairs of spectacles. There were his leather rattlesnake guards and Teed's many varieties of business cards. The string of cursive letters after Teed's name was longer than the name itself: Cyrus R. Teed, AM, PhD, LL, D, D. One room held paintings, including a portrait of Abie Andrews. Skeletal antique typewriters sat in a glass display case.

Just a few feet from the typewriters, a plastic bin waited to catch rain, evidenced by a stain on the ceiling. The roof leaked. All these years, the artifacts had been kept rather than preserved.

Dauray said that the artifacts couldn't stay. They would slowly make their way to the state historic site. The foundation had been waiting for the state to have room for the items.[37]

Recently, Scott Ritter reflected on his conversations with Michel during the winter of 1979, when he was twenty-five and she wanted him to be involved, wanted him to do . . . *something* to keep the Koreshans alive, he'll never know quite what. "She used to talk in riddles," he said.[38]

"If I regret anything, it's that there was this trust. And the people who were left blew it. They didn't care enough."

Dauray has said the foundation's bad rap was due to his predecessors. Bigelow, especially, had created a public relations nightmare for him to deal with, he said. He referred to the time before he ran the foundation as "B.C." (before Charles) and said the foundation had moved on, but he acknowledged that there were still critics. "I find it ironic," he said in 2012, "that many people who complain the loudest are quiet about being the recipients of our donations. Had I not come here, the foundation would be broke."[39]

When he took over, the assets were ten million dollars. Twelve years later, they had fallen to only three million. The fall parallels the story of any company heavily invested in real estate in the 2000s in southwest Florida. But in the single year that the assets suffered the largest drop, Dauray took his highest salary.[40]

Dauray seemed genuinely enthusiastic about the history of the Koreshans. He credited Teed's charisma for all that the Koreshans accomplished. "You don't bring people to a swamp with rattlesnakes and chiggers and build an empire," he said. "He damn near did it. If he had lived ten more years, Koreshanity would be a $5 billion operation," Dauray said, referring to the success of Teed's business ventures and the value of the land he amassed.[41]

Dauray has a wry sense of humor, and he sometimes uses Cyrus Teed's language when he talks. "Teed would have launched Koreshanity," he said. "Because when you're going 18,700 miles per hour in orbit, there's centrifugal force that keeps you going."[42]

In 2010, Dauray, on behalf of the foundation, sold the Koreshan cemetery and surrounding land, which lie inside Pelican Sound Golf & River Club. Bigelow had held back that land when she sold to WCI Communities, the developer of Pelican Sound, though she did nothing to maintain it.

The cemetery had long been a point of contention in Estero. In 2001, the wife of a descendant told a reporter she was upset that the foundation hadn't maintained it. When Dauray heard of the descendant's dissatisfaction, he told the reporter, "It's her relative. Tell her to go clean the damn thing herself." Later, he told the reporter he was willing to talk to anyone who would call him about maintaining the graveyard.[43]

The graveyard lies within the beautiful development of terrace houses, villas, and estate homes with lawns that are generously irrigated and meticulously landscaped. Until very recently, the only indication of the cemetery was a small white sign reading "Koreshan Cemetery #2." Cemetery #1 is on nearby Audubon land, unmaintained and inaccessible. Behind the small sign, fans of saw palmetto and a tangle of scrub oaks hide the clearing. A sandy path knotted with roots leads to the place where fifty-seven bodies are buried, including those of Allen Andrews, Berthaldine Boomer, Henry Silverfriend, Teed's sister Emma, George Hunt, and Vesta Newcomb. At one time, each of these had a simple wooden marker, but they were obliterated by rain and searing sun. A handful of the graves are marked with stones added later by descendants.

The cemetery's sale price was $250,000. According to Jim Whitmore, Pelican Sound's general manager, his company hadn't wanted the cemetery. It tried to purchase only the surrounding four and a half acres. But the foundation wasn't willing to do that, Whitmore said.[44]

When asked why he sold the cemetery, Dauray said it wasn't serving a beneficial purpose. "This isn't Graceland we're talking about." The folks at Pelican Sound told him that only five or so people visit it every year.[45]

Dauray was asked how selling the cemetery was in line with the foundation's mission to preserve Koreshan history. He shrugged and said, "It's being preserved."[46]

And it is, but not by the College of Life Foundation. Pelican Sound, the new owner, applied for a historic designation, hand-cleared it with the help of an archaeologist, commissioned a cultural resource survey, determined the exact boundaries and ensured a proper buffer, fenced it, widened the path, and is working to create a preservation easement. The public will have access, Pelican Sound will maintain it, and a historic marker will explain its history. "It looks better than it ever has," Whitmore said. "Now that we look at it, we're happy we purchased it, because at least we can keep it in good shape."[47]

In another move that seemed far afield from the foundation's mission of protecting the Koreshan legacy, it donated $150,000 to sponsor a golf tournament fundraiser benefiting Art of the Olympians, a nonprofit foundation that promotes Olympic ideals. It was the foundation's largest single charitable contribution in 2012, and it dwarfed the other giving that year.[48]

The contribution caught the attention of a reporter at the *News-Press*, and once again, the Koreshans and the press were at loggerheads. Dauray explained the contribution by saying that the Koreshans would have supported the golf tournament.

"The Koreshans acknowledged that man is both a physical and spiritual being," Dauray said to the *News-Press*. "I think the Koreshans would be very pleased that we have continued to foster their ideals and their thinking."[49]

Dauray told the reporter he saw the foundation's role not as operating a museum but as supporting environmental, educational, and cultural programs. The reporter pointed out that Dauray had not made the IRS aware of this. The *News-Press* ran a photo with the story, of cobwebs strung across the back door of the foundation headquarters.[50]

In 2012 there was a noticeable shift. Peg Egan, the secretary/treasurer of the College of Life, proposed that the foundation offer historical kayaking tours on the Estero River and Bay and hikes on Mound Key. This plan was in motion before the *News-Press* story ran, Egan said, but the foundation wasn't ready to go public with it. Egan is a master naturalist with experience leading field trips. No one was giving tours on the river, she said. "And it's a living museum."[51]

Dauray and the other officer approved her plan. The foundation put a kayak trailer and a Jeep on the books; bought a domain name; and began offering the tours. On the tax returns, the mention of a museum was dropped, and the wording reflected the tours. So did the sign out front. Today, it's clear from the road what the foundation is about.[52]

Perhaps the single most historic event was when Egan joined the board of Friends of the Koreshan State Historic Site. No one ever imagined that someone from the College of Life would sit on the board of Friends. Egan was voted onto the board unanimously. The members cheered, she said. They hugged her. Finally, reconciliation was happening after nearly thirty-five years. Furthermore, the foundation directed money to support more activities related to the Koreshan and Calusa legacies.

Egan said that the squabbles between the park and the foundation had gone on so long that the two sides had forgotten what the fights were about. The split started, she said, when Michel removed artifacts from the state site. It continued when Bigelow took charge of the foundation and carried on under Dauray.[53]

There's a new manager at the state park, Steve Giguere, a former Koreshan ranger. He wants to see an interpretive center in the Koreshan general store, the cake-batter-colored building where the river meets the highway, where people once stopped to get mail, food, and, later, gas. If funding materializes, he says, visitors can come into the store and see the Koreshans in context—their artifacts, inventions, and advances. And when Giguere talks about funding, he includes the College of Life as a potential source.[54]

The foundation has moved to temporary offices. Soon, Egan says, it will be headquartered on the park grounds, where it will offer the eco-tours. Black mold has moved into the College of Life building, and Egan is working to remove all of the artifacts. Most of the objects will go to the state park and to the local university. Giguere went to the College of Life recently to decide what the state would take. He was most excited that the park would finally have Cyrus Teed's tombstone.[55]

Egan says she wants to see the settlement become the center of a historic district in Estero one day. She and another employee lead kayak tours and hikes, and they're planning youth programs in the summer with the park. The foundation is now preserving the legacy of the Koreshans and other pioneers. Visitors can paddle the river and bay, learning about the natural environment, the Calusa, and the Koreshans.[56]

Of course, positive media coverage has followed—something that was rare while Teed was alive. A recent story on the kayak tours begins with a scene on the Estero River as the writer paddles a kayak, watches beetles on the water, and feels the breeze before getting to what reporters call the nut graf, the point of the story: the foundation and the park are working together. "As we glide along the surface, breathing in nature, it's hard to imagine we are helping to tear down invisible fences."[57]

The settlement's biggest challenge, Giguere says, is getting people to visit. "History is a hard sell on the mass population," he said. And perhaps the Koreshans' history is tougher than most, because people dismiss them.[58]

"I often hear people refer to the Koreshans as 'crazy,'" Giguere said. Their beliefs were unusual, he said, but not for that time period, when theology was different. The Koreshans were educated people who believed that society was on the verge of collapse. So they came to south Florida to build their own utopia. "Is that so crazy?" he asked.[59]

That Teed brought his people to Florida seems poetic, given that the state's growth depends on a steady stream of visitors and incoming residents—an influx, the word Teed used when he predicted an important arrival of people or spirits. He envisioned that Estero would have such an influx.

It's happening. A recent market assessment predicted that Estero will grow faster than other areas of Lee County. Hertz is building its global headquarters here, and a new Walmart is going up near the College of Life. "In the next decade," Dauray told a reporter, "we (Estero) will be an urban center, like it or not."[60]

The village is once again incorporated, giving residents more control over its leadership, how it spends its money, and its look—which developers like.

"No offense to Lee County," a developer from Miami-Dade recently told a reporter, "but I [am] attracted to Naples-Bonita Springs-Estero, and mostly because it is clean and new. Most places in Florida are congested and old."[61]

On the Estero River, upstream from the settlement and downstream from where the citrus packinghouse once stood, is a spiritual center called Happehatchee. "Happe" means luck, or to come upon by chance, and that's how the Koreshans liked to believe Gustave Damkohler found Estero: that he happened upon it, though there's strong evidence he had a map and a surveyor. "Hatchee" means river or creek. People go to the Happehatchee Center for yoga, tai chi, crystal bowl meditation, sweat lodges, drum circles, or labyrinth walking. The place has the feel of a sleep-away camp and, in fact, it was Camp Caloosa for Girl Scouts from the 1940s to the 1960s. There is a swinging bridge over the Estero River strung with small bells that jingle lightly. Had you stood on the bridge more than a hundred years ago, barges full of citrus would have floated underneath you on the way to the bay and then to market.

The woman who founded Happehatchee was the late Ellen Peterson, an environmental activist who moved to Estero decades ago. She knew Hedwig Michel. And she remembered Vesta Newcomb showing up in her yard asking for money and food.[62]

In the early 2000s, as the College of Life bought up the land around her for Riverplace, Peterson didn't sell. The rest of her neighbors did. She set up a legal structure to ensure that her five acres would never be developed, because she believed it was sacred. On the plans for Estero on the River, there's a blank white rectangle jutting from the road to the water.

Many people believe that the land around the Estero River is special, and by that they mean more than peaceful and pretty. They describe it as something they feel. Descendant Scott Ritter said that when he's at the Koreshan State Historic Site, he feels it. "Of course, I'm genetically attached to the place—but the people who work there tell me they feel it too."[63]

The Koreshans, too, believed the area was sacred. Before them, so did the Calusa; Mound Key is thought to have been a ceremonial center. And today, some people believe Estero overflows with a special earth energy that can raise human consciousness and heal or inspire, like the power at Stonehenge or the invisible whirlpools of psychic energy in Sedona, Arizona. There is no rational scientific explanation for it.

Several years ago, a reiki master, channeler, and spiritual counselor came to southwest Florida when she was ill, and she is convinced that being here healed her. Later, she mapped the area and identified what she believes are sacred energy sites, determining that southwest Florida is a giant energy vortex, she told the *Naples Daily News*.[64]

To find the sites, she used dowsing, an ancient method for finding water or minerals underground. People who know about dowsing might envision someone walking behind a forked stick, looking for water. It's an occult art, in the sense of "occult" meaning to reveal something that is hidden. Those who do it say it's intuitive and that it involves a connection to the supernatural. It's looked on as a pseudoscience, like alchemy. It's based on a belief that something will be revealed to the person who practices it.

The woman who mapped southwest Florida scanned the area without being there. She did remote dowsing, using a map, a pendulum, and a system of asking questions and receiving answers. Her resulting map shows what she calls interdimensional doorways, star gates, earth chakras, and a site of ceremonial magic. Many of the sites, she believes, are safe havens in times of change. On her map, southwest Florida is busy with different colored lines, triangles, circles, and dashes.

Around Estero is a yellow circle and, at the center of it, a jagged yellow mountain, representing a crystal. Estero, she determined, lies on a crystal grid. People who work with crystals believe that grids amplify the universal life force, allowing them to focus energies on a particular purpose.

What could be more fitting? Cyrus Teed, the first time he saw Estero, called it the vitellus of the cosmogonic egg and determined that it was the safest place for the great battle that would lead to the end of the world.

Even people who don't believe in dowsing or sacred energy sites appreciate the odd, enchanting beauty of the Koreshan historic settlement. Osprey perch atop pines on the river banks to scan the water for glinting fish; bamboo grows at a Jack-and-the-Beanstalk rate; and a tortoise named Cyrus keeps watch at the entrance of his grassy mound. Every few years in late summer, the monkey puzzle tree releases heavy green bombs, each one crashing through the branches and landing with a thump on the earth.

Afterword

The man who makes life easy for you always has a
chance of making you believe anything.

—"Madness and Death Add to the Mystery of Koresh's
Tomb," *New York Times*, November 6, 1910

The media became a much larger part of this story than I ever imagined. There
was no one else—not even Teed—who provided a through line from beginning to end. Followers came and went, but those newspaper reporters were
relentless—and as lively as characters come, especially the early, anonymous
ones in Chicago, hiding in the bushes, peering into windows, getting interviews
by pretending to be people they weren't. These newsmen and women were the
lens through which the public saw Teed and his followers. They melded into
a composite character—someone who was, by turns, a hysterical, pompous,
biased, and fair-minded Peeping Tom. It was an unreliable narrator, but at
points in the chronology, it was all I had.

In Fort Myers, there they were again, this time not anonymous. The media
took the form of Philip Isaacs, the editor of the *Fort Myers Press*, who realized,
too late, that he was a puppet of the most influential family in town.

The Koreshans joined the media character, too, by starting the *American
Eagle*, and the two newspapers wrestled like a dyspeptic, bothered monster.

When Jo Bigelow sold Koreshan land, the very newspaper that began covering Teed in 1893 sent a reporter to the foundation in 1996. Coverage continued
through the years—events at the park, changes at the foundation—and this
time the reporters were my colleagues, people I e-mail, call, and follow on Twitter. Finally, I myself entered the story when I wrote about the foundation for a
local magazine.

Were Teed alive today, he would make full use of the media. A born blog-
ger, he'd post essays on theology for his small band of followers. He would be

hopeless at Twitter, but, seeing its value, he would assign the task of tweeting to someone else—maybe Allen Andrews. He might start his own television show on public access or stream it on the Internet. He would love how easy it is to be a publisher with full control over his message.

But beyond his corner of the Internet, he would have no control. Just as the newspapers couldn't resist covering him at the turn of the nineteenth century, the media would not ignore him today. A cloistered figure who craves attention, leads a community surrounded by mystery and suspicion, claims to be celibate, champions advances in technology, and gets into occasional scrapes? He and his followers would make the news, subjects of ridicule and curiosity, a way for television networks to fill time on morning shows and slow news days.

1. "Cyrus Teed is making a fortune in real estate. We'll sit down with his financial advisor, Henry Silverfriend, to learn how."
2. "Medical electricity is making a comeback, providing pain relief for millions."
3. "Cyrus Teed admits that he experimented with sex in his twenties."
4. "Could your next-door neighbor be in a cult?"

In a lecture announcement in 1903, Teed asked, "Are Brains Necessary?" Not very.

Given infinite media narratives, I prefer the explanation of the world that doesn't make me angry—information I agree with. If I'm not careful, I'll fall into a thought tribe. I've made a career of trying to avoid that—deconstructing the news, finding facts, and seeking credible sources. Often, it's a fool's errand—fighting the yearning to live in a knowable world. I think that's what pulled me to write about the Koreshans.

I spent years trying to figure out how they could believe such strange ideas. Because here's the thing: they didn't seem crazy to me. They were educated, cultured, and middle to upper class, and I'd like to believe that those qualities can protect someone from irrational beliefs and actions. That's my hollow earth belief, or was.

The Koreshans worked and suffered and devoted their lives to Koreshanity, and it meant everything to them. Now they're gone, and it doesn't seem right that their history is evaporating. The more I researched, the more they came to life and the more there was to discover. They left journals and letters and lecture announcements and photos and even accounting ledgers. I became so obsessed with research that my husband told our friends he was one of the many men who lost his wife to Cyrus Teed.

The followers believed that the street fight in downtown Fort Myers in 1906 caused Teed's death two years later. Based on what we know today, that's highly unlikely. I spoke to a neurologist and laid out for her Teed's symptoms and his health history all the way back to the temporary paralysis he suffered in Virginia during the Civil War when he was twenty-three. I told her that Teed's followers believed his death was from a hemorrhage due to the fight. She said it didn't explain the symptoms of his nerve pain. It's possible there was a connection between the fight and the nerve pain, she said, but the pain would not have killed him. It isn't fatal.

We will never know what caused his death. It might have been a tumor in his neck or even an overdose of laudanum, the neurologist said. But it almost certainly was not Mr. Sellers. The Koreshans could not have known this.[1]

I mention this because it shows a larger truth about the Koreshans, about any like-minded community for that matter. Taken out of context, beliefs can seem outlandish. Put into context, they make more sense.

At the time the Koreshans lived, people wanted to *feel* religion as opposed to simply practicing it. Scientific discoveries threatened to kill faith. People flocked to the cities as industry grew and provided jobs—and living in those cities was exhilarating and terrifying. Gathered there, people looked for answers. They saw abuse of workers. The Koreshans believed that the moral fabric of the world was deteriorating. The need for reform felt vital and immediate.

Perhaps scariest of all were advances in medicine—strong drugs and sophisticated techniques were replacing traditional treatments. It's no accident that Mary Baker Eddy's theories about healing through the practice of Christian Science became popular. People were open to new ideas and answers, and these often came in the form of lectures. As Theodore Dreiser noted, there were many lecturers to choose from in big cities.

So it made perfect sense that on an afternoon in early September in Chicago someone would attend a lecture on mental healing and be fascinated by a guest speaker who knew how the brain worked, who understood Swedenborg, and who proposed with certainty that our minds could heal us. And the place smelled delectable.

The fact that followers were primed for Teed's message was helpful for understanding how Koreshanity could take root, but it didn't explain Teed. That is, why people would choose him, specifically. The followers still don't seem crazy to me, but he does. Why did they not dismiss him as delusional?

When I told a friend I wanted to figure that out, she said, "He was charismatic.

That's all you need. Plain and simple. And he made them feel that their lives had value."

Charisma is anything but plain and simple. Even the dictionary definition leads straight to God—*kharis*, Greek for favor or grace. A gift from God.

This is where my research hit a wall. I couldn't see Teed's charisma. It certainly didn't come through in his writing, which was nearly incomprehensible. There were plenty of accounts about his penetrating eyes (confirmed by portraits) and his ability to cast a spell (impossible to experience firsthand). Jennie Andrews, in her journal, often wrote that the followers were elated when he was with them and bereft when he was away.

I saw Teed in a dream once, very briefly. I guess this was inevitable, having spent so many waking hours researching him and reading his letters. In the dream, he was standing in front of me in a restaurant buffet line, and he made a passing remark about the green beans, something you'd say to a stranger, I don't remember exactly what. He turned toward me only slightly. And then I was awake and he was gone.

Seeing the picture of Teed's dead body was a turning point for me. There were four glass plate negatives. One was broken on its way to Tallahassee, but the other three were intact. When I saw the body, the eyes tightly closed, his lips pushed outward like a cleft fig, his brown, shiny skin, I had a visceral reaction. They *really* believed. I had known it intellectually. But seeing what they saw, and knowing that they watched his body for days and waited for signs, I saw his power, and it was spooky. Even in death—at least in those first days—he had a hold over his followers. They believed in him so intensely that they shut out what was in front of them. They adjusted their beliefs to line up with what they thought they were seeing. The stories they told in their letters showed that they had agreed on certain symbols—Horos, hieroglyphics, the chrysalis.

I sent photos of Cyrus Teed's body to the Lee County Medical Examiner and asked a forensic investigator what was happening to his body when the believers saw the hieroglyphics. How could they have thought they saw a new arm forming underneath the blister on the old one? There were answers for everything, but none of them fully explained what the Koreshans—and now I—had felt.

I discovered there was a candy factory in the basement of the former church when I spotted a brief mention of it in a blurry image of a *Chicago Herald* story about the convention. There was no indication of what kind of candy was made in the factory, and I wanted to know. This was a huge moment in Teed's life, when, after decades of effort, he attracted followers. The sweetness of the candy was a metaphor, and putting the smells in the scene would bring it alive. I wanted readers to feel what it was like to be inside that church.

I couldn't simply write that the people in the audience smelled candy. That would evoke nothing. The specific aromas were vital. Thanks to the news reports, I had the name and address of the church but not the candy company. Googling (and *not* "feeling lucky"), I discovered that there had just been an exhibit on the history of candy in Chicago. I wrote the researcher behind the exhibit, Leslie Goddard, and asked whether she knew the name of the factory in the old Church of the Redeemer at the intersection of Washington Boulevard and Sangamon Street. As I composed the e-mail, I considered the possibility that this stranger would think I was crazy. I also considered the possibility that I *was* crazy, that my education had not protected me at all from becoming irrational.

Goddard responded quickly. She knew the name of the company—Berry's Confectionery. More thrilling, she sent me an image of the church, the place where you might say Koreshanity was born. Goddard said I had helped her, too. She hadn't known whether the factory took up the whole building. "Can you imagine trying to sit through a lecture with the smell of fresh candy wafting through the air?!!" she wrote.[2]

I stared at the photo for a long while. In it, a white horse clops past the steps of the building toward the intersection, pulling a carriage. On the brick wall of the old church, on either side of the arched window above the entrance, are the words "How Good. Berry's Candies. State & Adams." How odd that Leslie Goddard and I, strangers, connected over a long-ago scent inside a building that no longer exists, in a city where two strangers—John Berry and Cyrus Teed—lived more than a hundred years ago.

I found an advertisement for Berry's in a Chicago paper and read over the offerings—cream caramels, French nougat, marshmallow drops, Spanish peanut brittle, rose cream almonds. I have never wanted so much to enter a portal into a different time and place. After all, as a child, one of my favorite books was *The Lion, the Witch and the Wardrobe*. I stared at the grainy black and white candy ad on my computer screen and imagined stepping through the words and into the shop on State Street, opposite the Palmer House. I would walk in, hand the clerk twelve cents, and order an ice cream soda with grated pineapple, along with a pound of pure broken candy.

I took a screenshot of the ad and sent it to a friend who is a food expert. She told me how different candies are made and which ingredients have aromas strong enough that they could travel to a sanctuary on the next floor, where this new man with an exciting message was holding up his Bible and speaking in front of a chart of the human brain. I could envision him, and I could smell the church, feel the pews, hear the people. I had my scene.

Two years later, I discovered that Teed must have spent more time in the Church of the Old Redeemer than I had imagined. When I was putting this book to bed, something incredible happened. Peg Egan at the College of Life Foundation was clearing out the building Hedwig Michel built, and she brought several boxes of books to the library of the university where I teach. Many of the books were not salvageable, having moldered for decades in poor conditions. But many can be preserved, and the library is rescuing them.

Special Collections Librarian Melissa Minds VandeBurgt invited me to look at the books—but not to touch them. I did not have the proper tools or training, and they were fragile, and I was liable to be too rough in my excitement. So I looked with my hands clasped behind my back. There were bound issues of the *Flaming Sword* with color covers; all manner of textbooks; works by Teed, including his novel, *The Great Red Dragon*; a chart of the left hemisphere of the brain; and a pamphlet of Victoria's speech "Woman's Restoration to Her Rightful Dominion." Various followers had made notations in the margins of many of the books. The paper was speckled and stained, the covers were worn, and the bindings on many of them were broken or in the process of coming apart.

Laid open on a white pillow at the end of one table was a Bible—a very old one. Copyright 1884. I bent over it and—I don't know why—sniffed it. She did, too.[3]

"What is that?" Melissa asked me. She said it smelled different from any book she had ever run across.

"It's rose and vanilla and caramel," I said.

"You're right!" she said, and she looked at me, astonished. She didn't know the story, so I explained to her about the church, the candy factory in the basement, and Teed's big break. I asked her whether it was really possible that this was the smell of the candy.

"Obviously," she said, gesturing to the Bible.

The paper was decaying, and the binding was breaking down. She thought she could slow down the book's aging but not stop it. The aroma has already lasted more than a lifetime, longer than the Koreshans. What she was telling me was that the smell, this sweet, mute testament, won't be there forever.

Acknowledgments

I was thrilled when the University Press of Florida expressed an interest in this book and am very fortunate to have worked with the people there. Dennis Lloyd was generous and kind from day one, even as he recovered from a biblical rainstorm that hit the Miami Book Fair. Amy Gorelick helped shape the early chapters. Meredith Babb's brilliant editing suggestions transformed the manuscript into a story I'm proud of, as did Virginia Garrison's precise corrections and comments. Catherine-Nevil Parker and her team of alchemists turned electrons into an actual book, which Romi Gutierrez and Rachel Doll worked diligently to publicize. I am forever grateful to all of them. Thanks also to Louise OFarrell, Elaine Otto, and Robert and Cynthia Swanson.

Mike Widner, former archivist at Koreshan State Historic Site, was a godsend with his knowledge of the Koreshans and his willingness to take questions, find documents, and do detective work on short notice. Bethanie Telesz at the State Archives of Florida interrupted her work on the archives to answer my endless requests. Both Mike and Bethanie understood what I needed, sometimes before I did, and their enthusiasm charged my batteries.

I'm in debt to scholars Lynn Rainard, Howard Fine, and Elliott J. Mackle, whose theses and journal articles were indispensable. Quentin Quesnell, with his book *Early Estero*, helped more than he will ever know. I'm grateful to the following journalists at the *News-Press* and *Naples Daily News*: Amy Bennett Williams, Charlie Whitehead, Chad Gillis, and Lee Melsek.

Many archivists, librarians, curators, historians, researchers, and experts were generous with their time and gifts. They include Beth Golding, Jim Powers, Gerri Reaves, Ryan McPherson, Leslie Goddard, Nicole Steeves, Melissa Minds VandeBurgt, Kaleena Rivera, Lauren McCraney, Christian Goodwillie, Doug Farley, Peggy Nickell, Sherry Kilgore, John Miller, Carol Ann MacMaster, Steven Machlin, Eileen Schwartz, Pricilla Doyle, and LeAnne McDaniel. Local historians Woody Hanson, Jeff McCullers, Mimi Straub, the members of the Estero Historical Society, and Ellen Peterson all offered valuable knowledge.

Koreshan descendants Bill Grace and Scott Ritter provided a vital connection to the past, as did current and former employees at Koreshan State Historic Site: Stephen Giguere, Andy Tetlow, Peter Hicks, Kate Anthony Zajanc, and Mike Heare. Gustave Damkohler's relative Gary Damkoehler provided me with letters, photos, and important research at the eleventh hour. Thank you to the many volunteers at the park who made me feel welcome and who shared my fascination with the Koreshans, including Ron Westcott, Joan McMahon, and Elizabeth Brown. Thanks also to Peg Phillips and Charles Dauray at the College of Life Foundation.

Molly Lyons helped bring this idea into being by sharpening the proposal and soliciting feedback. Lynne Barrett, my longtime mentor, encouraged me to write a flash version of the story, published in *Tigertail, a South Florida Annual*. David Sendler and John Dufresne provided inspiration. This book renewed my friendship with Dan Wakefield, to whom I'm grateful for his kind, incisive, and often funny advice.

My colleagues at Florida Gulf Coast University shared expertise on everything from turtles to morphine to the history of Honduras. I owe much to Judd Cribbs for guarding my off time. Rick Kenney gave encouragement, and my students showed enthusiasm when I needed it most: on the home stretch. Thank you to the university administration for the sabbatical that allowed me much-needed time.

Thanks also to my good friends. Karyn Everham helped me see what the book was about. Elena Ruiz, very early on, told me she couldn't wait to read it, and this made me want to finish it so that she could. Thank you to the many friends who endured my derailing of conversations by saying, "You know, that reminds me of Cyrus Teed . . .": Sasha Wohlpart, Jim Wohlpart, Win Everham, Karen Tolchin, Tom DeMarchi, Martha Rosenthal, Debbie Lewis, Maria Roca, Sharon Isern, Scott Michael, Nico Michael, and Elspeth McCulloch. Andrew Golden helped me see the structure. Leonard Nash, Colleen Ahern-Hettich, and Michael Hettich listened and brainstormed.

Thank you, Mom and Dad, for reading to me, taking me to the library, and allowing me to check out all the books I could carry. And to my brother, Chip, who introduced me to Ray Bradbury and Kurt Vonnegut and who was my first subject.

Thank you to Henry Brown. And most of all, to my husband—astonishing poet, gentle soul, my joy.

Abbreviations

AE	*American Eagle*
BB	*Bonita Banner*
BCI	*(Bartow, Fla.) Courier-Informant*
BDN	*Bonita Daily News*
CDN	*Chicago Daily News*
CH	*Chicago Herald*
CJ	*Chicago Journal or Chicago Evening Journal*
CSJ	*Christian Science Journal*
CT	*Chicago Tribune or Chicago Daily Tribune*
CTH	*Chicago Times-Herald*
CTimes	*Chicago Times*
DN	*(Oshkosh, Wis.) Daily Northwestern*
EHS	*Estero Historical Society newsletter*
FGCU	*Koreshan Collection, Florida Gulf Coast University*
FMP	*Fort Myers Press*
FS	*Flaming Sword*
FTU	*Florida Times-Union*
GS	*Guiding Star*
GSL	*Gulfshore Life*
IO	*Inter Ocean or Daily Inter Ocean*
IT	*(New Orleans) Item-Tribune*
KSHS	*Koreshan State Historic Site Archives, Estero, Fla.*
KU	*Koreshan Unity Papers, State Archives of Florida, Tallahassee*
LMG	*(LeMars, Iowa) Globe*
MSM	*Mental Science Magazine and Mind-Cure Journal*
NDN	*Naples Daily News*
NP	*(Fort Myers, Fla.) News-Press*
NY	*New Yorker*
NYT	*New York Times*

NYW	*(New York) World*
OET	*Oakland Daily Evening Tribune or Oakland Evening Tribune*
PD	*Pittsburg Dispatch*
PDN	*Pittsburgh Daily News*
PL	*Pittsburgh Leader*
PS	*Popular Science*
SDJ	*Syracuse Daily Journal*
SDN	*Salem Daily News*
SFC	*San Francisco Chronicle*
SH	*Syracuse Herald*
SLT	*Salt Lake Tribune*
SS	*Syracuse Standard*
TMT	*Tampa Morning Tribune*
TP	*(New Orleans) Times-Picayune*
TS	*(Tallahassee) Sun*
TT	*Tampa Tribune*

Notes

Prologue: The Man in the Bathtub

1. Descriptions of Teed's death and body come from letters written by Dr. J. Augustus Weimar, December 24, 1908; Jennie Andrews to Evelyn Bubbett, December 24, 1908; William McCready to Lovelle McCready, December 26, 1908; Dr. J. Augustus Weimar to "Elizabeth," December 27, 1908; Christine Hamilton to "Dear Kind Friends," December 29, 1908; "Abby" to "Jennie," December 1908; Dr. J. Augustus Weimar to DeCoursey Clinchy, December 30, 1908; statement of death, Dr. William Hanson and J. E. Brecht, M.D., December 23, 1908; and Anastasia, "A Testimony of Faith," December 25, 1908, KU papers. When I visited the Koreshan Unity archives at the State Archives of Florida in 2012, the collection was being processed and there were no box or folder listings. Wherever a researcher would have trouble finding documents, I have provided the box and folder numbers. A guide to the KU papers can be found here: https://www .floridamemory.com/collections/koreshan/.

2. Press coverage of Teed's death comes from the following: "Dr. Cyrus Teed Dead: Has Passed Away and Is No More," FMP, December 24, 1908; "Koresh I. Is Dead," CT, December 25, 1908; "Koresh I. Is Dead," NYT, December 25, 1908; "Dr. Teed Has Not Risen," NYT, December 27, 1908.

3. "Disciples Await New Breath of Life," TMT, December 25, 1908.

4. Emerson to Carlyle, October 30, 1840, Concord, in *The Correspondence of Thomas Carlyle and Ralph Waldo Emerson, 1834 to 1872*, vol. 1, section 58.

5. Twain and Warner, *The Gilded Age: A Tale of Today*.

6. Henry Silverfriend, 1898, in Berrey, "The Koreshan Unity," 37.

7. Information about David Koresh and the Branch Davidians comes from the following: Malcolm Gladwell, "Sacred and Profane: How Not to Negotiate with Believers," NY, March 31, 2014; J.B. Smith, "Scholars Tackle 'Cult' Questions 20 Years after Branch Davidian Tragedy," WacoTrib.com, April 13, 2013, http://www.wacotrib.com/news/ religion/scholars-tackle-cult-questions-years-after-branch-davidian-tragedy/article_ a3fa463e-d1b4-5eda-b49e-95327bc276d7.html?mode=story; Ashley Fantz, "18 Years after Waco, Davidians Believe Koresh Was God," CNN, April 14, 2011, http://www.cnn .com/2011/US/04/14/waco.koresh.believers/.

8. Dr. J. Augustus Weimar to "Elizabeth," December 27, 1908, KU papers.

Chapter 1. The Illumination

1. Remini, *Joseph Smith*, 1.

2. Information about the history of religion in America during the nineteenth century comes from Fuller, "Cosmology," 196–204, and Cross, *The Burned-Over District*.

3. Cross, *The Burned-Over District*, 87–89.

4. Ibid., 356.

5. Information about Swedenborg comes from Cross, *The Burned-Over District*, 341–44; and Swedenborg, *The New Jerusalem*, 155–56.

6. "Three Forms of Thought," NYT, November 29, 1897.

7. Declaration of Sentiments, Woman's Rights Convention, Seneca Falls, N.Y., July 19–20, 1848, in Stanton, *History*, vol. 1, chapter 4.

8. Bruce Sherwood (relative of Cyrus Teed) to Bruce Pennington (author of *King Koresh*), May 4 and May 26, 1981, KSHS.

9. Seventh Census of the United States, 1850 (National Archives microfilm publication M432, 1009 rolls); Records of the Bureau of the Census, record group 29 (National Archives, Washington, D.C.). Ancestry.com, Census Place, New Hartford, Oneida, N.Y. (roll M432-562; page 263B; image 531), http://search.ancestry.com/cgibin/.sse.dll?h=7706569&db=1850usfedcenancestry&indiv=try.

10. Information about hoggees and their work responsibilities, pay, and hours comes from Doug Farley (former director of the Erie Canal Discovery Center), telephone conversation and e-mails with author, June 5, 2012, and June 5, 2014.

11. Allen H. Andrews, untitled memoir, 1, FGCU. The document portion of FGCU Library's Koreshan collection, comprising two boxes at the time I visited, had not been processed. Wherever a researcher would have trouble locating an item, I have provided the box number and the name written on the folder.

12. "A Synopsis of Discourses Delivered by Dr. Cyrus Teed of the Koreshan Unity on Dec. 11 and 13 at Mt. Lebanon, N.Y.," *Manifesto*, March 1892. The *Shaker Manifesto* was the official monthly publication of the United Society of Believers from 1871 to 1899. It was published under different titles: the *Shaker* (1871–1872), *Shaker and Shakeress* (1873–1875), the *Shaker* (1876–1877), the *Shaker Manifesto* (1878–1882), and *Manifesto* (1883–1899). A full run can be found in the Special Collections of Hamilton College in Clinton, N.Y., http://elib.hamilton.edu/shaker-publications.

13. Bruce Sherwood to Bruce Pennington, May 26, 1981, KSHS; Hicks, "Cyrus Teed"; Rea, *Koreshan Story*, 5; Tsani "Bear" Yonah, "100 Years of Koreshan Unity," BB, October 19, 1994.

14. Information about Teed's Civil War service, his injury, and his discharge comes from his Certificate of Disability for Discharge, Army of the United States, October 15, 1863, KSHS, http://koreshan.mwweb.org/blog/?p=109; Rea, *Koreshan Story*, 1.

15. Register of Graduates of the Eclectic Medical College of the City of New York, in *Medical Eclectic*, July 15, 1876, 223.

16. Information about eclectic medicine comes from Haller, *Medical Protestants* and *Profile*.

17. Haller, *Profile*, 112.

18. Teed, *The Immortal Manhood*, 25; "The World Is Hollow and We Are Living on the Inside of the Shell," CT, December 18, 1887.

19. "Teed Slow about Rising," SH, December 27, 1908.

20. All quotations from Teed's account of the visit from the angel are from Teed, *Illumination*.

21. Rev. 12:1, 12:5 (King James Version).

22. Representative James Abram Garfield, speech to the U.S. House of Representatives, December 16, 1867, in John Clark Ridpath, *The Life and Work of James A. Garfield* (1881), 216.

23. Leslie L. Luther (historian in Moravia, N.Y.) to Howard D. Fine, December 28, 1967, in Fine, "Koreshan Unity," 20.

24. Fort Myers psychiatrist Dr. Steven Machlin in discussion with author, July 16, 2014.

25. Jones, "The God Complex," 205.

26. Ibid., 207, 216.

27. Ibid., 212.

28. Ibid.

29. Ibid., 222.

30. Teed, *Illumination*, 22.

Chapter 2. Inside the Earth: New York, 1869–1886

1. "A Synopsis of Discourses Delivered by Dr. Cyrus Teed of the Koreshan Unity on Dec. 11 and 13 at Mt. Lebanon, N.Y.," *Manifesto*, March 1892, 67.

2. Andrews, untitled memoir, 1, FGCU.

3. Carmer, "The Great Alchemist," 269.

4. A. H. Andrews, "Reminiscences of a Charter Member," FS, October, November, December 1945. *The Flaming Sword* was a periodical published by the Koreshan Unity (Chicago and Estero, Fla.) from 1889 to 1948. Record group 900000, collection N2009-3, boxes 247–77, KU papers.

5. Ibid.

6. Carmer, "The Great Alchemist," 269.

7. Cyrus Teed to A.W.K. Andrews, June 21, 1879, KU papers.

8. Cyrus Teed to Emma Norton, August 7, 18—, KSHS.

9. Cyrus Teed to Emma Norton, January 5, 1879, KSHS.

10. Cyrus Teed to Emma Norton, December 6, 1878, KSHS.

11. Ibid.

12. Holloway, *Heavens on Earth*, 92.

13. Arndt, *George Rapp's Successors*, 111.

14. Cyrus Teed to A.W.K. Andrews, June 1, 1880, KU papers.

15. Cyrus Teed to A.W.K. Andrews, June 7, 1880, KU papers.

16. Cyrus Teed to A.W.K. Andrews, December 2, 1879, KU papers.

17. Davis, *History of the National Woman's Rights Movement*, 31.

18. Jer. 31:22.

19. A. H. Andrews, "Reminiscences of a Charter Member," FS, October, November, December 1945.

20. Cyrus Teed to Emma Norton, March 18, 1879, KSHS; tenth census of the United States, 1880 (National Archives microfilm publication T9, 1,454 rolls); records of the Bureau of the Census, record group 29 (National Archives, Washington, D.C.); Ancestry.com, Census Place, Sandy Creek, Oswego, N.Y. (roll 915, family history film 1254915, page 99A, enumeration district 264, image 0199), http://search.ancestry.com/cgibin/sse.dll?h=4675766&db=1880usfedcen&indiv=try.

21. Cyrus Teed to Emma Norton, June 18, 1879, KSHS.

22. Cyrus Teed to A.W.K. Andrews, December 2, 1878, KU papers.

23. Cyrus Teed to Emma Norton, June 18, 1879, KSHS.

24. McCready, "Folks We Knew," 14; Cyrus Teed to Emma Norton, March 18, 1879, KSHS.

25. Cyrus Teed to Emma Norton, January 22, 1879, KSHS.

26. Cyrus Teed to Emma Norton, n.d., KSHS.

27. Jesse Teed to Sarah Teed, December 23, 1882, KSHS; Jesse Teed to Emma Norton, April 13, 1889, KSHS.

28. Cyrus Teed to Emma Norton, August 7, 18—, KSHS.

29. Cyrus Teed to recipient unknown (possibly Emma Norton), n.d., KSHS.

30. Cyrus Teed to Emma Norton, September 3, 1880, KSHS.

31. Cyrus Teed to A.W.K. Andrews, various, January 2, 1877 to September 2, 1880, KU papers.

32. Cyrus Teed to Emma Norton, January 10, 1882, KSHS.

33. Cyrus Teed to Emma Norton, June 26, 1881, KSHS.

34. Rea, *Koreshan Story*, 4.

35. Jesse Teed to Emma Norton, March 30, 1884, KSHS.

36. Ibid.

37. "Sure He Is the Prophet Cyrus," NYT, August 10, 1884.

38. Altonen, "Medical Electricity."

39. White, *Medical Electricity*, 148.

40. Ibid., 133, 185.

41. Ibid., 134.

42. "Letters Patent for an alleged new and useful improvement in Electro-Therapeutic Apparatus," Commissioner of Patents, July 31, 1883, KU papers.

43. White, *Medical Electricity*, 57–58.

44. "Half an Hour in 'Heaven,'" CTimes, May 5, 1892.

45. The story about Mrs. Cobb that follows comes from "Theology and Medicine: How a City Physician Combines Them," SDJ, August 9, 1884.

46. "Sure He Is the Prophet Cyrus," NYT, August 10, 1884; "Still Sure He Is a Prophet," SDJ, August 11, 1884.

47. "Theology and Medicine: How a City Physician Combines Them," SDJ, August 9, 1884.

48. "Sure He Is the Prophet Cyrus," NYT, August 10, 1884.

49. "Laying Claim to Divine Power," SS, August 10, 1884.

50. Rahn, "Brief Outline," 28.

51. Jesse Teed to Emma Norton, April 4, 1885, KSHS.

52. Rahn, "Brief Outline," 29.

53. Cyrus Teed to A.W.K. Andrews, June 18, 1885 to July 2, 1886, KU papers.

Chapter 3. It Must Be Good; It's Made in a Church

1. Cyrus Teed to Emma Norton, September 7, 1886, KSHS; "Parades Out of Chicago," CT, September 7, 1886.

2. Miller, *City of the Century*, 473.

3. Ibid., 473–74.

4. "Workingmen Rejoice: A Demonstration Participated in by More than 13,000 Men," CT, September 7, 1886.

5. Cyrus Teed to Emma Norton, September 7, 1886, KSHS; Ryan McPherson (archivist, Baltimore & Ohio Railroad Museum), e-mail messages to author, July 10–11, 2012; Rahn, "Brief Outline," 30.

6. Ryan McPherson, e-mail messages to author, July 10–11, 2012.

7. Miller, *City of the Century*, 423–24; Larson, *Devil in the White City*, 35.

8. Robinson, *Map of Chicago*, 1886.

9. Weather page, CT, September 8, 1886.

10. Cyrus Teed to Emma Norton, September 7, 1886, KSHS; "'Mental' Healing," CT, June 4, 1886.

11. Phillips, *Churches*, 568; "Berry's Candy Factory Building during a Strike," CDN, September 12, 1903, photo.

12. Leslie Goddard (author of *Chicago's Sweet Candy History*), e-mail message to author, July 9, 2012; "The Cure Won't Work," CH, September 12, 1886; Berry's display advertisement, CT, October 24 and 31, 1897; J.A.B., "In the Wake of the News: Do You Remember Way Back When?" CT, April 3, 1922.

13. "Mental Scientists to Have a Convention," CH, September 4, 1886; "Discoursing on the Brain," CH, September 13, 1886.

14. "The Mind-Healers," CT, September 11, 1886.

15. "The Convention," MSM, October 1886, 13, AC—0151, KSHS, http://koreshan .mwweb.org/virtual_exhibit/vex3/ac-0151.pdf; Mary Baker Eddy, "Questions Answered," CSJ, October 1886, 160; E. Hopkins, "What Is Plagiarism?" CSJ, July 1885, 81.

16. "The Convention," MSM, October 1886, 14.

17. "The Mind-Healers," CT, September 11, 1886.

18. "The Convention," MSM, October 1886, 14; "The Mind-Healers," CT, September 11, 1886.

19. "The Convention," MSM, October 1886, 14.

20. "The Mind-Healers," CT, September 11, 1886; "'Mental' Healing," CT, June 4, 1886.

21. "The Cure Won't Work," CH, September 12, 1886; Andrews, untitled memoir, 6.

22. "The Cure Won't Work," CH, September 12, 1886; "Mental Scientists to Have a Convention," CH, September 4, 1886.

23. "Mental Scientists to Have a Convention," CH, September 4, 1886; Berry's display advertisement, CT, October 24 and 31, 1897; Leslie Goddard, e-mail message to author, July 9, 2012.

24. "Mental Scientists to Have a Convention," CH, September 4, 1886; "The Cure Won't Work," CH, September 12, 1886.

25. "The Cure Won't Work," CH, September 12, 1886; "The Mental Scientists," CT, September 12, 1886.

26. "The Cure Won't Work," CH, September 12, 1886.

27. "Discoursing on the Brain," CH, September 13, 1886.

28. Dreiser, *Dawn*, 557.

29. Ibid.

30. "Discoursing on the Brain," CH, September 13, 1886.

31. "Madness and Death Add to the Mystery of Koresh's Tomb," NYT, November 6, 1910.

32. "Discoursing on the Brain," CH, September 13, 1886.

33. Ibid.

34. Rahn, "Brief Outline," 31.

35. "An Unfortunate Question," CT, September 14, 1886.

36. "An Unfortunate Question," CT, September 14, 1886.

37. "An Unfortunate Question," CT, September 14, 1886; "A Giant in the Camp," MSM, October 1886, 19.

38. "Tidings from the West: Report Them," MSM, October 1886, 18.

39. Gottschalk, *Emergence*, 103–4; "A Protest from a Mental Scientist," CT, September 17, 1886.

40. "Are Brains Necessary?," lecture announcement, July 1903, record group 900000, collection N2009-3, box 319, folder 17, KU papers.

41. Rainard, "Name of Humanity," 13.

42. "How to Get Ahead of Death: The World's College of Life—What the Kore-shanists Propose to Do," CT, November 17, 1886.

43. Ibid.

44. "Cyrus, the Son of Jesse," CT, April 10, 1887.

45. Ibid.

46. Ibid.

47. Cyrus Teed to Emma Norton, March 1887, KSHS; Rahn, "Brief Outline," 34.

48. Society Arch-Triumphant, meeting announcement, record group 900000, collection N2009-3, box 324, folder 25, KU papers; Rahn, "Brief Outline," 34.

49. Cyrus Teed to Emma Norton, March 1887, KSHS.

50. Ibid.

51. Ibid.

Chapter 4. The Watchmen of Chicago

1. Details and dialogue for the Benedict story and the related trial come from the following: "A 'Koreshan' Fatality," CT, February 22, 1888; "Held to the Grand Jury," CT, February 23, 1888; "Mustard and Miracles," CT, February 26, 1888; "A Faith-Cure 'Doctor' Is Arrested," NYW, February 23, 1888; and C. W. Leigh, M.D., letter to the editor, PS, May 6, 1889.

2. "A 'Koreshan' Fatality," CT, February 22, 1888.

3. Ibid.

4. Information about Leigh's visit, the death, autopsy, and the postmortem investigation is from "A 'Koreshan' Fatality," CT, February 22, 1888.

5. Information about the coroner's inquest, the jury decision, and Teed's arrest and release is from "Held to the Grand Jury," CT, February 23, 1888.

6. "The College of Life," CJ, September 18, 1889.

7. The entire account of the suit between Ida and Harry Ordway is from "Mrs. Ida Ordway's Case," CT, February 3, 1888.

8. Cyrus Teed to A.W.K. Andrews, December 26, 1887, KU papers.

9. Cyrus Teed to A.W.K. Andrews, January 11, 1888, KU papers.

10. A.W.K. Andrews to Margaret Harmon, March 23, 1888, AM-0153, KSHS.

11. Virginia Andrews to Margaret Harmon, June 1, 1889. AM-0153, KSHS.

12. A. H. Andrews, "Reminiscences of a Charter Member," FS, October, November, December 1945.

13. Rahn, "Brief Outline," 35.

14. "A Synopsis of Discourses Delivered by Dr. Cyrus Teed of the Koreshan Unity on Dec. 11 and 13 at Mt. Lebanon, N.Y.," *Manifesto*, March 1892, 67; Rahn, "A Brief Outline," 38.

15. The quotations from the exchange between Teed and the reporter in this section come from "The College of Life," CJ, September 18, 1889.

16. Douglas, *Everglades*, 302.

17. "Blasphemy and Folly," CT, July 20, 1890.

18. Psychiatrist Steven Machlin, M.D., in conversation with author, July 16, 2014.

19. "Teed Is on the Move," CJ, April 15, 1892.

20. "The College of Life," CJ, September 18, 1889.

21. Andrews, untitled memoir, 10–11.

22. Duncan, *Culture and Democracy*, 53.

23. "The College of Life," CJ, September 18, 1889.

24. Stead, *If Christ Came to Chicago!*, 327.

25. Schudson, *Discovering the News*, 65, 68–69.

26. Ibid., 69–70.

27. Ibid., 70–71; "Blasphemy and Folly," CT, July 20, 1890.

28. "Cyrus Is Coming Home," CH, August 30, 1891.

29. "A Tribute to Journalism," PD, July 31, 1890.

30. J. S. Sargent, "From Friends at Estero, Fla.," FS, January 21, 1898, 12; R. W., "The Flaming Sword the Clearest Search-Light," FS, March 4, 1898, 13.

Chapter 5. Opportunity

1. All quotations from letters among Abie Andrews, Virginia "Jennie" Andrews, and Margaret Harmon are from the following: Margaret Harmon to Virginia Andrews, March 22, 1888; A.W.K. Andrews to Margaret Harmon, March 23, 1888; and Virginia Andrews to Margaret Harmon on the following dates: June 1, 1889, October 10 and November 27, 1892, January 13, 1895, and February 5 and 11, 1895, AM-0153, KSHS.

2. "A Minister Warned by White Caps," NYT, May 9, 1889; untitled, CT, July 24, 1890.

3. Jennie Andrews kept a multivolume journal on behalf of the Unity, "Annals of the Koreshan Home." Only one volume, no. 3, survives in the KU papers. All journal entries and quotations recorded by Jennie Andrews are from that volume; Virginia Andrews, "Annals," February 7, 1892; "A Synopsis of Discourses Delivered by Dr. Cyrus Teed of the Koreshan Unity on Dec. 11 and 13 at Mt. Lebanon, N.Y.," Manifesto, March 1892, 67.

4. "He Can Do Nothing with Her," CT, November 21, 1891.

5. Ibid.; Miller v. Teed, Case G. 103382, Circuit Court of Cook County, Ill.; and Miller's Declaration in same, 1–5, in Fine, "The Chicago Years," 222.

6. "He Can Do Nothing with Her," CT, November 21, 1891.

7. "The Injustice of the Chicago Press," FS, June 1897, 419; Fine, "The Chicago Years," 223.

8. "The Science of Life," SH, July 13, 1890.

9. "The Injustice of the Chicago Press" and "Credit to the Chicago Journal," FS, June 1897, 418–19.

10. "The Science of Life," SH, July 13, 1890.

11. All quotations from Margaret Harmon to her husband, Allen, come from her letters to him on December 1 and 8, 1890, AM-0153, KSHS.

12. "The Koreshan God," SFC, October 16, 1891.

13. "A Chicago Messiah," OET, January 14, 1891.

14. "Has Disciples in Chicago," CT, February 12, 1891.

15. Ibid.

16. "Teed Says That He Will Be Killed," CT, March 3, 1892.

17. "Teed's Trip to Heaven," CT, May 17, 1891.

18. Cyrus Teed to A.W.K. Andrews, June 7, 1880, KU papers.

19. Earthquake descriptions are from Holden, A Catalogue of Earthquakes; Virtual Museum of the City of San Francisco, "San Francisco Earthquake History 1880–1914"; and Bennett, "Vacaville-Winters Earthquakes . . . 1892."

20. "Teed Is on the Move," CJ, April 15, 1892.

21. "A Celibate Combine," SFC, February 26, 1892; "'Cyrus' Teed's Ways," IO, September 13, 1891.

22. Jesse Teed to Emma Norton, November 14, 1891, KSHS.

23. "Koreshan Exposures," SFC, October 15, 1891; "The Koreshan God," SFC, October 16, 1891.

24. "Teed Is on the Move," CJ, April 15, 1892.

25. "Trustee Duss Talks," PD, November 16, 1891; Fred C. Datton, "A Master of Millions," LMG, December 18, 1891.

26. "Teed Is on the Move," CJ, April 15, 1892.

27. PL, October 25, 1891, in Carmer, "The Great Alchemist," 270–71.

28. Ibid.

29. "Economy and Dr. Teed," FS, January 16, 1892; "Messiah Teed Makes a Rich Haul," CT, October 27, 1891; "The Economite Society's Millions Safe," SDN, November 17, 1891.

30. Duss, *Harmonists*, 286.

31. "An Economite Denounces Dr. Teed," CT, January 3, 1892.

32. "Economy's Big Day," PD, February 15, 1892; Virginia Andrews, "Annals," February 10, 1893, KU papers.

33. "They Did Not Join 'Koresh' Teed," CT, February 16, 1892; "Fascinated by Teed," SLT, January 10, 1892; "Sidney Miller," FS, January 16, 1892.

34. "Teed Is on the Move," CJ, April 15, 1892.

35. Jennie's conversation with Teed about the Shakers, the description of the march, the visits from Gates and Cantrell, and the attempted confederations with other societies are from her "3rd Volume of Annals of the Koreshan Home," KU papers.

36. The description of Teed's visit and lectures to the Shakers is from "A Synopsis of Discourses Delivered by Dr. Cyrus Teed of the Koreshan Unity on Dec. 11 and 13 at Mt. Lebanon, N.Y.," *Manifesto*, March 1892, 66–68.

37. Virginia Andrews, "Annals," February 21, 1892, KU papers.

38. Beinecke, "America and the Utopian Dream."

39. "A Celibate Combine," SFC, February 26, 1892.

40. Ibid.

41. Virginia Andrews, "Annals," March 6, 1892, KU papers.

42. Daniel Offord, "North Family, July 1892," *Manifesto*, August 1892, 183.

43. Untitled, *Manifesto*, October 1892, 220–22, 229–31.

44. Ibid.

45. FS, August 13, 1892, in Untitled, *Manifesto*, October 1892, 230.

46. "Father Henrici Dead," NYT, December 26, 1892; "Angels Are in Luck," CT, December 27, 1892.

47. Duss, *Harmonists*, 296.

48. Ibid., 297.

Chapter 6. The White City

1. Descriptions of the Hilliard house come from McCready, "Memories," 28–36.

2. Virginia Andrews, "Annals," March 27, 1892, KU papers.

3. "Koreshan Converts," SFC, March 17, 1892.

4. "A Koreshan Move," SFC, December 15, 1891.

5. Earthquake descriptions are from the Virtual Museum of the City of San Francisco, "San Francisco Earthquake History 1880–1914"; Bennett, "Vacaville-Winters Earthquakes . . . 1892."

6. "Teed Is on the Move," CJ, April 15, 1892; Virginia Andrews, "Annals," April 15, 1892, KU papers.

7. "Teed Is on the Move," CJ, April 15, 1892.

8. "Teed May Be Tarred," CT, May 1, 1892.

9. Virginia Andrews, "Annals," May 10, 1892, KU papers; "Teed May Be Tarred," CT, May 1, 1892.

10. "Teed May Be Tarred," CT, May 1, 1892; "Dr. Teed Will Move," CT, May 3, 1892.

11. Unidentified death threat, undated, record group 900000, collection N2009-3, box 229, folder 1, KU papers.

12. Virginia Andrews, "Annals," April 28–29, 1892, KU papers; "Teed Is on the Move," CJ, April 15, 1892.

13. "California's Koreshan Converts," CT, May 4, 1892; Virginia Andrews, "Annals," May 3, 1892, KU papers.

14. "Here's Koresh King of Fakirs," TS, March 2, 1907, quoting "a Chicago paper" that reported on the arrival of the San Francisco contingent.

15. "Half an Hour in 'Heaven,'" CTimes, May 5, 1892. All information and dialogue for the interaction among Teed, Silverfriend, and Woodhull is covered in this CTimes article.

16. Ibid.

17. Ibid.

18. "Cyrus Hasn't Reached 'Heaven,'" CT, May 6, 1892.

19. Ibid.

20. "Dr. Teed Grows Enthusiastic," CT, May 7, 1892; Virginia Andrews, "Annals," March 22, May 3, and May 6, KU papers.

21. Virginia Andrews, "Annals," May 10, 1892, KU papers; "Dr. Beck Now Has His Revenge," CT, May 11, 1892.

22. Virginia Andrews, "Annals," October 18, 1892, KU papers.

23. Judges 6:11; Virginia Andrews, "Annals," March 27, 1892, KU papers; McCready, "Memories," 30.

24. "Wanted to Be a Goddess," CJ, June 9, 1892; Sidney C. Miller's Declaration in *Miller v. Teed*, Case G. 103382, Circuit Court of Cook County, Ill., in Fine, "The Chicago Years," 222.

25. Virginia Andrews, "Annals," May 26, 1892, KU papers.

26. "How to Deal with Teed," CT, May 21, 1892.

27. "They're After Teed," CT, May 15, 1892.

28. "Bombs for Dr. Teed," CT, May 16, 1892.

29. Ibid.

30. Virginia Andrews, "Annals," May 15, 1892, KU papers.

31. Virginia Andrews, "Annals," May 15 and 18, 1892, KU papers.

32. Sinclair, *Profits*, 127; Virginia Andrews, "Annals," May 15, 1892, KU papers.

33. "Messiah Teed Is Arrested," CT, May 19, 1892; "Teed's Angry Victims," SFC, May 19, 1892.

34. Virginia Andrews, "Annals," May 18, 1892, KU papers; "They're After Teed," CT, May 19, 1892.

35. "They're After Teed," CT, May 19, 1892.

36. Virginia Andrews, "Annals," May 26, 1892, KU papers; "Teed's Angry Victims," SFC, May 19, 1892.

37. "The Other Side," FS, May 21, 1892.

38. "They Defend Teed," CT, May 23, 1892; "Teed to His Angels," CT, May 30, 1892; "Will Push the Prosecution of Teed," CT, May 26, 1892; "Money to Prosecute Teed," CT, May 27, 1892.

39. Virginia Andrews, "Annals," May 28, 1892, KU papers.

40. Virginia Andrews, "Annals," May 30, 1892, KU papers.

41. Virginia Andrews, "Annals," October 24, 1892, KU papers.

42. Virginia Andrews, "Annals," September 14, 1892, KU papers.

43. Virginia Andrews, "Annals," October 1, 1892, KU papers.

44. Virginia Andrews, "Annals," September 30 and October 1, 1892, KU papers.

45. Virginia Andrews, "Annals," October 17, 1892, KU papers.

46. Virginia Andrews to Margaret Harmon, October 10, 1892, AM-0153, KSHS; Virginia Andrews, "Annals," September 21, 1892, KU papers.

47. Virginia Andrews, "Annals," October 20, 1892, KU papers.

48. Information about requiring a permit to leave the house is from Virginia Andrews, "Annals," November 11, 1892, KU papers. Information and dialogue from the women's disagreement over Victoria's divinity comes from Andrews's "Annals" from the following dates: December 18 and 20, 1892, and January 10, 15, and 17, February 4, 10, and 12, and March 10, 14, and 29, 1893.

49. Cyrus Teed to "Brother Daniel," December 19, 1893, record group 900000, collection N2009-3, box 228, folder 61, KU papers.

50. Virginia Andrews, "Annals," December 20, 1892, KU papers.

51. Virginia Andrews, "Annals," June 21, 1892, KU papers.

52. Cyrus Teed to "Brother Daniel," December 19, 1893, record group 900000, collection N2009-3, box 228, folder 61, KU papers.

53. Ibid.

54. Ibid.

55. Fine, "Chicago Years," 36; "Burglars Explore Teed's 'Heaven,'" CT, May 25, 1893.

56. The account of this meeting comes from Virginia Andrews, "Annals," January 15, 1893, KU papers.

57. Ibid.

58. "Let the Fires of Purification Continue to Burn," Brother George (Hunt), undated, record group 900000, collection N2009-3, box 234, folder 52, KU papers.

59. "Beth-Ophrah, Friday, August 11, 7:30 p.m. 1893," A. M. Potter. These are notes from the meeting of the concilium, KU papers.

60. Cyrus Teed to "My Dear Daughters of Zion in Jerusalem," June 27, 1896, KSHS.

61. "Provides an Annex: Dr. Teed Conducts a Children's Branch to His 'Heaven,'" CT, July 17, 1893.

62. Mrs. L. S. Boomer, "In a Defense of Dr. Teed's Teachings," CT, July 21, 1893.

63. Berthaldine S. Boomer, "Out of the Old Order into the New," AE, December 1978.

64. Ibid.

Chapter 7. The Homesteader

1. Damkohler, *Estero, Fla. 1882*, 4, KSHS.

2. Historical information about Punta Rassa comes from Andrews, *Yank Pioneer*, 14; James Powers, research historian, Southwest Florida Museum of History, e-mail to author, December 20, 2012; and Lee County Southwest Florida Parks and Recreation, "Historic Punta Rassa."

3. Quesnell, *Early Estero*, 10. Information about Gustave Damkohler's finding the land and his homesteading arrangement also comes from Quesnell, *Early Estero*, 13–17, 52–71.

4. Andrews, *Yank Pioneer*, 14.

5. Rea, *Koreshan Story*, 16.

6. Ibid., 17; Damkohler, *Estero, Fla. 1882*, 4.

7. Damkohler, *Estero, Fla. 1882*, 8.

8. Ibid., 20.

9. Quesnell, *Early Estero*, 70.

10. Florida Department of Agriculture, Seventh Census of the State of Florida 1945, 10, as cited by Williamson, *Florida Politics in the Gilded Age: 1877–1893*, 163.

11. Boomer, "Out of the Old Order into the New," AE, December 1978.

12. "A Big Colony," BCI, October 26, 1893.

13. Gustave Damkohler's plans to sell the land and his estimate of its value come from testimony and exhibits in *Gustave Damkohler v. Koreshan Unity*, filed in the Sixth Judicial Circuit Court, Lee County, Florida, April 15, 1897, KSHS.

14. Information about the meeting at Punta Rassa and the property deal comes from the following: Damkohler, *Estero, Fla. 1882*, 22–24; Boomer, "Out of the Old Order into the New," AE, December 1978; depositions and exhibits in *Damkohler v. Koreshan Unity*; and Rea, *Koreshan Story*, 19–24.

15. A. G. Ordway to Gustave Damkohler, November 18, 1893, and C. R. Teed to Gustave Damkohler, November 23, 1893. Both letters are exhibits in *Damkohler v. Koreshan Unity*.

16. Unless otherwise noted, the description, dialogue, and deal made on the porch come from testimony in *Damkohler v. Koreshan Unity*.

17. Rea, *Koreshan Story*, 22.

18. Damkohler, *Estero, Fla. 1882*, 22.

19. The trip to Estero and their arrival are documented in Boomer, "Out of the Old Order into the New," AE, January 1979, and in Damkohler, *Estero, Fla. 1882*, 22–23.

20. Boomer, "Out of the Old Order into the New," AE, January 1979.

21. Douglas, *The Everglades*, 302.

22. Hinds, *American Communities*, 472; Quesnell, *Early Estero*, 21–23.

23. Damkohler, *Estero, Fla. 1882*, 23.

24. Ibid.; Quesnell, *Early Estero*, 72.

25. No title, FMP, January 4, 1894.

26. Information about the Koreshans' first time in Estero comes from Damkohler, *Estero, Fla. 1882*, 22–27; Boomer, "Out of the Old Order into the New," AE, January 1979.

27. Boomer, "Out of the Old Order into the New," AE, January and February 1979.

28. Damkohler, *Estero, Fla. 1882*, 23; Boomer, "Out of the Old Order into the New," AE, January and February 1979.

29. Boomer, "Out of the Old Order into the New," AE, February 1979.

30. Ibid.

31. Ibid.

Chapter 8. Under the Canopy of Heaven

1. Material about the trip from Chicago to Estero and arrival in Estero comes from Andrews, untitled memoir, 17–19; Giles, "Vesta: A Tribute," 29–33. The sons of thunder reference to James and John is from Mark 3:17.

2. Andrews, *Yank Pioneer*, 2.

3. Early memories of being in Estero come from the following: McCready, "Memories," 65; C. S. Baldwin to E. A. Graham, February 22 through March 11, 1894, which appeared in AE, October 1978; Andrews, untitled memoir, 21; and Allen H. Andrews, "Replying to E. E. Damkohler," AE, June 30, 1927.

4. C. S. Baldwin to E. A. Graham, February 22 through March 11, 1894, which appeared in AE, October 1978.

5. Andrews, untitled memoir, 21.

6. Damkohler, *Estero, Fla. 1882*, 28.

7. Andrews, *Yank Pioneer*, 9.

8. Larson, *Devil in the White City*, 335.

9. Stead, *If Christ Came to Chicago!*

10. Boomer, "Out of the Old Order into the New," AE, November 1978.

11. "His New Jerusalem," CH, April 8, 1894.

12. Ibid.

13. "Master's Lecture at Hickory Island, Dec. 25, 1894," record group 900000, collection N2009-3, box 230, folder 20, KU papers.

14. *Koreshan Unity: Communistic*, 2–3, 9, 12–13, 14–16.

15. Ibid.

16. Untitled, CT, March 24, 1895, 28.

17. No title, FMP, June 28, 1894.

18. Andrews, *Yank Pioneer*, 11.

19. Damkohler, *Estero, Fla. 1882*, 26.

20. Andrews, *Yank Pioneer*, 14.

21. The conversation between Damkohler and L'Amoreaux is from testimony in *Damkohler v. Koreshan Unity*.

22. Damkohler, *Estero, Fla. 1882*, 26.

23. "The Koreshan Community," W. W. Foose, FMP, September 13, 1894.

24. The conversations between Damkohler, Teed, and Victoria about the transfer of property come from testimony and exhibits in *Damkohler v. Koreshan Unity*.

25. Acts 5: 1–11.

26. Damkohler, *Estero, Fla. 1882*, 23–24.

27. Virginia Andrews to Margaret Harmon, January 13 and February 5, 1895, AM-0153, KSHS.

28. Virginia Andrews to Margaret Harmon, February 5, 1895, AM-0153, KSHS.

29. Ibid.

30. Ibid.

31. Virginia Andrews to Margaret Harmon, February 9, 1895, AM-0153, KSHS.

32. Virginia Andrews to Margaret Harmon, November 27, 1892, AM-0153, KSHS.

33. Virginia Andrews to Margaret Harmon, February 11, 1895, AM-0153, KSHS.

34. Quesnell, *Early Estero*, 82.

35. Information about the dispute over the Estero Island land, including letters from Damkohler to the land commissioner in Tallahassee, comes from Quesnell, *Early Estero*, 79–83, 125–33.

36. Rahn, "A Brief Outline," 52; "A Visit to the Koreshan Unity at Estero," FMP, April 16, 1896.

37. "A Visit to the Koreshan Unity at Estero," FMP, April 16, 1896.

38. FS, October 1896, in Berrey, "The Koreshan Unity," 50–52.

39. Damkohler, *Estero, Fla. 1882*, 28.

40. Allen H. Andrews, "Replying to E. E. Damkohler," AE, June 30, 1927; Damkohler, *Estero, Fla. 1882*, 28–29.

41. Allen H. Andrews, "Replying to E. E. Damkohler," AE, June 30, 1927.

42. Damkohler, *Estero, Fla. 1882*, 29.

Chapter 9. Our Cosmic Egg

1. Teed and Morrow, *The Cellular Cosmogony*, 1905, 9. This edition of the book included Ulysses G. Morrow as a co-author. However, in the 1922 edition, Teed appears as the sole author and mention of Morrow is entirely removed in spite of the fact that Morrow's work remained in the book verbatim. For this reason, the endnotes make a distinction between the 1905 edition, which credits Morrow, and the 1922 edition, which does not.

2. "A Demo-Pop Reconstruction Plan," CT, November 28, 1896.

3. Isa. 40:12.

4. Information and quotes about Ulysses Morrow come from the following: Hay, "The Rectilineator," 18; McCready, "Folks," 13; "Profile: The Koreshans' [*sic*] Daughter,"

NP, January 23, 2005; "Pair Looks Back upon Fifty Years of Married Life," TP, July 3, 1936; Hermann Deutsch, "Cult Believes Entire Universe Is Housed in Hollow Sphere," IT, January 5, 1936, reprinted in *Field Theory Publicity*, 3–6.

5. Letter from Ulysses G. Morrow, FS, May 1895, excerpted in Allen Andrews, "Prof. Morrow a Plagiarist," FS, March 1936, 14–15.

6. Descriptions of the team's tests come from Teed and Morrow, *The Cellular Cosmogony*, 1905, 64–76.

7. Ibid., 76.

8. These dimensions are documented in Teed and Morrow, ibid., 5.

9. Ibid., 83.

10. The rectilineator is described and diagrammed in Teed and Morrow, ibid., 36–39, 92–96.

11. "Device to Test the Earth's Shape," CT, September 28, 1896.

12. Untitled, NYT, November 24, 1896.

13. The disagreement between Gustave and Teed is from testimony in *Damkohler v. Koreshan Unity*.

14. Ulysses Morrow to Evelyn Bubbett, January 25, 1897, published in AE, July 1980 to January 1981.

15. The nickname for the Naples Beach camp comes from a photograph in the KU papers, http://www.floridamemory.com/items/show/257362. Descriptions of how the tests were conducted come from Teed and Morrow, *The Cellular Cosmogony*, 1905, 97–111.

16. Morrow's descriptions of the work on the beach are from his letters to Evelyn Bubbett, January 25 and one undated, and February 1, 6, 19, 22, and 26, 1897, published in AE, July 1980 to January 1981.

17. Ulysses Morrow to Evelyn Bubbett, no date, 1897, published in AE, July 1980 to January 1981.

18. Ulysses Morrow to Evelyn Bubbett, January 25, 1897, published in AE, July 1980 to January 1981.

19. Ulysses Morrow to Evelyn Bubbett, no date, 1897, published in AE, July 1980 to January 1981.

20. Ibid.

21. Andrews, *Yank Pioneer*, 29–30.

22. Ulysses Morrow to Evelyn Bubbett, February 6, 1897, published in AE, July 1980 to January 1981.

23. Teed and Morrow, *The Cellular Cosmogony*, 1905, 111.

24. Ibid., 110, 114.

25. "Sparks from the Wires," CT, October 12, 1894.

26. Teed and Morrow, *The Cellular Cosmogony*, 1905, 117.

27. "Proof That We Live Inside the Globe," CTH, July 25, 1897; "The Koreshan Expedition," FMP, July 22, 1897; "Living Inside of the Earth," DN, March 18, 1899, 12.

28. Teed and Morrow, *The Cellular Cosmogony*, 1905, 138, 146.

29. Ibid., 134–44.

30. Carmer, "The Great Alchemist," 262.

Chapter 10. In the Outside World

1. Memories of the Damkohlers' early days in Estero are from Damkohler, *Estero, Fla. 1882.*

2. *Damkohler v. Koreshan Unity.*

3. Ibid.

4. Ibid.

5. Ibid.; Quesnell, *Early Estero,* 77–78.

6. "The 'Koreshan' Leader Wins," FMP, July 1, 1897, originally printed in CJ.

7. Letter from Cyrus Teed in Chicago to George Hunt in Estero, June 27, 1898, KSHS; Quesnell, *Early Estero,* 86.

8. Untitled, FMP, April 29, 1897; "Misery in Estero," FMP, August 5, 1897, originally appeared in PDN, May 19, 1897.

9. "Misery in Estero," FMP, August 5, 1897; Cyrus Teed to George Hunt, August 29, 1898, KSHS; Harriet Wright, "Another Teed Victim Heard From," letter to the editor, FMP, December 15, 1898.

10. "Misery in Estero," FMP, August 5, 1897; Cyrus Teed to George Hunt, August 29, 1898, March 24, 1899, and January 28, 1902, KSHS; *Damkohler v. Koreshan Unity.*

11. "Misery in Estero," FMP, August 5, 1897.

12. Ibid.; "Washington Heights Wishes to Get Rid of Teed," CT, February 24, 1896.

13. "Mrs. Watson Exposes Teed," FMP, October 25, 1906.

14. "Washington Heights Wishes to Get Rid of Teed," CT, February 24, 1896; "Imperialism Run Mad," NYW, November 17, 1895; "Teed Defies His Foes," CT, March 9, 1896; "The Koreshans in Florida," NYT, March 1, 1896.

15. "Teed Defies His Foes," CT, March 9, 1896.

16. Memories of the McCreadys' experiences are from McCready, "Memories," and McConnell, "Growing-Up Days."

17. McConnell, "Growing-Up Days," 24.

18. Ibid., 45.

19. McCready, "Memories," 18.

20. Ibid., 7.

21. Ibid., 18–19.

22. Ibid., 18.

23. Ibid.

24. Ibid., 22–23; "A Notorious Criminal Attacks Koreshanity," FMP, January 5, 1899, reprinted from FS.

25. McCready, "Memories," 22–23.

26. "A Notorious Criminal Attacks Koreshanity," FMP, January 5, 1899.

27. "A Theosophical Problem," NYT, February 2, 1896.

28. McCready, "Memories," 23; Cyrus Teed to George Hunt, December 30, 1898, KSHS.

29. "A Notorious Criminal Attacks Koreshanity," FMP, January 5, 1899; McConnell, "Growing-Up Days," 62.

30. McCready, "Memories," 48.

31. "Old Friend in a New Role," FMP, Supplement, December 15, 1898, reprinted from the *New York Herald*.

32. Ibid.

33. Ibid.; "Is This Another Colony on the Koreshan Order for Lee County?" FMP, November 24, 1898.

34. "Princess Edietha [*sic*] Loleta," FMP, December 1, 1898. (The correct spelling is "Editha.")

35. "The Princess Furnishes Another Chapter on the Doings of 'Dr.' Teed," FMP, December 8, 1898.

36. "A Notorious Criminal Attacks Koreshanity," FMP, January 5, 1899.

37. Harriet F. Wright, "Arraigns Dr. Teed," letter to the editor, FMP, January 19, 1899.

38. Untitled, FMP, December 15, 1898.

39. Ibid.

40. Cyrus Teed to George Hunt, November 21, 1899, KSHS.

Chapter 11. At Last

1. Cyrus Teed to George Hunt, 1897, KSHS.

2. Cyrus Teed to George Hunt, January 20, 1899, KSHS.

3. "Henry D. Silverfriend told me," Claude Rahn, July 1933, unpublished page, box 2, folder: "Cyrus Teed," FGCU.

4. "'Rev.' Mrs. Castle Lectures on Koreshanity," FMP, February 2, 1899.

5. Cyrus Teed to George Hunt, February 24, 1899, KSHS; Civil War Records: Military and Pension, Cyrus R. Teed, from the holdings of the National Archives, AM-0154, KSHS.

6. Cyrus R. Teed, "Debtor's Schedule," *Parsons v. Teed*, in Fine, "The Koreshan Unity," 40.

7. Cyrus Teed to George Hunt, March 24, 1899, KSHS.

8. Cyrus Teed to George Hunt, June 23, 1900, KSHS.

9. Andrews, *Yank Pioneer*, 37.

10. Ibid., 38.

11. Ibid., 12.

12. "Estero," FMP, November 15, 1900; McConnell, "Growing-Up Days," 96.

13. "The Koreshan Unity: General Information Concerning Membership and Its Obligations," in Herbert and Reeves, *Koreshan Unity Settlement*, 29.

14. Marie's memories of coming to Estero are from McCready, "Memories" and McConnell, "Growing-Up Days."

15. McConnell, "Growing-Up Days," 71.

16. McCready, "Memories," 54.

17. Ibid., 55.

18. McConnell, "Growing-Up Days," 75.

19. Ibid., 77.

20. Mackle, "The Koreshan Unity," 94–95.

21. Cyrus Teed to George Hunt, September 18, 1902, KSHS.

22. Victoria Gratia to Mary, undated, box 2, folder: "Victoria Gratia," FGCU.

23. "Let the Fires of Purification Continue to Burn," Brother George (Hunt), undated, record group 900000, collection N2009-3, box 234, folder 52, KU papers.

24. Cyrus Teed to George Hunt, June 13, 1902, KSHS.

25. FMP, June 12, 1902; Cyrus Teed to George Hunt, June 7, 1903, KSHS.

26. Cyrus Teed to George Hunt, June 13, 1902, KSHS.

27. Ibid.

28. "He Is Messiah No Longer!" FMP, January 23, 1902.

29. Marie's memories of the typhoid epidemic are from McCready, "Memories," 68–72, and McConnell, "Growing-Up Days," 102–10.

30. McConnell, "Growing-Up Days," 102–10.

31. "Two Hundred Koreshans at Estero," FMP, November 26, 1903.

32. "Koreshan Daily Graces," Estero, Fla.: Koreshan Unity Press, no date, 2 and 4, as cited in Mackle, "The Koreshan Unity," 96-97.

33. Mackle, "The Koreshan Unity," 97–98.

34. "Madness and Death Add to the Mystery of Koresh's Tomb," NYT, November 6, 1910.

35. All details and quotes about the railroad coming to Fort Myers are from "Fort Myers Celebrates," FMP, February 25, 1904.

36. "Gala Day in Fort Myers," FMP, April 30, 1903.

37. "Florida as a Great World-Center," FS, June 13, 1905.

38. Veritas, "Tin-Shop and Laundry," FMP, July 21, 1904.

39. All information from the prospectus is taken from Koreshan Unity Co-operative, *The Solution of Industrial Problems*.

40. Ibid., 79–83.

41. Mackle, "The Koreshan Unity," 135.

42. All information about the incorporation fight comes from numerous articles in FMP on these dates: August 4, 11, 18, and 25 and September 1, 8, and 15, 1904.

43. Schauer, Hafner, and Frantz, "Valuable Property Owned by Outsiders," letter to the editor, FMP, August 18, 1904.

44. Veritas, "The Coming City of Estero," FMP, August 25, 1904.

45. "Object to Coming Under Control of a Koreshan Municipality," letter to the editor, FMP, August 25, 1904.

46. Brother Ezra to Brother Joseph, December 8, 1906, in "Estero in 1906: The Report of a Shaker Visitor," AE, May 1979.

47. "Another Letter from Anti-Koreshans," FMP, September 1, 1904; "The Government of Estero," FMP, September 1, 1904.

48. "Party of Cranks," FMP, September 1, 1904.

49. Cyrus Teed, "The Truth Concerning Estero," letter to the editor, FMP, September 8, 1904.

50. Douglas, *Everglades*, 303; Veritas, "Park Grounds at Estero," FMP, September 29, 1904.

51. Veritas, "Amusements at Estero," FMP, December 22, 1904.

52. Hinds, *American Communities*, 476.

53. O.E.S., "A Visit to Estero," FMP, May 25, 1905, as reprinted in FS, June 13, 1905.

54. Beecher, *Douglas Arthur Teed*; O.E.S., "A Visit to Estero," FMP, May 25, 1905, as reprinted in FS, June 13, 1905.

55. Douglas Arthur Teed, "The Lost Muse," 1890, KL-0081, KSHS.

56. Giles, "Vesta: A Tribute," 32.

57. Marie's memories of packing and of her sisters leaving come from McCready, "Memories."

Chapter 12. Fight

1. Descriptions of politics in Lee County, Isaacs's hiring, the competition between the papers, and coverage of Edison come from Grismer, "The Story of Fort Myers," 154–55, 158.

2. Information about the Hendrys' attempts to pass bond issues and Isaacs's moves to block them is from Grismer, "The Story of Fort Myers," 202–4.

3. Slander letter to Cyrus Teed, undated, anonymous (signed "Your Hater"), item ID AM-0192, KSHS.

4. Information in this section about the Democratic primary, the election of 1906, and the pledge voters were required to sign come from Mackle, "The Koreshan Unity," 102–5; Mackle, "Cyrus Teed and the Lee County Elections," 7–8; and "The Pledge Required of the Koreshans," FMP, May 31, 1906.

5. Details about the formation of the *American Eagle*, the printing operation, and the press fight with Isaacs are from Andrews, *Yank Pioneer*, 43–48; Anderson, "The American Eagle," 20–34; Mackle, "The Koreshan Unity," 81–84, 101–21.

6. Lead editorial, AE, June 7, 1906.

7. "The Gospel According to St. Isaacs," AE, June 7, 1906.

8. Andrews, *Yank Pioneer*, 44.

9. A. H. Andrews, "Open Letter to *Florida Times-Union*," AE, June 14, 1906.

10. Information about the Hendrys' attempts to pass another bond issue and Isaacs's opposition, culminating in his resignation, is from Grismer, "The Story of Fort Myers," 202–4.

11. Ross Wallace, "Reaching the Vitals," AE, August 16, 1906; "1906—Political Situation," notes by Claude Rahn, undated, box 2, folder: "Koreshan politics," FGCU.

12. "A Summing Up," AE, September 20, 1906; "Koresh in Politics," FMP, September 27, 1906.

13. "The Sphinx Has Spoken" and untitled, AE, October 4, 1906.

14. Descriptions of the telephone call, the exchange in the street, and the two street fights, including dialogue, come from affidavits sworn by Cyrus R. Teed, C. Addison Graves, W. Ross Wallace, Claude J. Rahn, Rollin W. Gray, Roland Sander, and George Henry Danner, AE Supplement, November 8, 1906; AE, October 18 and 25, November 1 and 8, 1906; FMP, October 18 and 25, 1906; Mackle, "The Koreshan Unity," 114–20; and Mackle, "Cyrus Teed and the Lee County Elections," 5–17.

15. "Teed Starts a Street Fight!" FMP, October 18, 1906.

16. Ibid.

17. Affidavit sworn by W. Ross Wallace, AE Supplement, November 8, 1906.

18. Koresh, "A Put-Up Job," AE, October 18, 1906.

19. "Teed Starts a Street Fight!" FMP, October 18, 1906; "Teed Poses as Martyr," FMP, October 18, 1906, reprinted from CTimes, unknown date.

20. "Teed Starts a Street Fight!" FMP, October 18, 1906.

21. "Came Near Lynching Teed," FMP, October 25, 1906, reprinted from CTimes, May 18, 1892; "Will Investigate Koresh," FMP, October 18, 1906, reprinted from CTimes, unknown date.

22. "Proof of Teed's Rascality," FMP, October 25, 1906.

23. Ibid.

24. "In the Editorial Perspective," FS, October 1906.

25. "Will Myers Redress the Wrong?" AE, October 25, 1906.

26. "Bombastes Teed's Ultimatum," FMP, November 1, 1906.

27. Koresh, "The Political Contest in Lee County," FS, November 6, 1906; "Reincarnation of Koresh," FMP, November 8, 1906.

28. "Here's Koresh King of Fakirs," TS, March 2, 1907.

29. "Koresh Receives the Kibosh—Kicks," FMP, March 21, 1907, reprinted from TS, March 16, 1907.

30. "Advice to Koresh: Let the People of Lee County Alone," FMP, March 28, 1907.

31. "'Old Cy's' Pet Scheme Knocked Out!" FMP, May 23, 1907.

32. Grismer, The Story of Fort Myers, 203, 275–348.

33. AE, October 10, 1907, in Mackle, "The Koreshan Unity," 125.

Chapter 13. City of the Blessed

1. Eileen Schwartz, M.D., neurologist, in conversation with author, September 3, 2014.

2. Teed, The Great Red Dragon, 148.

3. Ibid.; untitled notes by C. J. Rahn, undated, KU papers.

4. Wells, The War in the Air; Teed, The Great Red Dragon, "Publisher's Note."

5. Teed, The Great Red Dragon, "Publisher's Note."

6. Exchanges between Arthur and his father come from these letters: D. Arthur Teed to "Dear Father," May 10, 1907, and October 31, 1908; propositions for settlement, May 10, 1907, and October 29, 1908; compromise settlement, November 17, 1908, KU papers.

7. Virginia Andrews, "Annals," November 28 and December 27, 1892, KU papers; D. Arthur Teed to "Dear Father," May 10, 1907, KU papers.

8. D. Arthur Teed to "Dear Father," May 10, 1907, KU papers.

9. Fort Myers psychiatrist Dr. Steven Machlin in discussion with author, July 16, 2014.

10. Henry Silverfriend to "My Dear Master," June 27, 1907, KU papers; Henry Silverfriend to "Dear Master," October 26, 1907, KU papers.

11. Henry Silverfriend to "My Dear Master," January 26, 1908, FGCU; Henry Silverfriend to "My Dear Master," November 18, 1908, KU papers.

12. Henry Silverfriend to "My Dear Master," January 26, 1908, FGCU.

13. Ibid.

14. Bill Foley, "Millennium Moments: Feb. 1, 1908," FTU, February 1, 1999.

15. Pension record for Cyrus Teed, application number 34622, certificate number D3385. Civil War Records: Military and Pension, Cyrus R. Teed, from the holdings of the National Archives, AM-0154, KSHS.

16. Cyrus Teed to Evelyn Bubbett, undated, record group 900000, collection N2009-3, box 228, folder 13, KU papers; Cyrus Teed to George Hunt, May 17, 1908, KSHS.

17. Cyrus Teed to Evelyn Bubbett, undated, record group 900000, collection N2009-3, box 228, folder 13, KU papers.

18. Cyrus Teed to Evelyn Bubbett, July 3 and 22, 1908, and undated, record group 900000, collection N2009-3, box 228, folder 13, KU papers.

19. Cyrus Teed to Evelyn Bubbett, undated, record group 900000, collection N2009-3, box 228, folder 13, KU papers; Cyrus Teed to Orline Thacher, May 6, 1906, KU papers.

20. Cyrus Teed to Evelyn Bubbett, July 22, 1908, KU papers.

21. Ibid.

22. Ulysses Morrow to "My dear friend Mr. Manley," September 21, 1938, AM-0181, KSHS.

23. Cyrus Teed to Evelyn Bubbett, July 22, 1908, KU papers.

24. Ibid.; "Death of the Master," Claude Rahn, undated, box 2, folder: "Cyrus Teed," FGCU.

25. "Excerpt from the Master's letter written in Washington, D.C. to the people at Estero," 1908, KU papers.

26. Ibid.

27. Ibid.

28. The account of Teed and Victoria's arrival in Estero comes from "Death of the Master" and "Master and Victoria Returned Home to Estero," Claude Rahn, undated, box 2, folder: "Cyrus Teed," FGCU.

29. William McCready to Lovelle McCready, December 26, 1908, KU papers.

30. "Solar Festival Entertainment," A Guest in the *American Eagle*, FS, November 15, 1908; "Solar Festival Program: October 18, 1908, A.K. 69," FS, November 15, 1908. The reading of the work *Armageddon* mentioned in "Solar Festival Entertainment" above likely refers to one of these three publications in the KU papers, record group 900000, collection N2009-3: "Call to the Battle of Armageddon in the Koreshan Church" (box 245, folder 3); "Armageddon: The Last Battle" (box 242, folder 7); or "The Battle of Armageddon" (box 242, folder 10).

31. "The Solar Festival Services," Elizebeth [*sic*] Robinson, FS, November 15, 1908, 23, KSHS.

32. Ibid.; compromise settlement, November 17, 1908, KU papers.

33. Henry Silverfriend to "My Dear Master," November 18, 1908, KU papers.

34. Ibid.

35. The scene of the band visit to play for Teed comes from "Death of the Master," Claude Rahn, undated, box 2, folder: "Cyrus Teed," FGCU.

36. Descriptions of Teed's dying, his death, and his body come from letters written by Christine Hamilton to Jennie Campbell, December 1, 8, and 16, 1908; Etta Silverfriend to Evelyn Bubbett, December 17, 1908; Evelyn to James (Bubbett?), December 22, 1908; Dr. J. Augustus Weimar, writing to "Sisters and Brothers," December 24, 1908; Virginia

Andrews to Evelyn Bubbett, December 24, 1908; William McCready to Lovelle Mc-Cready, December 26, 1908; Dr. J. Augustus Weimar to "Elizabeth," December 27, 1908; Christine Hamilton to "Dear Kind Friends," December 29, 1908; "Abby" to "Jennie," December 1908; and Dr. J. Augustus Weimar to DeCoursey Clinchy, December 30, 1908. All letters are from KU papers.

37. Christine Hamilton to Jennie Campbell, December 16, 1908, KU papers.

38. Christine Hamilton to Jennie Campbell, December 8, 1908, KU papers.

39. Christine Hamilton to Jennie Campbell, December 1, 1908, KU papers.

40. Accounts of Teed's paroxysm, his cries, and his conversation with Emma are from William McCready to Lovelle McCready, December 26, 1908, KU papers, and Christine Hamilton to "Dear Kind Friends," December 29, 1908, KU papers.

41. Victoria Gratia "To my people, and disciples of Koresh, Shepherd and Stone of Israel," December 20, 1908, KU papers.

42. Ibid.

43. Ibid.

44. Gay, "The Last Words of the Master," undated, record group 900000, collection N2009-3, box 172, folder 14, KU papers.

45. Virginia Andrews to Evelyn Bubbett, December 24, 1908, KU papers.

46. Ibid.

47. Ibid.; "Abby" to "Jennie," December 1908, KU papers.

48. Information about Victoria's return to Estero comes from the following: Christine Hamilton to "Dear Kind Friends," December 29, 1908; "Abby" to "Jennie," December 1908, KU papers.

49. "Abby" to "Jennie," December 1908, KU papers.

50. Dr. J. Augustus Weimar to DeCoursey Clinchy, December 30, 1908, KU papers.

51. Christine Hamilton to "Dear Kind Friends," December 29, 1908, KU papers.

Chapter 14. After Koresh

Epigraph: Author's Remarks from *Under the Banner of Heaven: A Story of Violent Faith* by Jon Krakauer, copyright © 2003 by Jon Krakauer. Used by permission of Doubleday, an imprint of the Knopf Doubleday Publishing Group, a division of Penguin Random House LLC. All rights reserved.

1. "Dr. Teed Predicted His Own Death," FS, January 15, 1909, KSHS.

2. "This Day in History," December 28, 1908, http://www.history.com/this-day-in-history/earthquake-rocks-sicily; "Dr. Teed Predicted His Own Death," FS, January 15, 1909, with Teed's prediction reprinted from an article in the FS, March 26, 1892; Junius R. Van Duzee, "Astronomic and Cosmic Phenomena: Coordinating and Contemporaneous with the Death of Dr. Teed," FS, February 15, 1909, 56–57.

3. E. Benson Steele, "Concerning Dr. Teed's Death," FS, February 15, 1909.

4. E. Benson Steele, "The Koreshan Lunar Festival," FS, May 15, 1909.

5. Sister Josephine to Sister Orline (Thacher), Tacy, and others, February 4, 1923. FGCU.

6. Material about the Order of Theocracy comes from the following: Berrey, "The Koreshan Unity," 41–42 and various issues of the *Double-Edged Sword*, KU papers. Material about Gus Faber's claim that Teed conferred the leadership to him comes from

Carmer, "The Great Alchemist," 280–81, and from Evelyn Bubbett to Imogene Bubbett-Rahn, October 12, 1913, KU papers. Material about Edgar Peissart can be found in Shaw, *Octavia*, 124–50, and in numerous publications that appear to have been written by Peissart, located in the H. W. Manley Collection, Edgar S. Peissert [*sic*] Material, AM-0180, http://koreshan.mwweb.org/virtual_exhibit/vex2/A8807C1C-A7E5-4FDD-8F58-119715718220.htm, KSHS.

7. H. W. Manley to Ulysses Morrow, September 11, 1938, KSHS.

8. U. G. Morrow to "My dear friend Mr. Manley," September 21, 1938, AM-0181, KSHS.

9. Allen Andrews, "Prof. Morrow a Plagiarist," FS, March 1936, 14–15, KSHS; Teed and Morrow, *The Cellular Cosmogony*, 1905, 5–6; Teed, *The Cellular Cosmogony*, 1922.

10. "Madness and Death Add to the Mystery of Koresh's Tomb," NYT, November 6, 1910.

11. Descriptions of the hurricane, its effects on the tomb, and the cleanup come from the following: Evelyn Bubbett to "My Dear Ones—Gene, Claude and Laurie," October 26, 1921; and Evelyn Bubbett to Gene (Imogene Bubbett), November 5, 1921, KU papers.

12. Evelyn Bubbett to "My Dear Ones—Gene, Claude and Laurie," October 26, 1921, KU papers.

13. Ibid.

14. The story of the light bulb anniversary dinner is from AE, June 6, 1929, excerpted in Rose Gilbert, "Community Current Events," FS, July 1940, KSHS. The Edisons' lunching at the Rustic Tea Garden is covered in a few "Community Current Events" write-ups in the *Flaming Sword*, e.g., May 1931, KSHS. A visit from Paul Sargent is covered by Max E. Arendt, "Community Current Events," FS, June 1932, KSHS.

15. Christina Cepero, "Ford's Link to Koreshans Strengthened," NP, December 23, 2005; "When Henry Ford Visited the Koreshan Unity," *Historic Bonita & Estero*, Historic Publications, no date, 7.

16. Raw film from Fox Movietone News, April 13, 1930, KSHS, http://koreshan.mwweb.org/blog/?p=463.

17. "Transplanting Botanicals to Koreshan Gardens," *Historic Bonita & Estero*, Historic Publications, no date, 4.

18. "In returning to the Unity, I must confess . . . ," Claude Rahn to unknown, November 4, 1936, box 2, folder: "A. Andrews," FGCU.

19. D. J. Richards, "Community Current Events," FS, October 1936, KSHS.

20. "Life in the Unity," Unofficial Site of the Koreshan State Historic Site, last modified December 13, 2010, http://koreshan.mwweb.org/blog/?p=344.

21. Franklin Jacke obituary, NP, April 1, 1936.

22. A. H. Andrews, "Evicted," letter to the editor, NP, undated, KU papers; A. H. Andrews, "Andrews to Fight," letter to the editor, NP, June 8, 1950; various AE articles in January and NP in February 1948; unsigned (Allen Andrews) to Hearst Publications, May 1949, KU papers.

23. "Number of Members of the Koreshan Unity January 29, 1948," authored by one or more of these officers of the Unity, Laurence Bubbett, Hedwig Michel, and Lou Staton, AM-0144, KSHS. The legal documents for Silverfriend are summarized here on the KSHS website: http://koreshan.mwweb.org/gene/notes/n0000013.htm.

24. L. M. Bubbett to "Friends and Subscribers to the *Flaming Sword*," April 25, 1949, AM-0158, KSHS.

25. "Andrews Arrested; Wrecked Plant Stand," NP, June 7, 1950.

26. Andrews, *Yank Pioneer*, 514; Allen Andrews's last will and testament, September 12, 1951, KU papers.

27. Rea, *Koreshan Story*, 69.

28. Comments about Michel provided, in conversation with the author, by Bill Grace, June 24, 2009, and by Mimi Straub, ca. March 9, 2010.

29. Conrad Schlender, handwritten note, December 4, 1948, record group 900000, collection N2009-3, box 72, folder 5, KU papers.

30. Scott Ritter, in conversation with author, September 2, 2014.

31. All quotations in this section from Scott Ritter and his father, Bob, are from the author's interviews with both on February 2, 2010, and with Scott Ritter on September 2, 2014.

32. "Reader's Report," anonymous peer reviewer for this book, University Press of Florida, November 6, 2013.

33. Carmer, "The Great Alchemist," 287.

34. Ibid.

35. Carmer, "The Great Alchemist," 287–88.

36. Carmer, "The Great Alchemist," 288.

37. Ibid.

38. Claude Rahn to Hedwig Michel, March 3, 1960, KU papers.

39. Hedwig Michel to Claude Rahn, February 19, 1960, KU papers.

40. Dunning, "A Visit with Miss Vesta," 3–5.

41. Giles, "Vesta: A Tribute," 31–32.

42. Dunning, "A Visit with Miss Vesta," 3–5; Scott Ritter, in conversation with author, September 2, 2014; Ellen Peterson (Estero resident), in conversation with author, December 23, 2009; and Bill Grace, in conversation with author, June 24, 2009.

43. Acreage and prices come from Quesnell, *Early Estero*, 95; *State of Florida Koreshan State Historic Site Unit Management Plan*, 57.

44. Rahn, "A Brief Outline," 51.

45. Minutes of the annual meeting of the Board of Directors of the Koreshan Unity Inc., October 26, 1980, KU papers; Rea, *Koreshan Story*, 71.

46. Mormino, *Land of Sunshine*, 9.

Chapter 15. Florida Forever

1. Andrews, *Yank Pioneer*, 489.

2. McCready, "Growing-Up Days," 73.

3. Dirr, *Dirr's Trees and Shrubs for Warm Climates*, 45.

4. Holloway, *Heavens on Earth*, 217–18, 230.

5. Shawn Holiday and Kathy Becker, "We Live Inside," GSL, October 1995, 24–31.

6. Bill Grace's memories of his interactions with Jo Bigelow come from a conversation with the author, August 13, 2014.

7. Holiday and Becker, "We Live Inside," GSL, October 1995; Kate Zajanc (former

museum curator at Koreshan State Historic Site), e-mail exchange with author, September 1, 2014.

8. Peter Hicks (retired ranger, Koreshan State Historic Site), e-mail exchange with author, August 20–21, 2014; Holiday and Becker, "We Live Inside," GSL, October 1995.

9. Holiday and Becker, "We Live Inside," GSL, October 1995.

10. Bill Grace, in conversation with author, August 13, 2014.

11. Holiday and Becker, "We Live Inside," GSL, October 1995.

12. Andrea Stetson, "Koreshan Lands Dwindling," NP, June 30, 1996; Lee Melsek, "Charity Starves Koreshan History," NP, July 27, 1997.

13. Melsek, "Charity Starves Koreshan History" and "Cemetery Alive with Overgrowth," NP, July 27, 1997.

14. Editorial, "New Stewards Needed to Preserve Koreshan Legacy," NP, July 27, 1997; Laura J. Cummings Gates, "Experience Estero: Historical Kayaking along the Estero River," Estero Lifestyle Magazine, July 2014.

15. Holiday and Becker, "We Live Inside," GSL, October 1995.

16. I interviewed Dauray twice, most recently in 2012. Late that year, I wrote an article about the Koreshans for Gulfshore Life magazine. Following this, I was interviewed by a News-Press reporter for a story about the College of Life. Both stories questioned the activities of the foundation. I then tried to contact Dauray for this book, and he made himself unavailable. When I asked whether I could use a photo of him for the book, I was forwarded the following statement: "Using my picture would not be a concern if I had confidence that the accompanying copy would be factual. Your disparaging comments about me in both your Gulfshore Life article and subsequent input in the News-Press article were both inflammatory and inaccurate. Therefore, I deny your request." I e-mailed him, asking what the inaccuracies were in the GSL story, asking him about the foundation's mission, and asking whether there was anything he would like the reading public to know. There was no answer. I called, and he didn't return my phone call. I spoke with the foundation's secretary, who relayed that he would not speak to me for this book.

17. This description and the quotes below it come from Charles Runnells, "Koreshan Group Has Devoted Administrator," NP, May 8, 1999.

18. Ibid.; Erinn Hutkin, "New Administrator Discusses Plans for Koreshan Foundation," BB, April 17, 1999; Erinn Hutkin, "Foundation's First-Ever Executive Administrator Will Take Over Daily Operations Jan. 4," BB, January 2, 1999.

19. Charlie Whitehead, "Koreshan Unity Foundation: Group Plans Development at Historic Site," NDN, September 25, 2000.

20. Lyn Millner, "Koreshans: The Legacy and the Questions," GSL, November 2012.

21. Chad Gillis, "The Koreshan Legacy," BDN, May 13, 2001.

22. Charlie Whitehead, "Koreshan Unity Foundation: Group Plans Development at Historic Site," NDN, September 25, 2000.

23. Ibid.

24. Chad Gillis, "The Koreshan Legacy," BDN, May 13, 2001.

25. Ibid.

26. Charlie Whitehead, "Lee, State Get Additional Time to Consider Estero Land Offer," NDN, May 29, 2002.

27. Lyn Millner, "Koreshans: The Legacy and the Questions," GSL, November 2012.

28. Charlie Whitehead, "College of Life Leaders Surprised to Learn State Votes to Pursue Their Property," BDN, March 4, 2003.

29. Ibid.

30. Ibid.

31. Amy Bennett Williams, "Profile," NP, March 13, 2005.

32. Description of the plans for Estero on the River comes from this site: "Estero on the River," last modified January 27, 2014, http://www.esterofl.org/Issues/Estero_on_the_River.htm.

33. Bill Grace, in conversation with author, June 24, 2009; Scott Ritter, in conversation with author, February 2, 2010; College of Life Foundation, Inc., 990-PF tax returns, 2010.

34. Florida Memory Blog, http://floridamemory.com/blog/2012/05/09/koreshan -unity-collection/ and http://floridamemory.com/blog/author/beth-and-bethanie/.

35. Peg Egan, in conversation with author, October 8, 2014, and November 19, 2014.

36. College of Life Foundation Inc., 990-PF tax returns for the years 1999–2012; Amy Bennett Williams, "College of Life Foundation Changing Direction," NP, November 25, 2012.

37. Lyn Millner, "Koreshans: The Legacy and the Questions," GSL, November 2012.

38. Scott Ritter, in conversation with author, September 2, 2014.

39. Lyn Millner, "Koreshans: The Legacy and the Questions," GSL, November 2012; Chad Gillis, "The Koreshan Legacy," BDN, May 13, 2001.

40. College of Life Foundation Inc., 990-PF tax returns for the years 1999–2012.

41. Lyn Millner, "Koreshans: The Legacy and the Questions," GSL, November 2012.

42. Ibid.

43. Lee Melsek, "Neglect Eats Away at Historic Cemetery," NP, September 9, 2001.

44. Jim Whitmore (general manager of Pelican Sound Golf & River Club), in conversation with author, September 8, 2014.

45. Lyn Millner, "Koreshans: The Legacy and the Questions," GSL, November 2012.

46. Ibid.

47. Jim Whitmore, in conversation with author, September 8, 2014.

48. College of Life Foundation Inc., 990-PF tax return for the year 2012.

49. Amy Bennett Williams, "College of Life Foundation Changing Direction," NP, November 25, 2012.

50. Ibid.

51. Peg Egan, in conversation with author, October 8, 2014.

52. College of Life Foundation Inc., 990-PF tax return for the year 2012; ICANN WHOIS domain name search: whois.icann.org.

53. Peg Egan, in conversation with author, October 8, 2014.

54. Steve Giguere (park manager, Koreshan State Historic Site), in conversation with author, September 8, 2014.

55. Peg Egan, in conversation with author, October 8, 2014; Steve Giguere, in conversation with author, September 8, 2014.

56. Peg Egan, in conversation with author, October 8, 2014.

57. Laura J. Cummings Gates, "Experience Estero: Historical Kayaking along the Estero River," *Estero Lifestyle Magazine*, July 2014.

58. Steve Giguere, in conversation with author, September 8, 2014.

59. Steve Giguere, e-mail to author, September 17, 2014.

60. Lindsay Downey, "Preserving History," NP, August 15, 2013.

61. Maryann Batlle, "Developers Speeding Up Projects before Estero Incorporation Vote," NDN, July 21, 2014.

62. Ellen Peterson, in conversation with author, December 23, 2009.

63. Scott Ritter, in conversation with author, September 2, 2014.

64. Jennifer Grant, "Sacred Sites," NDN, May 8, 2004.

Afterword

1. Eileen Schwartz, M.D., neurologist, in conversation with author, September 3, 2014.

2. Leslie Goddard, e-mail message to author, July 9, 2012.

3. Melissa Minds VandeBurgt, in conversation with author, October 31, 2014.

Bibliography

Primary Sources

Archival Documents

Andrews, Allen H. Untitled memoir. Undated manuscript. Adobe portable document file. FGCU.

Andrews, Virginia Harmon. "3rd Volume of Annals of the Koreshan Home, Chicago, Ill., commencing January 1, 1892." Unpublished. January 1, 1892, through March 31, 1893. Adobe portable document file. KU papers.

Boomer, Berthaldine S. "Out of the Old Order into the New." A report from the Koreshan Archives published in the *American Eagle* as "The Koreshan Unity Settlement." Edited by Hedwig Michel. November 1978–February 1979. KSHS.

Chicago Historical Society. The Haymarket Affair Digital Collection. http://www .chicagohistory.org/hadc/index.html.

Double-Edged Sword. Fort Myers, Fla.: Order of Theocracy, 1931 to 1934 (est.). Koreshan Unity Papers, State Archives of Florida, Tallahassee.

Flaming Sword. Chicago and Estero, Fla.: Guiding Star, 1889 to 1948. Koreshan Unity Papers, State Archives of Florida, Tallahassee.

Florida Memory Blog. *Florida Memory*. Division of Library and Information Services, Florida Department of State, Tallahassee. http://floridamemory.com/blog/tag/ koreshan-unity-collection/.

Giles, Lillian. "Vesta: A Tribute." In *Estero: The Life and Times*, by Jeff McCullers, 29–33. Unpublished. 1976. Adobe portable document file. KSHS.

Koreshan Archives. Koreshan State Historic Site, State of Florida, Estero. http://koreshan .mwweb.org/virtual_exhibit/index.htm.

Koreshan Collection. Florida Gulf Coast University Library Archives, Special Collections, and Digital Initiatives, Fort Myers.

Koreshan Unity Papers. State Archives of Florida, Florida Department of State, Tallahassee. https://www.floridamemory.com/collections/koreshan/.

Manifesto. East Canterbury, N.H.: The United Societies (The United Society of Believers), 1883–1899. Special Collections of Hamilton College, Clinton, N.Y. http://elib .hamilton.edu/shaker-publications.

McConnell, Marie McCready. "Growing-Up Days in a Celibate Community." Unpublished. 1976. Adobe portable document file. KSHS.

McCready, Marie. "Memories, Memories: Days of Long Ago." Unpublished. 1966. Adobe portable document file. KSHS.

———, ed. "Folks We Knew While in the K.U." Unpublished. 1966. Adobe portable document file. KSHS.

Rahn, Claude. "A Brief Outline of the Life of Dr. Cyrus Teed (Koresh) and of the Koreshan Unity." Unpublished manuscript. 1963. Adobe portable document file. KSHS.

Teed, Douglas Arthur. "The Lost Muse." Unpublished. 1890. Adobe portable document file. KSHS.

Published and Unpublished Sources

Andrews, Allen H. *A Yank Pioneer in Florida: Recounting the Adventures of a City Chap Who Came to the Wilds of South Florida in the 1890's and Remained to Grow Up with the Country.* Jacksonville: Press of the Douglas Printing Co. Inc., 1950.

Bellamy, Edward. *Looking Backward: 2000-1887.* 1888. Reprint edited by Matthew Beaumont. New York: Oxford University Press, 2009.

Carlyle, Thomas, and Ralph Waldo Emerson. *The Correspondence of Thomas Carlyle and Ralph Waldo Emerson, 1834 to 1872.* Vol. 1. Edited by Charles Eliot Norton. Project Gutenberg, 2004. http://www.gutenberg.org/cache/epub/13583/pg13583.txt.

Damkohler, E. E. *Estero, Fla. 1882: Memoirs of the First Settler.* Fort Myers Beach, Fla.: Island Press, 1967.

Davis, Paulina W., comp. *A History of the National Woman's Rights Movement, for Twenty Years, with the Proceedings of the Decade Meeting Held at Apollo Hall, October 20, 1870.* New York: Journeymen Printers' Co-operative Association, 1871.

Douglas, Marjory Stoneman. *The Everglades: River of Grass.* 1947. Reprint Sarasota, Fla.: Pineapple Press, 1988.

Dreiser, Theodore. *Dawn: An Autobiography of Early Youth.* 1931. Reprint edited by T. D. Nostwich. Santa Rosa, Calif.: Black Sparrow Press, 1998.

———. *Sister Carrie.* 1900. Reprint New York: Penguin Classics, 1994.

Dunning, Ernest. "A Visit with Miss Vesta." *Caloosa Quarterly* 3, no. 3 (September 1974): 3–5.

Duss, John S. *The Harmonists: A Personal History.* 1943. Reprint Ambridge, Pa.: Harmonie Associates, 1970.

Eddy, Mary Baker. *Retrospection and Introspection.* Boston: Trustees under the Will of Mary Baker G. Eddy, 1891.

Field Theory Publicity: The Earth Cell Concept. Kirksville, Mo.: Morrow-McManis, 1936.

Holden, Edward Singleton. *A Catalogue of Earthquakes on the Pacific Coast, 1769–1897.* Washington, D.C.: Smithsonian Institution, 1898. https://archive.org/details/acatalogue earthooholdgoog.

Jones, Ernest, M.D. "The God Complex." In *Essays in Applied Psycho-Analysis,* 204–26. London: International Psycho-Analytical Press, 1923. https://archive.org/details/EssaysOnAppliedPsycho-analysis.

Koreshan Unity: Communistic and Co-operative Gathering of the People. Chicago: Guiding Star, 1895.

Koreshan Unity: General Information Concerning Membership and Its Obligations. Chicago: Guiding Star, no date.

Koreshan Unity Co-operative. *The Solution of Industrial Problems.* Estero, Fla.: Guiding Star, 1907.

Lamoreaux, Leroy. *Early Days on Estero Island.* Fort Myers Beach, Fla.: Estero Island Press, 1967.

Lewis, Sinclair. *Elmer Gantry.* 1927. Reprint New York: Signet Classics, 2007.

Michel, Hedwig. *A Gift to the People.* Estero, Fla.: Koreshan Unity, 1961.

Morrow, Ulysses G. *Phonography; or, Phonetic Shorthand: What It Is, and How to Learn It.* Corning, Iowa: Self-published, 1888.

Moseley, Julia Winifred, and Betty Powers Crislip, eds. *Come to My Sunland: Letters of Julia Daniels Moseley from the Florida Frontier, 1882–1886.* Gainesville: University Press of Florida, 1998.

Moses, John, and Joseph Kirkland, eds. *The History of Chicago, Illinois.* Vol. 2. Chicago: Munsell, 1895.

Most, Johann. *The Beast of Property: The Curse of the World Which Defeats the People's Emancipation.* Tucson, Ariz.: See Sharp Press, 2007.

———. *The Social Monster: A Paper on Communism and Anarchism.* Tucson, Ariz.: See Sharp Press, 2007.

Phillips, George Searle. *Chicago and Her Churches.* Chicago: E. B. Myers and Chandler, 1868. Google eBook ed.

Pierce, Bessie Louise, ed. *As Others See Chicago: Impressions of Visitors, 1673–1933.* 2nd ed. Chicago: University of Chicago Press, 2004.

Ridpath, John Clark. *The Life and Work of James A. Garfield.* Philadelphia: P. W. Ziegler, 1881.

Robinson, E. *Robinson's Map of Chicago.* Northwestern University: Chicago Historical Society, 1886.

Sinclair, Upton. *The Jungle.* 1906. Reprint Cambridge, Mass.: R. Bentley, 1946.

———. *Profits of Religion: An Essay in Economic Interpretation.* 1917. Lexington, Ky.: Seven Treasures, 2008.

Stanton, Elizabeth Cady, Susan B. Anthony, and Matilda Joslyn Gage. *History of Woman Suffrage.* Vol. 1. Project Gutenberg 2009. http://www.gutenberg.org/files/28020/28020-h/28020-h.htm.

Stead, William T. *If Christ Came to Chicago! A Plea for the Union of All Who Love, in the Service of All Who Suffer.* Chicago: Laird & Lee, 1894.

Swedenborg, Emanuel. *The New Jerusalem and Its Heavenly Doctrine.* Boston: New-Church Union, 1907. Google eBook ed.

Teed, Cyrus [Koresh, pseud.]. *The Cellular Cosmogony; or, The Earth a Concave Sphere.* 3rd ed. Estero, Fla.: Guiding Star, 1922.

———. [Lord Chester, pseud.]. *The Great Red Dragon; or, The Flaming Devil of the Orient.* Estero, Fla.: Guiding Star, 1909.

———. *The Illumination of Koresh: Marvelous Experience of the Great Alchemist Thirty Years Ago, at Utica, N.Y.* Chicago: Guiding Star, n.d.

———.[Koresh, pseud.]. *The Immortal Manhood.* 2nd ed. Estero, Fla.: Guiding Star, 1909.

Teed, Cyrus [Koresh, pseud.], and U. G. Morrow. *The Cellular Cosmogony; or, The Earth a Concave Sphere.* 2nd ed. Estero, Fla.: Guiding Star, 1905.

Twain, Mark [Samuel L. Clemens], and Charles Dudley Warner. *The Gilded Age: A Tale of Today.* 1873. Reprint New York: Harper, 1901.

Wells, H. G. *The War in the Air.* 1908. Reprint edited by Patrick Parrinder. New York: Penguin Books, 2005.

White, William, M.D. *Medical Electricity: A Manual for Students.* New York: Samuel R. Wells, 1872. https://archive.org/details/39002011210441.med.yale.edu.

Wilde, Oscar. "The Soul of Man Under Socialism." New York: Max N. Maisel, 1915. https://archive.org/details/soulmanundersoco1wildgoog.

Wood, Horatio C. *Therapeutics: Its Principles and Practice.* 7th ed. of *A Treatise on Therapeutics.* Philadelphia: J. B. Lippincott, 1888.

Secondary Sources

Adams, Katherine. "Life inside the Earth: The Koreshan Unity and Its Urban Pioneers, 1880–1908." Master's thesis, Florida State University, 2010.

Altonen, Brian. "Medical Electricity." Public Health, Medicine, and History. Blog by Brian Altonen, MPH, MS. http://brianaltonenmph.com/6-history-of-medicine-and-pharmacy/hudson-valley-medical-history/1795-1815-biographies/quaker-shadrach-ricketson-md/medical-electricity/.

Anderson, Kenneth Edwin. "The American Eagle: A Unique Florida Weekly Newspaper." Master's thesis, University of Florida, 1970.

Arndt, Karl, J. R. *George Rapp's Successors and Material Heirs: 1847–1916.* Teaneck, N.J.: Fairleigh Dickinson University Press, 1971.

Beinecke Rare Book and Manuscript Library, Yale University. *America and the Utopian Dream.* Web exhibition, 2006. http://brbl-archive.library.yale.edu/exhibitions/utopia/.

Bennett, John H. "Vacaville-Winters Earthquakes . . . 1892: Solano and Yolo Counties." *California Geology* 40, no. 4 (April 1987):75–83.

Berrey, Richard S. "The Koreshan Unity: An Economic History of a Communistic Experiment in Florida." Master's thesis, University of Florida, 1928.

Carmer, Carl. "The Great Alchemist at Utica." In *Dark Trees to the Wind: A Cycle of York State Years,* 260–90. 1949. Reprint New York: David McKay, 1965.

Clark, Elmer T. *The Small Sects in America: An Authentic Study of Almost 300 Little-Known Religious Groups.* Rev. ed. Nashville: Abingdon Press, 1965.

Cross, Whitney. *The Burned-Over District: The Social and Intellectual History of Enthusiastic Religion in Western New York, 1800–1850.* Ithaca, N.Y.: Cornell University Press, 1950.

Dirr, Michael A. *Dirr's Trees and Shrubs for Warm Climates: An Illustrated Encyclopedia.* Portland, Ore.: Timber Press, 2002.

Douglas Arthur Teed: An American Romantic: 1860–1929. Exhibition catalogue compiled and written by Pamela Beecher. Elmira, N.Y.: Arnot Art Museum, 1982.

Duncan, Hugh Dalziel. *Culture and Democracy: The Struggle for Form in Society and Architecture in Chicago and the Middle West during the Life and Times of Louis H. Sullivan.* 2nd ed. New Brunswick, N.J.: Transaction, 1989.

Fine, Howard D. "The Koreshan Unity: The Chicago Years of a Utopian Community." *Journal of the Illinois State Historical Society* 68, no. 3 (June 1975): 213–27.

———. "The Koreshan Unity, Utopian Community: We Live Inside the World." Master's thesis, University of Notre Dame, 1972.

Fuller, Robert. "Cosmology." In *Religion in American History*, edited by Amanda Porterfield and John Corrigan, 190–209. West Sussex, UK: Wiley-Blackwell, 2010.

Goldsmith, Barbara. *Other Powers: The Age of Suffrage, Spiritualism, and the Scandalous Victoria Woodhull.* New York: Alfred A. Knopf, 1998.

Gottschalk, Stephen. *Emergence of Christian Science in American Religious Life.* Berkeley: University of California Press, 1973.

Grismer, Karl H. *The Story of Fort Myers: The History of the Land of the Caloosahatchee and Southwest Florida.* Fort Myers, Fla.: Island Press, 1982.

Haller, John S., Jr. *Medical Protestants: The Eclectics in American Medicine, 1825–1939.* Carbondale: Southern Illinois University Press, 1994.

———. *A Profile in Alternative Medicine: The Eclectic Medical College of Cincinnati, 1845–1942.* Kent, Ohio: Kent State University Press, 1999.

Hay, G. Earl. "The Rectilineator: Koreshan Efforts to Prove the Earth Is Concave." Estero, Fla.: Koreshan State Historic Site and Koreshan Unity Alliance, 1995. http://koreshan .mwweb.org/virtual_exhibit/vex3/ac-0131.pdf.

Herbert, G. M., and I.S.K. Reeves V. *Koreshan Unity Settlement, 1894–1977.* Winter Park: Architects Design Group of Florida, 1977.

Hicks, Peter. "Cyrus Teed." *The Koreshans.* Unofficial site of the Koreshan State Historic Site. http://koreshan.mwweb.org/teed.htm.

Hinds, William Alfred. *American Communities and Co-operative Colonies.* 2nd rev. Chicago: Charles H. Kerr, 1908.

Holloway, Mark. *Heavens on Earth: Utopian Communities in America: 1680–1880.* 2nd ed. New York: Dover, 1966.

Kitch, Sally L. *Chaste Liberation: Celibacy and Female Cultural Status.* Urbana: University of Illinois Press, 1989.

Krakauer, Jon. *Under the Banner of Heaven: A Story of Violent Faith.* New York: Anchor Books, 2004.

Lachman, Gary. *Swedenborg: An Introduction to His Life and Ideas.* New York: Tarcher, 2012.

Landing, James E. "Cyrus Reed Teed and the Koreshan Unity." In *America's Communal Utopias*, edited by Donald E. Pitzer, 375–95. Chapel Hill: University of North Carolina Press, 1997.

Larson, Erik. *Devil in the White City: Murder, Magic, and Madness at the Fair That Changed America.* New York: Random House, 2004.

Lee County Southwest Florida Parks and Recreation. "Historic Punta Rassa." Compiled by Joe A. Akerman Jr. and Butch Harrison. http://www.leeparks.org/pdf/Punta_ Rassa.pdf.

Mackle, Elliott J., Jr. "Cyrus Teed and the Lee County Elections of 1906." *Florida Historical Quarterly* 57, no. 1 (July 1978): 1–18.

———. "The Koreshan Unity in Florida, 1894–1910." Master's thesis, University of Miami, 1971.

Markel, Howard. *An Anatomy of Addiction: Sigmund Freud, William Halsted, and the Miracle Drug Cocaine.* New York: Vintage, 2012.

Miller, Donald L. *City of the Century: The Epic of Chicago and the Making of America.* New York: Simon & Schuster, 1996.

Mormino, Gary R. *Land of Sunshine, State of Dreams: A Social History of Modern Florida.* Gainesville: University Press of Florida, 2005.

Ohnemus, Catherine Anthony. "Dr. Cyrus Teed and the Koreshan Unity Movement." *CRM Magazine* 24, no. 9 (2001): 10–12.

Pitzer, Donald E., ed. *America's Communal Utopias.* Chapel Hill: University of North Carolina Press, 1997.

Quesnell, Quentin. *Early Estero.* Estero, Fla.: Estero Historical Society, 2002.

Rainard, Robert Lynn. "In the Name of Humanity: The Koreshan Unity." Master's thesis, University of South Florida, 1974.

———. "Conflict inside the Earth: The Koreshan Unity in Lee County." *Tampa Bay History* 3, no. 1 (1981): 5–16.

Rea, Sara Weber. *The Koreshan Story.* Estero, Fla.: Guiding Star, 1994.

Remini, Robert V. *Joseph Smith.* Penguin Lives series. New York: Penguin, 2002.

Schudson, Michael. *Discovering the News: A Social History of American Newspapers.* New York: Basic Books, 1978.

Shaw, Jane. *Octavia, Daughter of God: The Story of a Female Messiah and Her Followers.* New Haven: Yale University Press, 2011.

Simanek, Donald E. "Turning the Universe Inside-Out: Ulysses Grant Morrow's Naples Experiment." *D. Simanek's Pages: Myths and Mysteries of Science.* https://www.lhup.edu/~dsimanek/hollow/morrow.htm.

Solomon, Irvin D. "The New Life Is Here: The Koreshan Unity and Its Commercial Enterprises in South Florida, 1894-1961." *Communal Societies: Journal of the Communal Studies Association* 22 (2002): 45–66.

State of Florida Koreshan State Historic Site Unit Management Plan. State of Florida Department of Environmental Protection, Division of Recreation and Parks. August 6, 2003. http://www.dep.state.fl.us/parks/planning/parkplans/KoreshanStateHistoric Site.pdf.

Stein, Stephen J. *The Shaker Experience in America: A History of the United Society of Believers.* New Haven, Conn.: Yale University Press, 1994.

Virtual Museum of the City of San Francisco. "San Francisco Earthquake History, 1880–1914." http://www.sfmuseum.org/alm/quakes2.html.

Williamson, Edward C. *Florida Politics in the Gilded Age, 1877–1893.* Gainesville: University Presses of Florida, 1976.

Index

Union Station, Chicago, 99
United Society of Believers. *See* Shakers
Utica, New York, 13–16, 84

Vacaville, California, 97
VandeBurgt, Melissa Minds, 285
Vanderbilt, Cornelius, 100
Vear, William, 98
Verne, Jules, 30
Vesta. *See* Newcomb, Lillian
Victoria paddlewheel steamer, 191
Village Partners, 270, 271

W. W. Kimball & Co., 50
Waco, Texas, 9
Wallace, Ross, *167*, 193, 210, 230, 246; street fight
    with Sellers, S., 214–16, 282; Teed spiritual
    world message to, 232
The War in the Air (Wells), 222
Warner, Charles Dudley, 7
Warrenton, Virginia, 16
Washington, D.C.,: Gratia joined Teed in, 227;
    Gratia to stay in, 233; plans for Hollyrood
    colony in, 227, 229, 232; Teed letters to Estero
    about, 229; Teed settled in, 226–27; Teed's
    letters to Bubbett, E., chronicled life in, 227
Washington, George, 25
Washington Heights, 97, 104; reporters covered
    conflict in, 98–99; vigilance committee
    formed against Teed in, 98
Washington Heights mansion, 98; Andrews, J.,
    on move to, 96–97; Beth-Ophrah as name
    for, 103–4; *Chicago Evening Journal* report
    on Teed moving to, 97; Gratia as head of,
    104; for Koreshans, *94*, 96; "No Sorrow in
    Heaven" sung for, 102; occupant list of, 103
Washington Post, 227
Watch Tower and Herald of Christ's Presence, 120
Watson, Mattie: mass indignation meetings
    held by, 172; Teed's transgressions catalogued
    by, 172
WCI Communities, 274
Weaver, Moses, *167*
Weimar, Augustus, *1*, 10–11, 234; as doctor of

osteopathy, 2; Teed's suspended animation
    watched by, 2–3; as witness to changes in
    Teed's body, 4–5
"We Live Inside" slogan, xi, 154, 155
Wellington Hotel, Chicago, 100
Wells, H. G., 222, 223
Wells House, Utica, Teed's electro-alchemical
    laboratory of, 18–19
West, Catharine A., 169, 178
White, Anna, 112–13
White, William, on treatment for chorea, 35
White Caps, 71
Whitechapel Club, Chicago, 67
Whitmore, Jim, 274
Wilde, Oscar, 130
Women: Beth-Ophrah trouble among, 113–14;
    disenchanted with Teed, 65–66; Estero dorm
    for, *165*; as journalists, 99–101; as Koreshans
    followers, xi; New York state law regarding
    married, 14; in Second Great Awakening, 12;
    Spiritualists involvement in rights movement
    for, 14; Teed as advocate of equal rights for,
    62; Teed formalized appointments of, 114;
    Teed's strong power over, 8
Women's Rights Convention, Seneca Falls, 14
Woodhull, Victoria, 10; Andrews, J., on Teed
    and, 101–2; as controversial figure, 100–101;
    prominent in women's suffrage movement,
    101
Woolsey, Ella, 33, 34, 37, 61
World's College of Life. *See* College of Life
World's Parliament of Religions, 116
Wright, Harriet, 171, 178
Writing, Teed's inscrutable language in, 7

Yellow journalism, xii; newspaper articles about
    Teed's death, 5–6
"Yellow peril," 222, 230
Young Men's Christian Association, 26–27

Zajanc, Kate, 266
Zinc bathtub, 1, *240*, 249
Zion in Nauvoo, Illinois, 2
Zion's Watch Tower Tract Society, 123, 124, 145

Lyn Millner's radio stories and essays have been broadcast on National Public Radio's *Morning Edition* and *Weekend Edition* and on American Public Media's *Marketplace*. Her print work has appeared in *USA Today*, *Oxford American*, the *Hollywood Reporter*, and *Boca Raton* magazine. She teaches journalism at Florida Gulf Coast University.

CPSIA information can be obtained
at www.ICGtesting.com
Printed in the USA
LVHW091934111221
705838LV00003B/24